Twelve Select Overtures

Recent Researches in Music

A-R Editions publishes seven series of critical editions, spanning the history of Western music, American music, and oral traditions.

Recent Researches in the Music of the Middle Ages and Early Renaissance
    Charles M. Atkinson, general editor

Recent Researches in the Music of the Renaissance
    James Haar, general editor

Recent Researches in the Music of the Baroque Era
    Christoph Wolff, general editor

Recent Researches in the Music of the Classical Era
    Eugene K. Wolf, general editor

Recent Researches in the Music of the Nineteenth and Early Twentieth Centuries
    Rufus Hallmark, general editor

Recent Researches in American Music
    John M. Graziano, general editor

Recent Researches in the Oral Traditions of Music
    Philip V. Bohlman, general editor

Each edition in *Recent Researches* is devoted to works by a single composer or to a single genre. The content is chosen for its high quality and historical importance, and each edition includes a substantial introduction and critical report. The music is engraved according to the highest standards of production using the proprietary software MusE, owned by MusicNotes, Inc.

For information on establishing a standing order to any of our series, or for editorial guidelines on submitting proposals, please contact:

A-R Editions, Inc.
Middleton, Wisconsin

800 736-0070 (U.S. book orders)
608 836-9000 (phone)
608 831-8200 (fax)
http://www.areditions.com

Recent Researches in the Music of the Nineteenth and Early Twentieth Centuries, 35

Johann Nepomuk Hummel

Twelve Select Overtures

Arranged for Pianoforte,
Flute, Violin, and Violoncello

Edited by Mark Kroll

A-R Editions, Inc.
Middleton, Wisconsin

Performance parts are available from the publisher.

A-R Editions, Inc., Middleton, Wisconsin
© 2003 by A-R Editions, Inc.

All rights reserved. No part of this book may be reproduced or transmitted in any form by any electronic or mechanical means (including photocopying, recording, or information storage and retrieval) without permission in writing from the publisher.

The purchase of this edition does not convey the right to perform it in public, nor to make a recording of it for any purpose. Such permission must be obtained in advance from the publisher.

A-R Editions is pleased to support scholars and performers in their use of *Recent Researches* material for study or performance. Subscribers to any of the *Recent Researches* series, as well as patrons of subscribing institutions, are invited to apply for information about our "Copyright Sharing Policy."

Printed in the United States of America

ISBN 0-89579-519-1
ISSN 0193-5364

∞ The paper used in this publication meets the minimum requirements of the American National Standard for Information Sciences—Permanence of Paper for Printed Library Materials, ANSI Z39.48-1984.

Contents

Acknowledgments vi

Introduction vii
  Background vii
  The Arrangements viii
  The Editions viii
  Notes on Performance ix
  Comparison with the Original Overtures xi
  Notes xii

Plates xiii

Twelve Select Overtures
  1. Overture to Prometheus, *Ludwig van Beethoven* 3
  2. Overture to Die Zauberflöte, *Wolfgang Amadeus Mozart* 21
  3. Overture to Lodoïska, *Luigi Cherubini* 39
  4. Overture to Figaro, *Wolfgang Amadeus Mozart* 65
  5. Overture to Iphigénia, *Christoph Willibald Gluck* 88
  6. Original Overture, *Friedrich Heinrich Himmel* 107
  7. Overture to Sargino, *Ferdinando Paer* 133
  8. Overture, *Andreas Jakob Romberg* 153
  9. Overture to Der Freischütz, *Carl Maria von Weber* 184
  10. Overture to Euryanthe, *Carl Maria von Weber* 214
  11. Overture to Tancredi, *Gioachino Rossini* 238
  12. Overture to Anacreon, *Luigi Cherubini* 256

Critical Report 287
  The Source 287
  Editorial Methods 287
  Critical Notes 288

Acknowledgments

I would like to thank my friends and colleagues from Germany, the violinist Waltraut Wächter and the cellist Thomas Fritzsch, who first brought these arrangements to my attention and with whom I have performed these works in Europe, the Middle East, and North America. My deepest appreciation is given to violinist Carol Lieberman, my colleague and wife of thirty years. We have also performed these works, as well as almost all of the violin/keyboard repertoire, and have recorded much of this music, including Hummel's *Haffner* and *Linz* symphony arrangements. I express my gratitude to Professor Wendy Heller of Princeton University, who has provided invaluable and unlimited advice and assistance. Special thanks also to Holly Mockovak, Head of the Music Library at Boston University, for her help with microfilms and source material, and to Professor Richard Cornell for his assistance in making computer-generated copies of many of the overtures. I also thank Hugh Cobbe, Head of the Music Collections at the British Library, for making the source material available to me and for the generous approval for its use and reproduction.

Introduction

Background

Johann Nepomuk Hummel was one of the most important musicians in Europe during his lifetime.[1] His skills as a virtuoso pianist and his uncanny ability to improvise extemporaneously placed him among the great keyboard players of the day, including Beethoven, Dussek, and Moscheles. His solo tours throughout Germany, France, Austria, England, the Netherlands, Poland, and Russia made him one of the most well traveled musicians of the period. As a composer, Hummel's solo piano works, chamber music, concertos, and orchestral and vocal music were published by the major publishing houses, such as Peters, Schott, and Boosey, and they were frequently performed by the composer himself and by other artists, such as Liszt. Hummel was also an important teacher. His students included luminaries like Sigismund Thalberg, Ferdinand Hiller, Adolf von Henselt, and Carl Czerny, and his monumental treatise, *A Complete Theoretical and Practical Course of Instructions on the Art of Playing the Piano Forte,* which is essentially a summary of a lifetime of teaching, remains one of the most important contributions to the field.[2] Finally, Hummel was a tireless advocate for the protection of composers from the ongoing piracy practiced by publishers of the period, and he expended considerable effort trying to establish a composer's union and copyright protection. His steadfast dedication to this goal was so strong that he even lobbied Beethoven on his deathbed to support the cause.[3]

One aspect of Hummel's career that has been largely overlooked is his role as a conductor. Nepomuk served as kapellmeister to the Grand Duke of Weimar from 1819 until his death in 1837, and these were the happiest and most productive years of his life. His primary responsibilities were to lead performances at the court chapel, present private concerts at court, and direct operas at the famous court theater. Opera had assumed increasing importance in Weimar during this time, since the quality of dramatic productions at that theater had declined markedly after Goethe's resignation as director in 1818, and Hummel became quite busy on the podium. The list of operas he conducted includes Gluck's *Iphigénia en Aulide, Iphigénia en Tauride,* and *Alceste;* Mozart's *Don Giovanni, Die Zauberflöte, Le nozze di Figaro, La clemenza di Tito, Cosi fan tutte,* and *Die Entführung aus dem Serail;* Cherubini's *Medea* and *Lodoïska;* Spontini's *La vestale;* Paer's *Sargino;* Méhul's *Joseph;* Catel's *Semiramis;* Salieri's *Axur;* Sacchini's *Oedipe;* and Beethoven's *Fidelio*. Some of the earliest performances of Weber's *Der Freischütz* were given at the court theater under Hummel's direction, and his formidable energy was further acknowledged by the *Chronik des Weimarischen Hoftheaters,* which reported on 3 April 1819 that he had "conducted the fiftieth performance in Weimar of Mozart's *Don Giovanni*."[4] He also frequently conducted symphonies and concertos by Mozart, Haydn, and Beethoven.

Nevertheless, Hummel was forgotten shortly after his death, and his work is essentially unknown today. This is not surprising, since his accomplishments are overshadowed by his admittedly greater contemporaries—Mozart, Beethoven, and Haydn during his lifetime, and Liszt, Chopin, and Schumann shortly thereafter. However, Hummel is experiencing something of a revival, and his appropriate place in musical history is gradually being established.

As a composer, Hummel's music is frankly one of the least significant legacies of his career. The compositions are always skillful and sophisticated, and the piano writing is particularly brilliant, but except for a small number of first-class works which have entered the repertoire (e.g., the Septet, the Trumpet Concerto, the Piano Concerto op. 85, and some small salon pieces), the majority are lightweight and of interest primarily as period pieces or vehicles for virtuosic display. On the other hand, during a ten-year period between 1820 and 1830, Hummel produced a large number of arrangements for chamber ensemble of symphonies, concertos, and opera overtures. One could easily surmise that he did not consider this body of work to be particularly significant at the time, but they are indeed masterpieces of the genre.

The art of transcription has a long and fascinating history, extending from the keyboard versions of sixteenth-century vocal music to the intricate reworkings by Bach and Handel, but in the early decades of the nineteenth century there was a virtual explosion of arrangements. Several musical and social factors contributed to this. Since there was no radio, television, or recordings, an evening spent playing transcriptions was an ideal way for a rapidly growing middle class to learn and enjoy the newest compositions. Moreover, people living far from major cultural centers had few opportunities to attend a symphonic concert, and one can safely suggest that for every individual who actually heard a large orchestral or operatic work, hundreds experienced them only through arrangements. Thus, as soon as a large-scale composition had been premiered or published, an arrangement for small ensemble usually became available for home use. Sometimes the arrangements appeared *before* the original was heard![5] Furthermore, playing transcriptions was not only a popular form of private entertainment, but also at times an accepted mode of romantic courtship.

The majority of these transcriptions were written by competent "hacks," typically in piano four-hand versions, but when the task was placed in the hands of a great musician such as Hummel, the results could be quite different. Hummel was ideally suited for such an assignment. As Mozart's most famous student, Europe's renowned pianist, and a friend and colleague of Haydn, Beethoven, Weber, and others, Hummel had already conducted many of the pieces he would now arrange.[6] He therefore knew the works thoroughly from the perspective of both a composer and performer, and his transcriptions are not only skillful but also insightful. As a consummate craftsman and a reliable businessman, he did not let his ego interfere with the regular production of such seemingly mundane *Hausmusik*. The income they produced must have also pleased Nepomuk, who was as renowned for his astute business practices as for his musicianship (his estate at the time of his death was valued at more than eighty times that of his annual salary). The transcriptions probably took little time or effort, and he received £8.15.0 for each overture.

The Arrangements

The initial impetus for Hummel's arrangements came from one J. R. Schultz, a German or Austrian who settled in England in the early part of the century and established himself as an entrepreneur-publisher-musician. Schultz had earlier commissioned or published a number of original European compositions, including Beethoven's Variations op. 121a and Hummel's own Trio in E-major, op. 33, and he maintained a close collaboration with the publisher Peters on the continent. Beginning in 1820, Schultz commissioned from Hummel the first of what would eventually comprise more than fifty transcriptions. In August of that year he published, with Boosey, Hummel's arrangement of F. H. Himmel's Overture in C minor, in two versions, for piano four-hands and for a trio of piano, violin, and cello. Peters also published an edition of these works in Germany. During the ensuing decade Hummel would ultimately arrange five symphonies of Mozart, Symphonies nos. 1–7 of Beethoven, four Haydn symphonies, seven Mozart piano concertos (with additional ornamentation and cadenzas), the Beethoven Septet, and twenty-four opera overtures. He scored them all for piano, flute, violin, and cello, and all were written for Schultz in London.

Those who are familiar with Hummel's arrangements of Mozart's *Haffner* and *Linz* symphonies cannot but help admire the skill with which he reduces the classical orchestra of Mozart to an ensemble of four instruments, while at the same time preserving the essential music and character of the original.[7] Bernard Holland of the *New York Times,* in a review of my recording of these works, made the perceptive and witty observation that these arrangements were akin to viewing "Mozart through Hummel's fluoroscope."[8] That is, the "flesh" of the entire work is removed, but all the basic musical material, the "bones," remains clearly visible and, in fact, highlighted.

The same can be said, perhaps to a greater degree, about the arrangements of the overtures, in which Hummel was often confronted with a larger orchestra and a more amorphous formal structure than that of the symphonies of Mozart, Haydn, and Beethoven. For example, it is indeed a formidable challenge to squeeze the orchestra of Weber's *Der Freischütz* (i.e., two flutes, two oboes, two clarinets, two bassoons, trumpet, three trombones, timpani, and a full complement of strings) into the confines of an ensemble of flute, violin, cello, and piano. Yet even with his small forces, Hummel manages to capture both the essence and flavor of the orchestral experience. His choice of overtures is also significant. Hummel published two sets of twelve overtures, and each contains some of the best-known examples by the great masters (e.g., Mozart's *Le nozze di Figaro* and *Die Zauberflöte,* Weber's *Der Freischütz,* Beethoven's *Fidelio* and *The Creatures of Prometheus,* Rossini's *La gazza ladra*) as well as overtures by lesser composers who have long since disappeared into the pages of musical history, such as Paer, Romberg, Vogel, and Winter. In this sense, Hummel's arrangements provide an invaluable glimpse into the opera world of the first decades of the nineteenth century, a summary, if you will, of current musical tastes. These overture arrangements, like the transcriptions of Mozart and Beethoven symphonies, also provide a wealth of information about the performance practices of the period, including articulation, dynamics, tempo, and instrumental performance.

The Editions

The state of music publishing in the nineteenth century was complicated and byzantine at best, and chaotic or illegal at worst. Unauthorized or pirate editions appeared almost simultaneously with official publications, and composers were generally at the mercy of unscrupulous publishers.[9] The conditions in England were somewhat more stable and easily understood. To summarize briefly, English copyright law required that a publisher deposit one or more copies of a new work at Stationer's Hall in London. After such a deposit, the work would receive its certification and copies would be made for national and university libraries. Therefore, since no composition was allowed to be "entered at Stationer's Hall" without demonstrated proof of ownership, this certification should give a reasonable assurance that the volume was not a piracy.

The system, however, was hardly foolproof, and one cannot use the records in the Stationer's Hall with complete equanimity. Publishers might not deposit their works at all, or the high costs of depositing would deter them from entering more than one work in a series of compositions. This was the case with Hummel's *Twelve Select Overtures*. Only the first overture was officially deposited, perhaps on the assumption that the deposit and its protection would apply to the other eleven overtures. The second set of overture arrangements was never formally deposited.

Notes on Performance

Hummel provides generous indications for dynamics, phrasing, and articulation. It is not unusual to find identical passages played by two or more instruments notated with different phrasings and/or dynamics.[10] This is not necessarily a mistake nor should it be a source of confusion. The practice of nonuniform phrasing during the eighteenth and nineteenth centuries was much more common than is usually assumed; by this, composers sought to achieve variety in color and musical texture. Today's performers and editors should therefore avoid the temptation to smooth over these supposed "irregularities" by imposing uniformity in all parts. Likewise, the scoring of a passage might have a different dynamic in each of the four instruments. Here Hummel achieves subtle differences in dynamics and also distinguishes between principal or solo material and secondary or accompanying figures.

Questions about the realization of ornaments, choices of fingering, or, for that matter, most issues of execution can often be answered by going directly the source, that is, the relevant sections in Hummel's own treatise. For example, the trills in the arrangements, indicated by the signs *tr* or ∿ raise the eternal question about the starting note (i.e., whether to begin the trills from the main note or the upper auxiliary). Hummel answers this clearly and unequivocally in his treatise—all trills should begin with the main note. He writes:

> With regard to the shake, we have hitherto followed the practice of the ancient masters, and begun it always with the subsidiary note above; a custom to all appearances founded upon the earliest rules laid down for the voice in singing, and which were subsequently adopted for instruments. But . . . no reason exists that the same rules which were given for the management of the voice, must also serve for the piano-forte, without admitting of alternation or improvement. . . . [Therefore,] every shake should begin with the note itself, over which it stands, and not with the subsidiary note above, unless the contrary be expressly indicated.[11]

Moreover, he recommends that a termination be added to almost every trill, even if not expressly notated.

Hummel provides no metronome markings for the overtures, but this in itself should not be an impediment. Even when a composer does include metronome markings, he never expected that this number would be followed mechanically, in an unyielding and automatic manner. As in all good musical performance, tempo should be adjusted throughout a movement to reflect changes in character, texture, and musical context. Hummel, Beethoven, and other commentators were aware of the danger of being a slave to the metronome at the expense of the music. For example, in the autograph of his song "Nord oder Süd," Beethoven wrote that a metronome marking can apply only "to the first measures, for feeling also has its tempo and this cannot entirely be expressed in this figure."[12] Hummel himself writes in his treatise that

> many persons still erroneously imagine, that, in applying the metronome, they are bound to follow its equal and undeviating motions throughout the whole piece, without allowing themselves any latitude in the performance for the display of taste and feeling.[13]

Another thorny issue concerns the interpretation of the signs for staccato dot and the wedge or stroke. This question has been a continual source of controversy among editors, performers, and scholars, and many have concluded that the two signs are interchangeable and represent the same articulation. However, there is considerable evidence that this is not the case. For example, Louis Adam, the first Professor of Piano at the Paris Conservatoire, provides what seems to be a definitive answer to the question in his important *Méthode*.[14] He holds that there are three basic articulations (see example 1). Each is indicated by a different symbol, and each implies a distinctly different performance. In other words, these articulations *are* different and should be played accordingly in the arrangements.

Admittedly, some of the notation in *both* the arrangements and the originals is ambiguous, and knowledge of the performance practice of the period will be useful. For example, in the *Overture to Euryanthe*, triplet passages in one instrument are often accompanied by a dotted figure in another (e.g., mm. 1 and 5, as well as m. 199). As tradition dictates, the dotted rhythm should be adapted to the dominant triplet rhythm. That is, ♪♩ is performed as if it were written ♪♩. However, when the same dotted figure appears alone, independent of the triplet figure, the performer can decide whether a triplet or dotted realization is most appropriate (e.g., m. 15). In the *Overture to Sargino*, Paer (or Hummel) seems to be making an attempt to distinguish between these two rhythms by using a separate notation for each. That is, the rhythmic figure of ♪♩ implies a dotted performance, while the figure of ♪♩ was probably intended to be played as a triplet.

Hummel adds very few pedal indications in the piano part, but this should not be surprising. Contemporary accounts of his playing and the comments in his treatise make it clear that Hummel was very conservative with the pedal. He writes that

> a truly great Artist has no occasion for Pedals to work upon his audience by expression and power, . . . its employment [i.e., the damper pedal] however is rather to be

Example 1. Articulations as demonstrated in Louis Adam, *Méthode de piano de Conservatoire* (Paris, 1804)

recommended in slow than in quick movements, and only where the harmony changes at distant intervals: all other Pedals are useless, and of no value either to the performer or to the instrument.[15]

The pedal in these arrangements should therefore be used with great discretion, primarily for expressive purposes, or as an adjustment to a particular piano or acoustical space. On the other hand, one can find instances in the arrangements where Hummel instructs the pianist to hold the sustaining pedal much longer than one would expect, through many measures in which the harmonies change frequently (e.g., in the *Overture to Figaro,* mm. 280–82). Although this is contrary to the teachings of modern piano pedaling, it was a common practice during this time. The effect can be quite dramatic, especially when played on pianos of the period.

Regarding the choice of actual instruments, and particularly the piano, it is instructive to look at the resources available when these transcriptions appeared. The typical Viennese-style piano of the period 1820–30 (as represented by builders such as Graf, Walther, and Dulcken) had six or six and one-half octaves and could be fitted with a variety of pedals and special devices. These would usually include a sustaining pedal, an *una corda* (in which only one of three strings would be struck), and a *sordine* (to mute the sound by means of a cloth or other material placed on the strings). Pianos also had *due corda* pedals, which struck two strings rather than three, and special-effect pedals such as the *janissary,* which operated a drum and triangle built into the instrument. English instruments were equally large and complex, the best being made by Broadwood, and typically had six or six and one-half octaves and a full complement of pedals and devices. However, it is useful to remember that these transcriptions were primarily intended for home use and were most often played on instruments built for the typical middle-class household. A piano was part of the basic furnishings for any self-respecting bourgeois home in the early nineteenth century. These instruments were usually smaller square pianos, such as those ubiquitous house instruments built by Clementi and Co. in London or the "Nachttisch" (table) squares of Germany, but larger upright models such as the "giraffe" or "pyramid" piano were also popular.

The flutes in Hummel's time were made with a forest of materials, including boxwood, ebony, and ivory, and could have from one to eight keys. Theobald Boehm began his groundbreaking work on the flute in 1832. His conical bore and ingenious design transformed the instrument and established what is now the modern flute. The violin and cello would have been fitted with gut strings. A chin rest for the violin or an endpin for the cello was still optional, although becoming more typical, and the bow was of the early modern Tourte style. The prevailing pitch of the time would have fallen within the range of a′ = 427–30 cps, but there was really no standard diapason "a," and pitch varied from country to country, and even from city to city. Performers fortunate enough to play on instruments of the period will learn a great deal from the experience and find the realization of these works quite natural and satisfying. Needless to say, performance on a modern piano, flute, violin, and cello is an equally valid and acceptable approach to this repertoire.

It should be mentioned that these arrangements can also be performed on piano alone. Publishers were quite aware that a pianist living in a small village, far from a major city, might not have a full ensemble of instrumentalists to accompany him, and their good marketing sense motivated them to offer for sale solo piano versions of many of the transcriptions. For example, Hummel's transcriptions of Mozart's Symphony K. 543, which was originally scored for flute, violin, cello, and piano, was published by Schott in 1825 in solo piano format. Hofmeister similarly published a solo edition of Hummel's arrangement of the *Linz* Symphony, K. 425, around the same time. Since the bulk of the musical material was already contained in the piano part, a solo version would not compromise the integrity of the work and also made practical business sense.

Comparison with the Original Overtures

As we have noted, a comparison of the arrangements with the original overtures is instructive and revealing. It is beyond the scope of this introduction to describe all the similarities and differences, but a few examples are worth mentioning.

Overture to Prometheus (no. 1). Beethoven frequently uses the symbol *sf*, and less frequently *sfp*, but never the *rf* found in Hummel. Beethoven also only uses the staccato sign throughout, not the stroke; Hummel uses both. In measure 83, there is an interesting discrepancy between original and arrangement:

In measures 185 and 187 Hummel adds grace notes to the right hand of the piano part where none exist in the corresponding passage of the original. Hummel also makes a significant change to Beethoven's rhythms in measures 249–50:

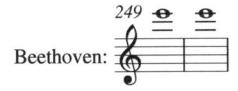

Overture to Die Zauberflöte (no. 2). Mozart uses only the staccato sign, never the stroke; Hummel's arrangement is generously articulated with both. The rhythm in measure 172 differs markedly in the two sources:

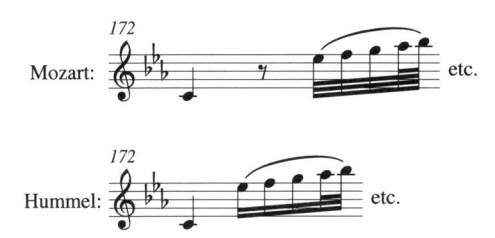

The time signature does not change from C to ¢ at the Allegro in measure 16 of the original, as it does in Hummel's arrangement.

Overture to Figaro (no. 4). Hummel often slurs passages where Mozart applies a staccato or uses no articulation at all. The turn figure of measure 14 in the arrangement is fully realized in the original score:

Overture to Der Freischütz (no. 9). There are numerous differences in articulations, dynamics, and tempo, such as the following:

M.	Weber	Hummel
88	*ff*	*cresc.*
91	*p*	*ff*
96	*con molto passione ff*	*fz*
105	no *fz*; overall dynamic is *f*	*fz*
160		
288	no tempo indication	*Più presto*
312	no tempo indication	*Ancora più stringendo*

Overture to Euryanthe (no. 10). Weber's Largo in measure 129 becomes Largo ma non troppo in the Hummel version. In measures 185–88, the Weber indicated *stringendo poco a poco*, followed by Tempo I in measure 189. There is no *stringendo* at this point in Hummel's arrangement, but there is an *accelerando* beginning at measure 197.

Notes

1. For an extended description of Hummel's life and character, see my introduction to Johann Nepomuk Hummel, *Mozart's* Haffner *and* Linz *Symphonies, Arranged for Pianoforte, Flute, Violin, and Violoncello*, ed. Mark Kroll, Recent Researches in the Music of the Nineteenth and Early Twentieth Centures, vol. 29 (Madison: A-R Editions, Inc., 2000). There is only one complete biography, Karl Benyovsky, *J. N. Hummel, Der Mensch und Künstler* (Bratislava: Eos, 1934). See also Joel Sachs, "Hummel in England and France" (Ph.D. diss., Columbia University, 1968).

2. This seminal work contains invaluable information about piano playing and performance practice in the nineteenth century. It was published simultaneously in English, French, and German. The English edition, *A Complete Theoretical and Practical Course of Instructions on the Art of Playing the Piano Forte* (London: Boosey, [1827 or 1828]), carries a dedication to King George. The German edition is *Ausführliche theoretisch practische Anweisung zum Pianoforte Spiel vom ersten Elementar-unterricht an bis zur vollkommensten Ausbildung* (Wien: T. Haslinger, 1828). The French edition is *Méthode compléte theorétique et practique pour le pianoforte* (Paris, 1829). For a complete discussion of the treatise, see Mark Kroll, "La Belle Execution," in *Festschrift for Robert Marshall*, ed. Roberta Marvin and Stephen Crist (Rochester: University of Rochester Press, forthcoming).

3. Hummel and Beethoven were such contrasting personalities that their relationship fluctuated between warm admiration and open hostility. For a complete description of their final meeting and reconciliation, see Anton F. Schindler, *Biographie von Ludwig van Beethoven*, (Münster, 1840; 3d ed. in 2 vols., Münster, 1860); translated from the 3d ed. by Constance Jolly and edited by Donald W. MacArdle, as *Beethoven as I Knew Him* (Chapel Hill: University of North Carolina Press, 1966), 387–90.

4. Benyovsky, *J. N. Hummel*, 90.

5. For example, Johann Peter Salomon, who commissioned Haydn's twelve *London Symphonies*, first published these works in piano trio arrangements, before both Haydn's arrival in London and the actual premiere of the symphonies. In this manner, Salomon was able to generate a large and knowledgeable audience for his distinguished guest.

6. Hummel conducted in Weimar at least fifteen of the twenty-four overtures he arranged: *Die Zauberflöte, Le nozze di Figaro, Iphigénia in Aulide, Der Freischütz, Euryanthe, Tancredi, Anacreon, Il matrimonio segreto, Opferfest, Don Giovanni, La clemenza di Tito, Fanchon, Il barbiere di Siviglia, L'italiana in Algeri,* and *Fidelio*. In addition, he conducted the *Jupiter* Symphony, a symphony by Haydn in E-flat which could have been no. 103, and Beethoven's Symphonies nos. 3, 5, and 6 (and 8, which he did not live long enough to arrange). Cited in Joel Sachs, "Authentic English and French Editions of Hummel," *Journal of the American Musicological Society* 25 (1972): 209 n. 30.

7. See Hummel, *Mozart's* Haffner *and* Linz *Symphonies*, and the author's recording of these symphonies, Wolfgang Amadeus Mozart and Johann Nepomuk Hummel, *Symphonies No. 35 (Haffner) and 36 (Linz)*, Mark Kroll and the Parlor Philharmonic, Boston Skyline Records, BSD 144.

8. Bernard Holland, "Mozart through Hummel's Fluoroscope," *New York Times*, 6 July 1997, sec. H, p. 26.

9. For a complete description of this perilous state of affairs, see Hummel, *Mozart's* Haffner *and* Linz *Symphonies*, xiii; and Sachs, "Authentic English and French Editions of Hummel."

10. To cite one example, in measure 67 of the arrangement of *Der Freischütz*, the flute and right hand of the piano share the same melody in unison, but each has a different articulation and phrasing; the violin and cello are also given two distinct accents and articulations.

11. Hummel, *A Complete Theoretical and Practical Course of Instructions*, part 3, chap. 2, pp. 2–3.

12. *Thayer's Life of Beethoven*, rev. and ed. Elliot Forbes (Princeton: Princeton University Press, 1967), 2:687–88.

13. Hummel, *A Complete Theoretical and Practical Course of Instructions*, part 3, chap. 5, p. 65.

14. Louis Adam, *Méthode de piano de Conservatoire* (Paris, 1804), art. 7, pp. 154–55.

15. Hummel, *A Complete Theoretical and Practical Course of Instructions*, part 3, chap. 3, p. 62.

Plate 1. Johann Nepomuk Hummel, *Twelve Select Overtures . . . Arranged for the Piano Forte, with Accompaniments of Violin and Flute and Violoncello* (London, [1821]), piano part, first page of *Overture to Prometheus*. Courtesy of the British Library, London.

Plate 2. Johann Nepomuk Hummel, *Twelve Select Overtures . . . Arranged for the Piano Forte, with Accompaniments of Violin and Flute and Violoncello* (London, [1821]), violin part, first page of *Overture to Euryanthe*. Courtesy of the British Library, London.

Twelve Select Overtures

1. Overture to Prometheus

Ludwig van Beethoven

Allegro molto con brio
pizz.
pizz.
Allegro molto con brio
arco
arco
Ped.

5

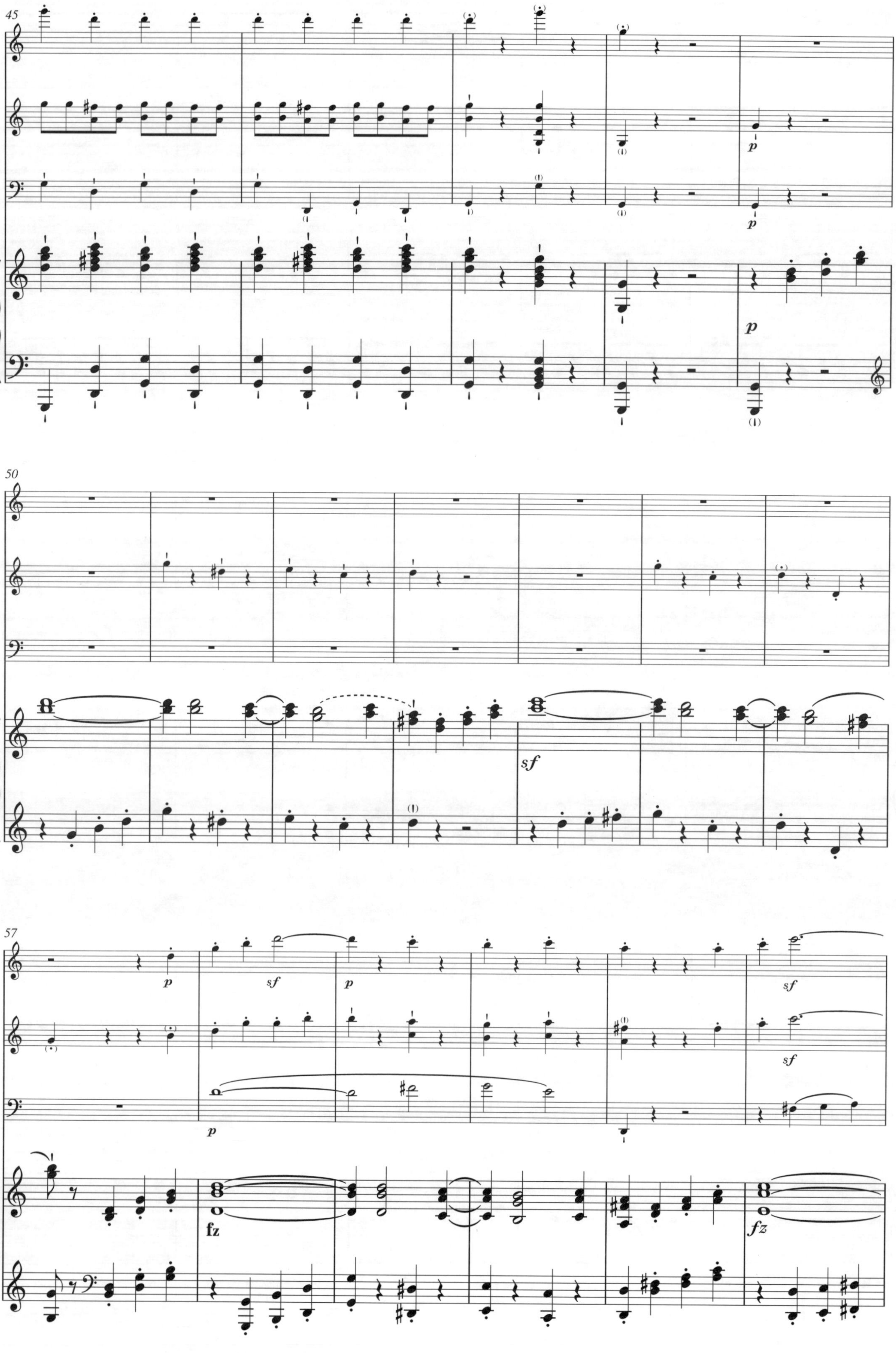
45
50
57
p
sf
fz

7

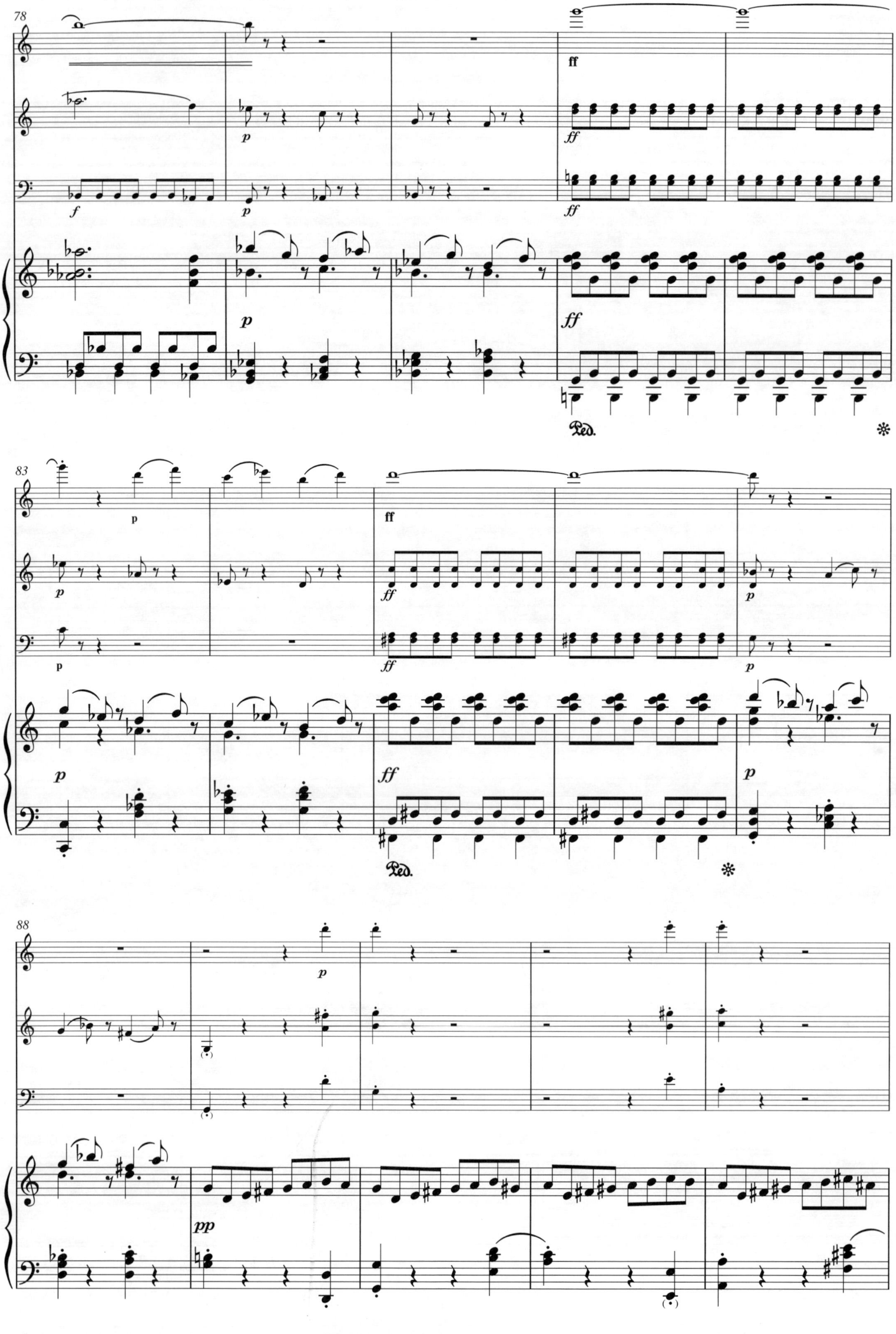
78
83
88
Ped.
Ped.

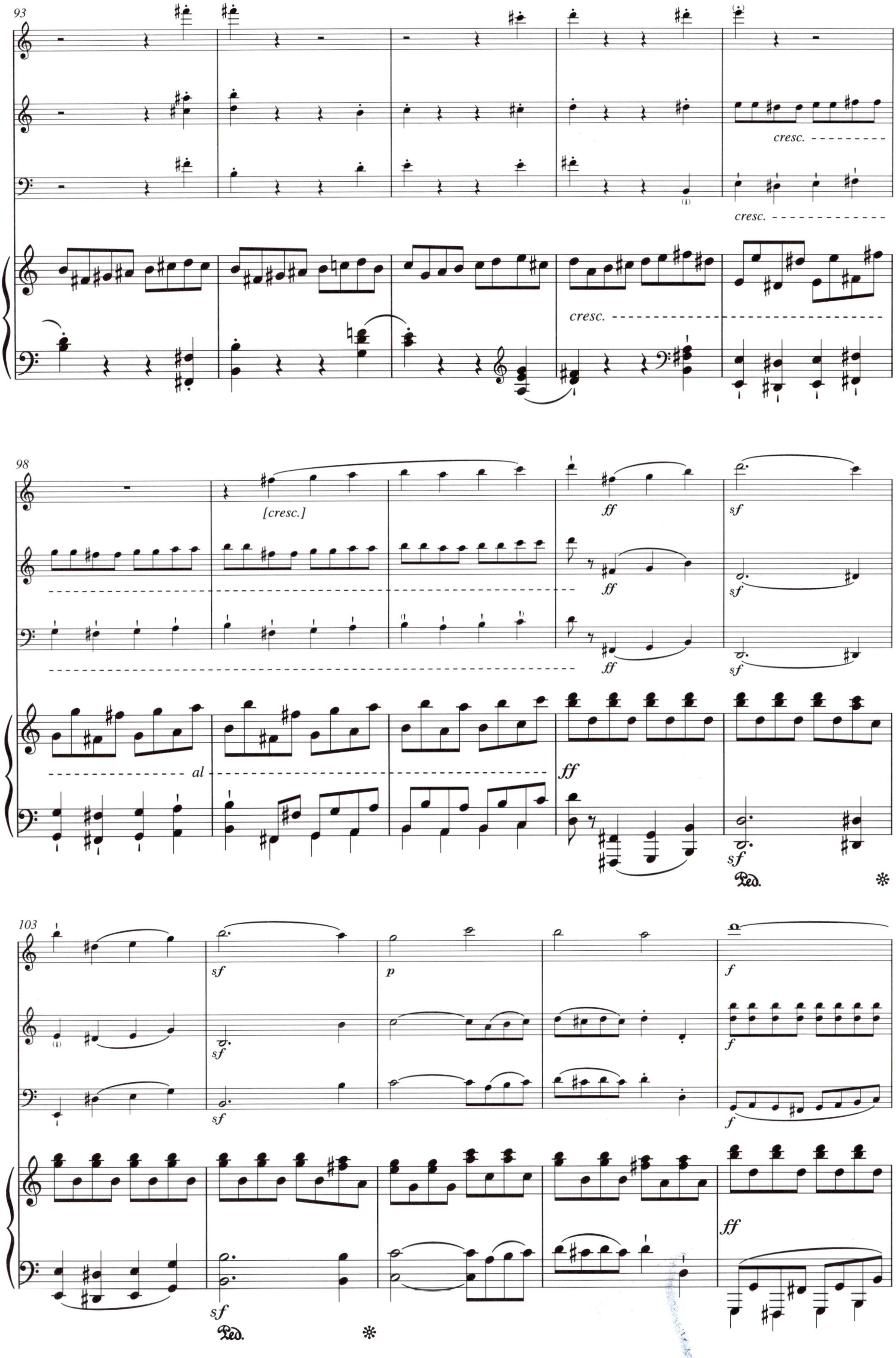
93
cresc.
cresc.
cresc.
98
[cresc.]
ff
sf
al
Ped.
103
p
f

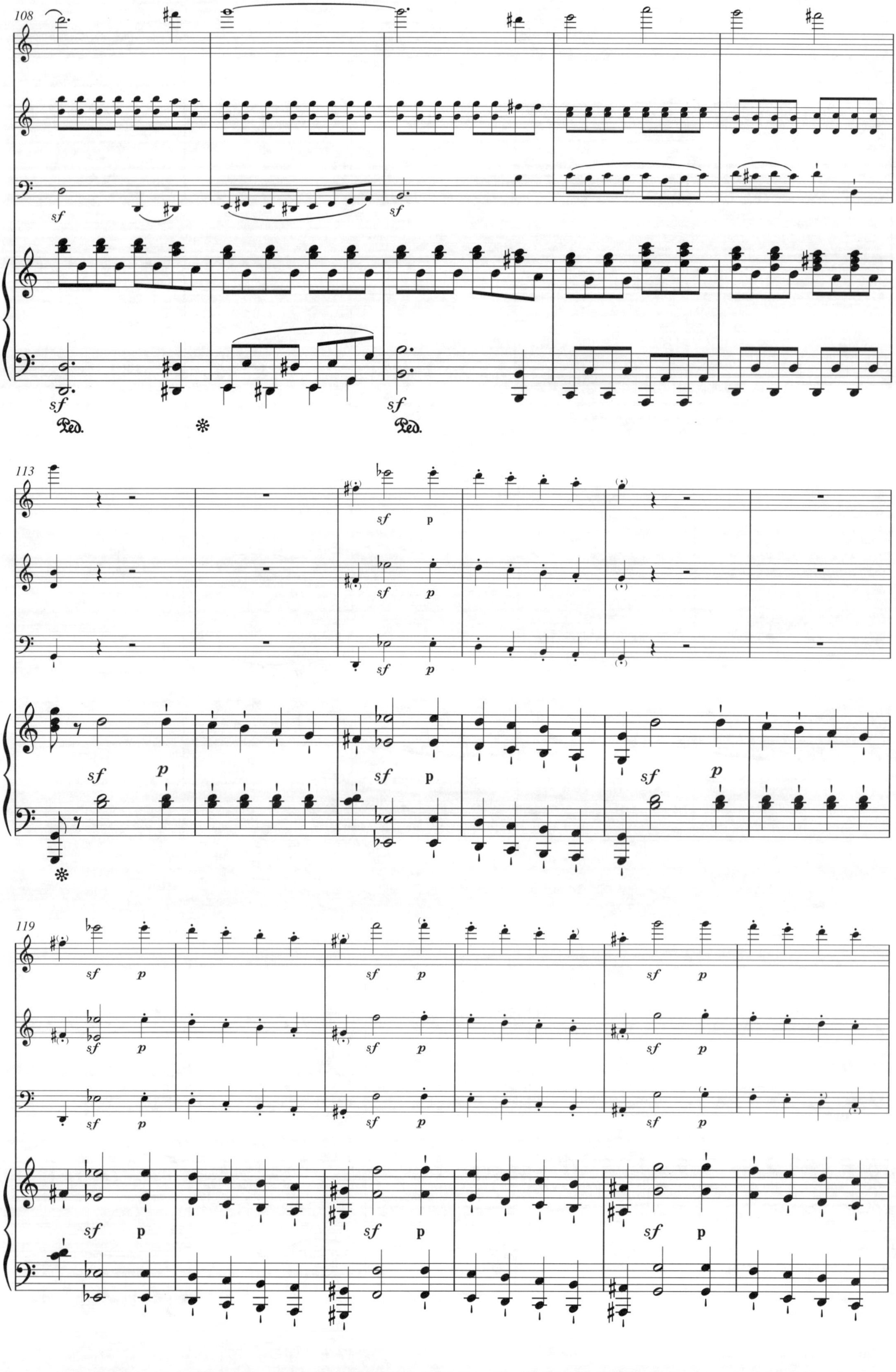
108
sf
Ped.
113
119
p

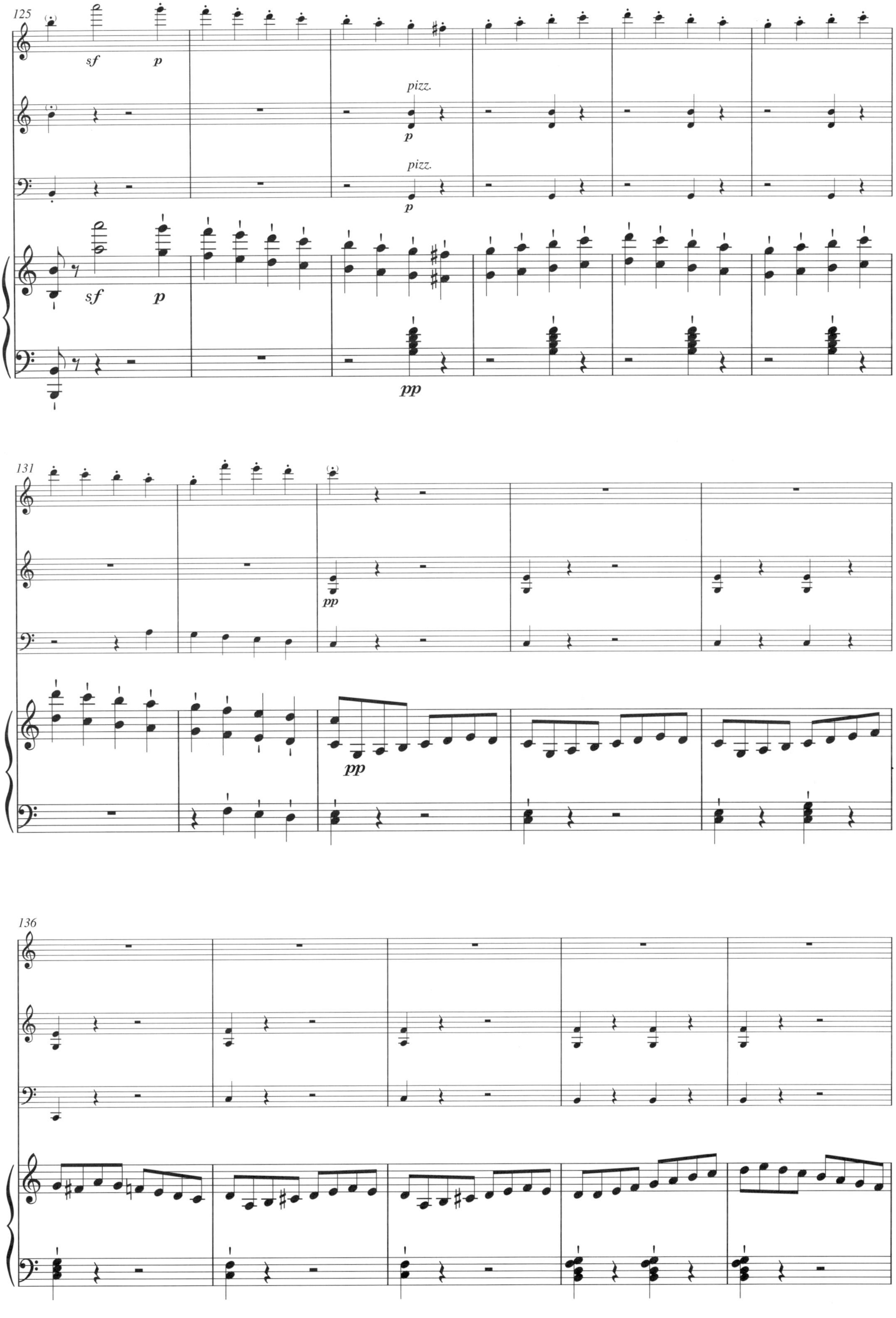
125
sf
p
pizz.
p
pizz.
p
sf
p
pp
131
pp
pp
136

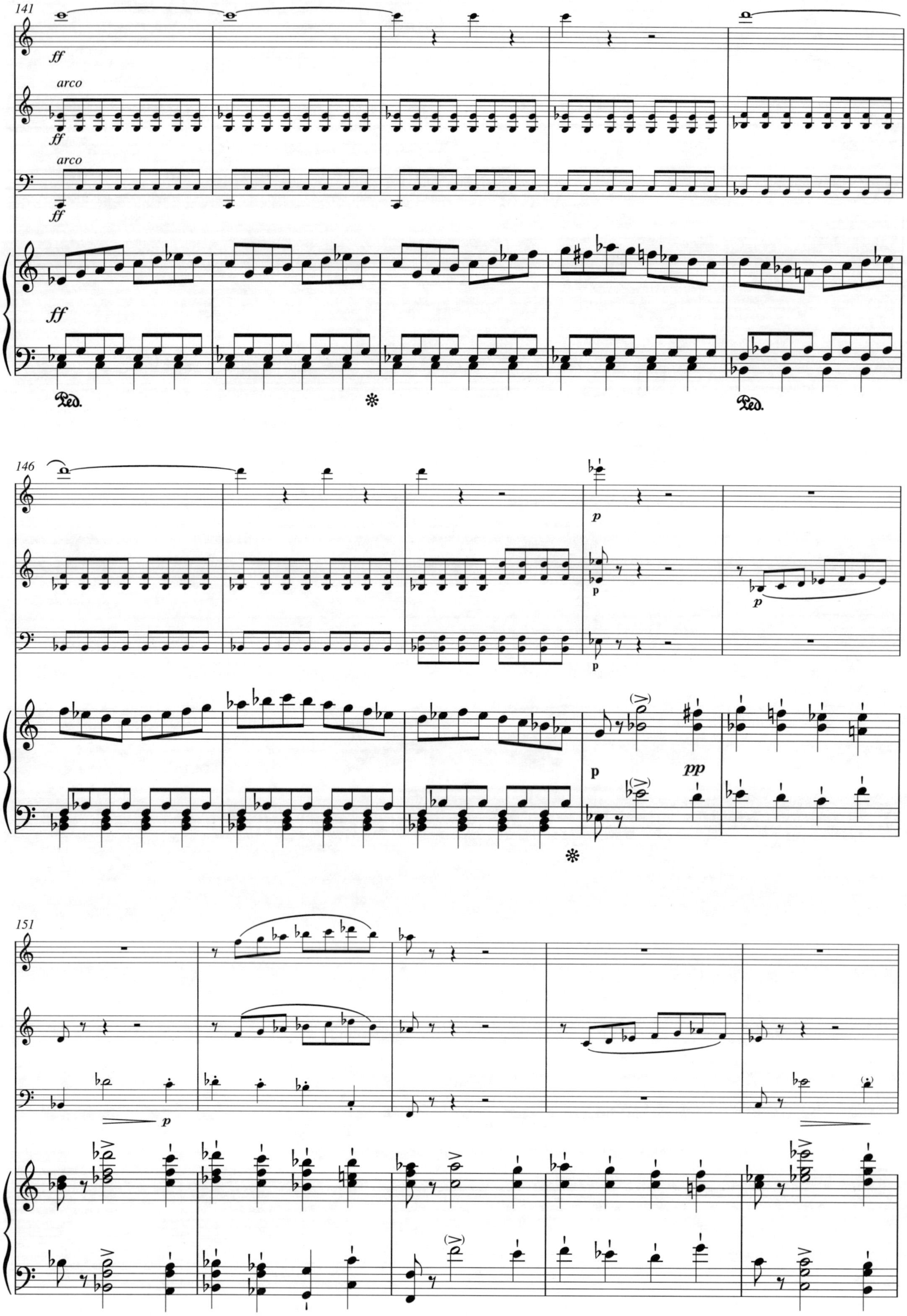
141
ff
arco
ff
arco
ff
ff
Ped.
Ped.
146
p
p
p
p
pp
151
p

13

14

15

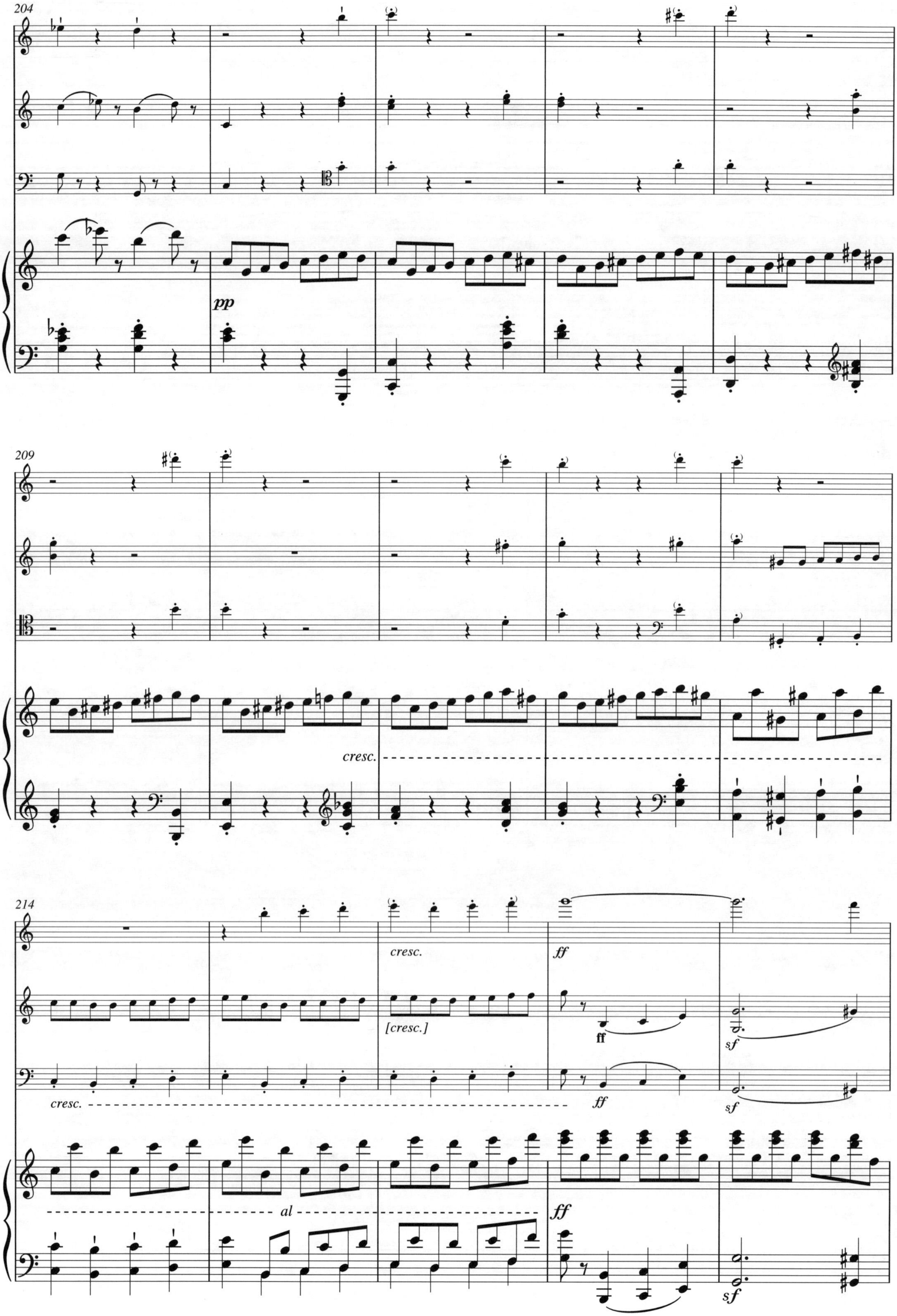
204
pp
209
cresc.
214
cresc.
[cresc.]
cresc.
al
ff
ff
ff
ff
sf
sf
sf

17

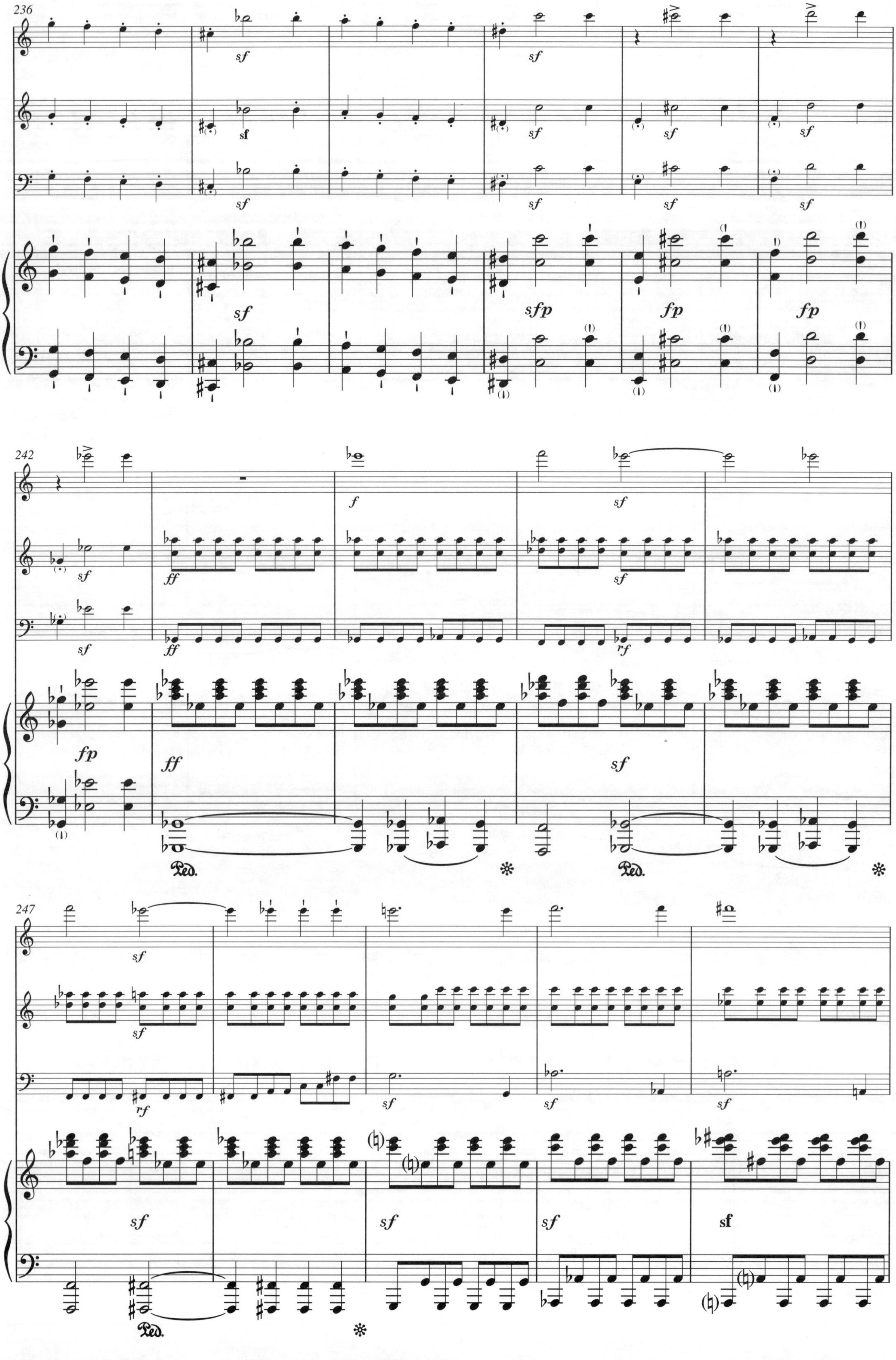
236
sf
sfp
fp
242
ff
f
rf
Ped.
247

252
p
p
p
257
p
mf
sul G
cresc.
cresc.
cre
scen
do
f
f
f
f
262
(sul G)
cresc.
ff
ff
ff
ff
sf
rf
sf
Ped.
*

267
sf
sf
rf
rf
rf
rf
rf
rf
rf
rf
8va
sf
f
ff
sfz
[Ped.
f
[Ped.
sf
sf
272
sf
sf
rf
rf
rf
f
rf
rf
rf
f
(8va)
f
f
sf
sf
sf
f
277
sf
sf
f
f
f
ff
f
f
f
f
f
ff
f
f
f
f
f
ff
f
f
f
f
f
ff
f
f

2. Overture to Die Zauberflöte

Wolfgang Amadeus Mozart

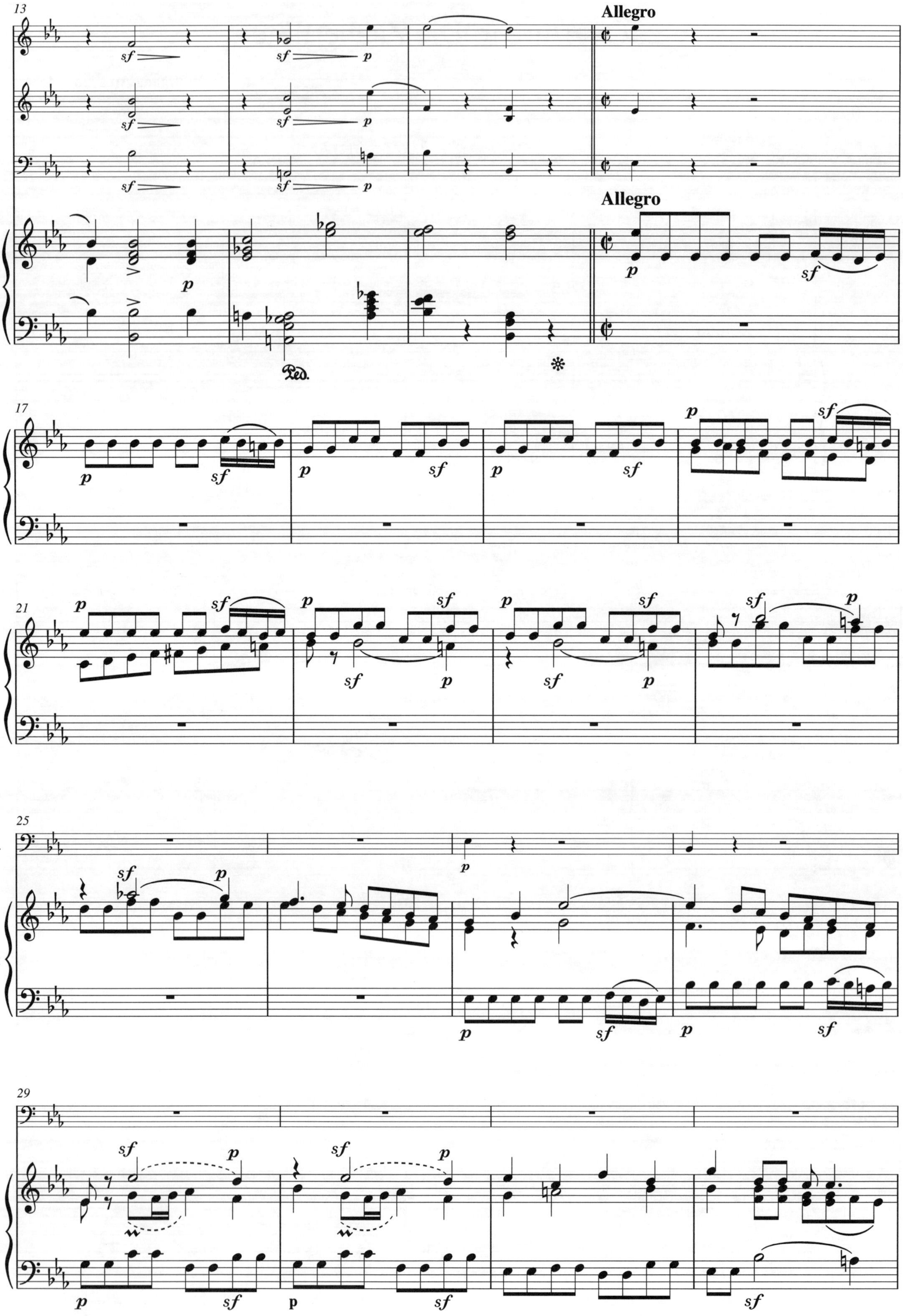
13
Allegro
Allegro
17
Pn.
21
25
Vc.
Pn.
29

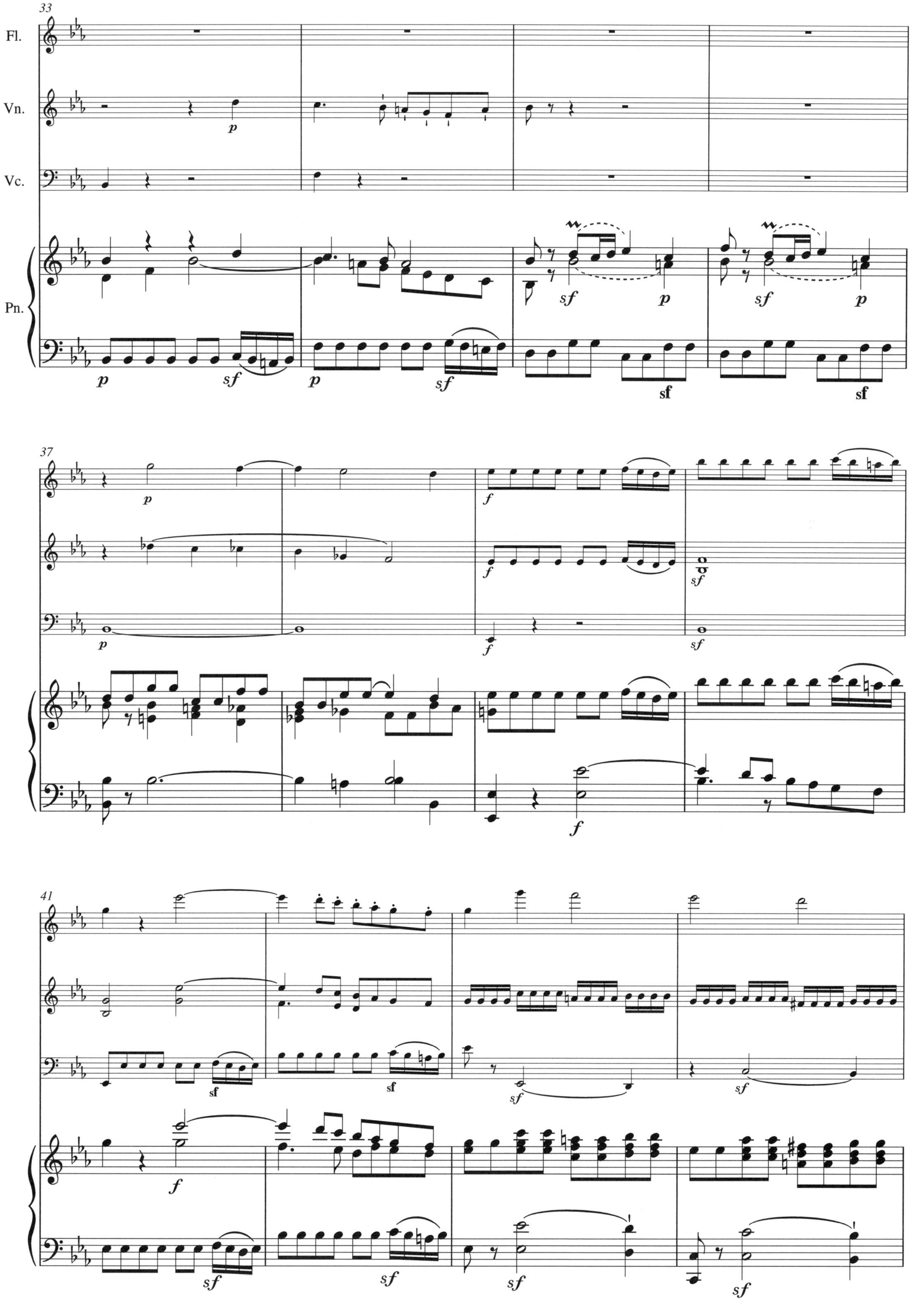
33
Fl.
Vn.
Vc.
Pn.
p
sf
37
f
41

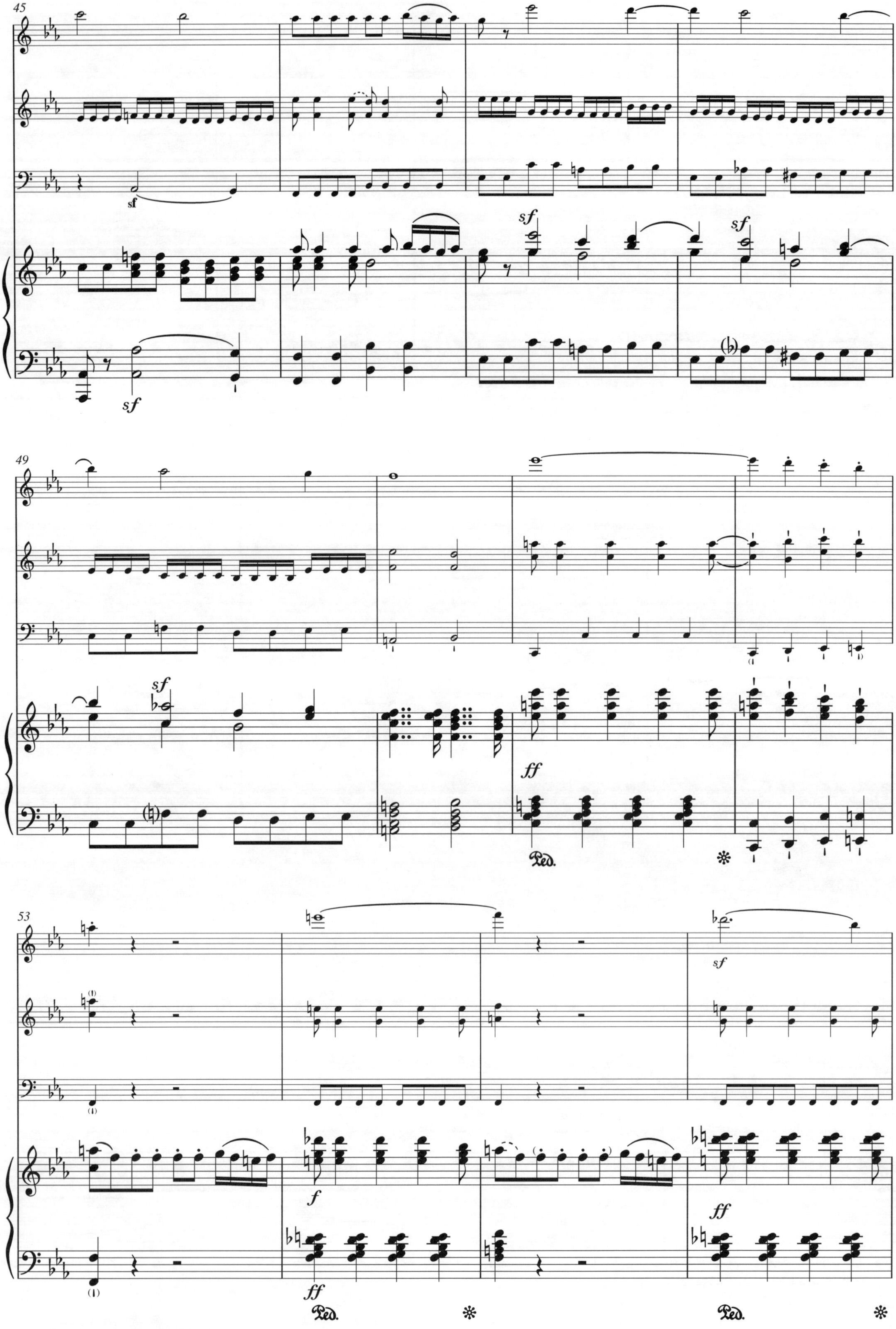
45
sf
sf
sf
sf
49
sf
ff
Ped.
53
f
sf
ff
ff
Ped.
Ped.

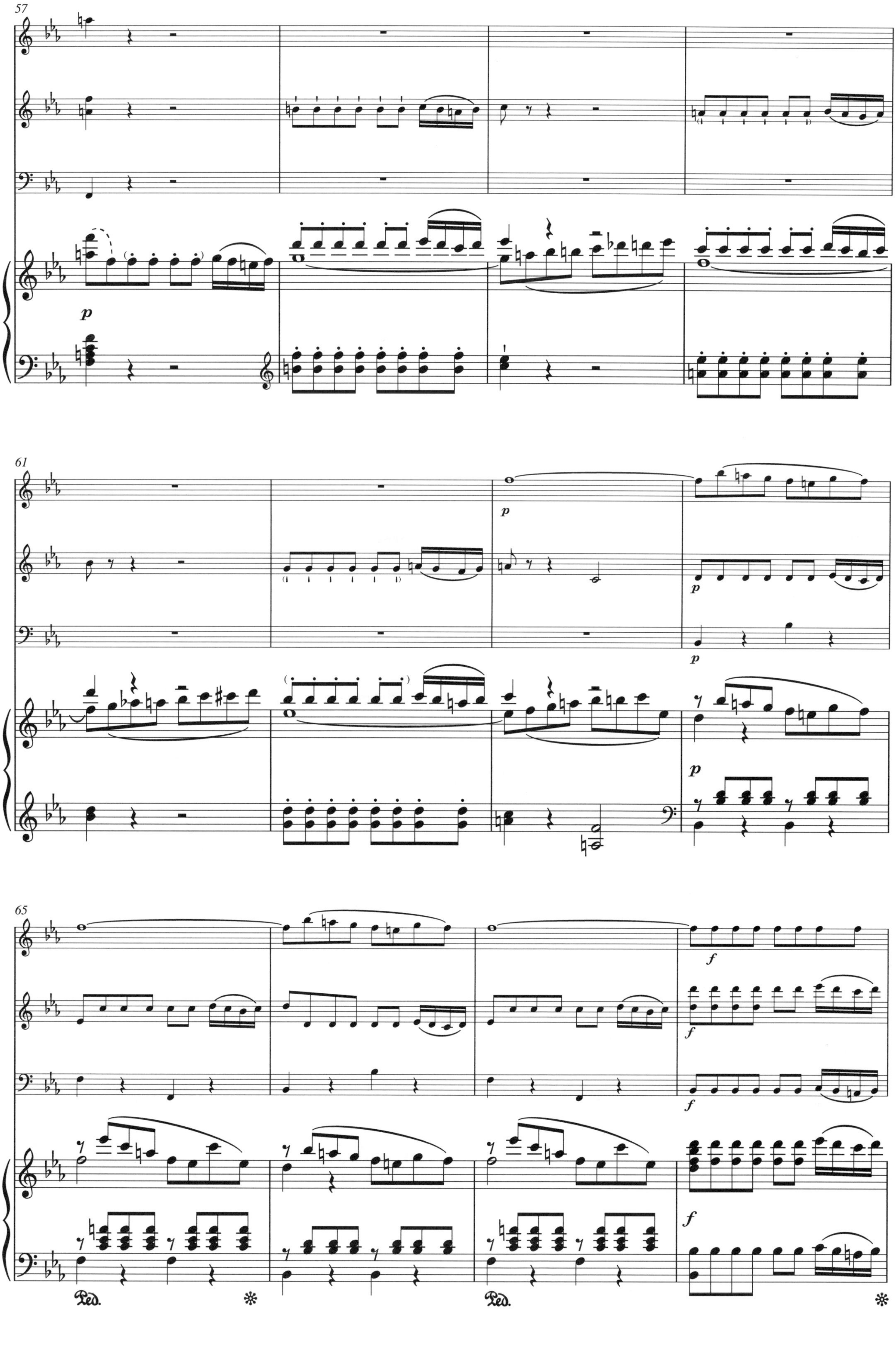
57
p
61
p
65
f
Ped.

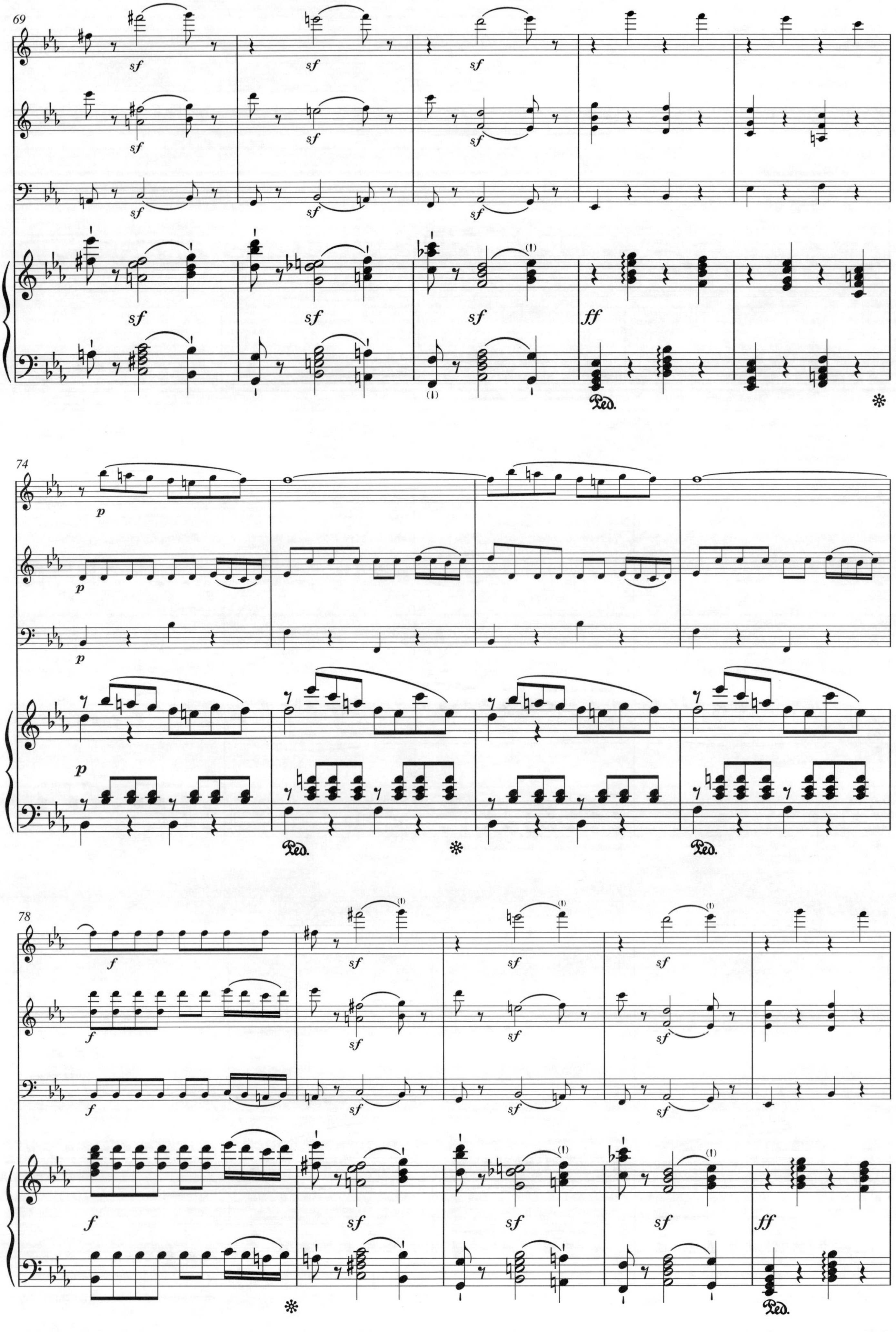
69
sf
ff
Ped.
74
p
Ped.
78
f
sf
ff
Ped.

27

28

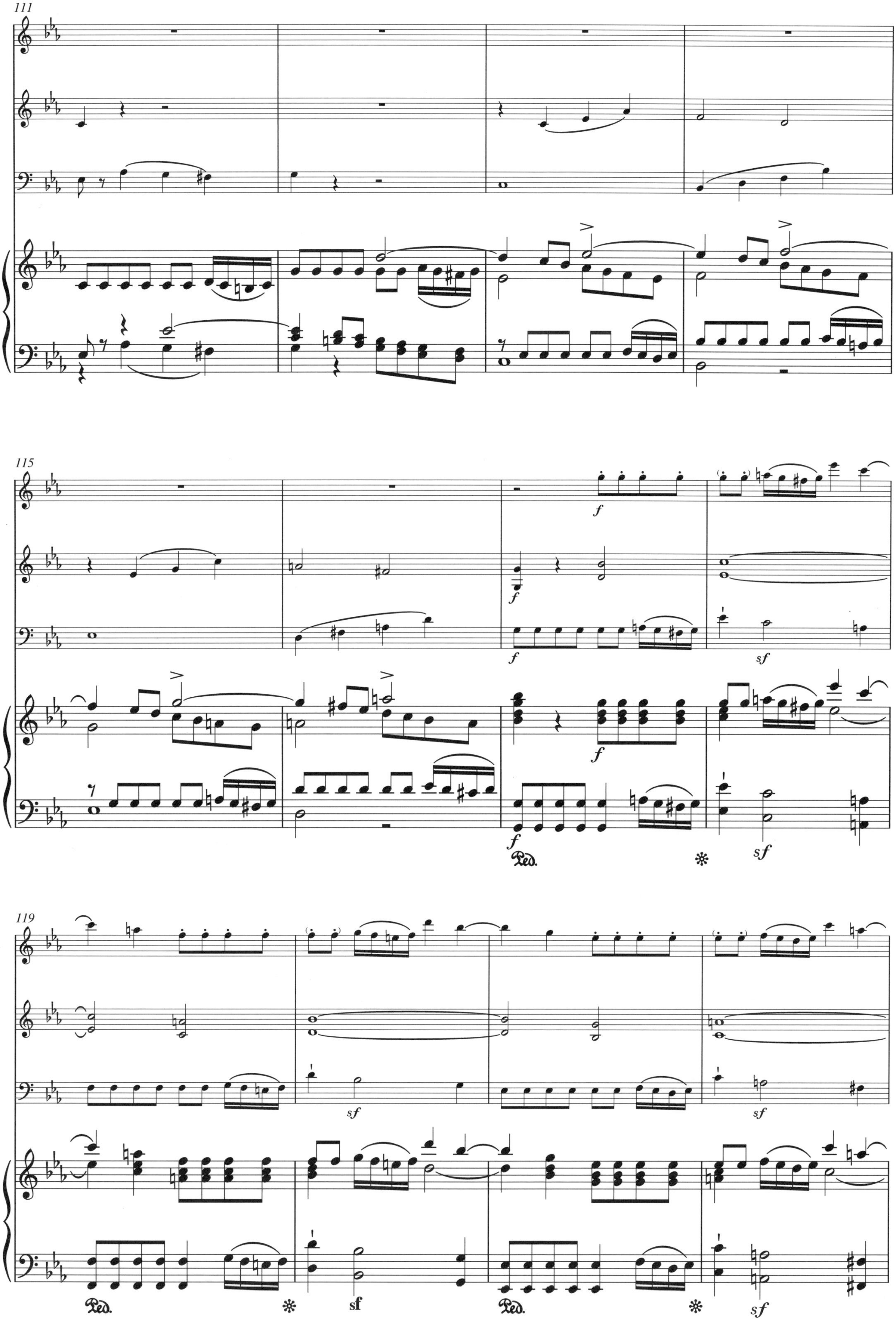
111
115
f
sf
Ped.
119
sf

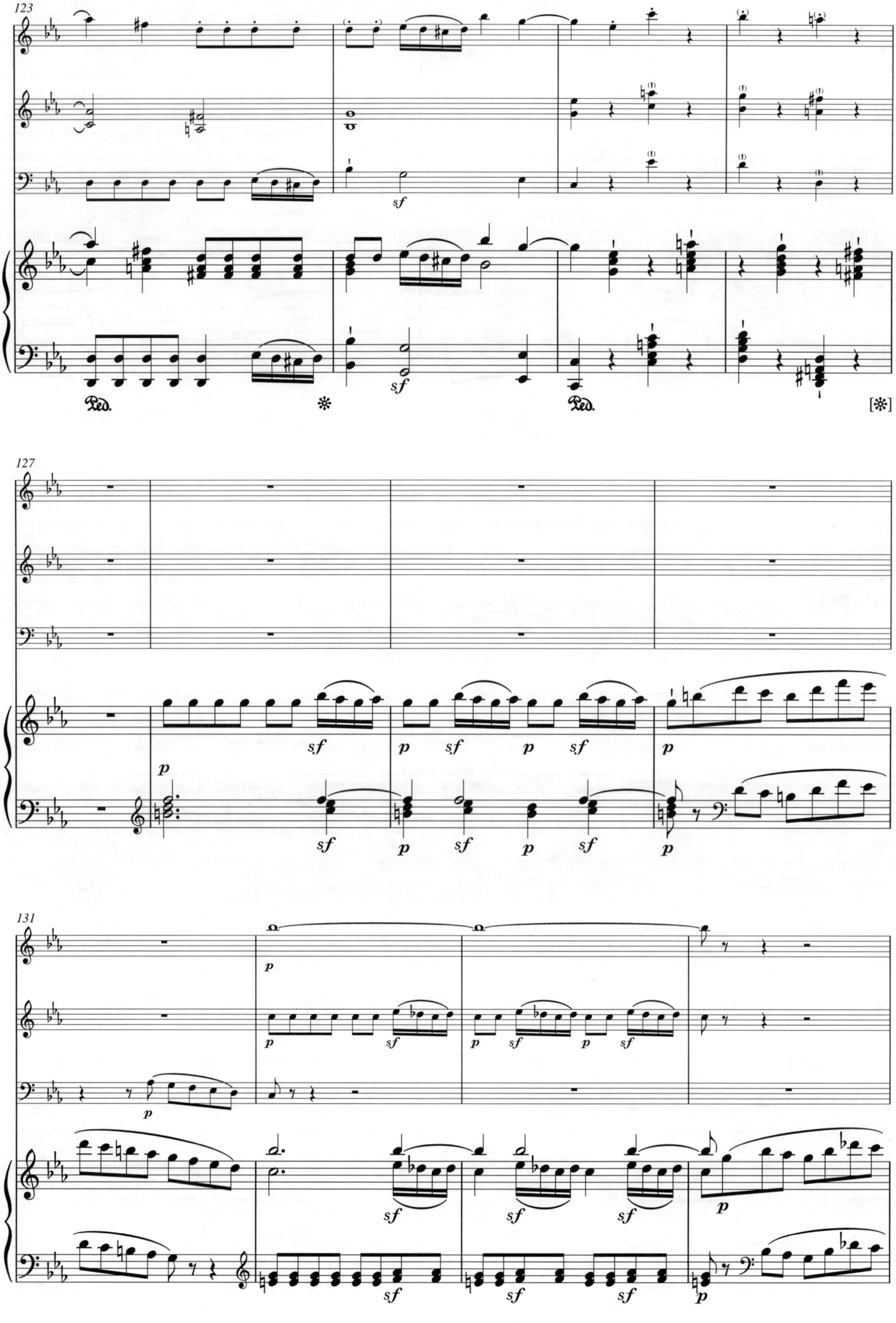
123
sf
Ped.
Ped.
127
p
sf
131
p
sf

31

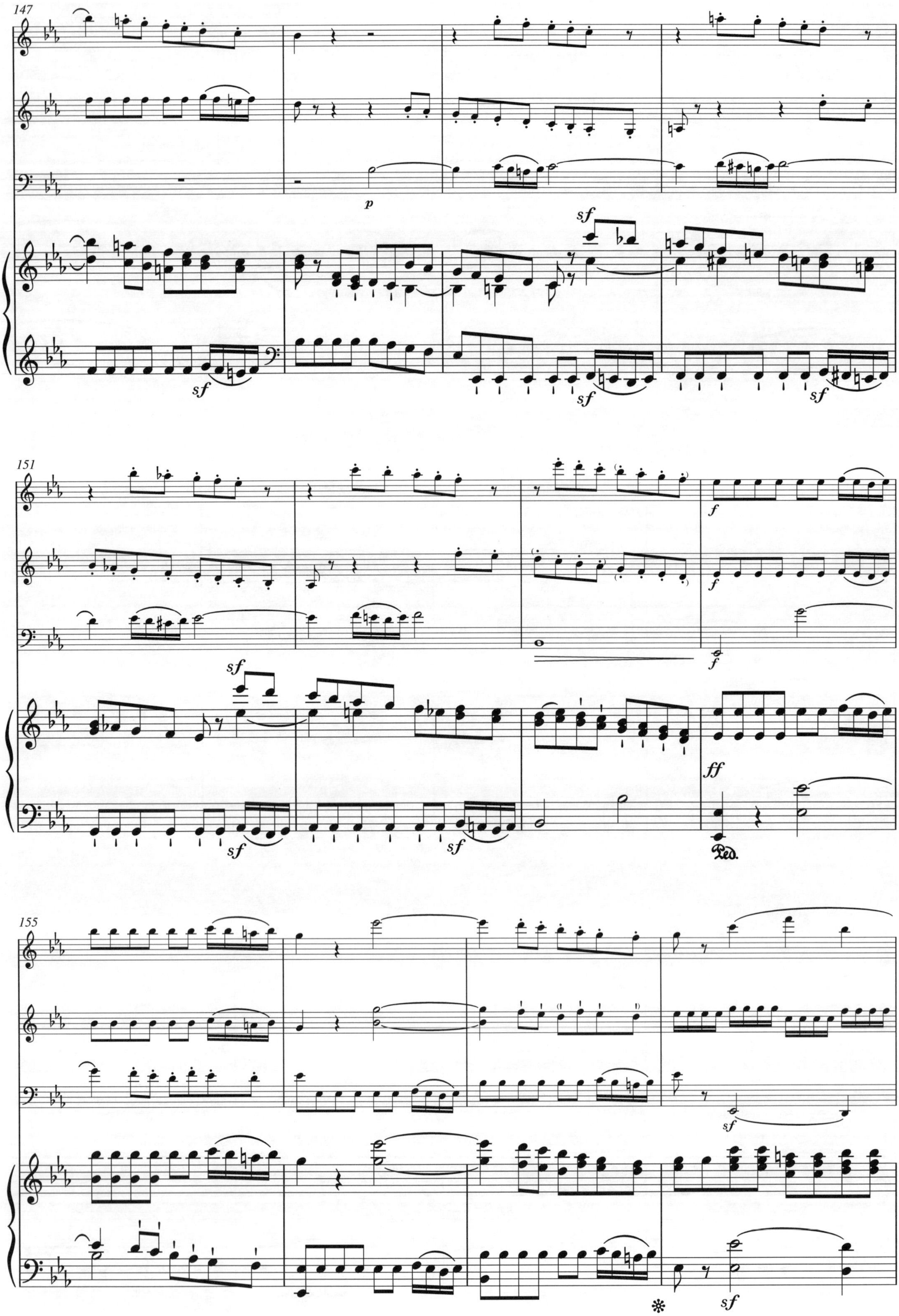
147
p
sf
151
f
ff
Ped.
155
sf

33

34

35

36

37

38

3. Overture to Lodoïska

Luigi Cherubini

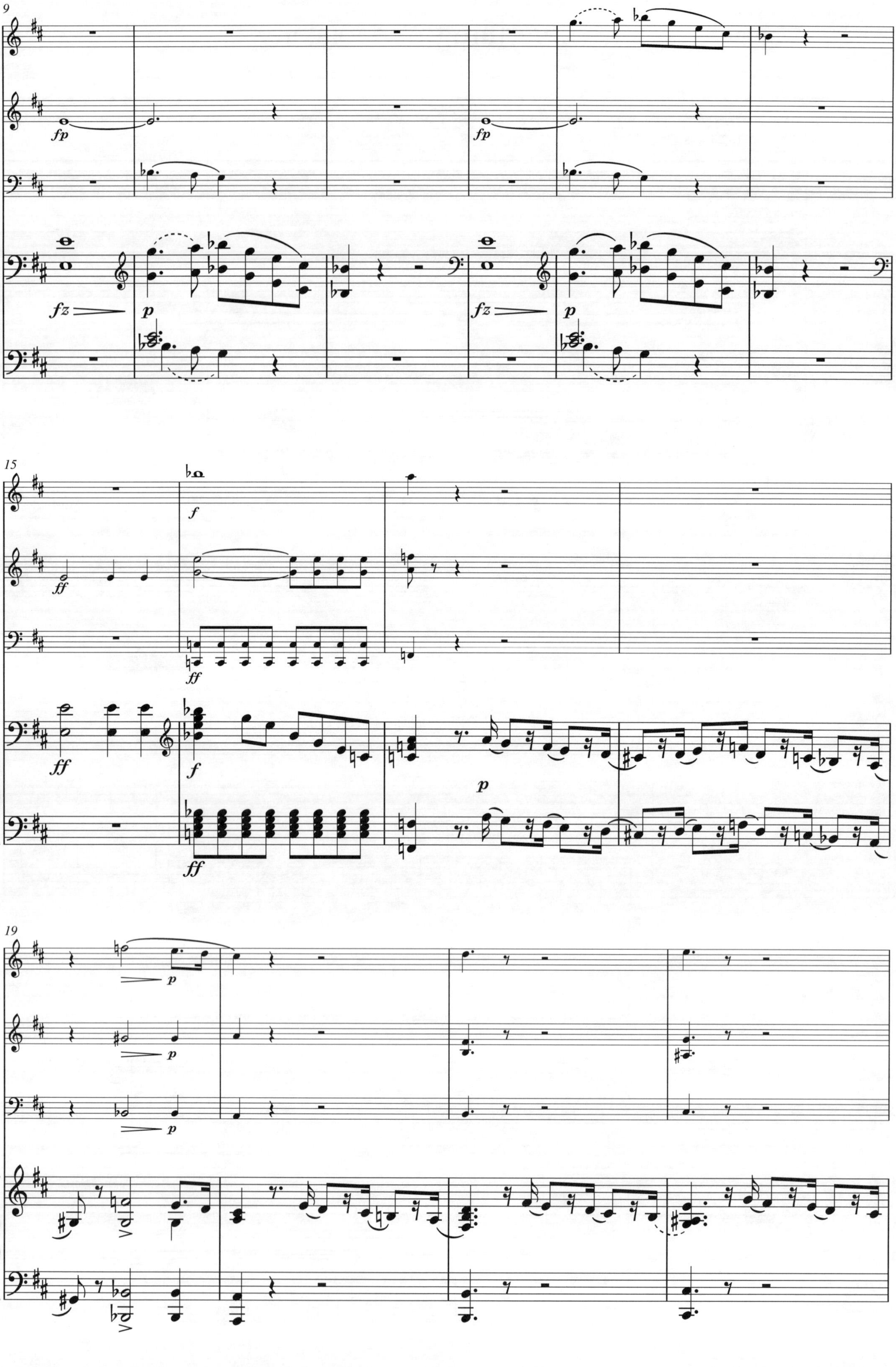

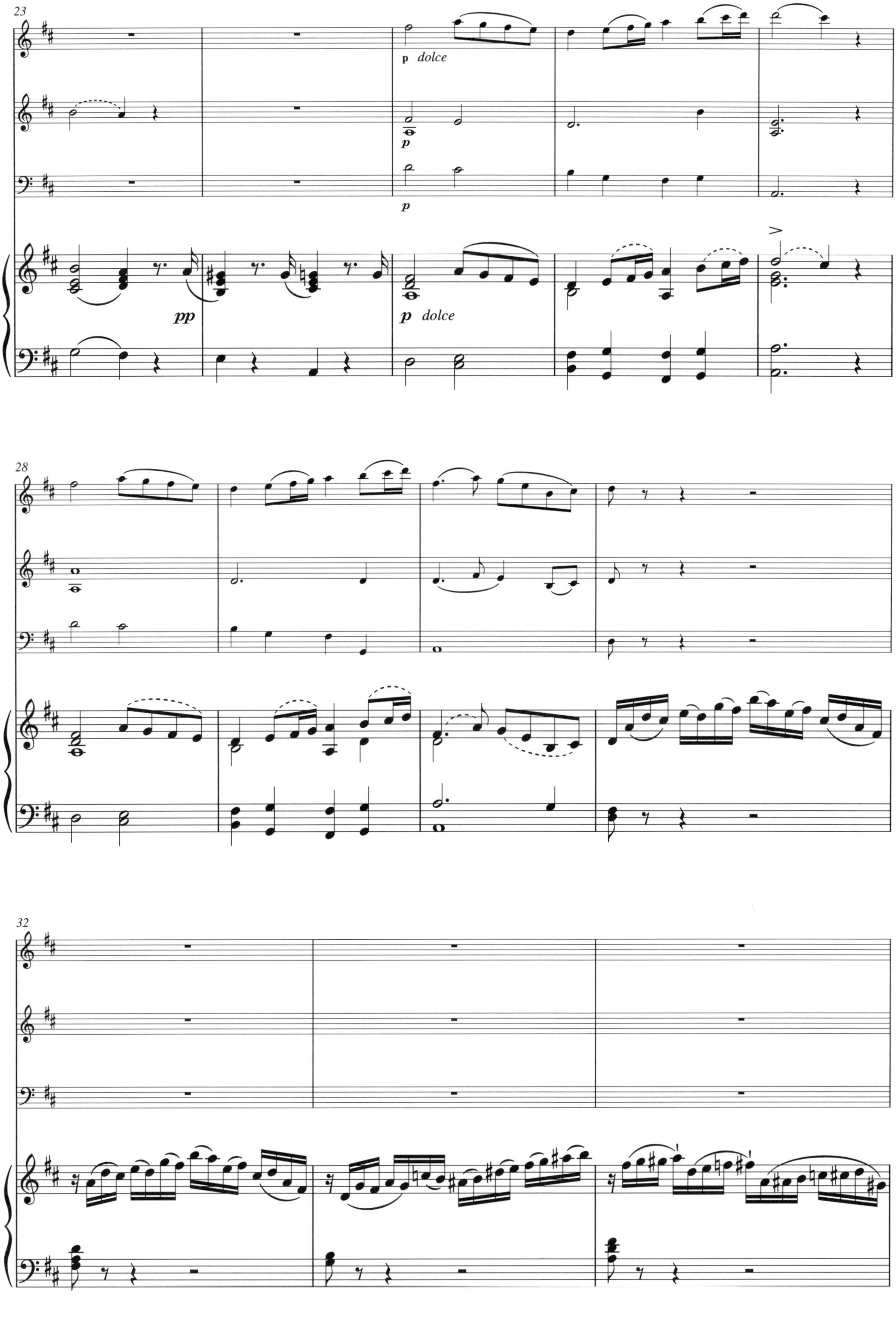
23
p dolce
p
p
pp
p dolce
28
32

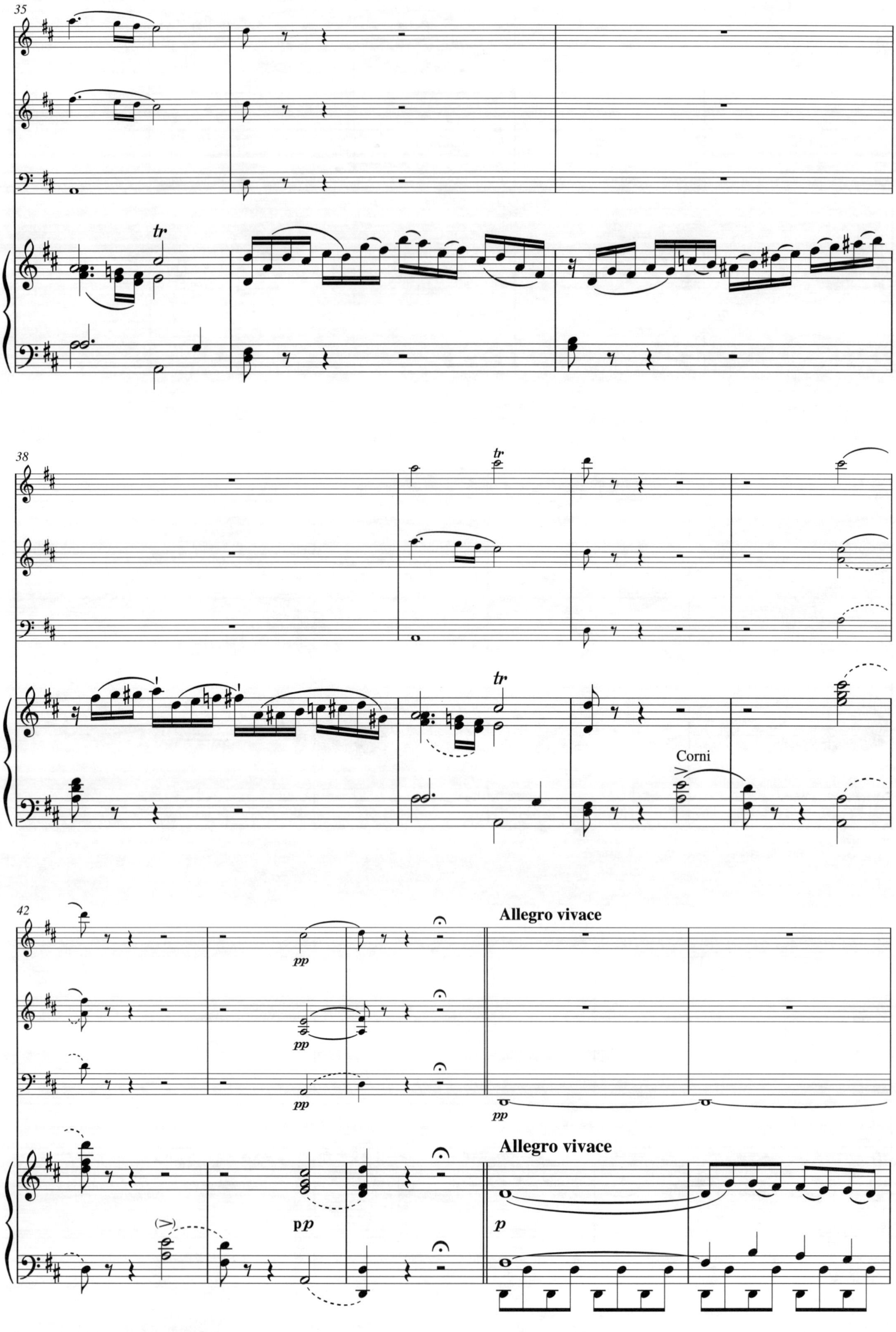
35
38
Corni
42
Allegro vivace
Allegro vivace

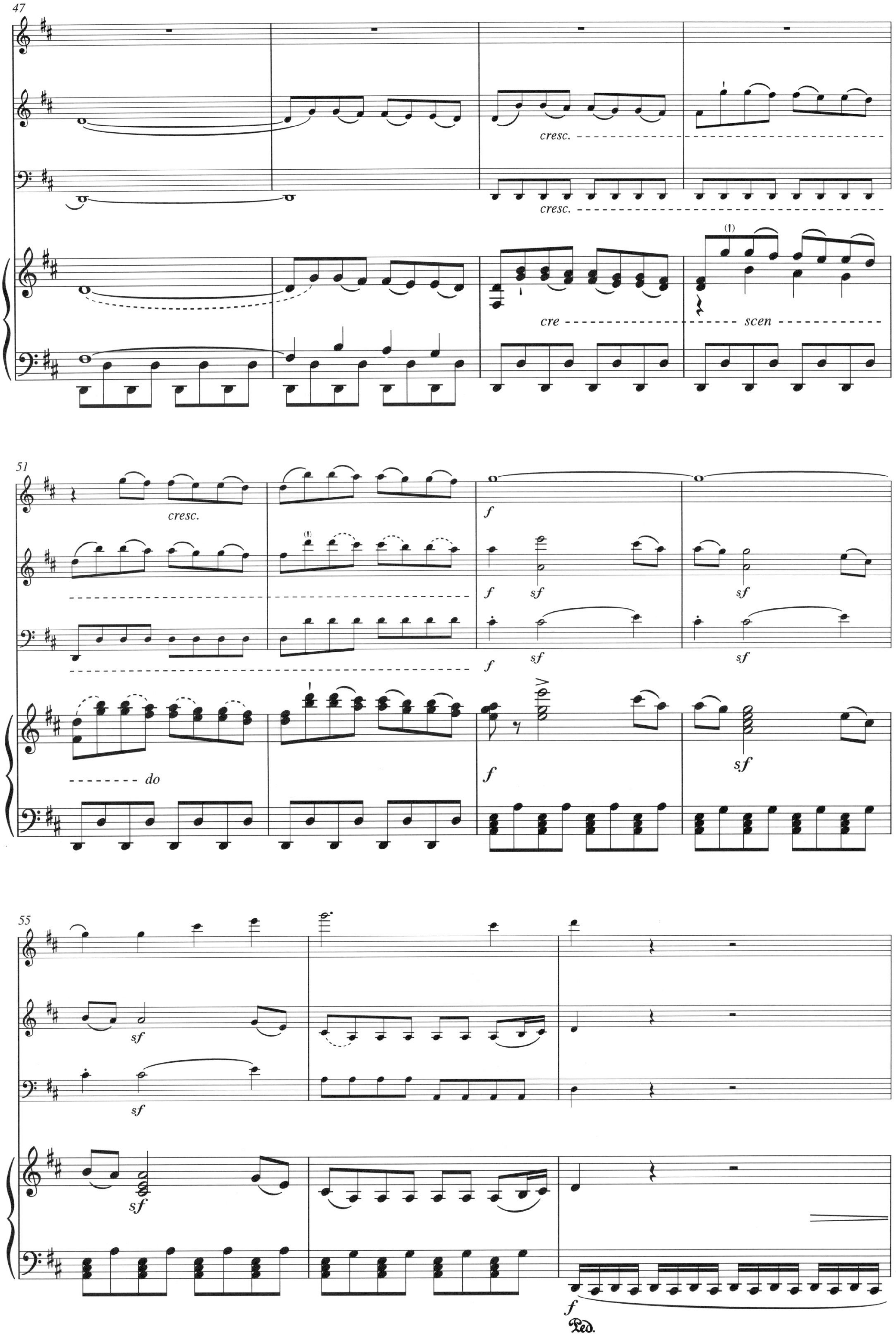
47
cresc.
cresc.
cre
scen
51
cresc.
do
f
sf
55
sf
f
Ped.

44

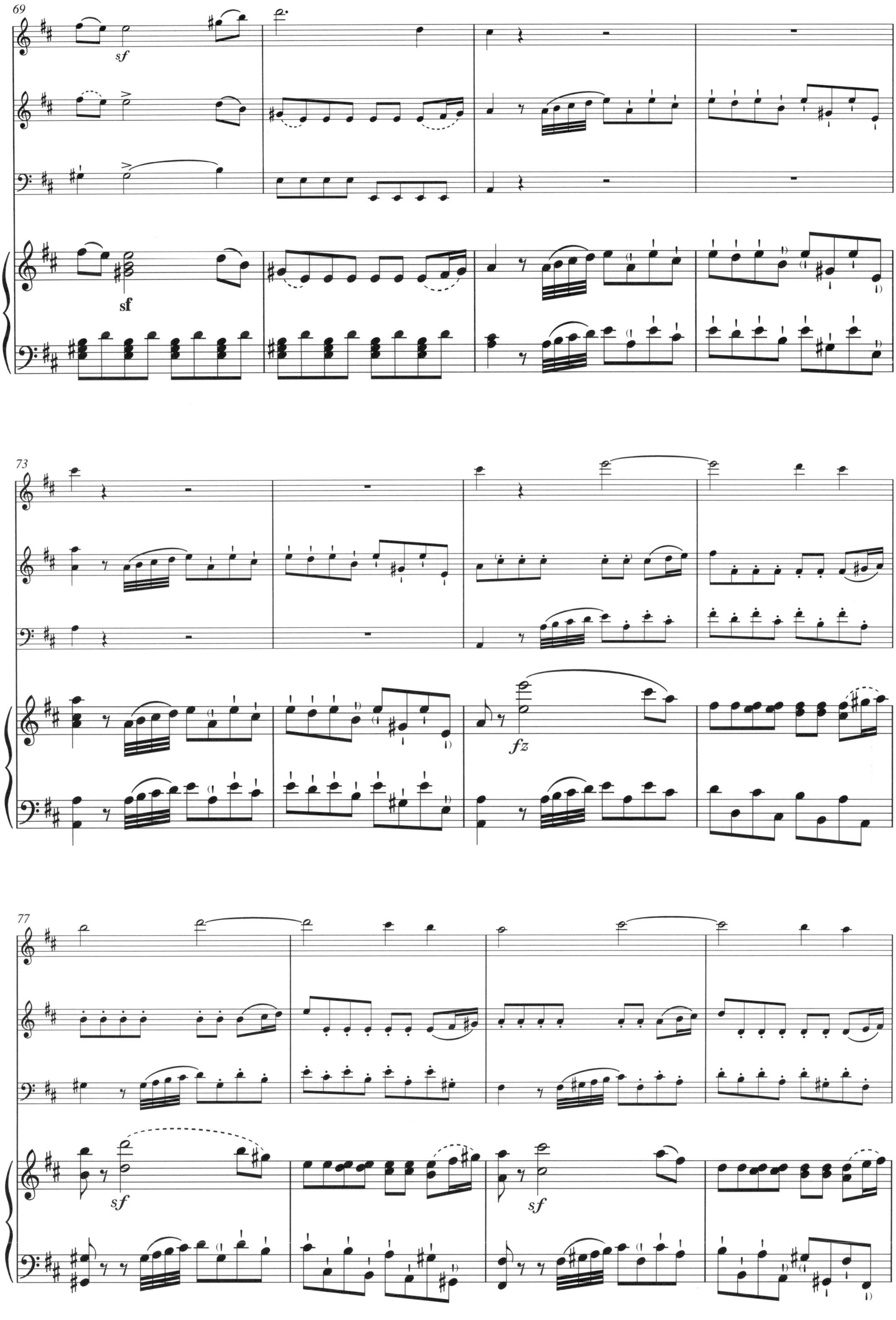
69
sf
sf
73
fz
77
sf
sf

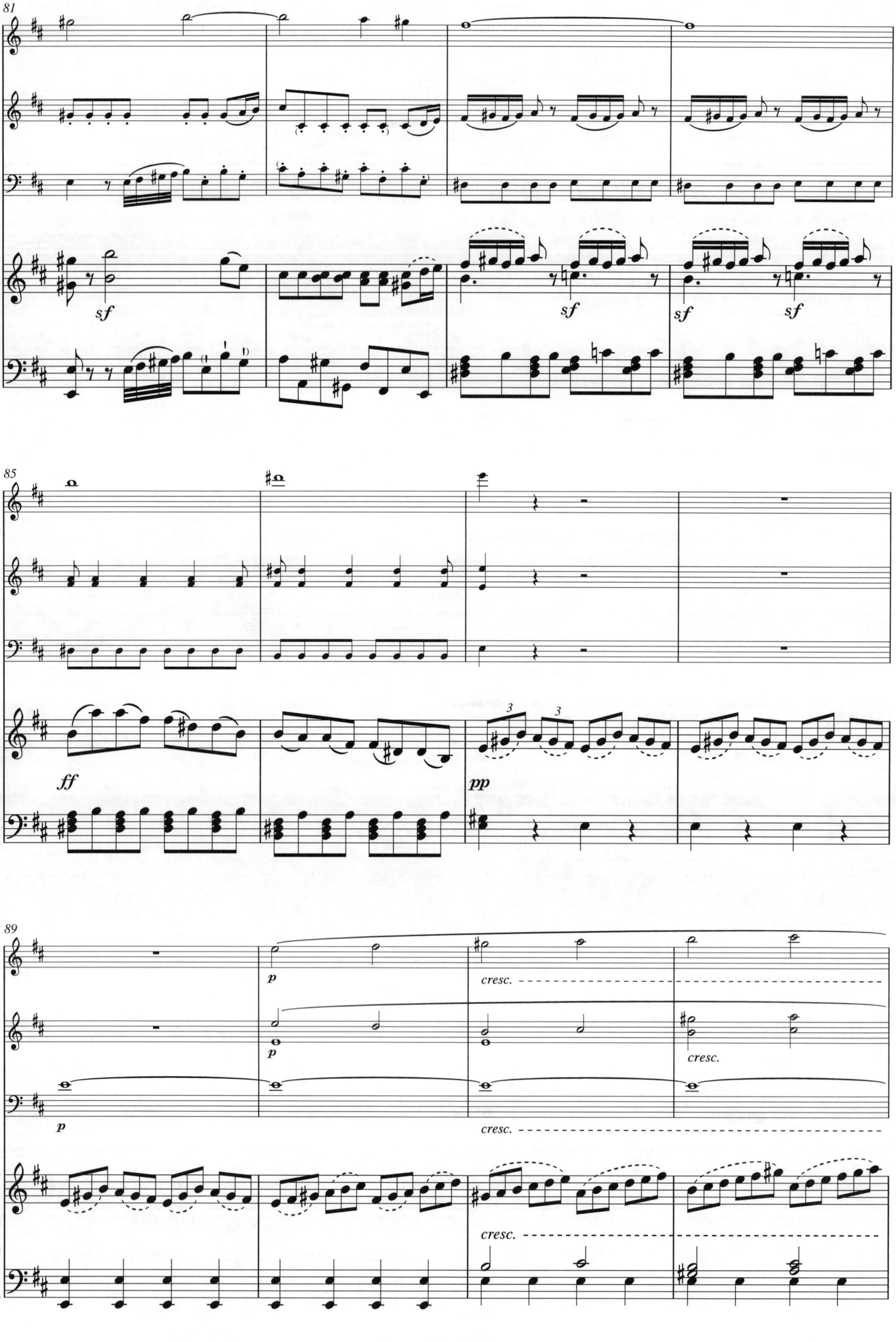
81
sf
sf
sf
sf
85
ff
pp
89
p
p
p
cresc.
cresc.
cresc.
cresc.

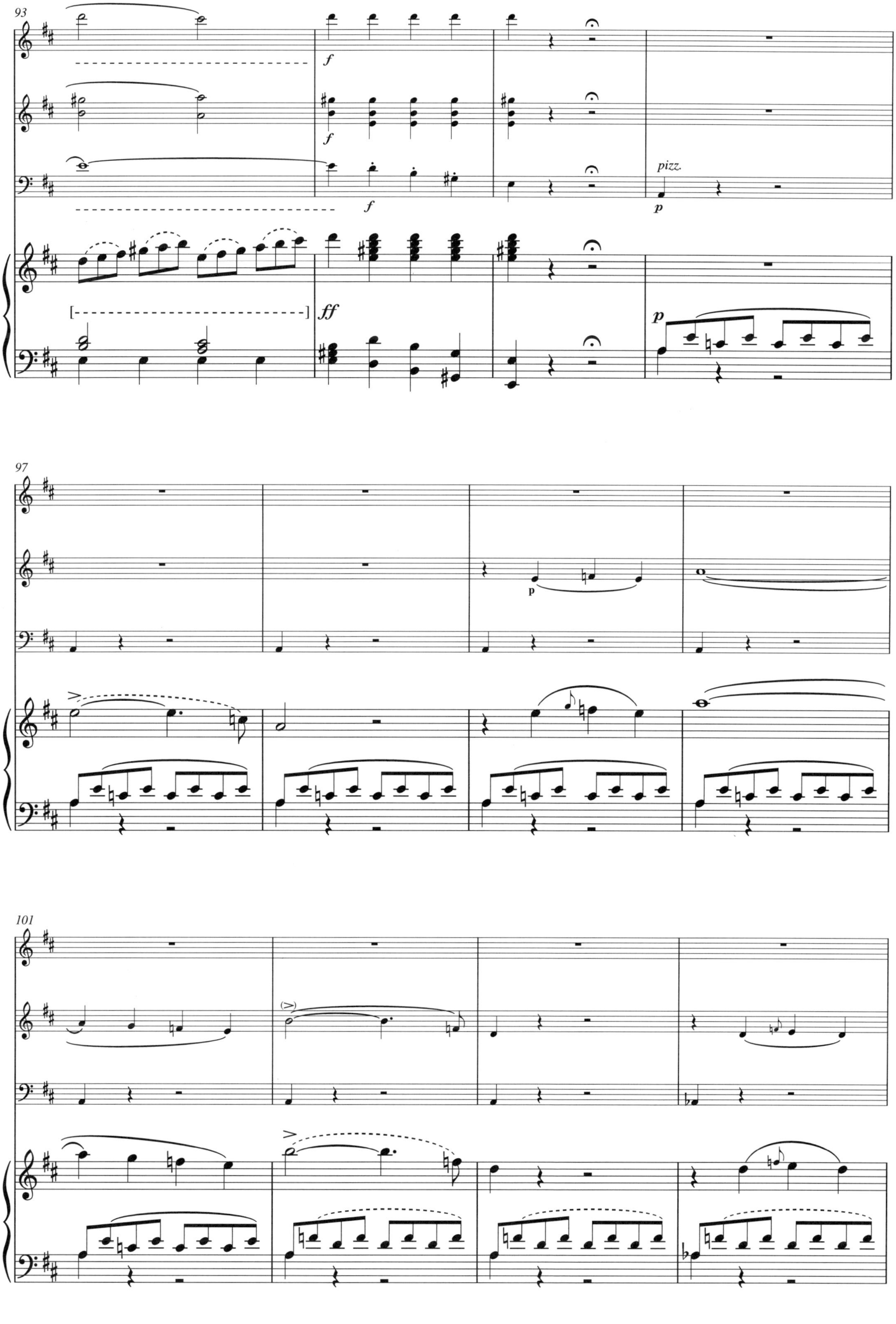
93
f
f
f
pizz.
p
ff
p
97
p
101

48

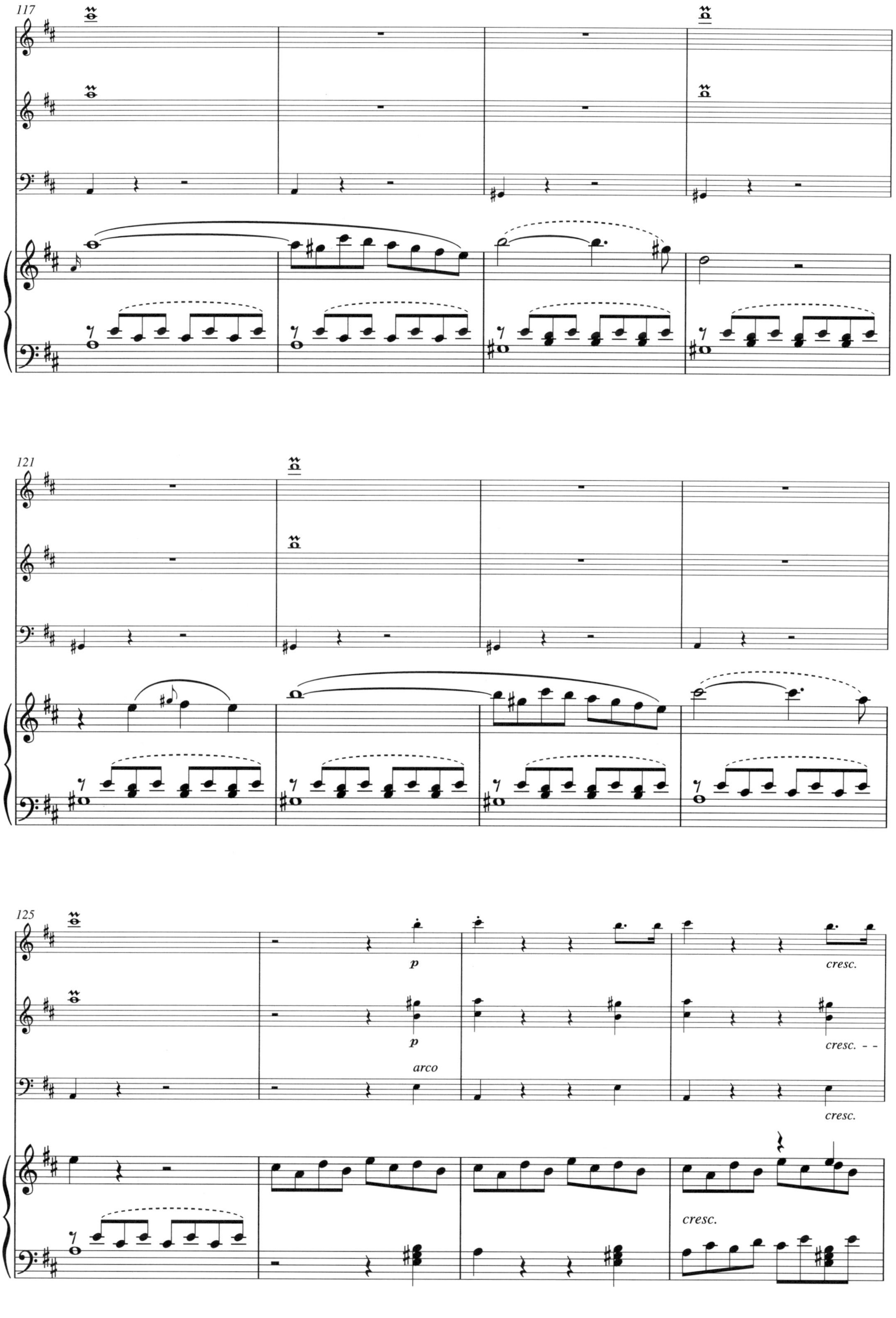
117
121
125
p
p
arco
cresc.
cresc. - -
cresc.
cresc.

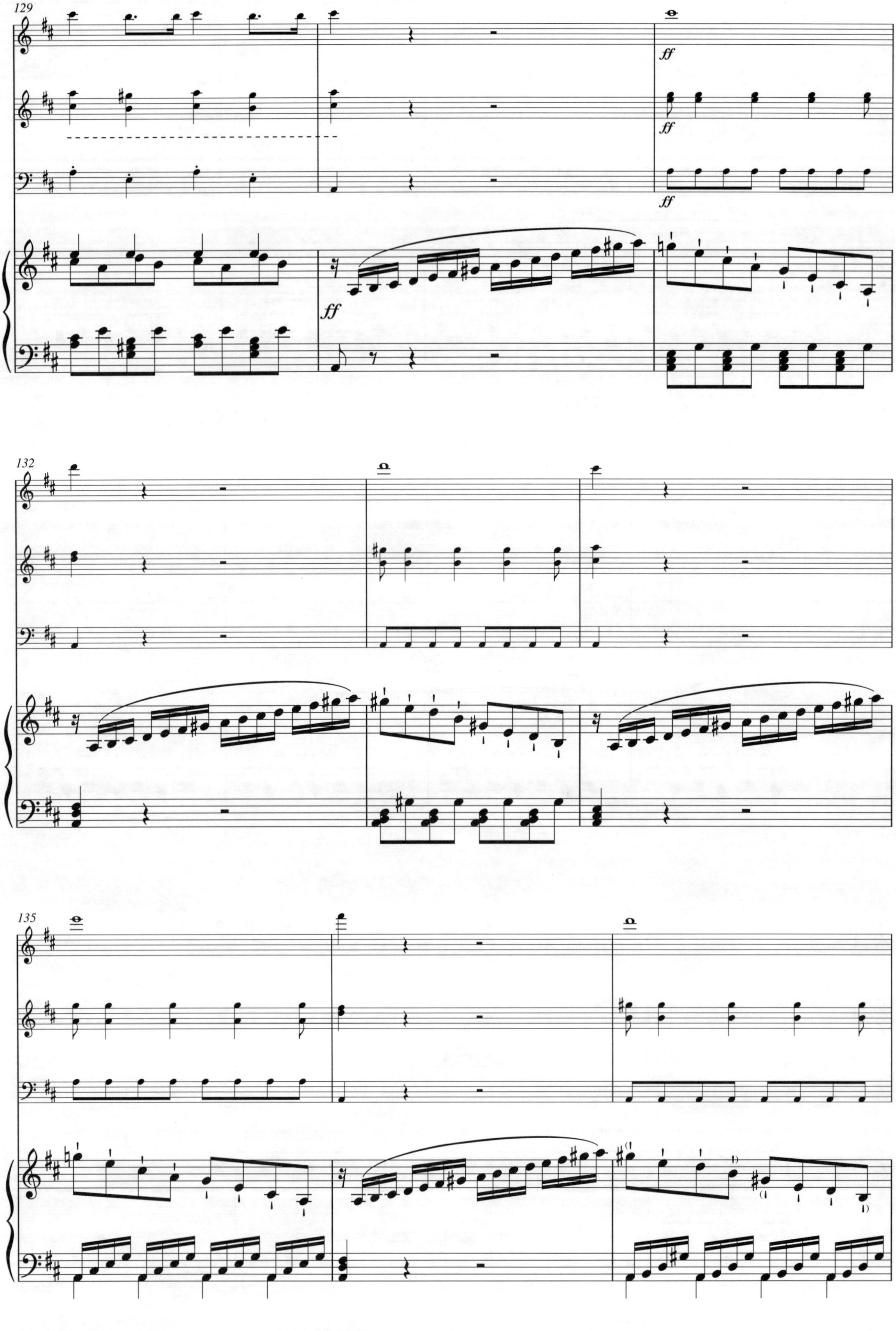
129
ff
ff
ff
ff
132
135

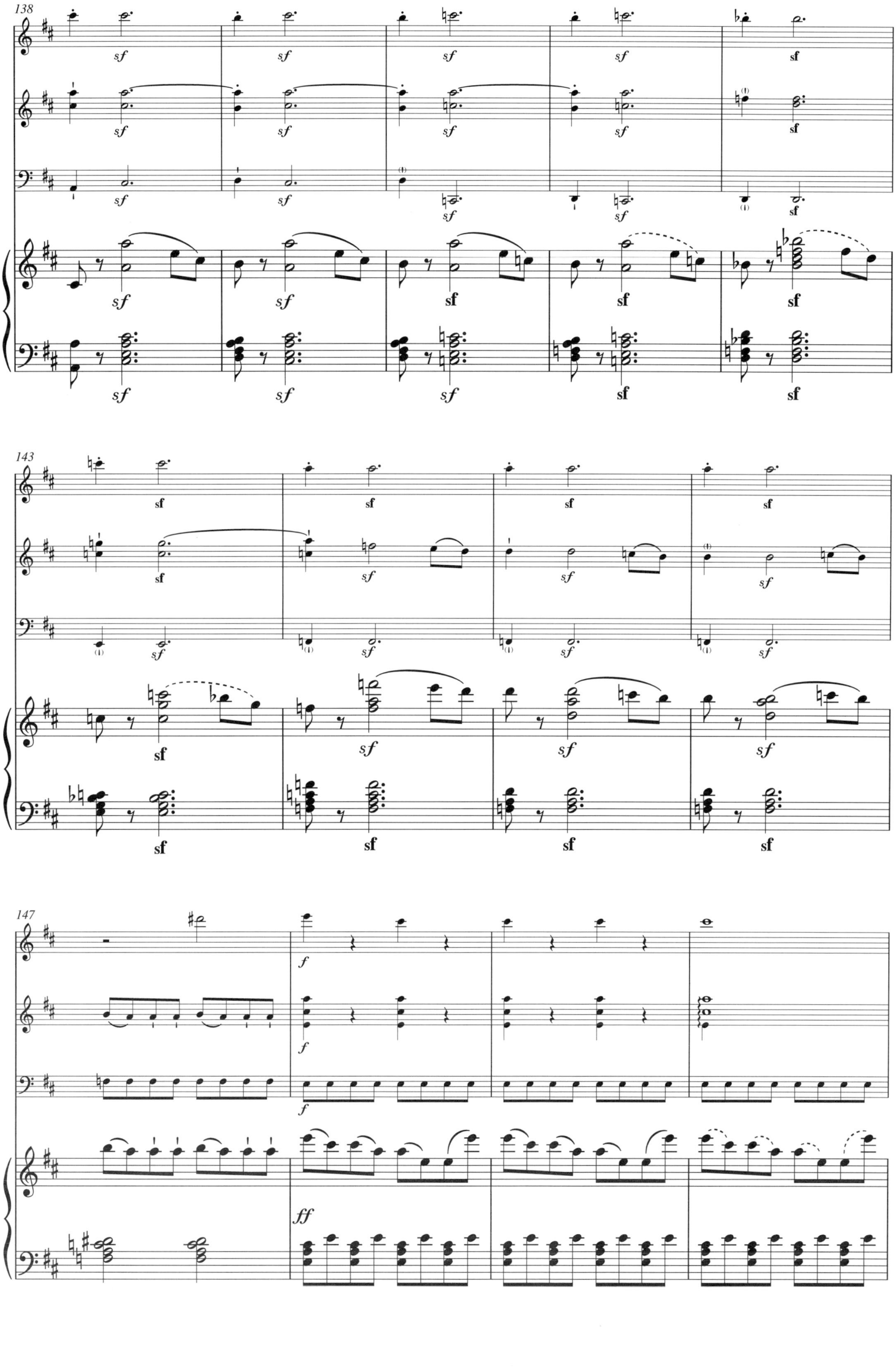
138
143
147

52

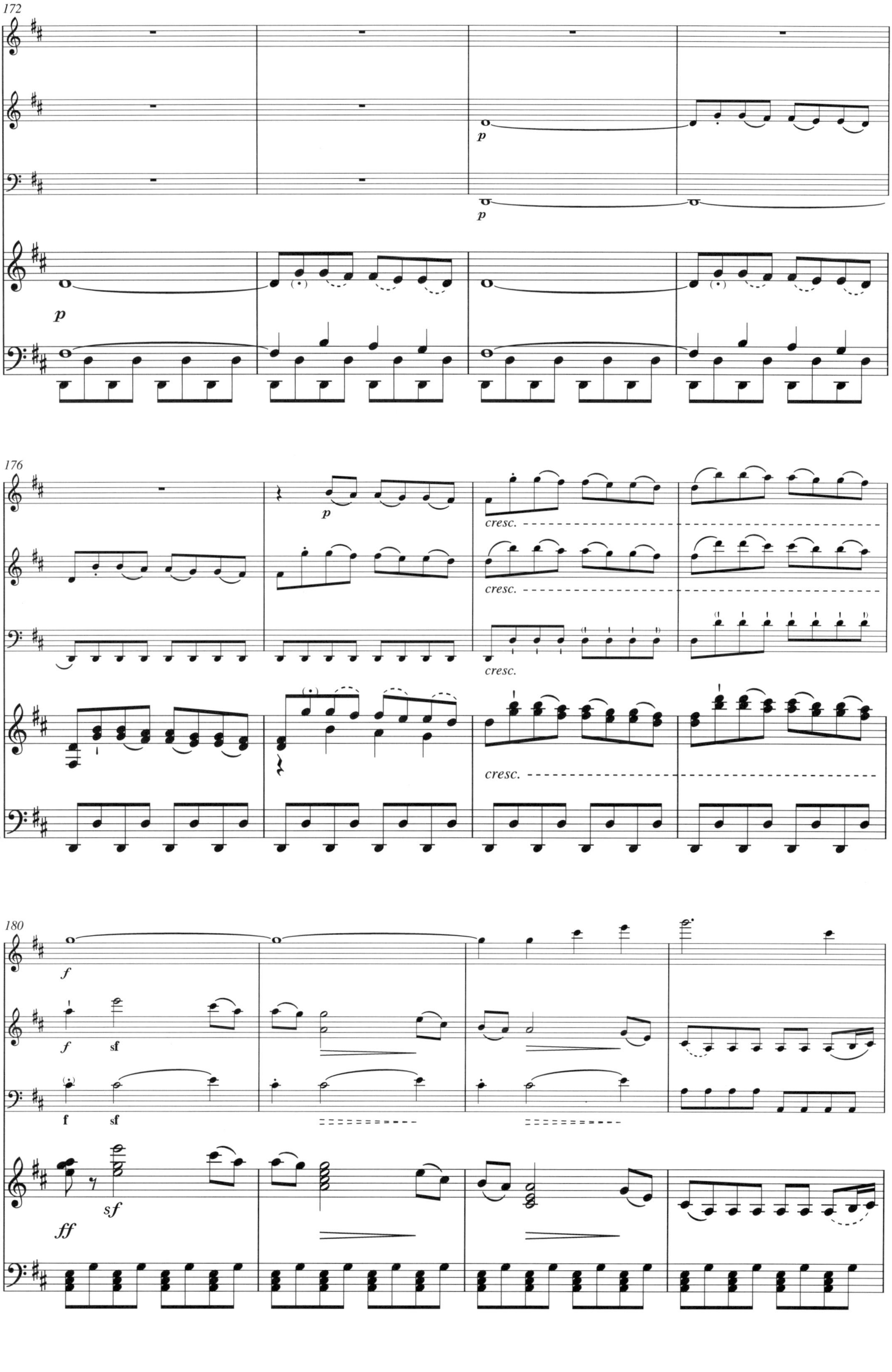
172
p
p
p
176
p
cresc.
cresc.
cresc.
cresc.
180
f
f
sf
f
sf
sf
ff

54

55

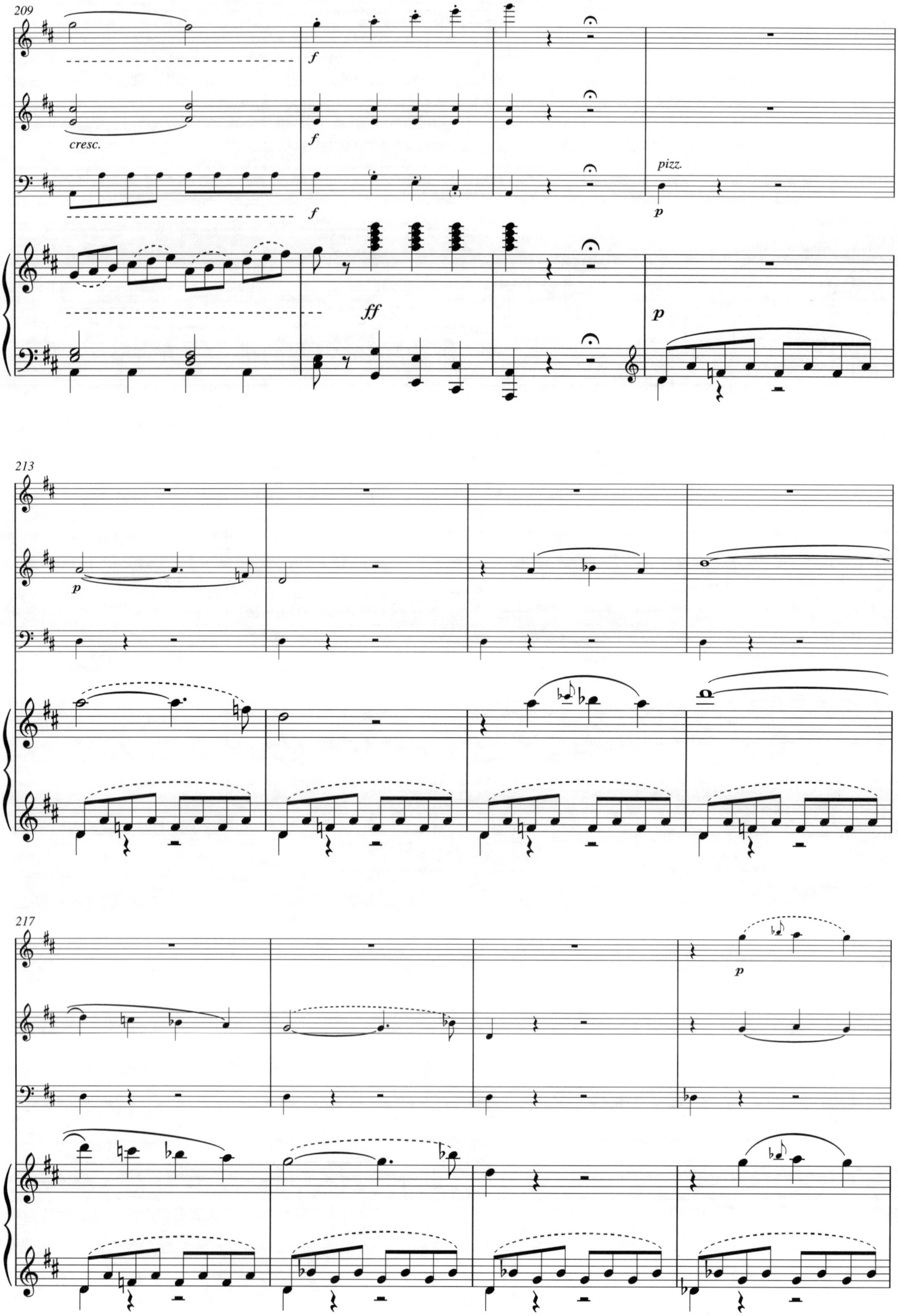
209
cresc.
f
f
f
ff
pizz.
p
p
213
p
217
p

57

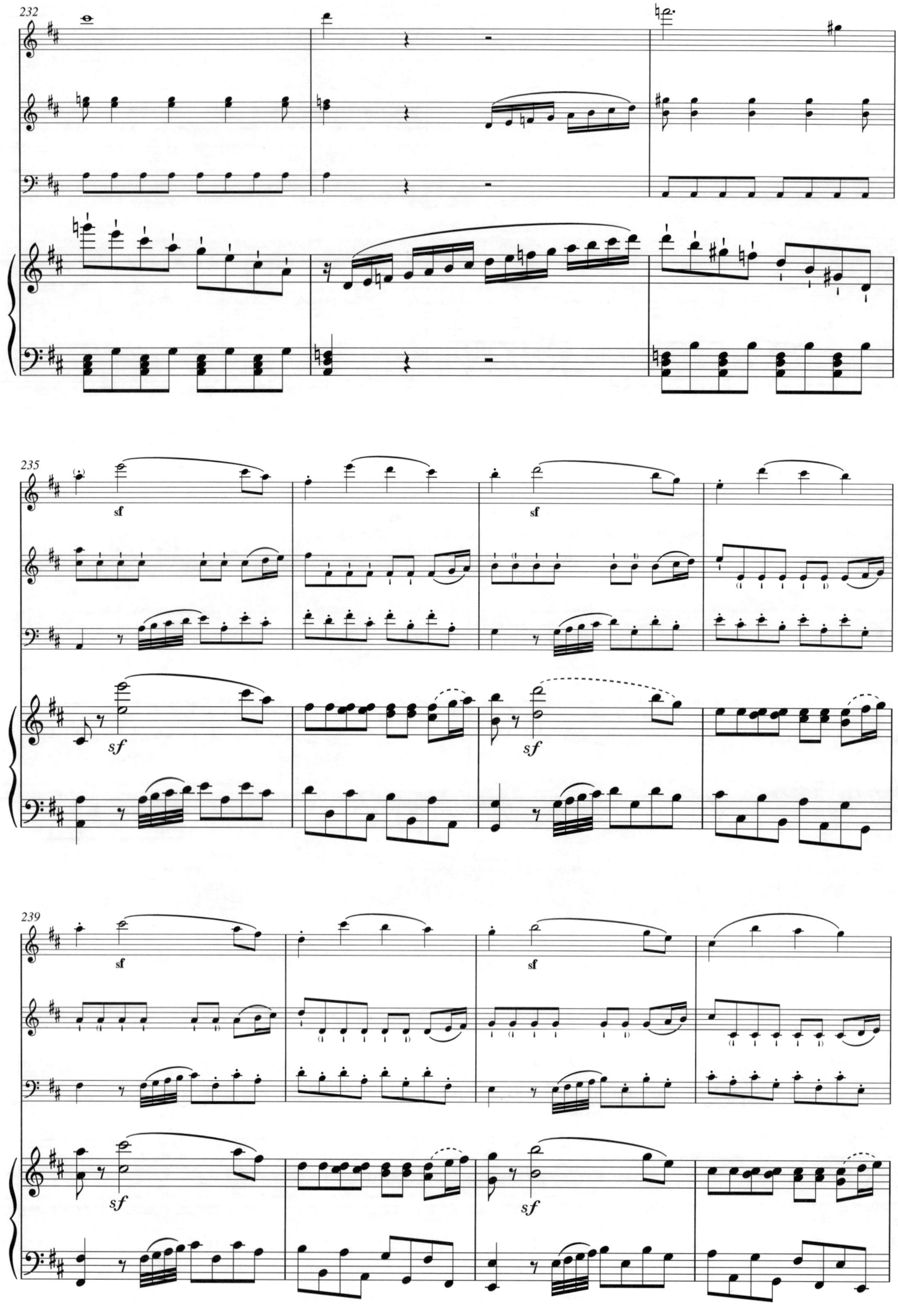
232
235
sf
sf
sf
sf
239
sf
sf
sf
sf

59

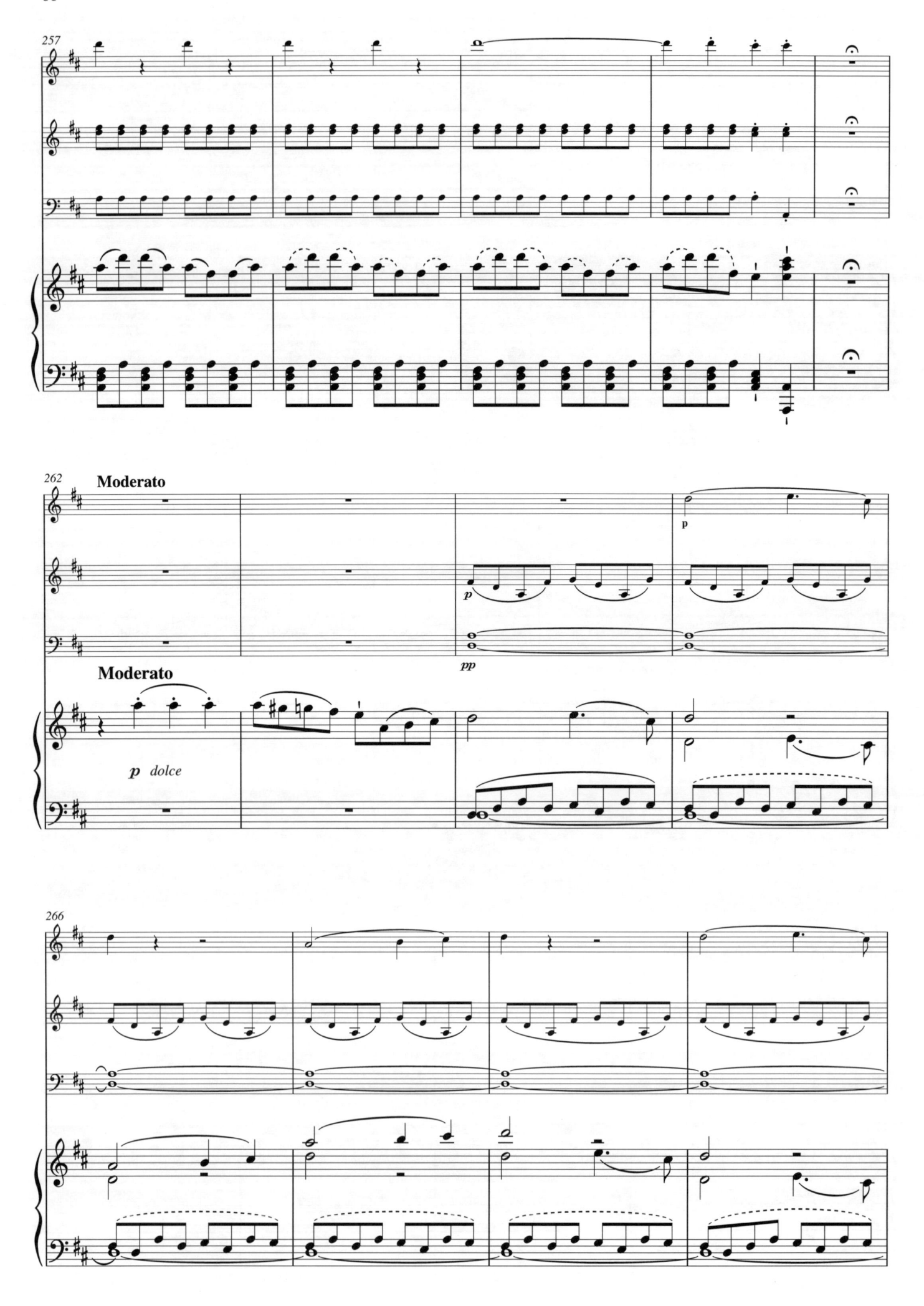
257
262
Moderato
p
p
pp
Moderato
p dolce
266

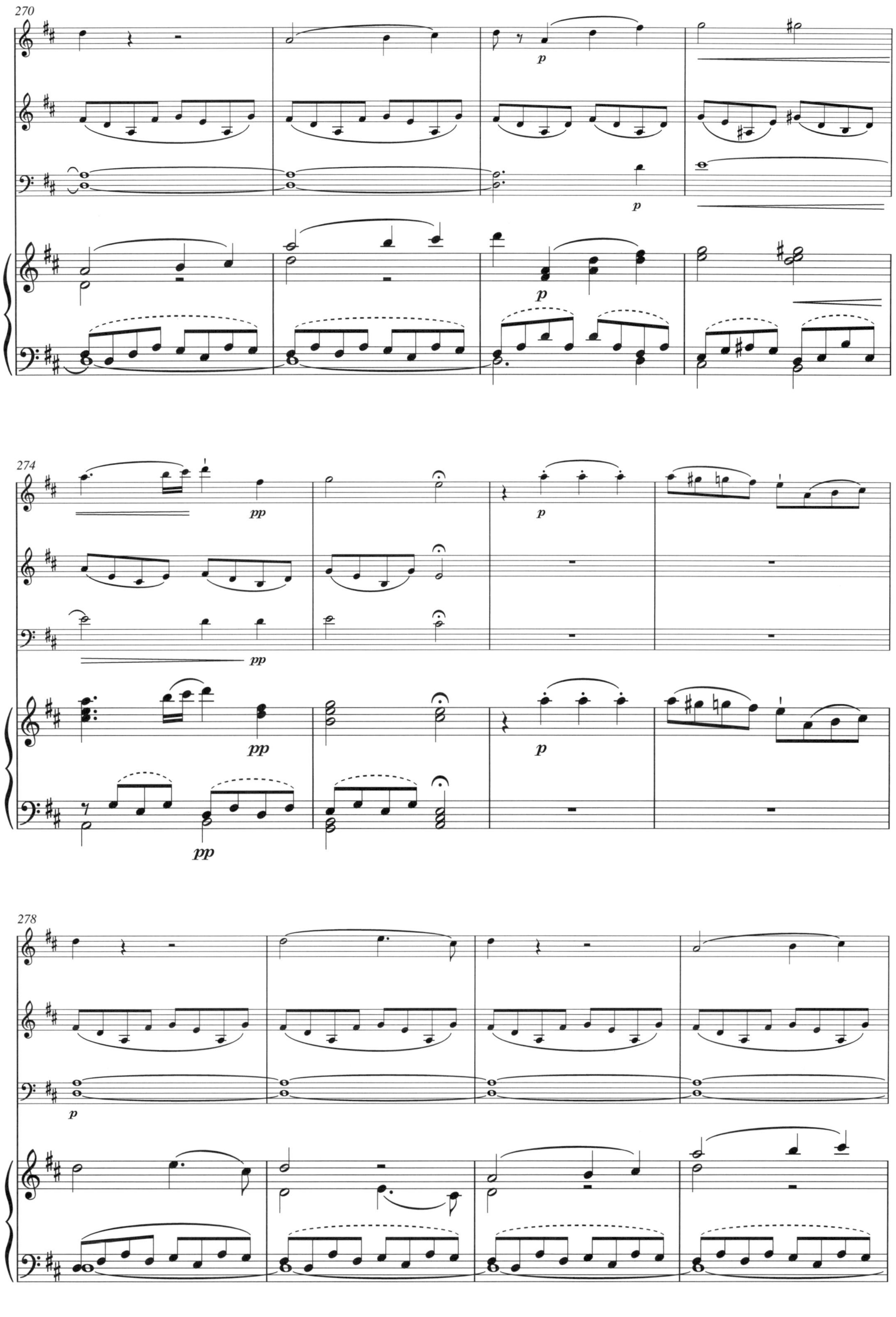
270
p
p
p
274
pp
pp
p
pp
pp
p
278
p

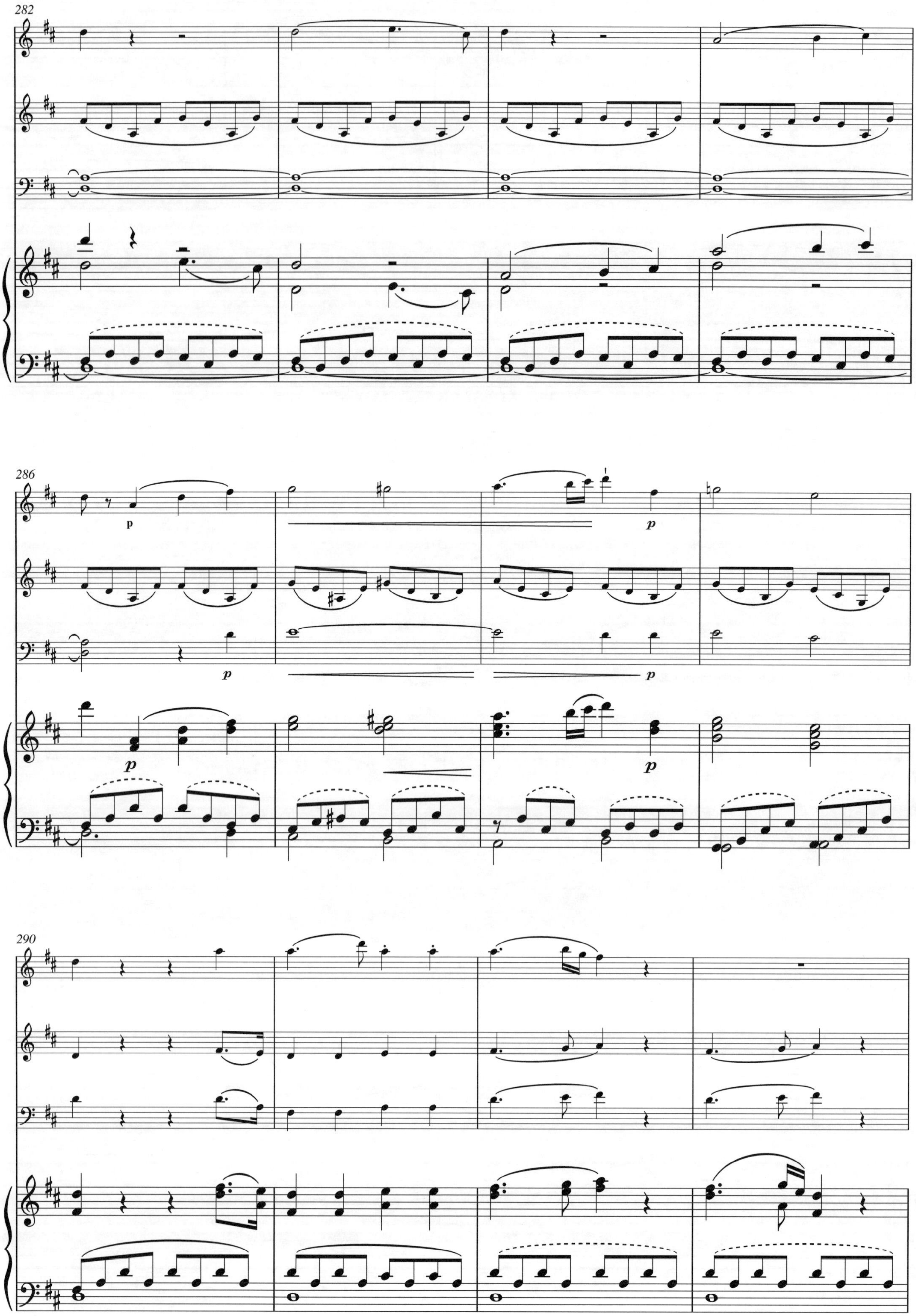
282
286
p
p
p
p
p
290

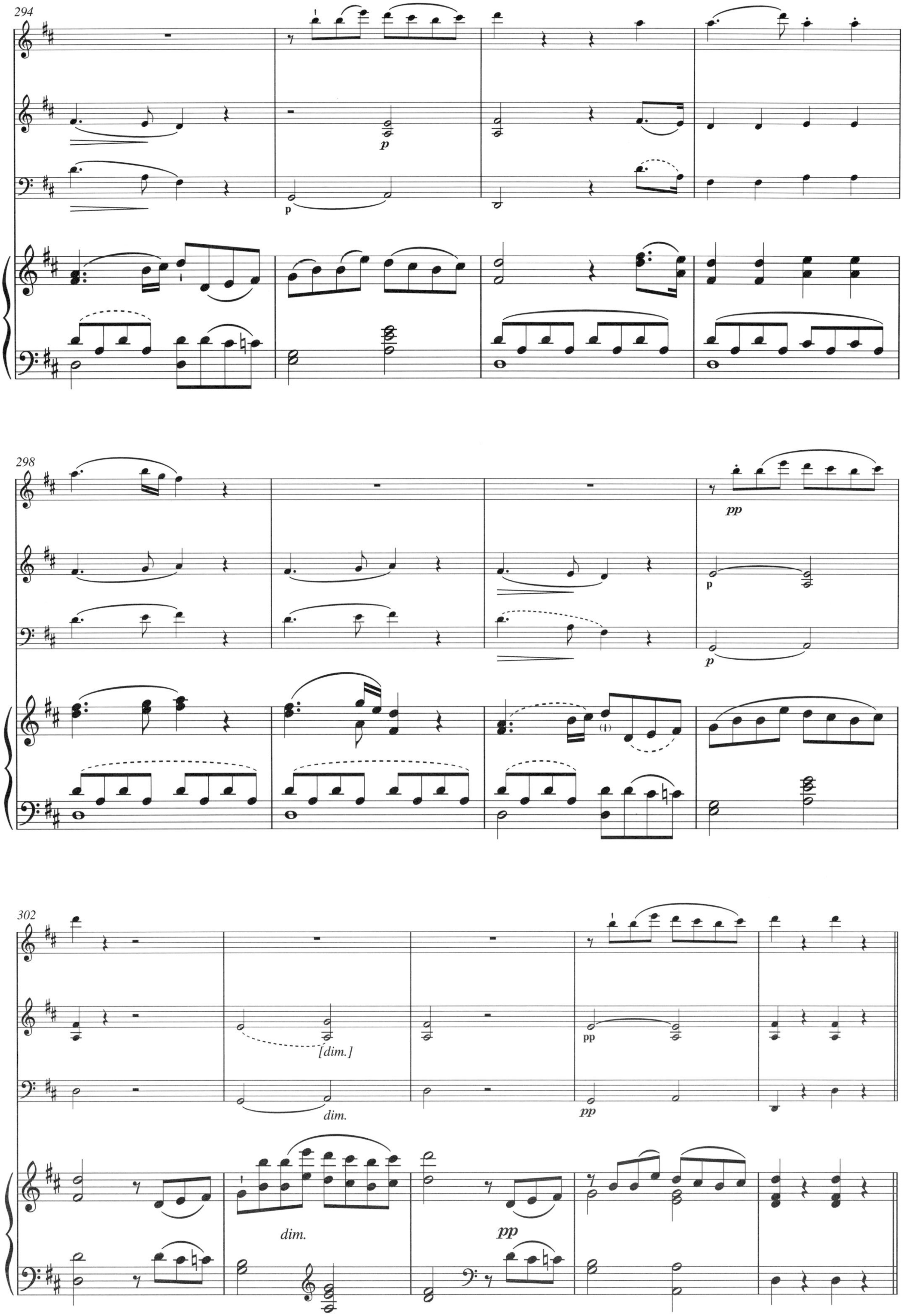
294
p
p
298
pp
p
p
302
[dim.]
dim.
pp
pp
dim.
pp

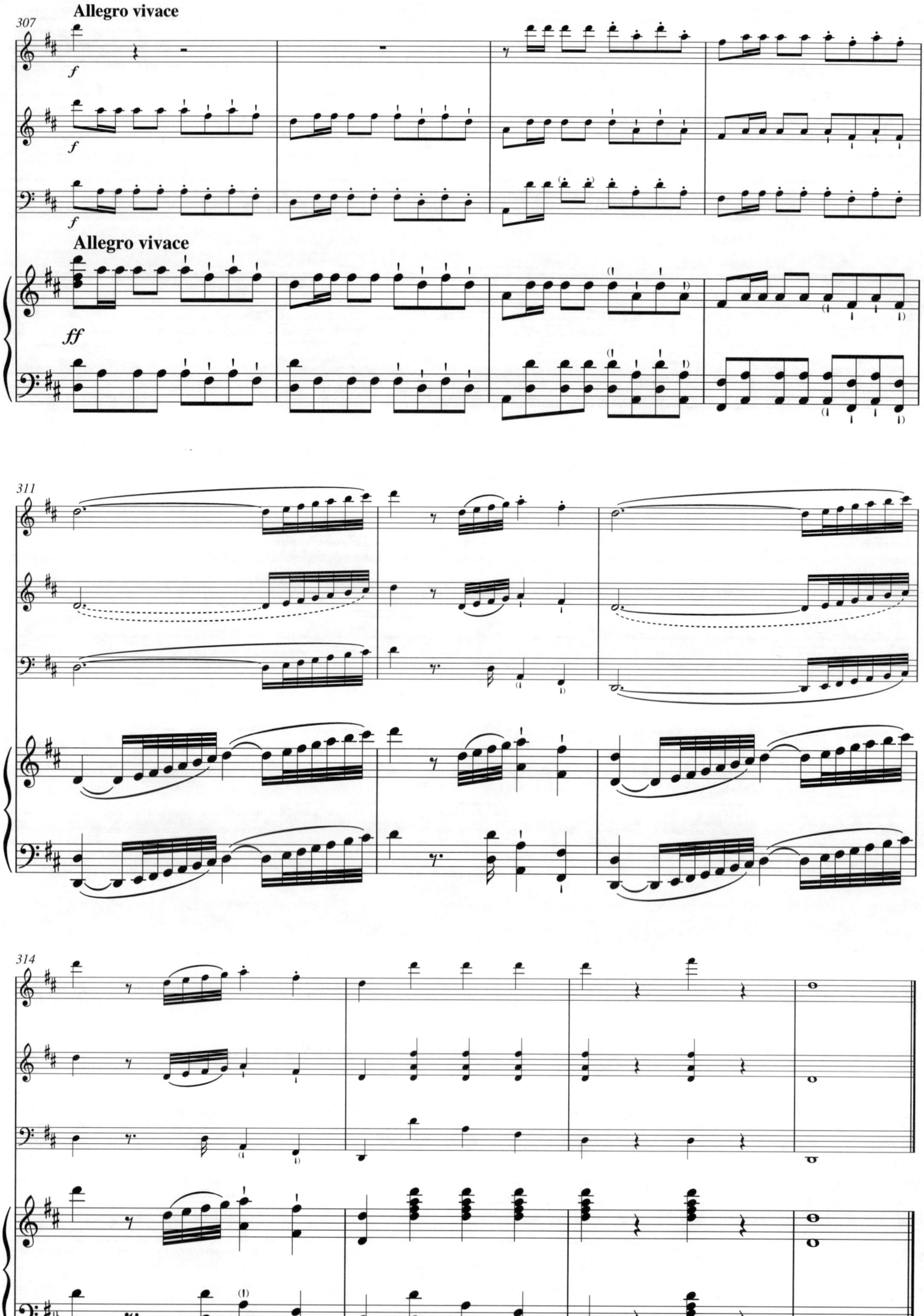
Allegro vivace
307
f
f
f
Allegro vivace
ff
311
314

4. Overture to Figaro

Wolfgang Amadeus Mozart

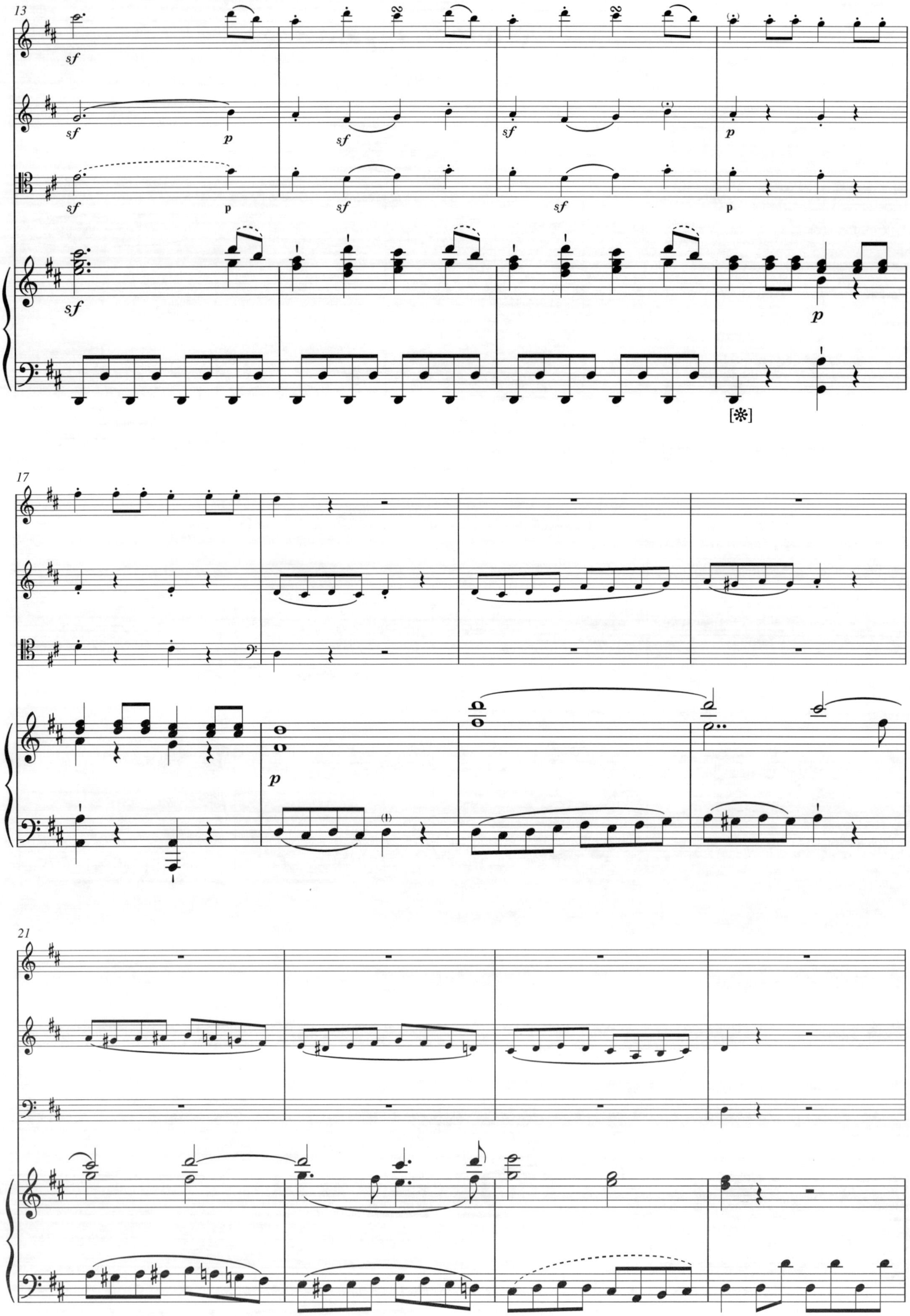
13
sf
sf p
sf p
sf
sf
sf
sf
sf
p
p
p
[※]
17
p
21

67

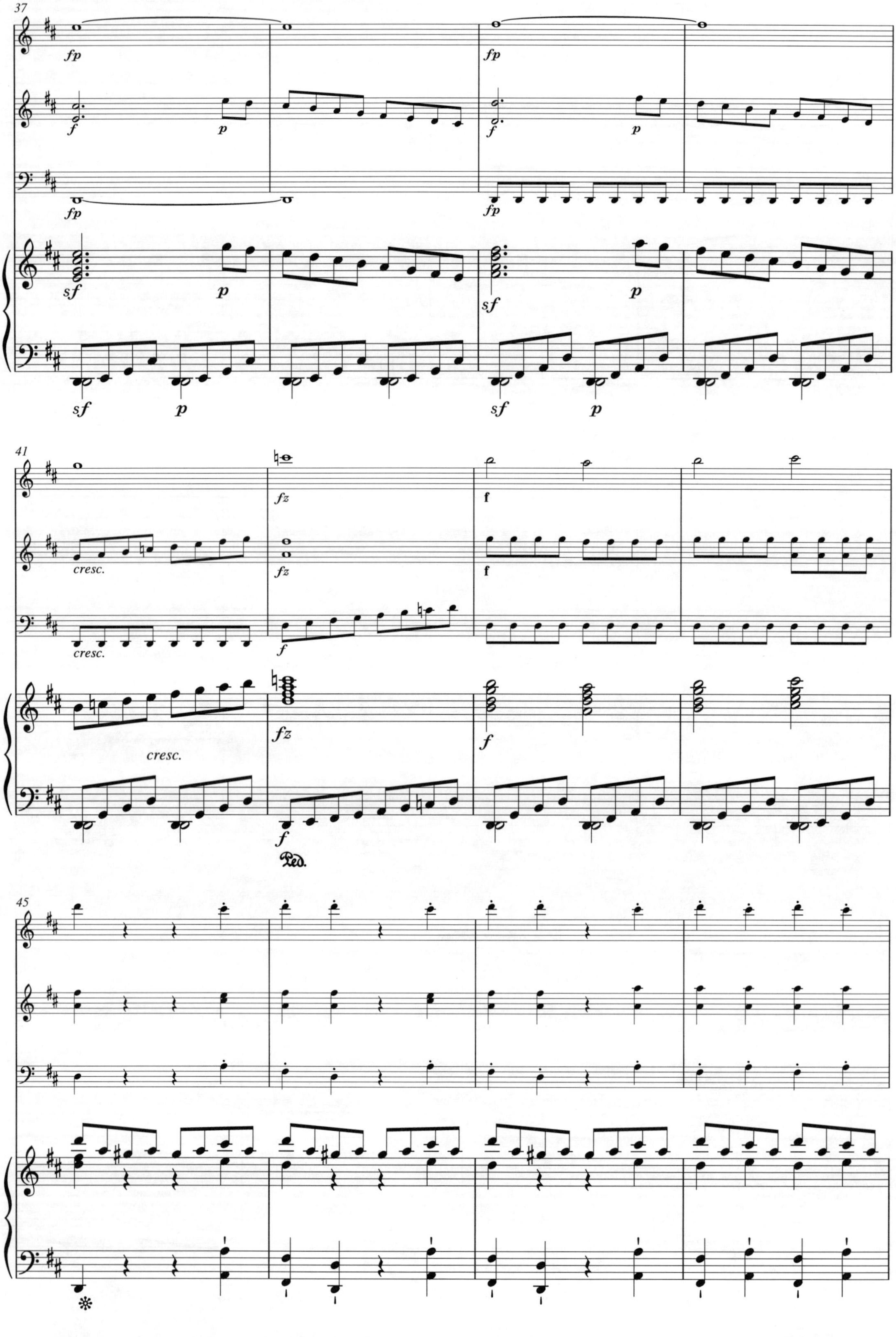
37
fp
f
p
fp
sf
p
sf
p
41
fz
f
cresc.
cresc.
fz
f
cresc.
fz
f
f
Ped.
45

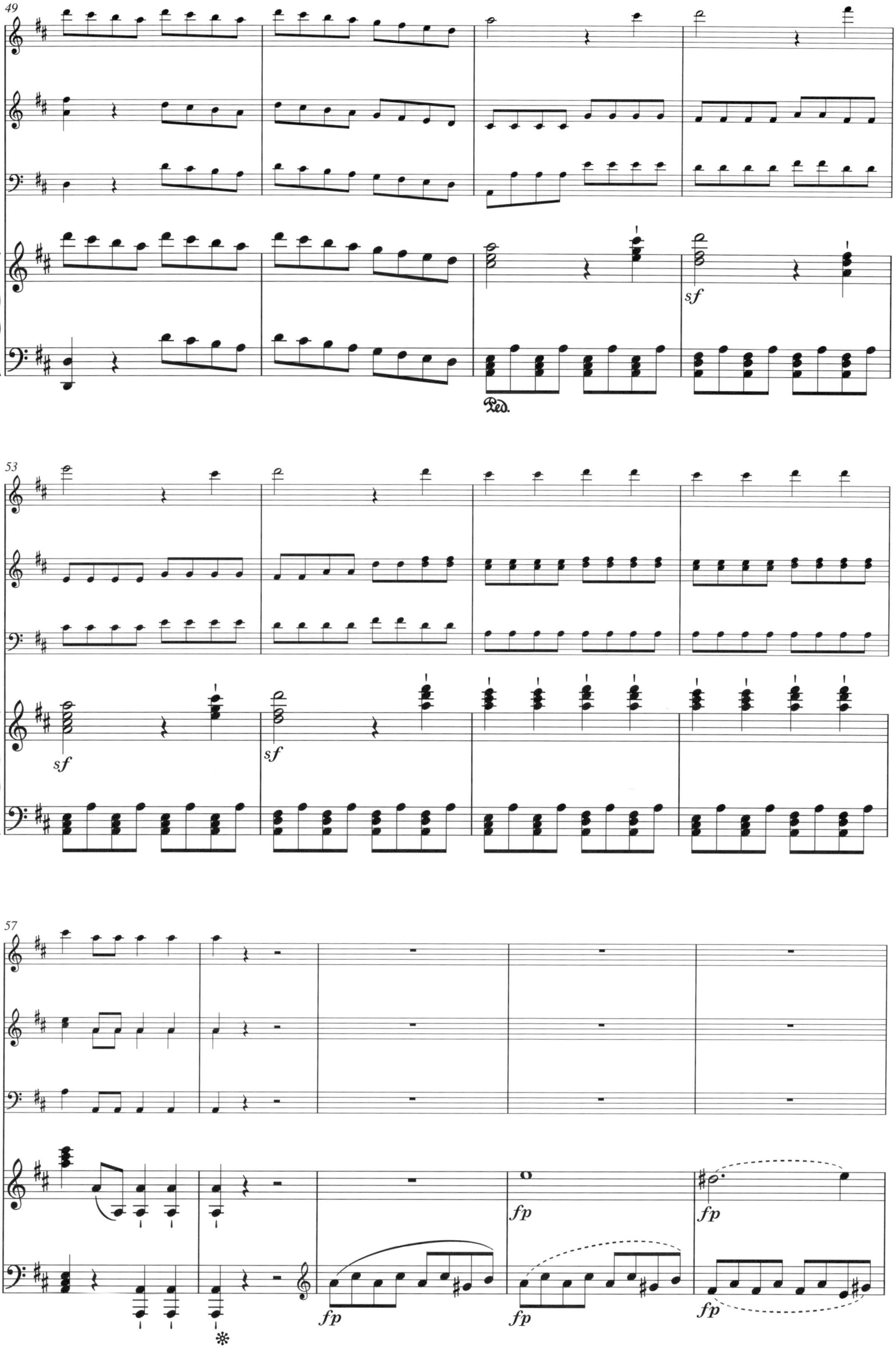
49
Ped.
sf
53
sf
sf
57
fp
fp
fp
fp
fp

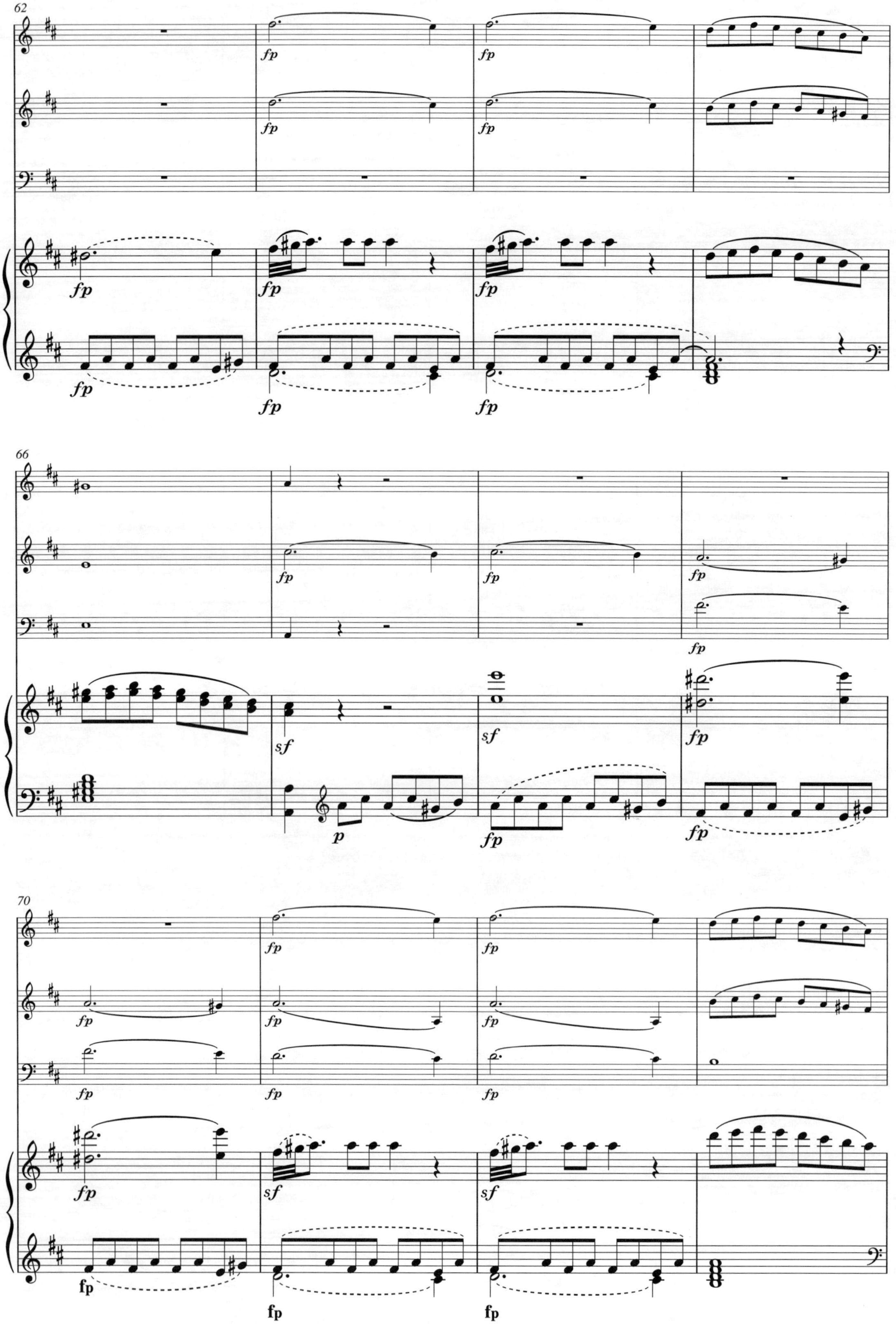
62
66
70

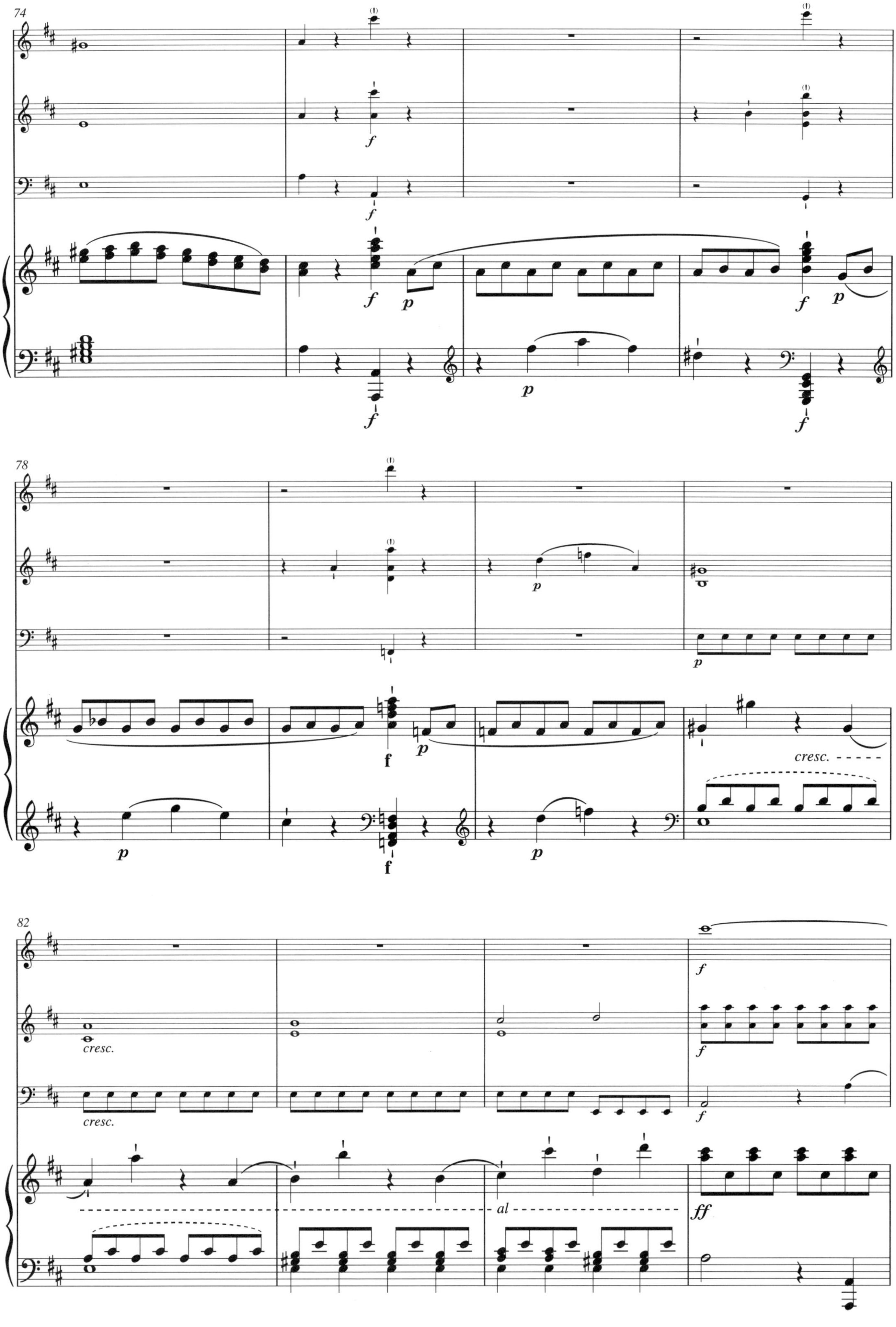
74
78
82
cresc.
cresc.
cresc.
al

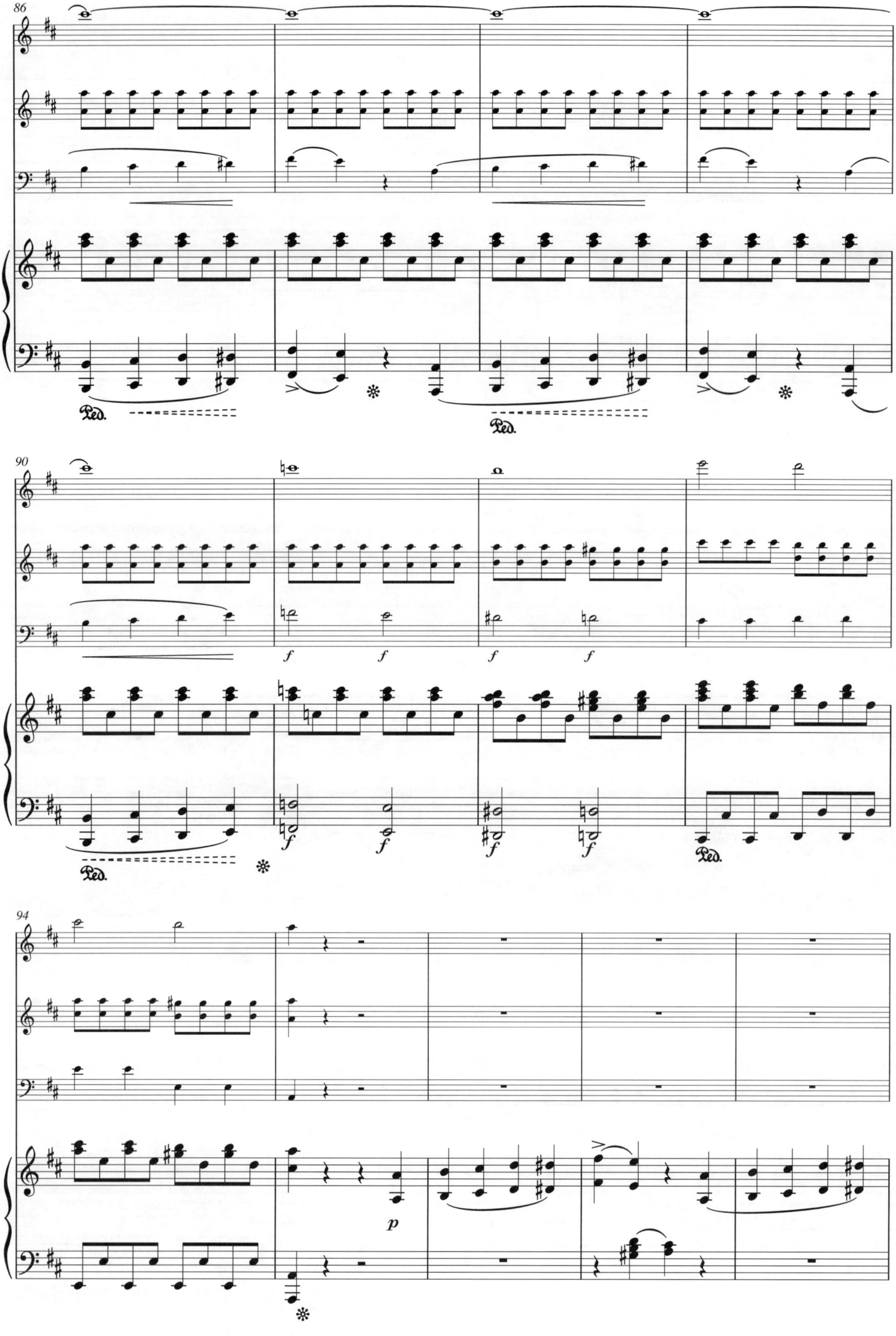
86
Ped.
Ped.
90
f
Ped.
94
p

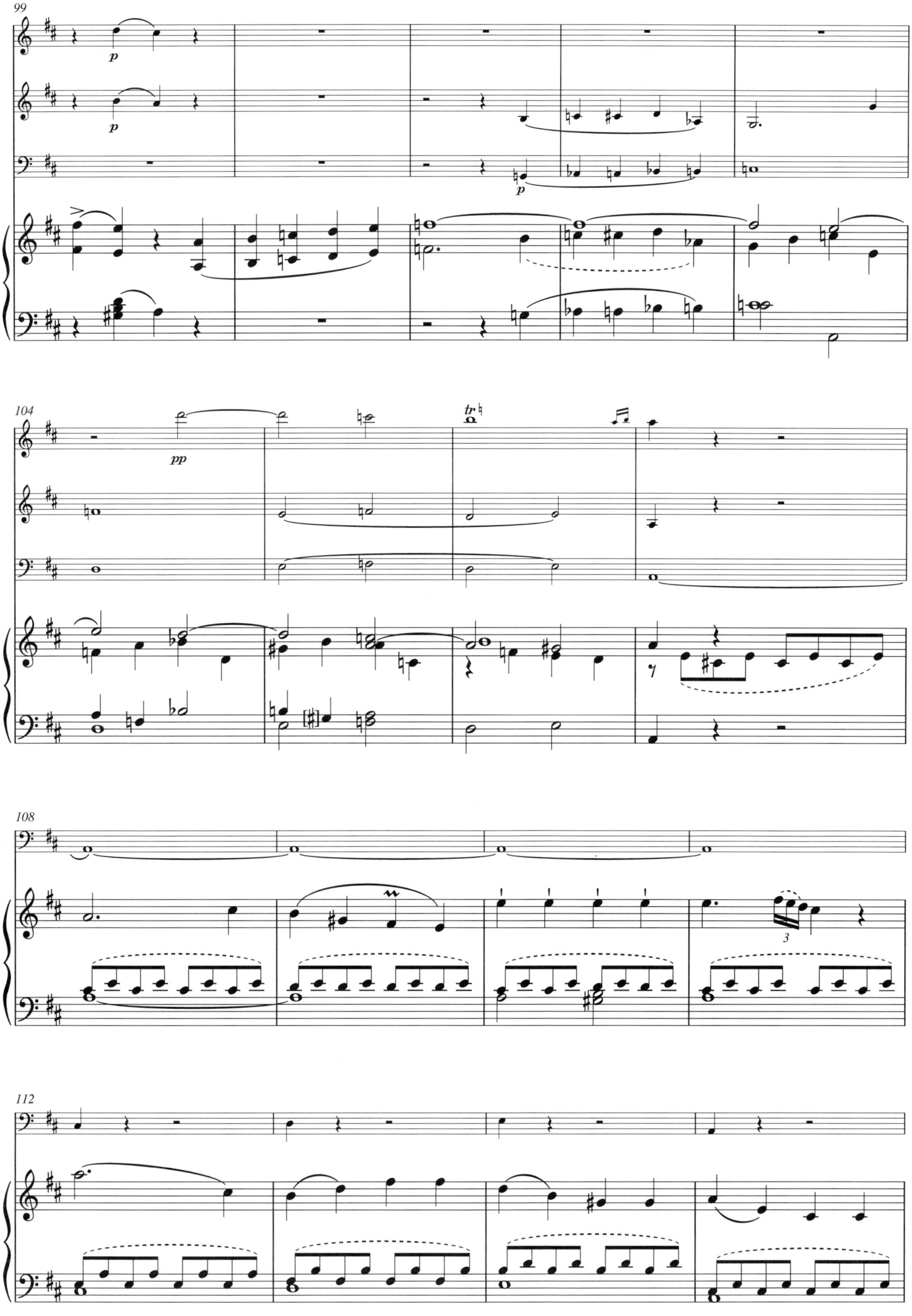
99
p
p
p
104
pp
tr
108
Vc.
Pn.
3
112

116
Fl.
Vn.
Vc.
Pn.
p
p
3
120
fp
fp
fz
fz
p
fz
p
Ped.
124
fp
fp
fp
fp
fp
fp
fz
p
fz
p
fz
p
fz
p
Ped.
Ped.

128
fp
fp
fp
fp
fz
fz
fz
p
fz
fz
p
fz
132
fp
ff
fp
ff
fz
ff
fz
ff
p
fz
Ped.
136
pp
pp
pp

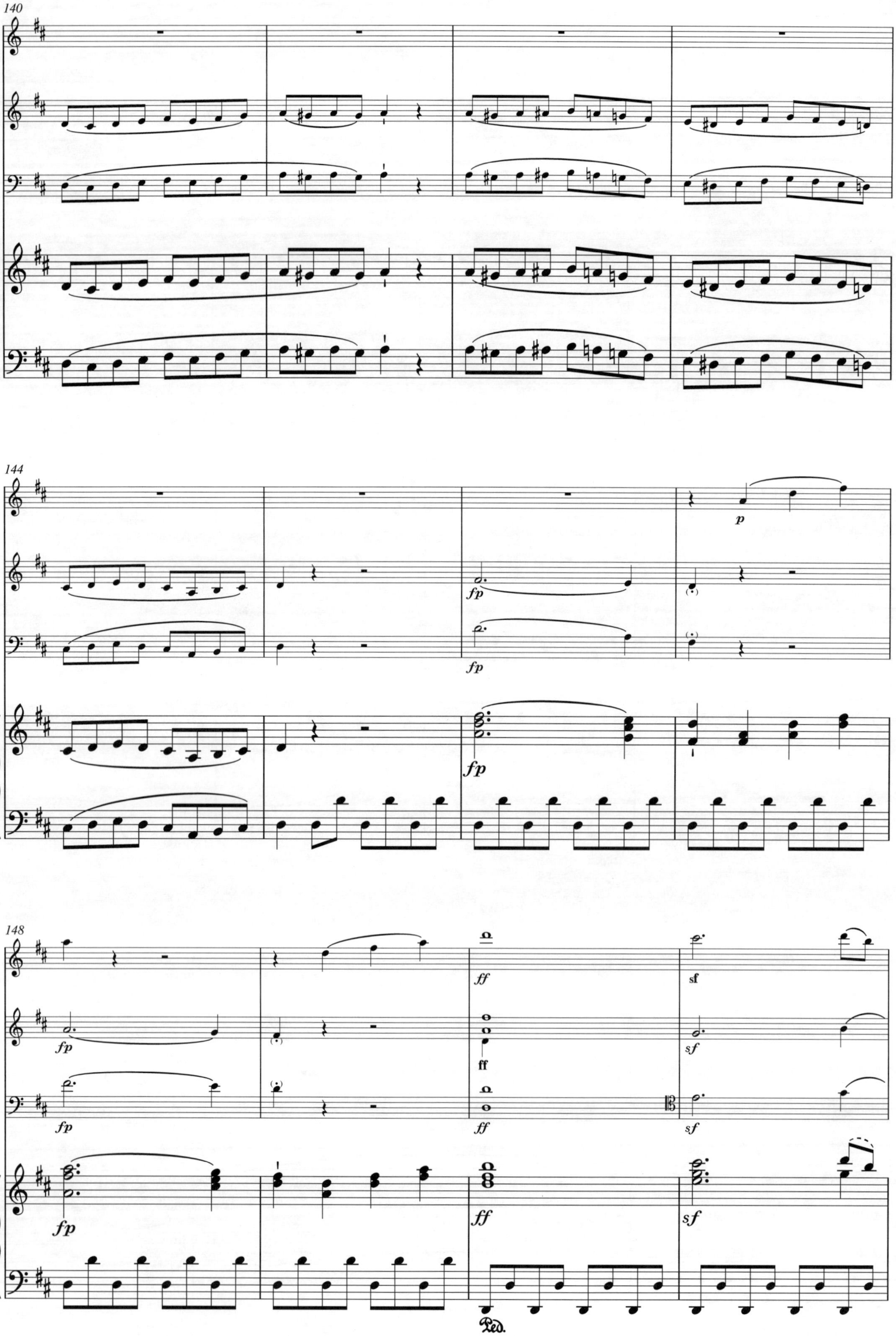
140
144
p
fp
148
ff
sf

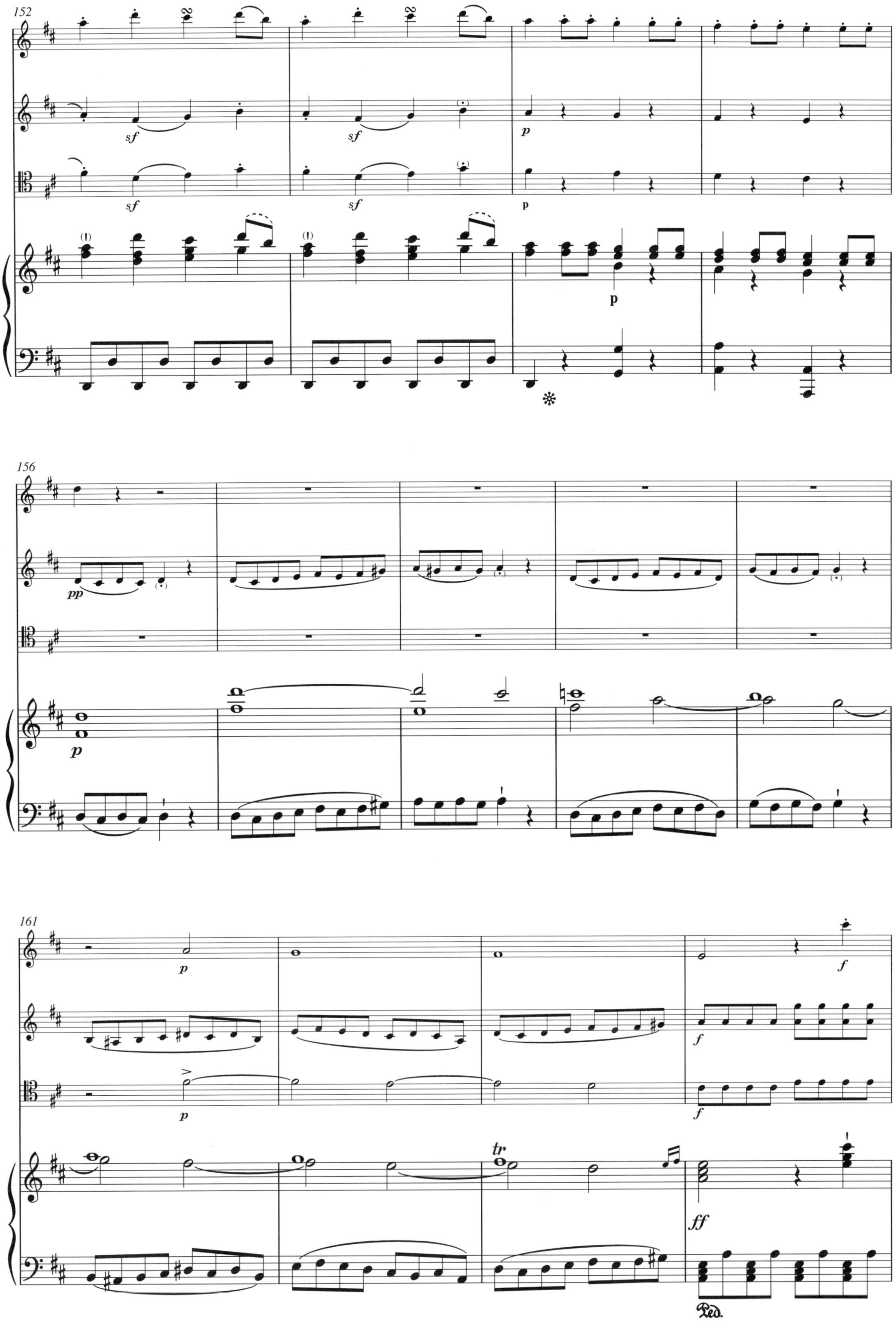
152
sf
sf
sf
sf
p
p
p
156
pp
p
161
p
p
f
f
f
tr
ff
Ped.

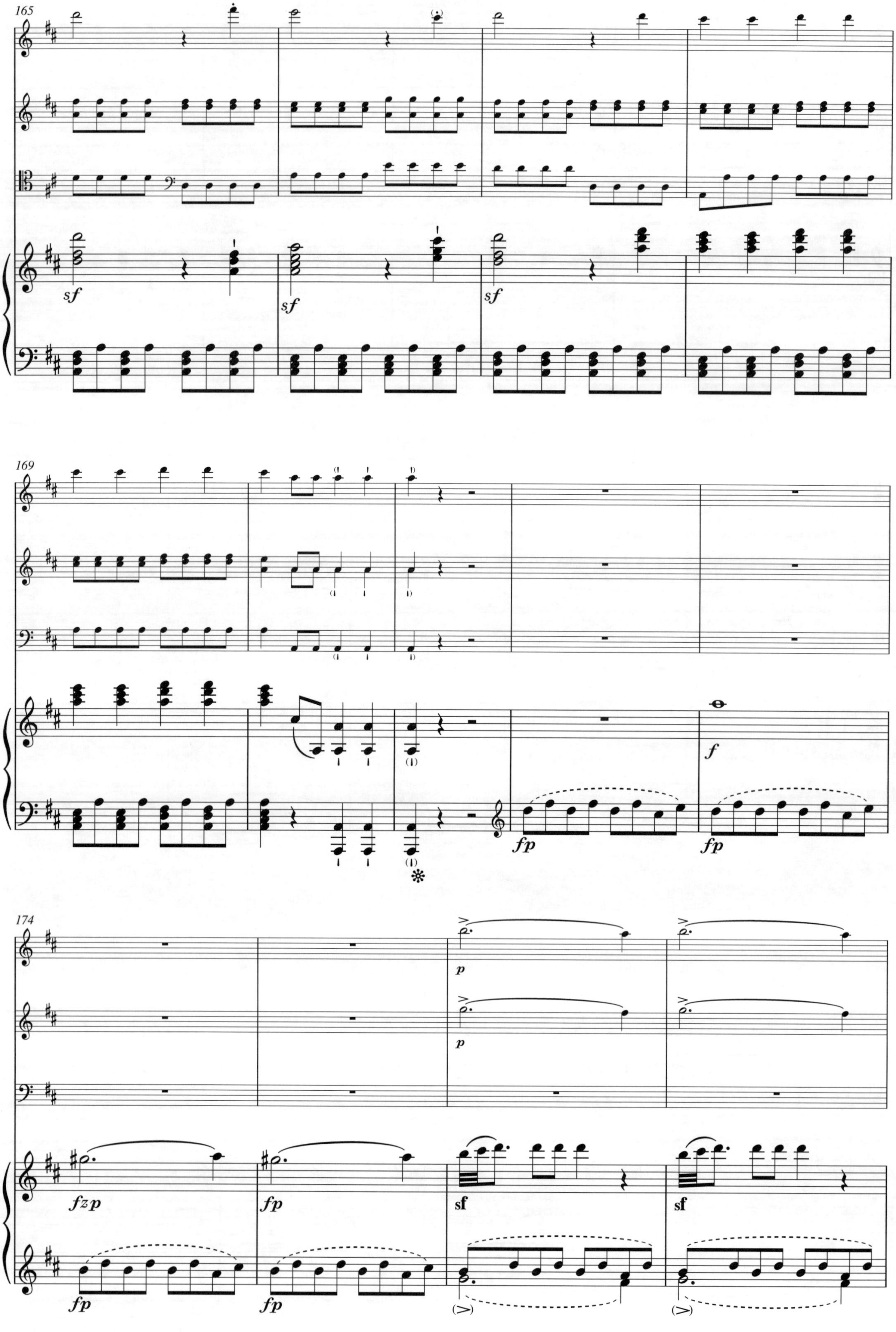
165
sf
sf
sf
169
f
fp
fp
174
p
p
fzp
fp
sf
sf
fp
fp

79

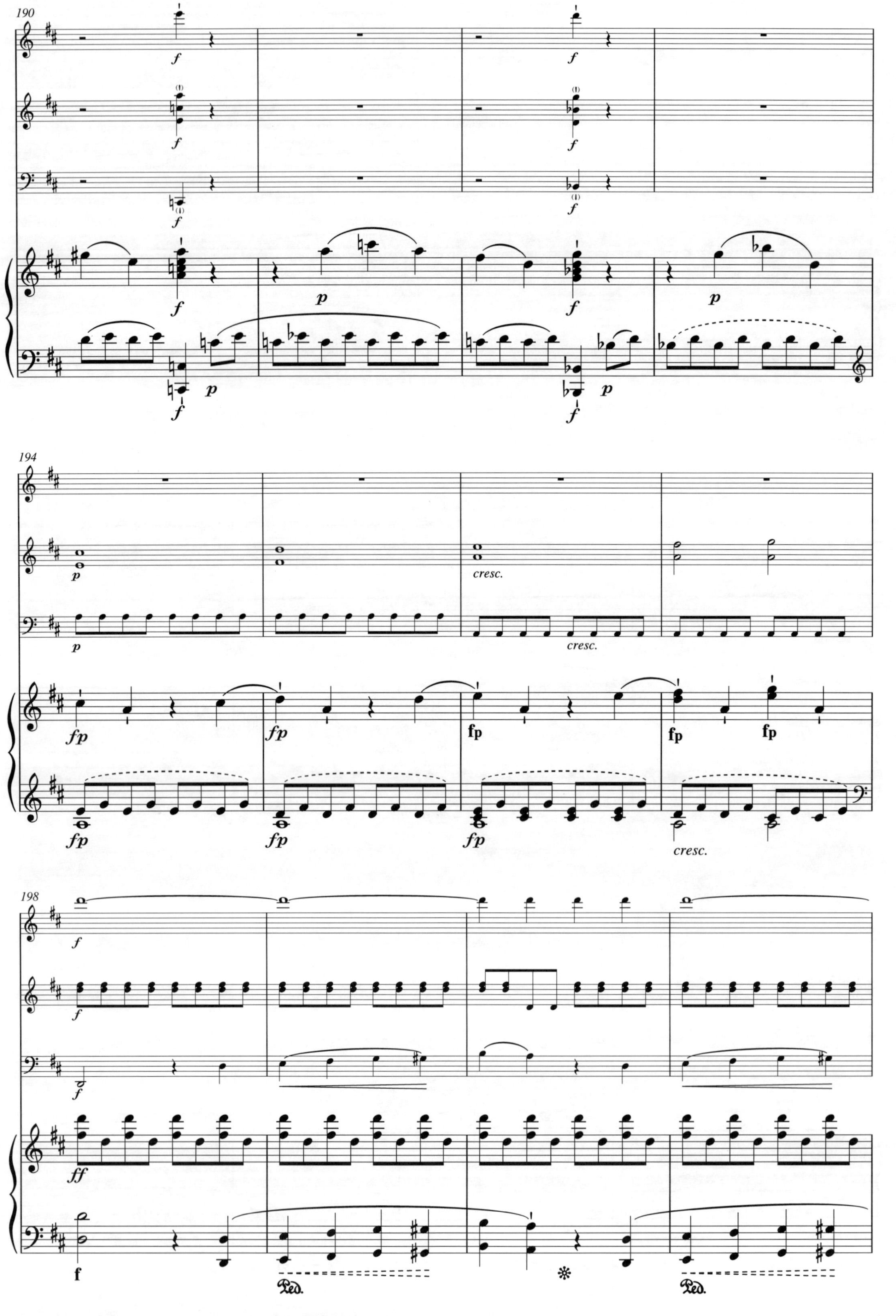
190
194
cresc.
198
ff
Ped.

81

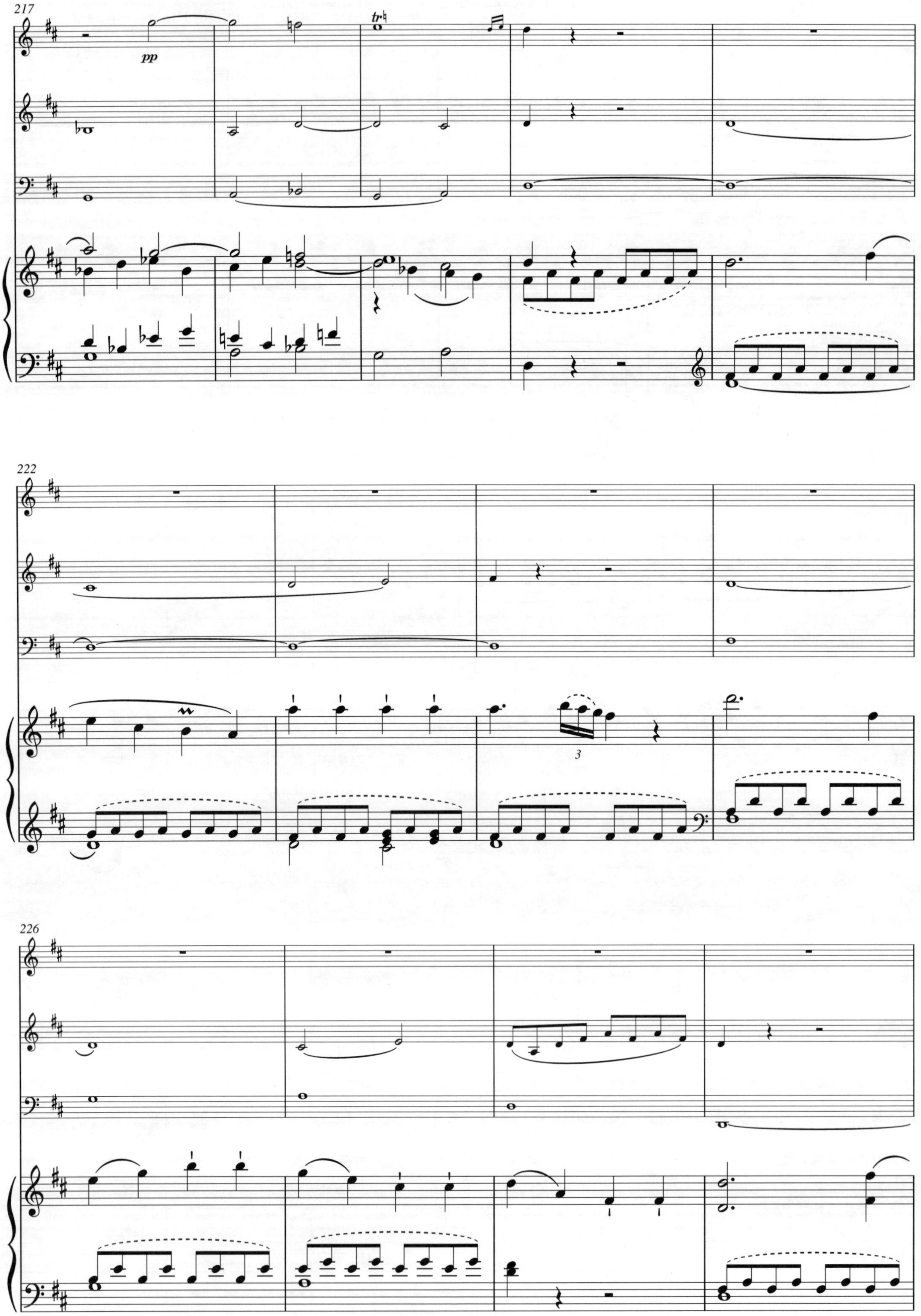
217
pp
tr
222
3
226

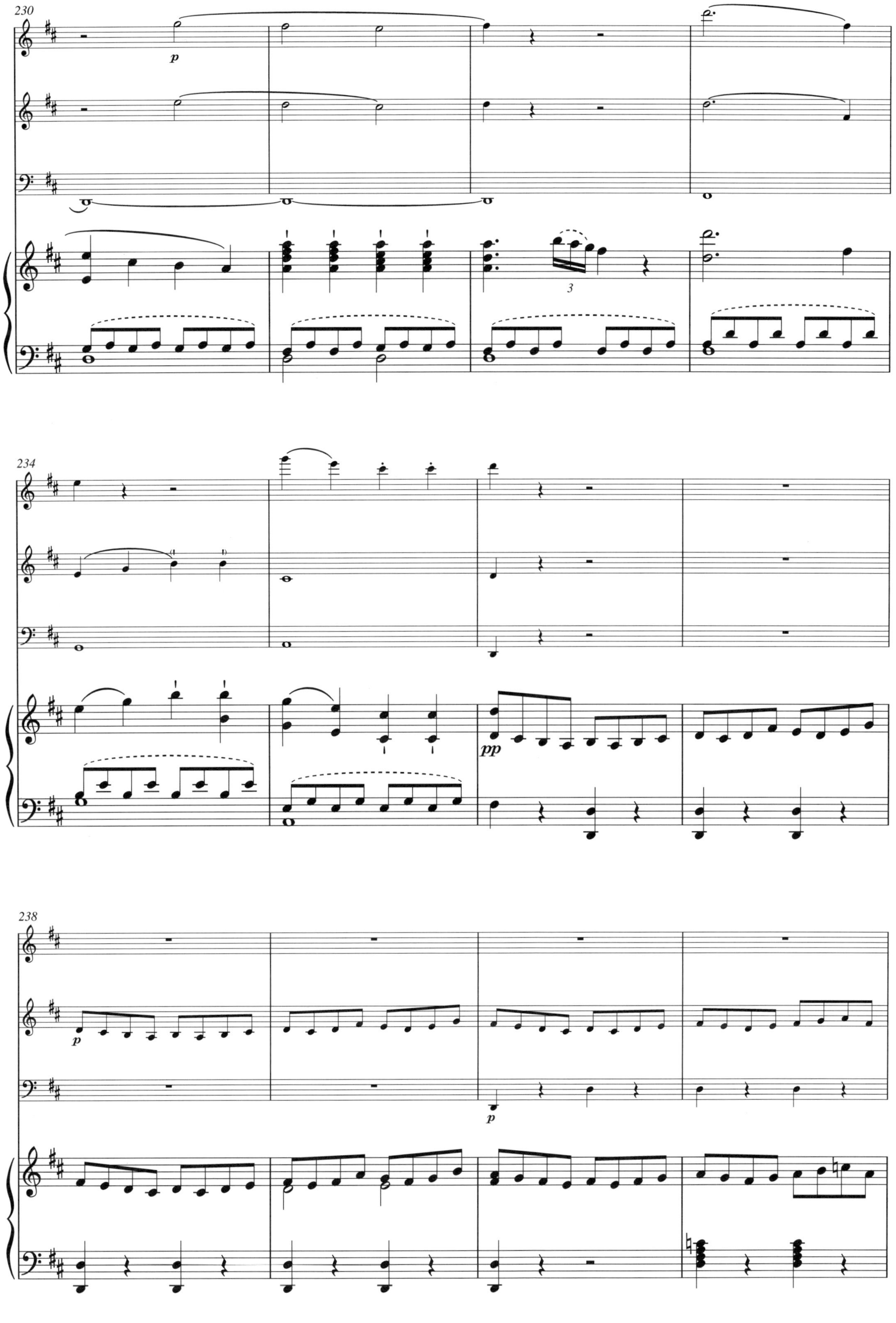
230
p
3
234
pp
238
p
p

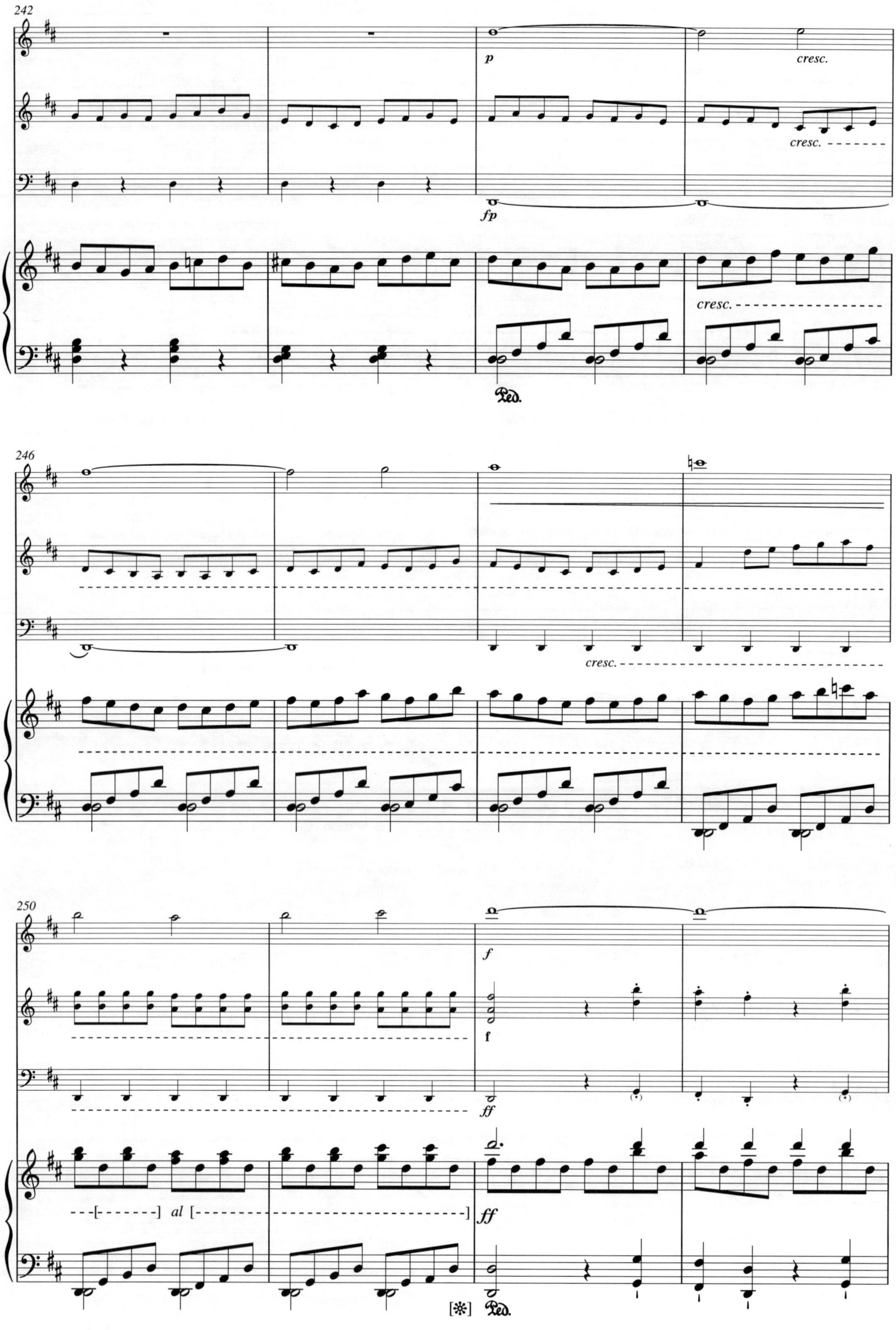
242
p
cresc.
cresc.
fp
cresc.
Ped.
246
cresc.
250
f
f
ff
ff
al
[※]
Ped.

85

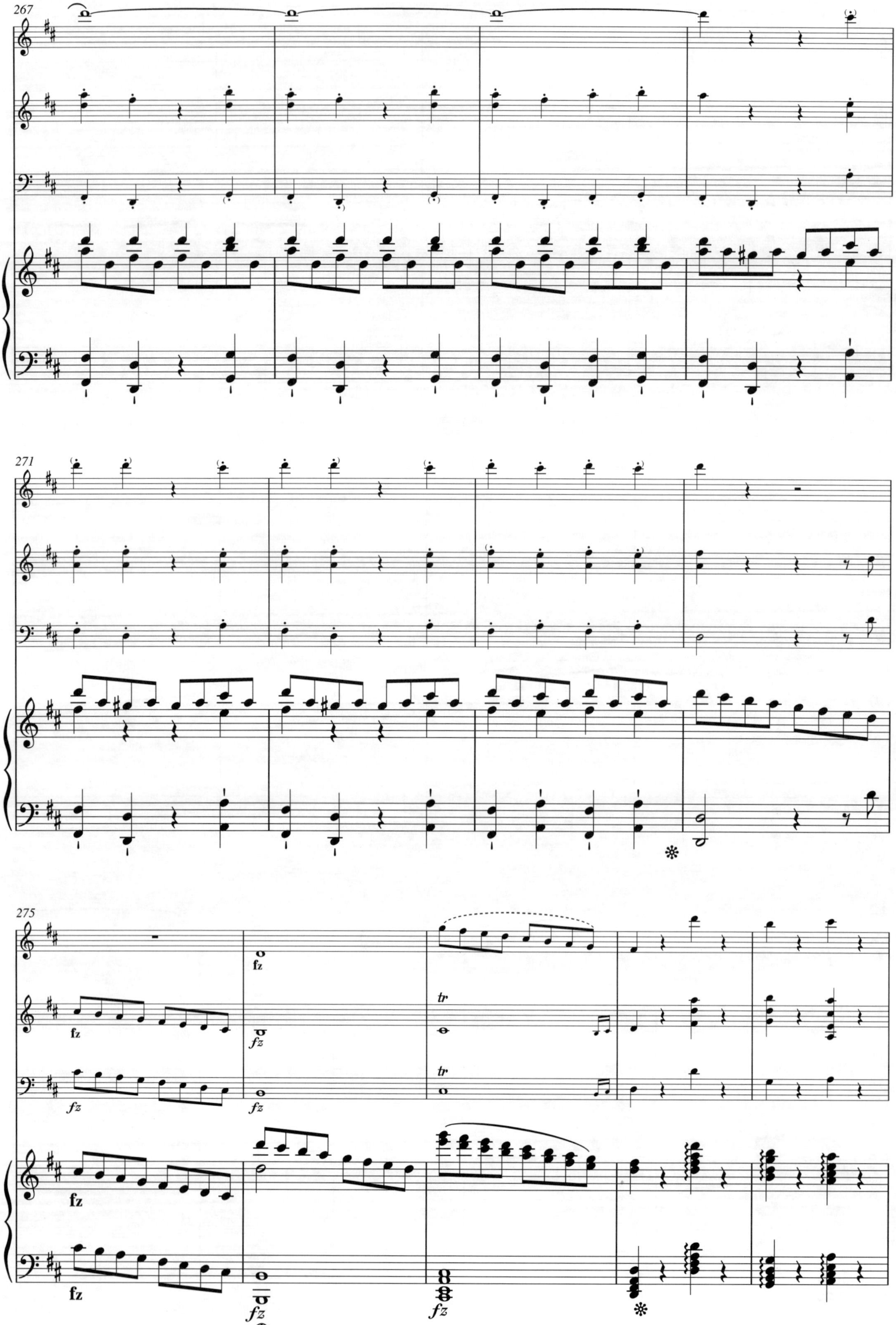
267
271
275
fz
tr
Ped.

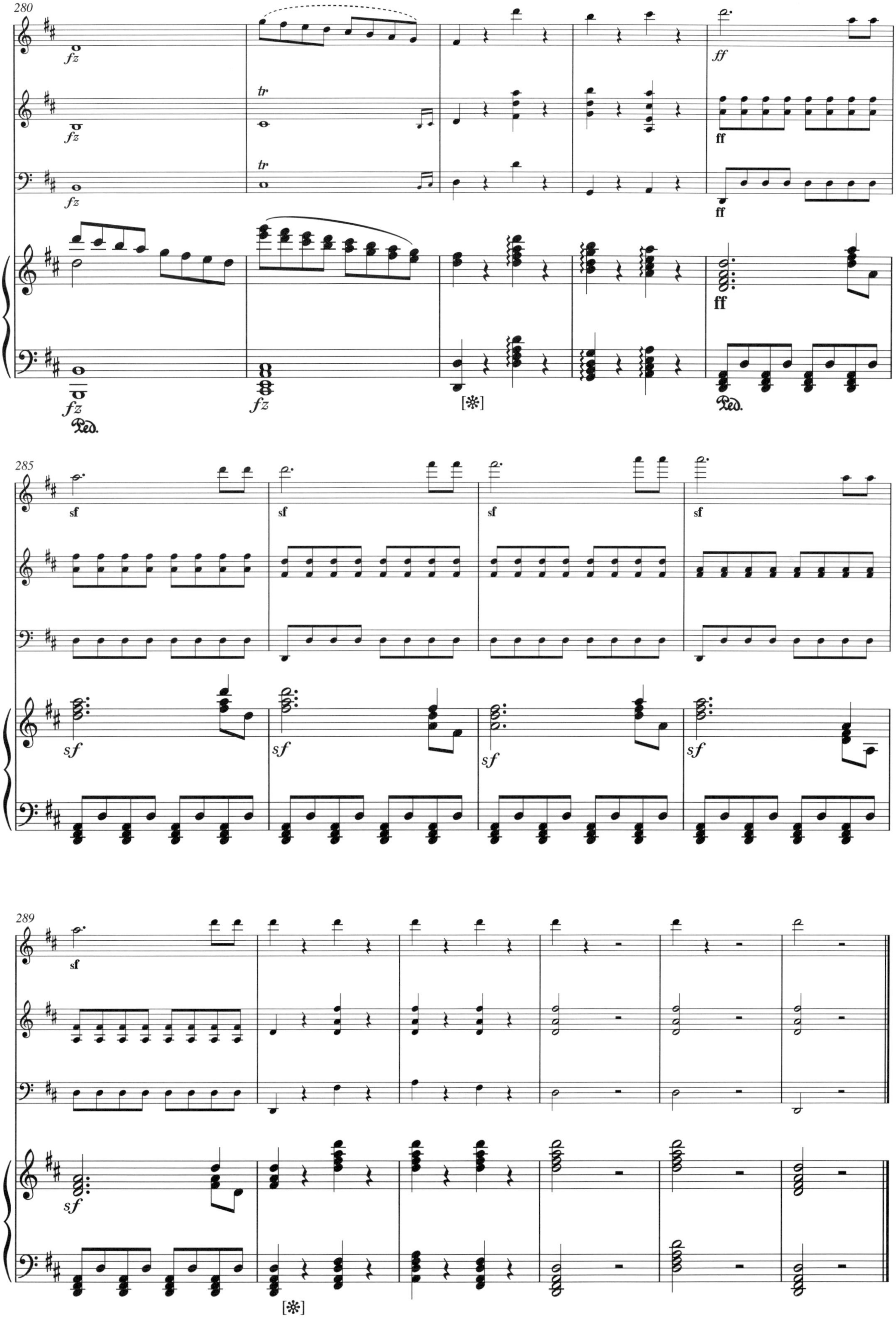
280
fz
tr
ff
Ped.
[※]
285
sf
289

5. Overture to Iphigénia

Christoph Willibald Gluck

89

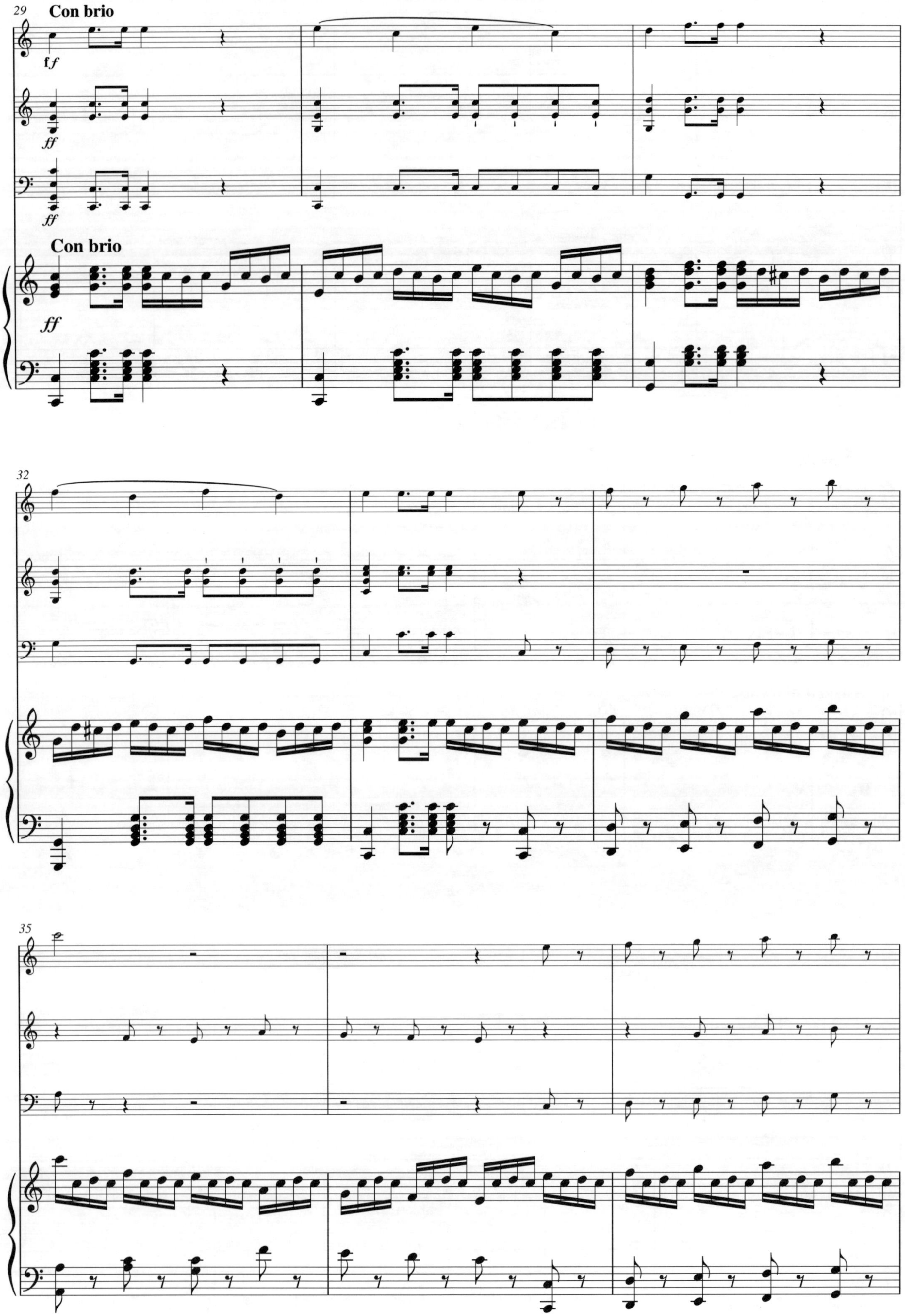
29
Con brio
ff
ff
ff
Con brio
ff
32
35

91

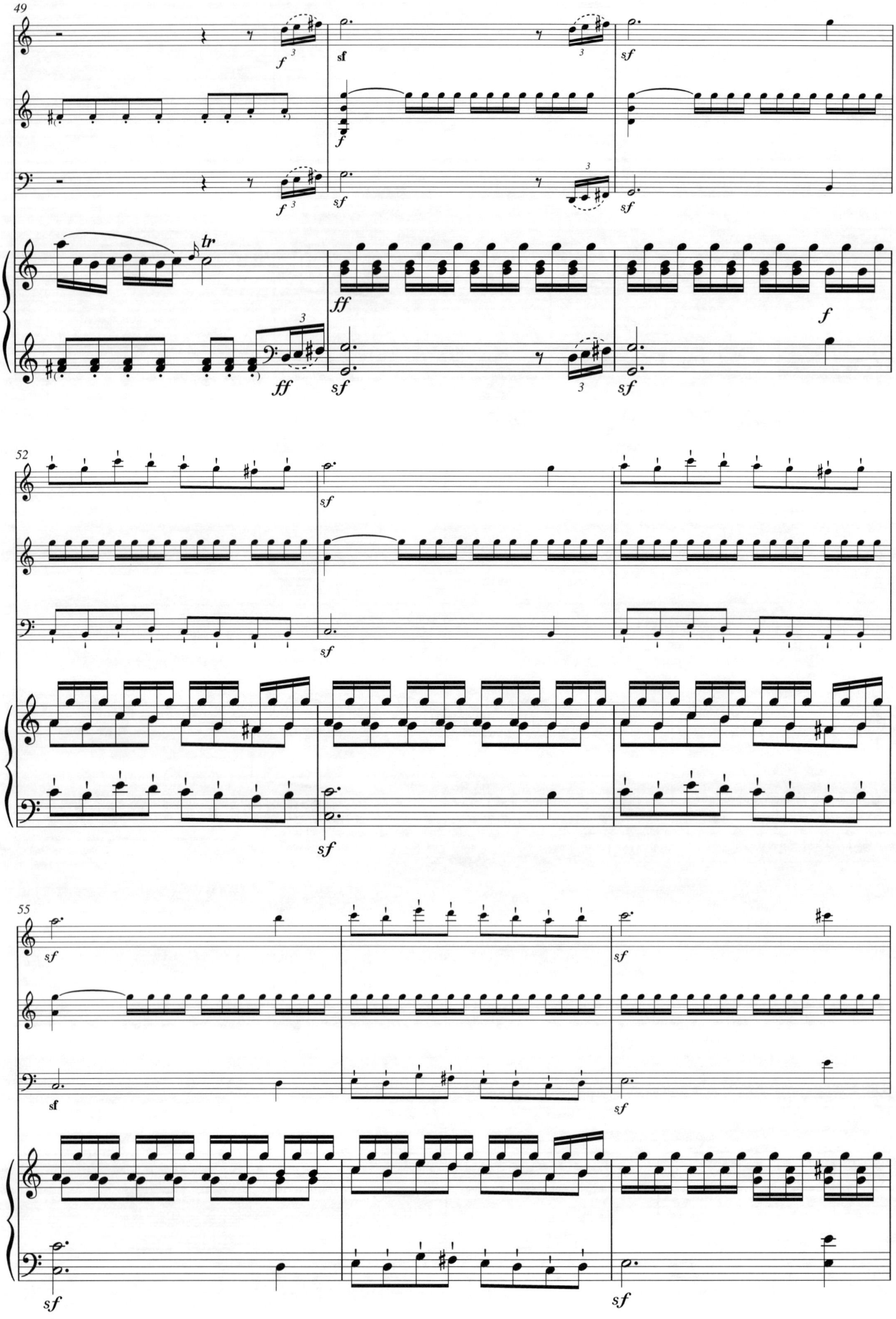

93

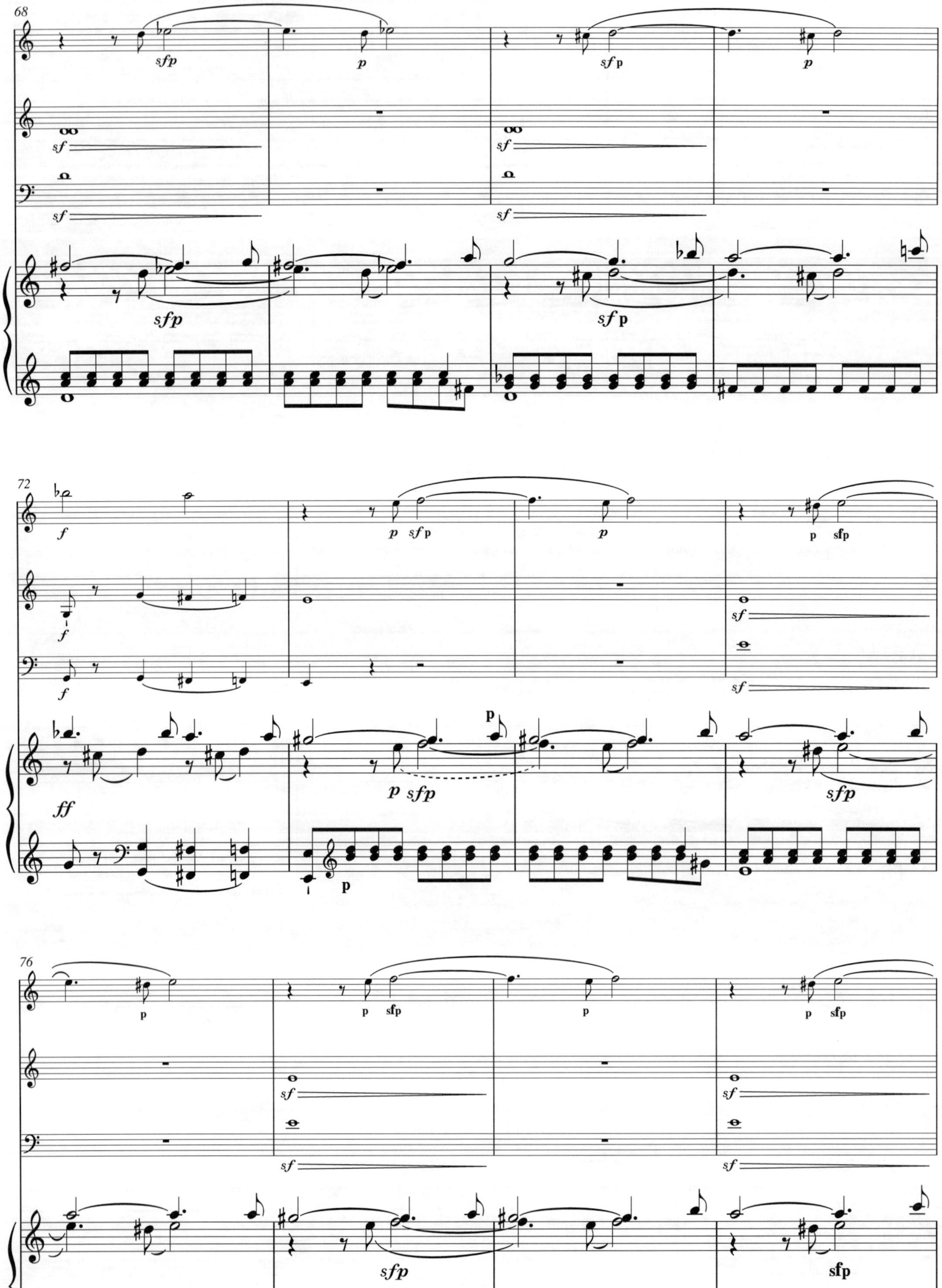
68
72
76

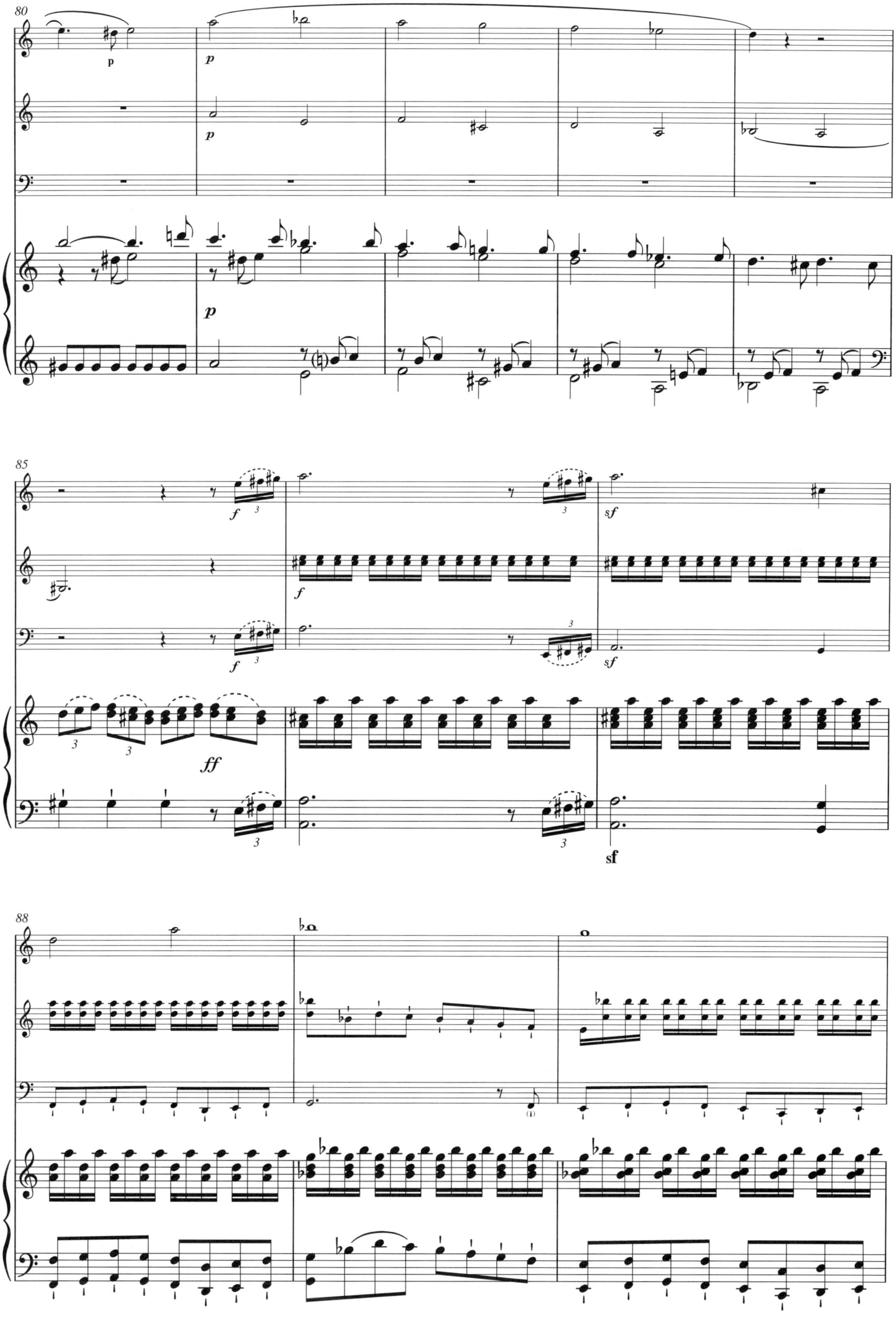
80
85
88

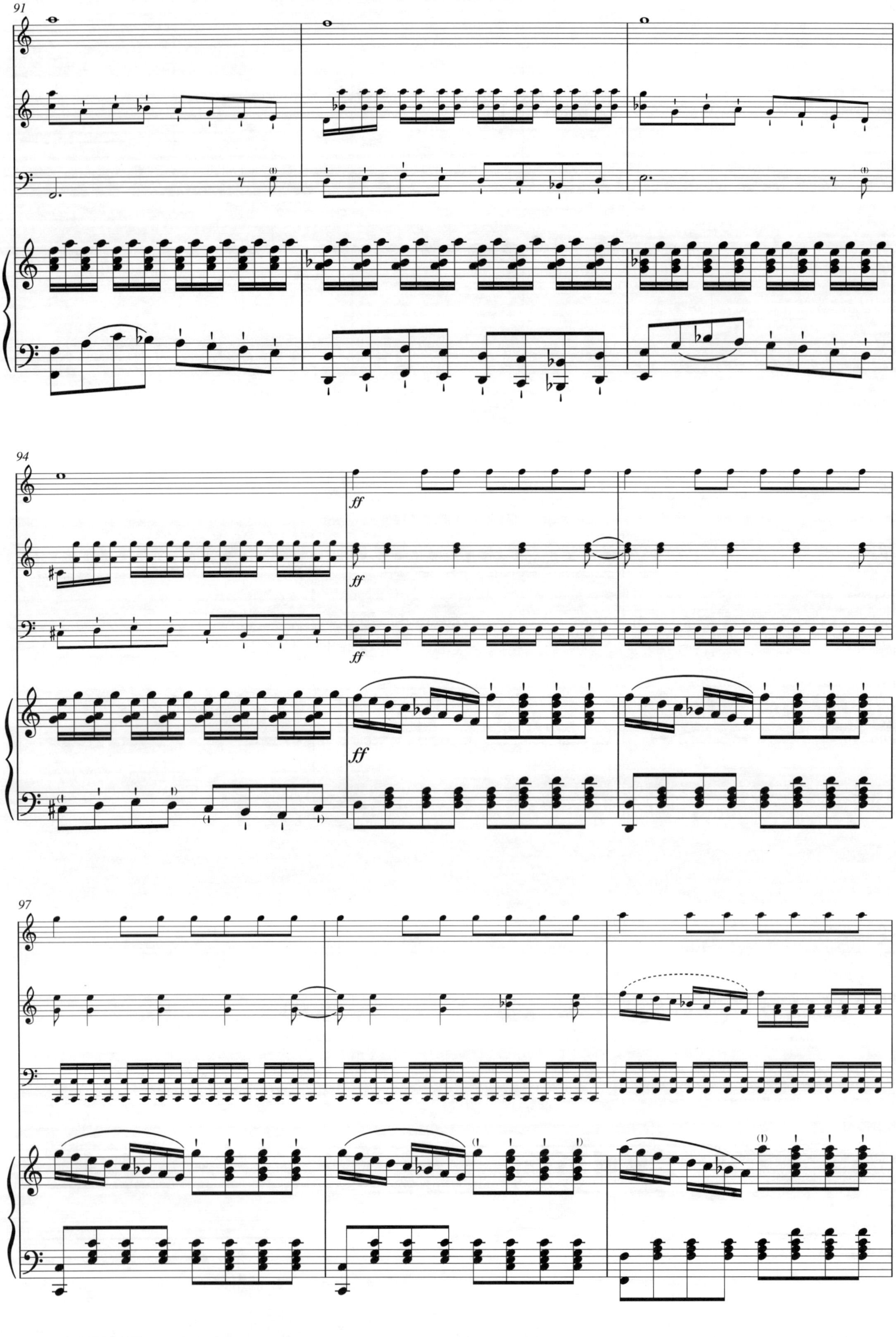
91
94
ff
ff
ff
ff
97

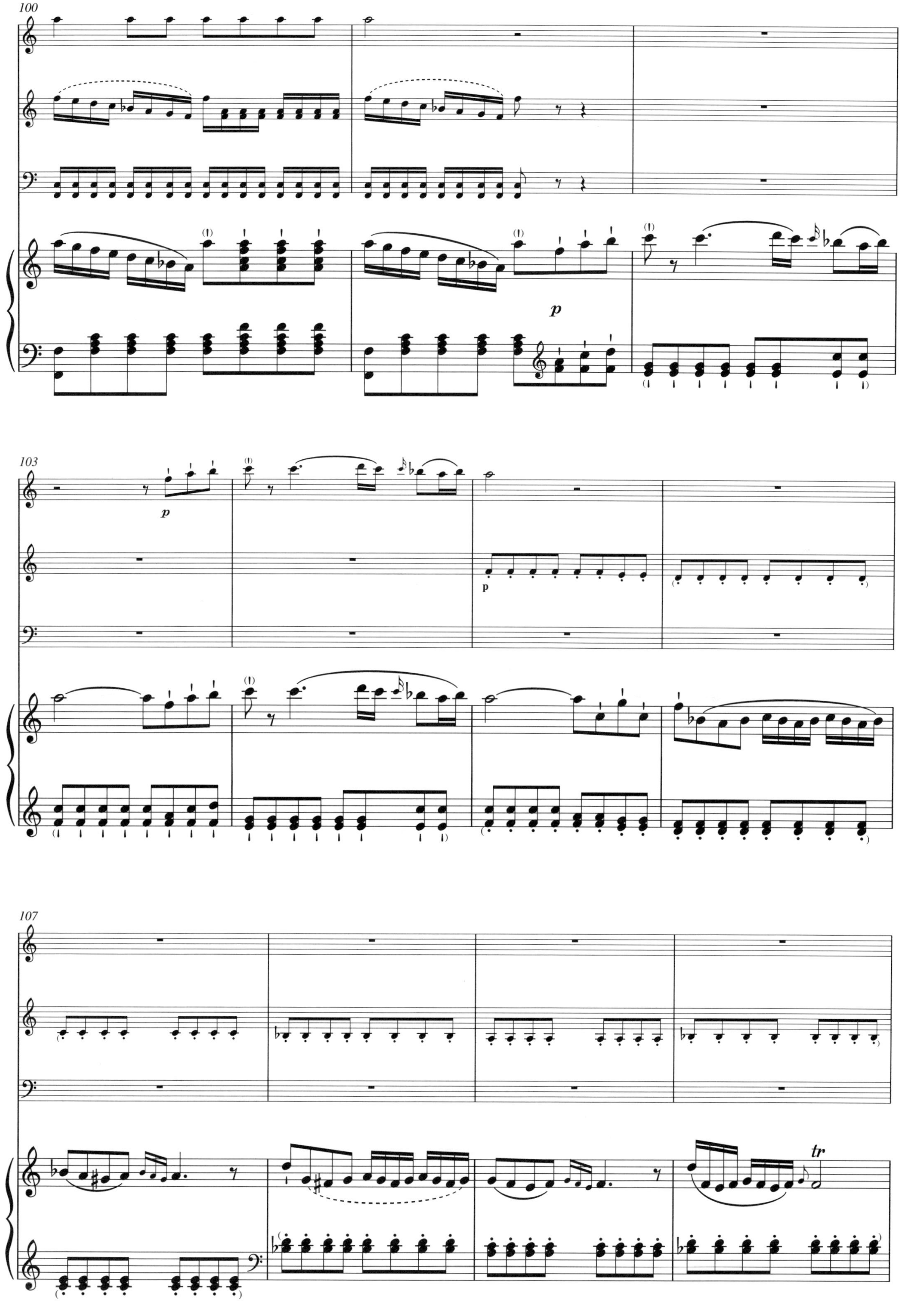
100
p
103
p
p
107
tr

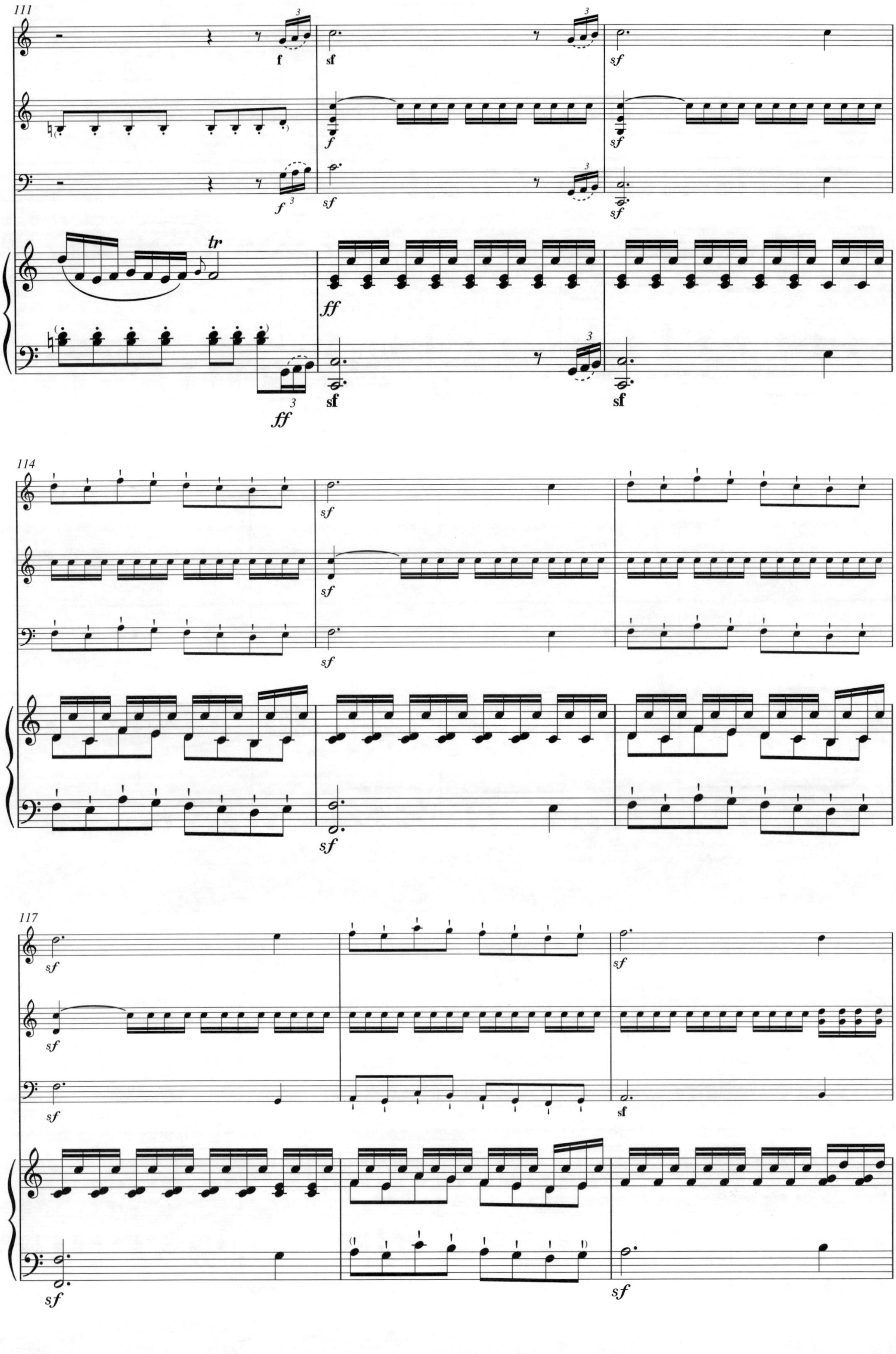
111
114
117

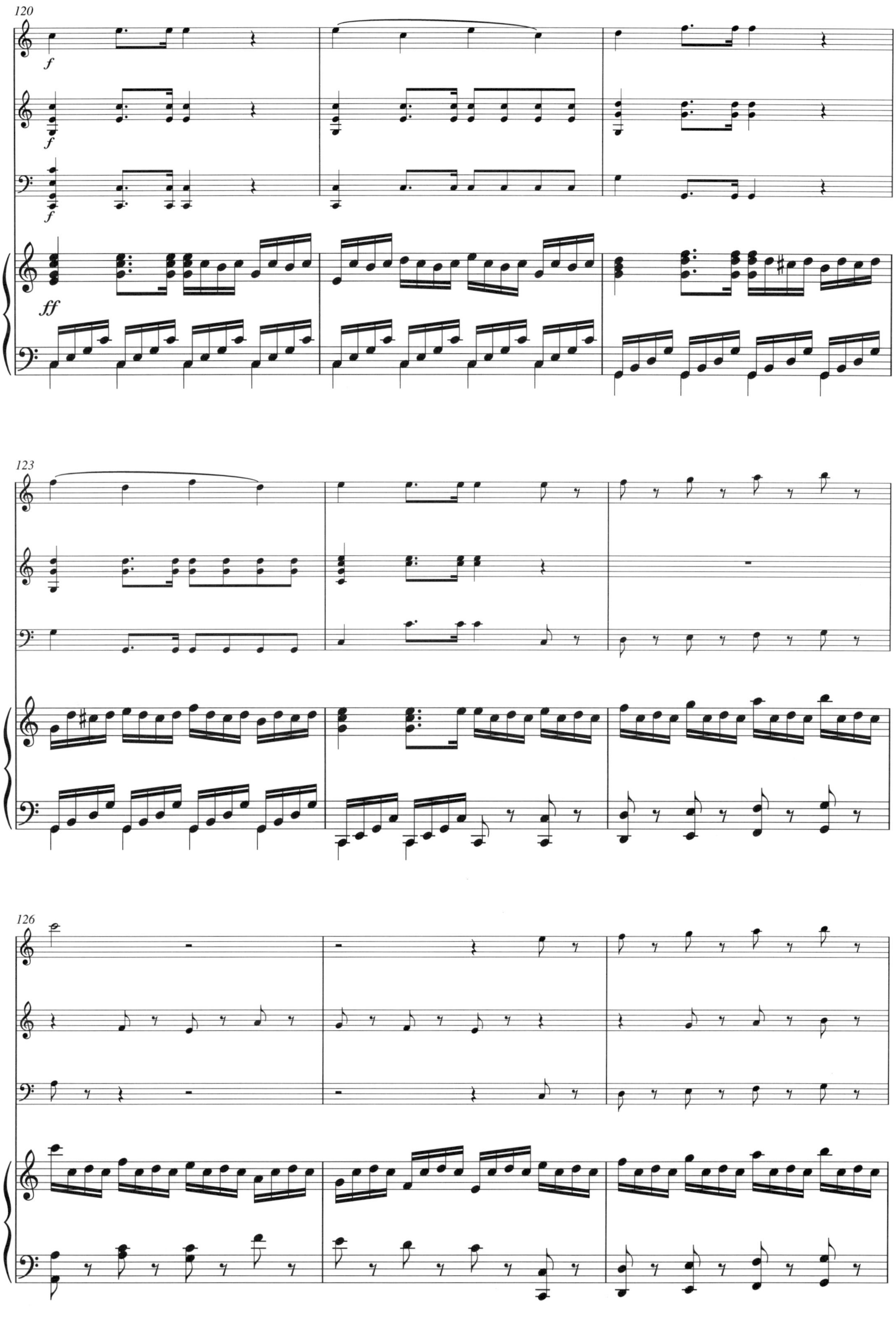
120
f
f
f
ff
123
126

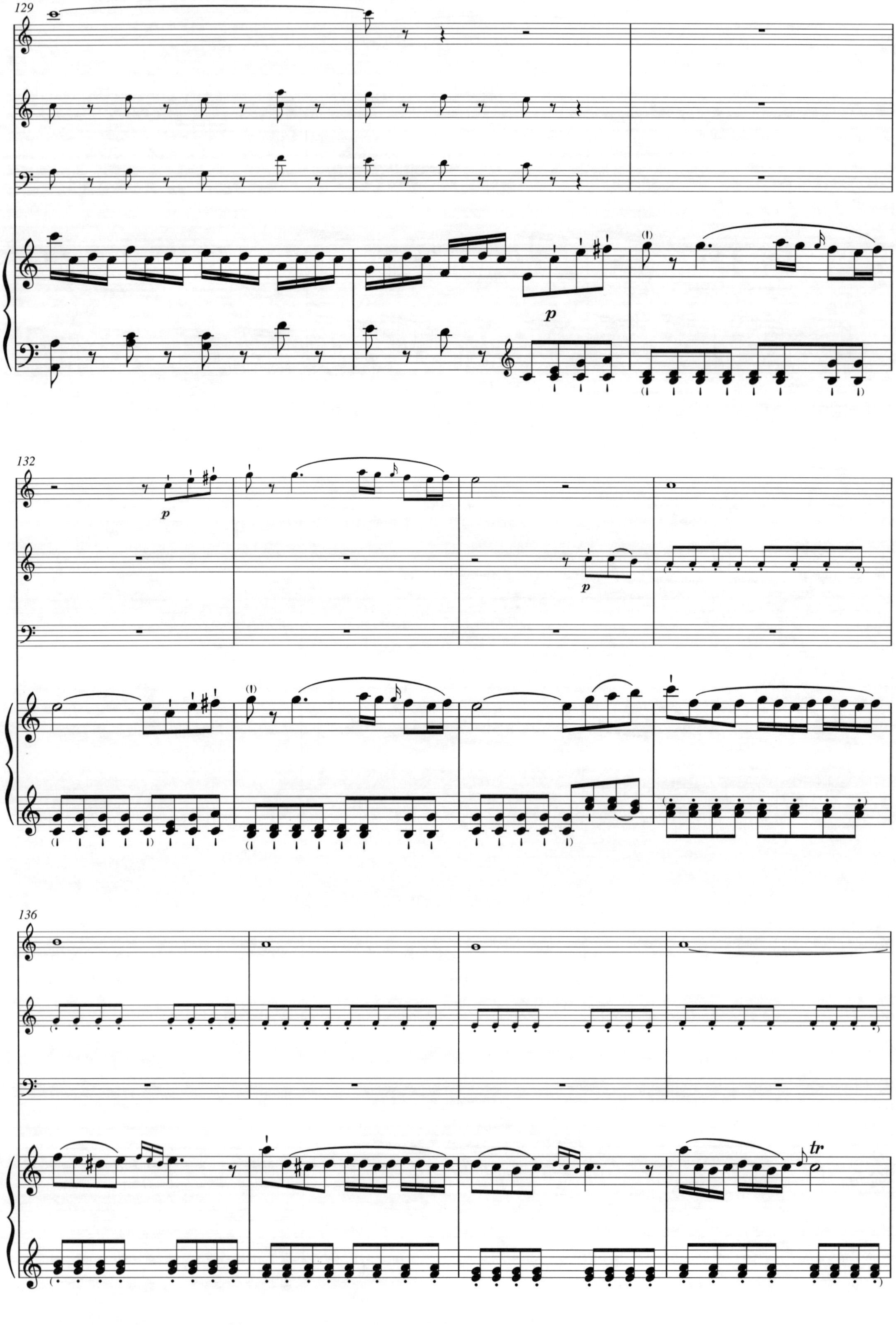
129
p
132
p
p
136
tr

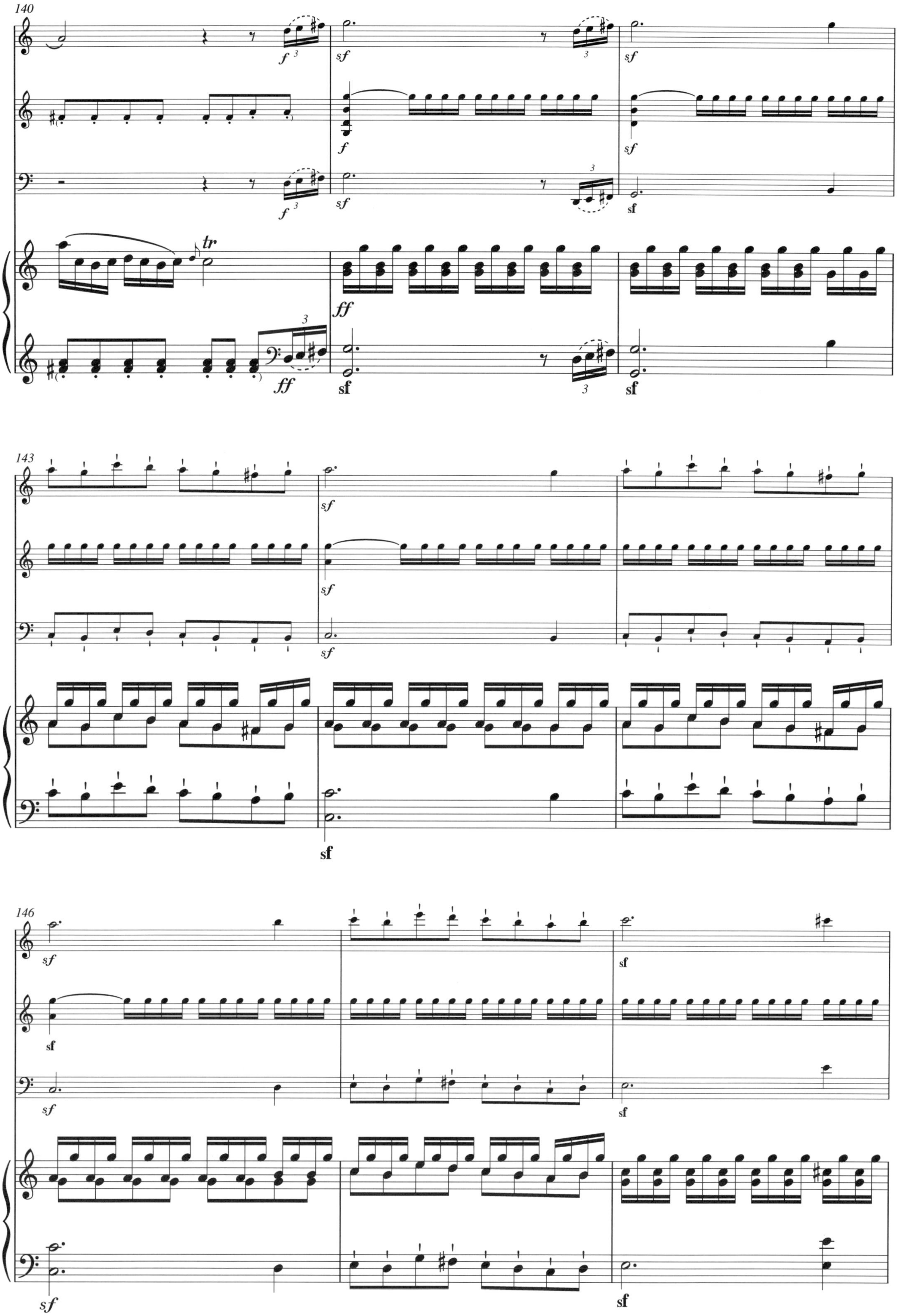
140
f
sf
tr
ff
143
146

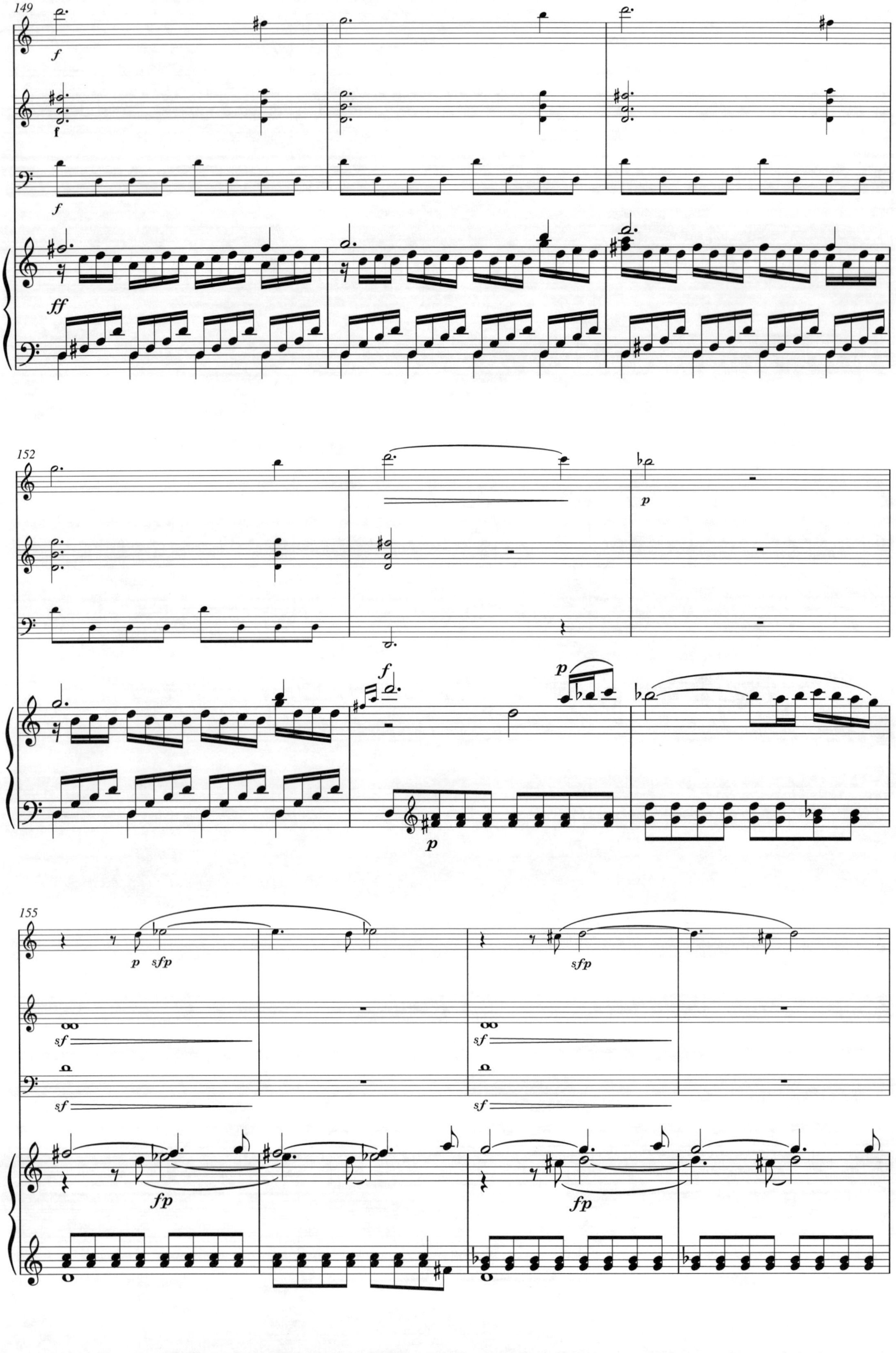
149
f
f
f
ff
152
p
f
p
p
155
p sfp
sf
sf
sf
sf
sfp
fp
fp

103

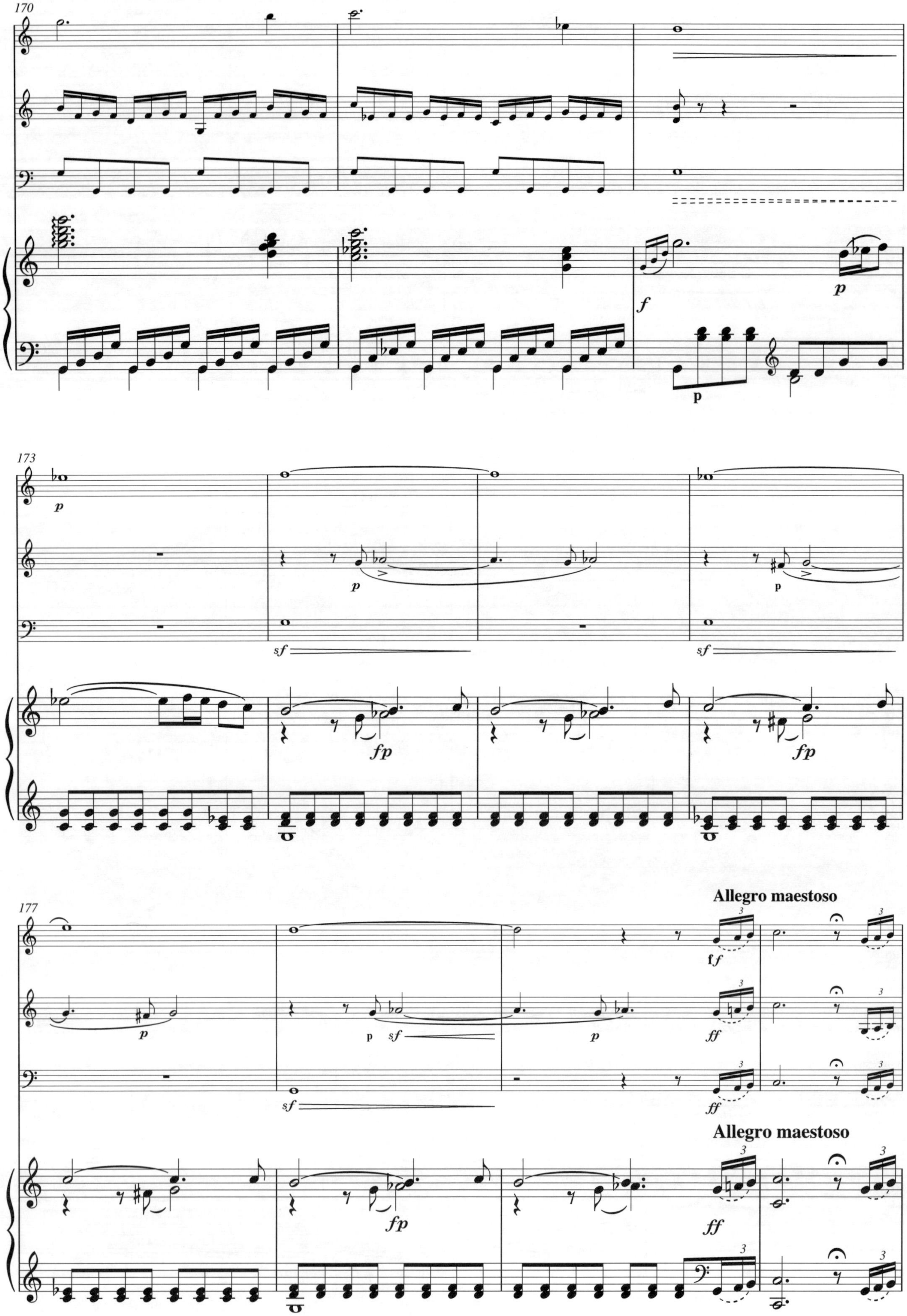
Allegro maestoso
Allegro maestoso

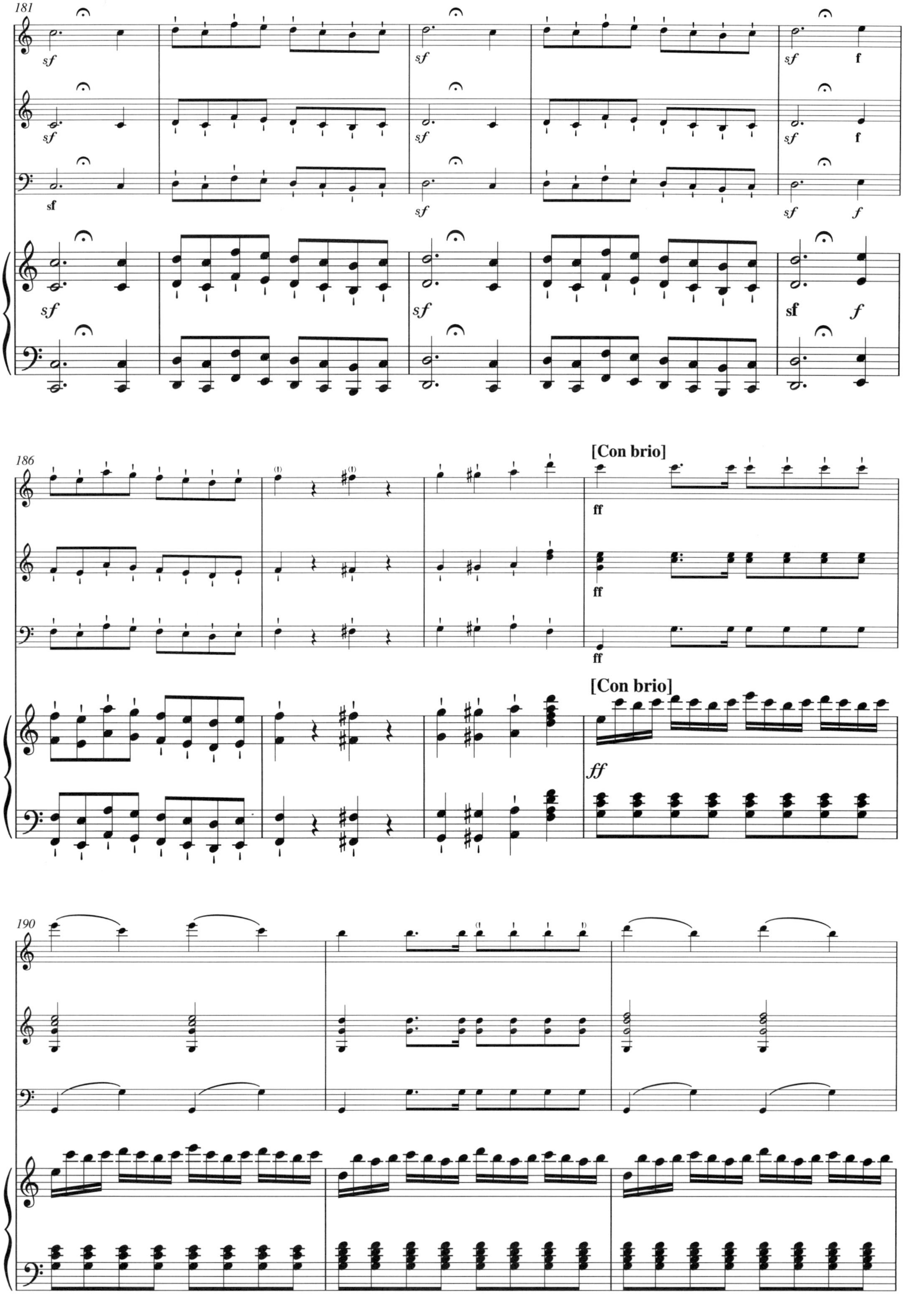
181
sf
f
186
[Con brio]
ff
[Con brio]
ff
190

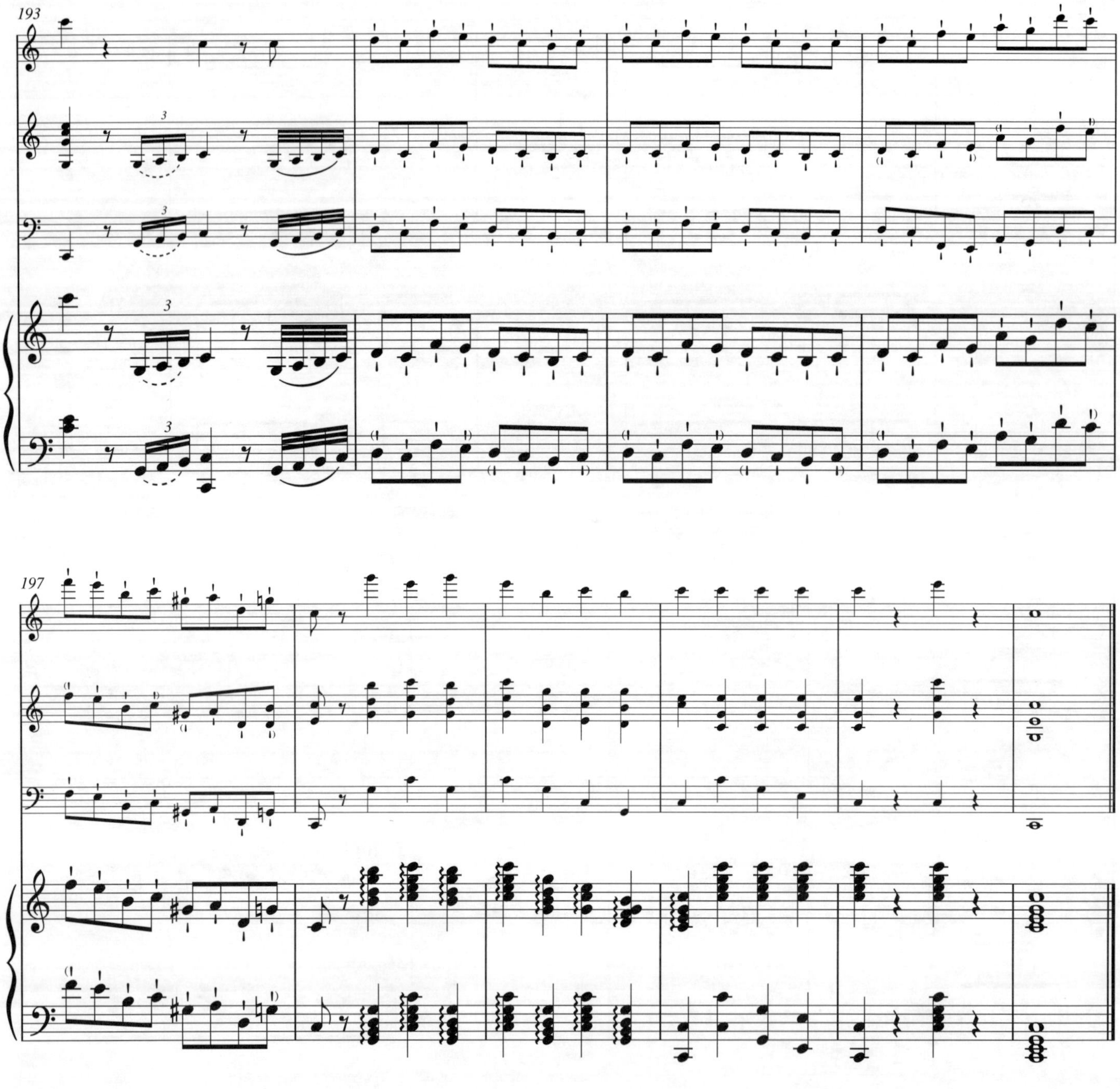
193
197

6. Original Overture

Friedrich Heinrich Himmel

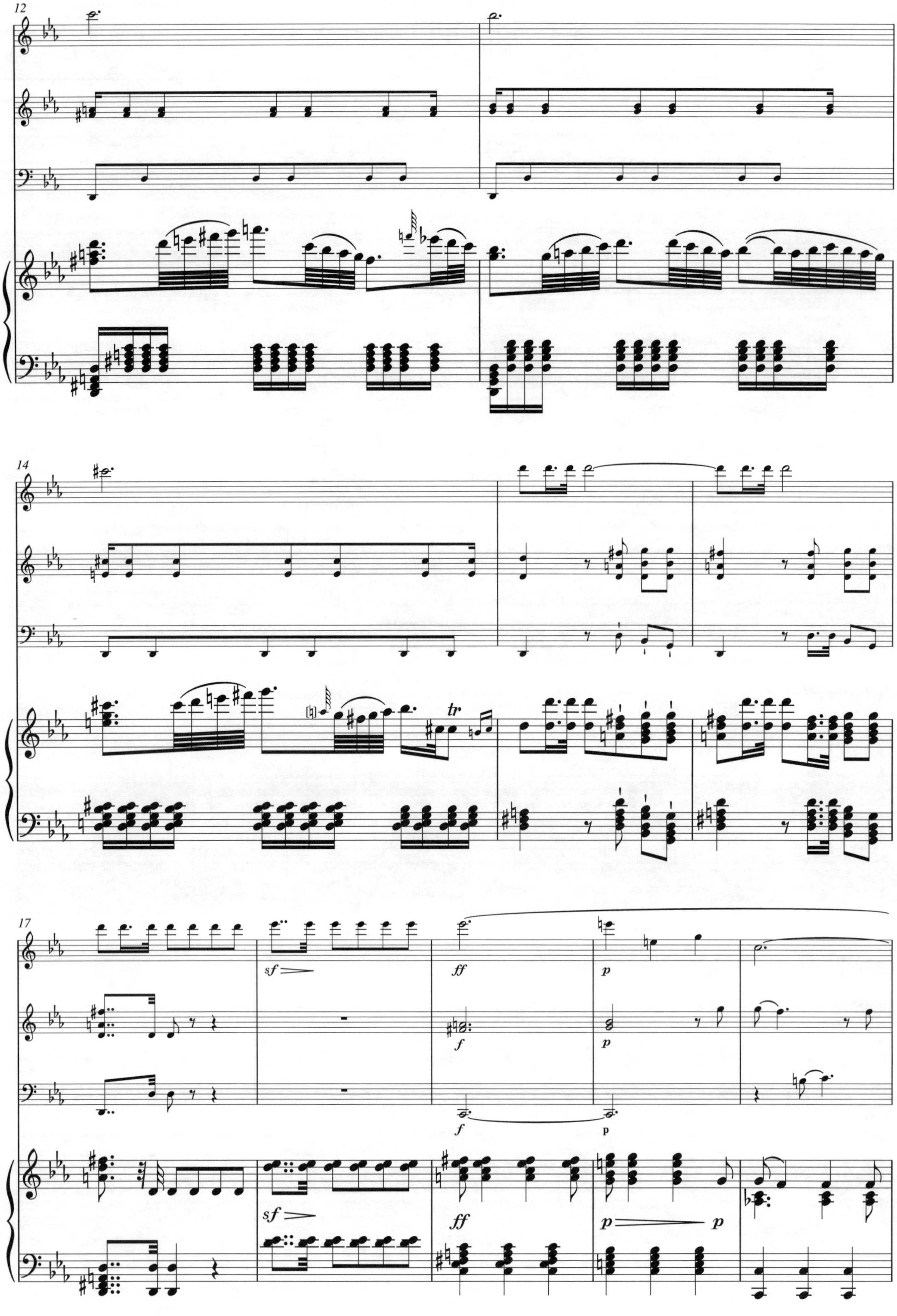
12
14
tr
17
sf
ff
p
f
ff
p
sf
ff
p
p
p

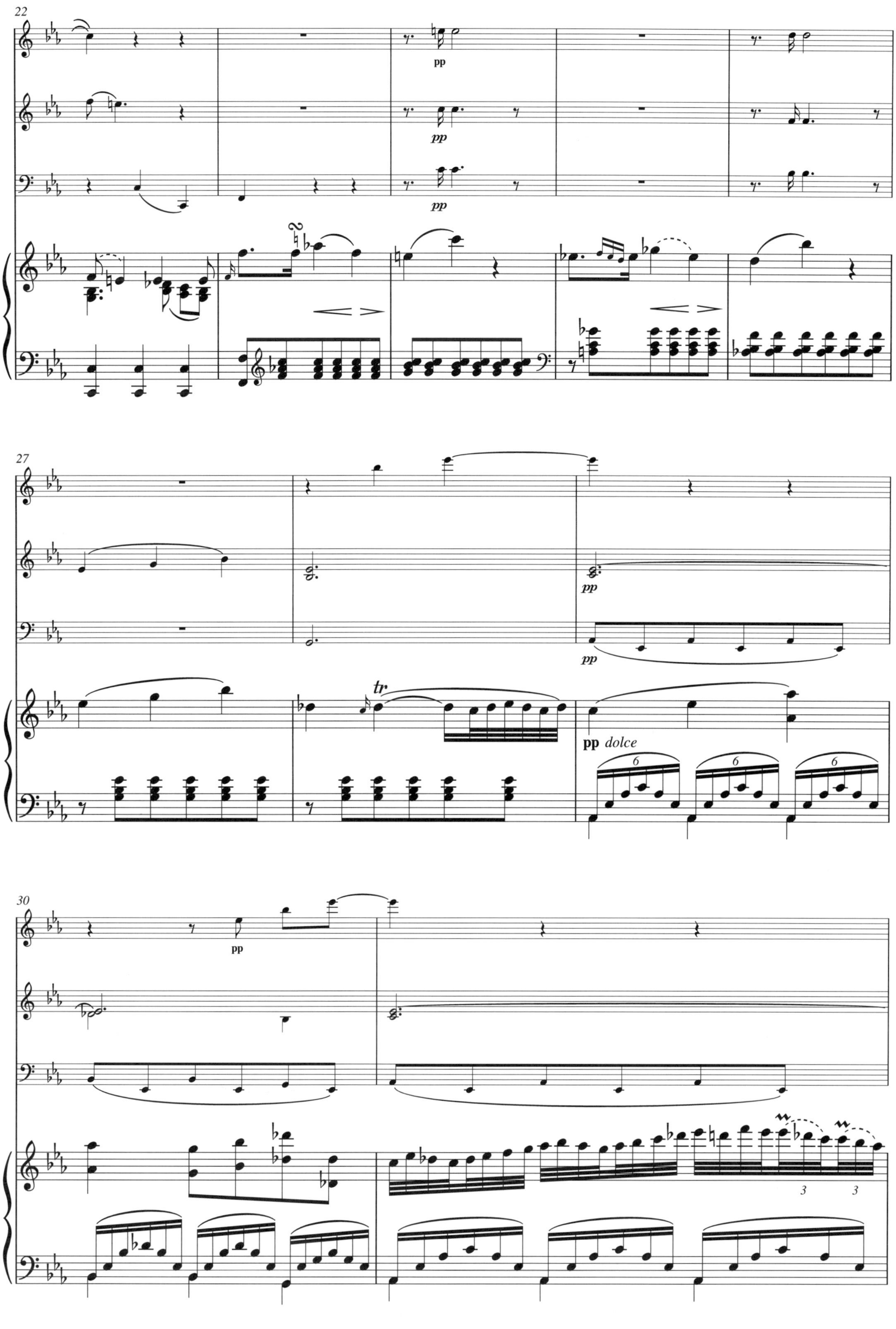
22
pp
pp
pp
27
tr
pp
pp
pp dolce
6
30
pp
3

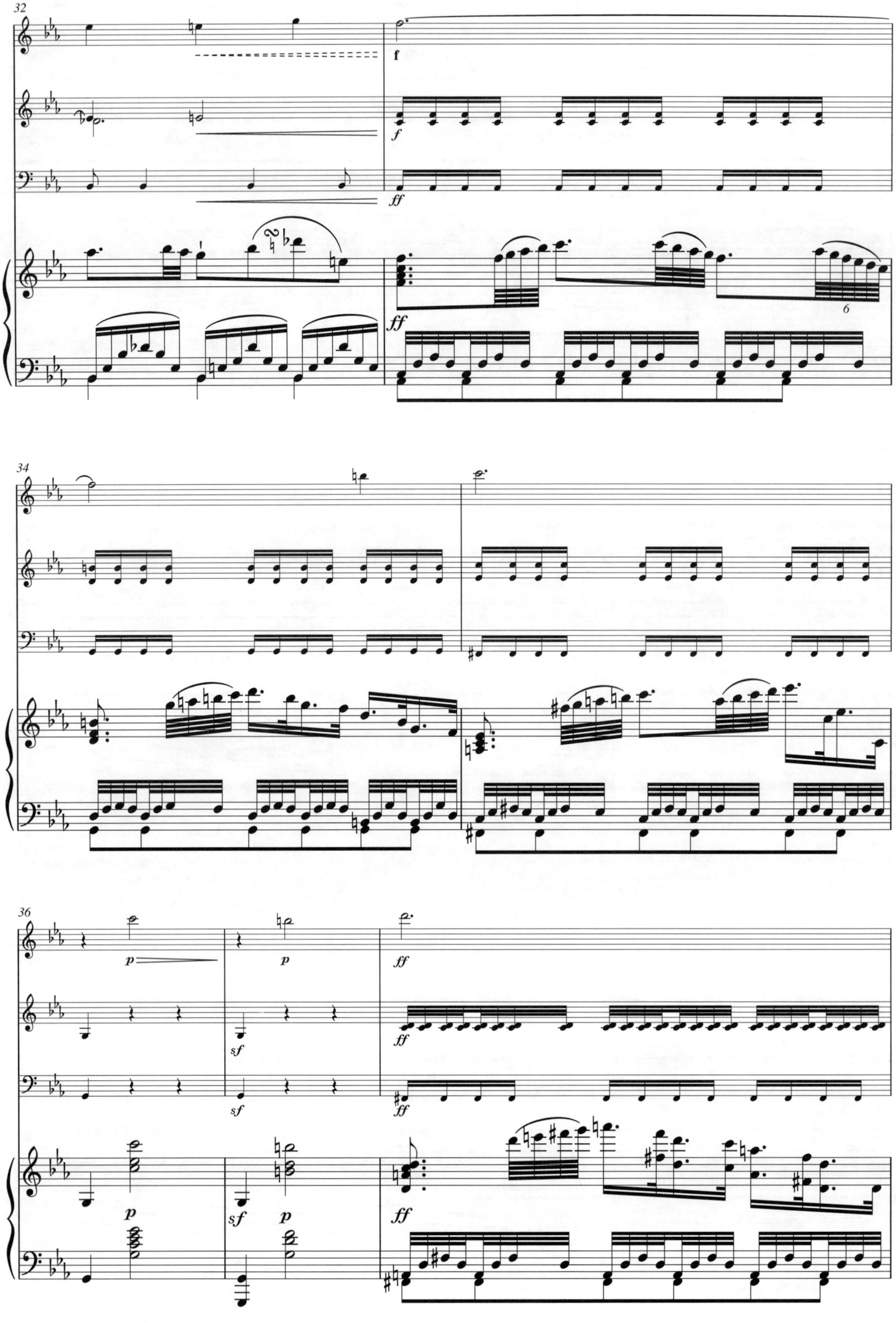

39
pp
dim.
pp
pp
pp
42
Allegro marcato e con brio
mf
mf
mf
Allegro marcato e con brio
mf
46
ff
ff
f

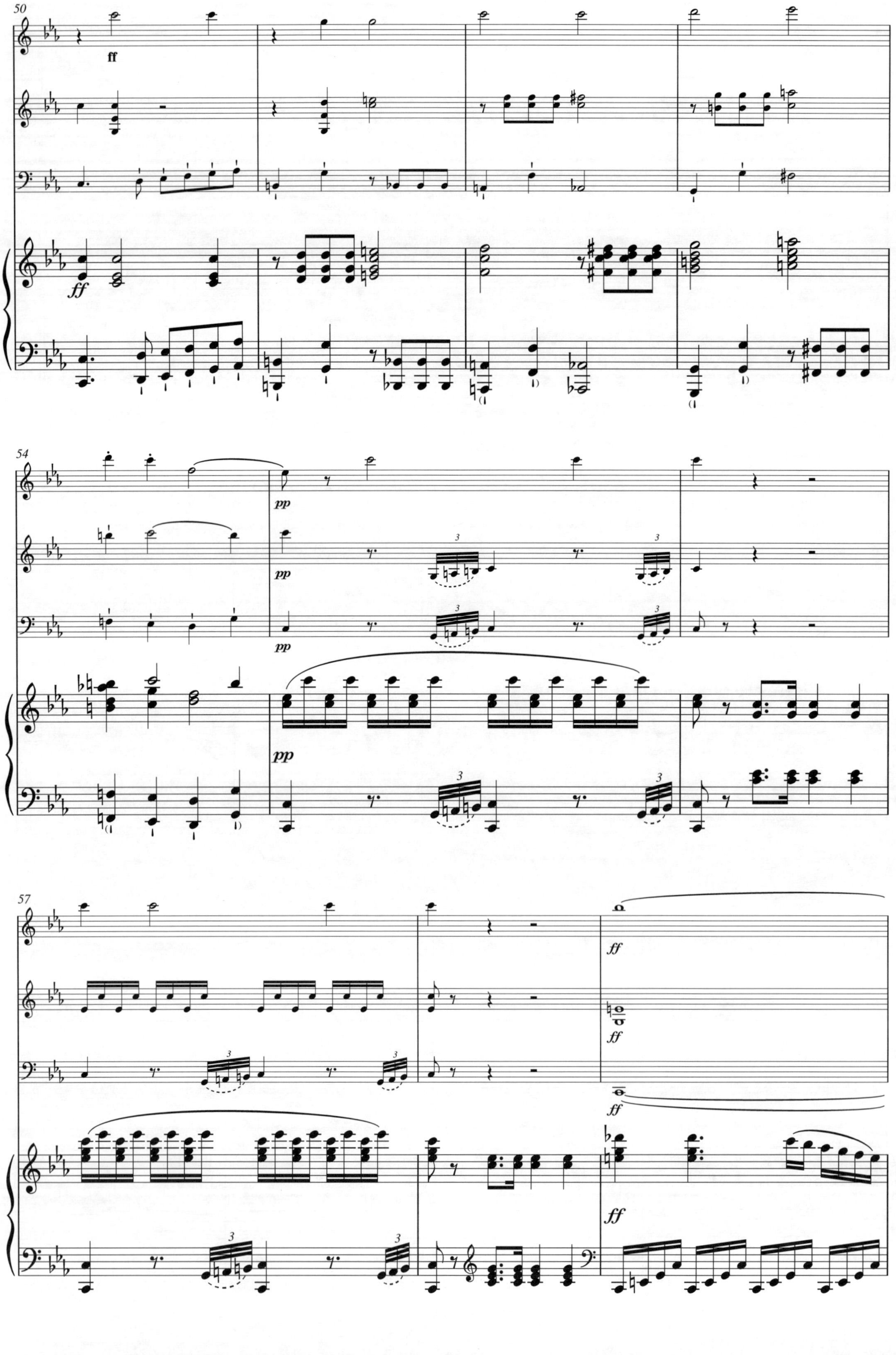
50
ff
ff
54
pp
pp
pp
pp
57
ff
ff
ff
ff

113

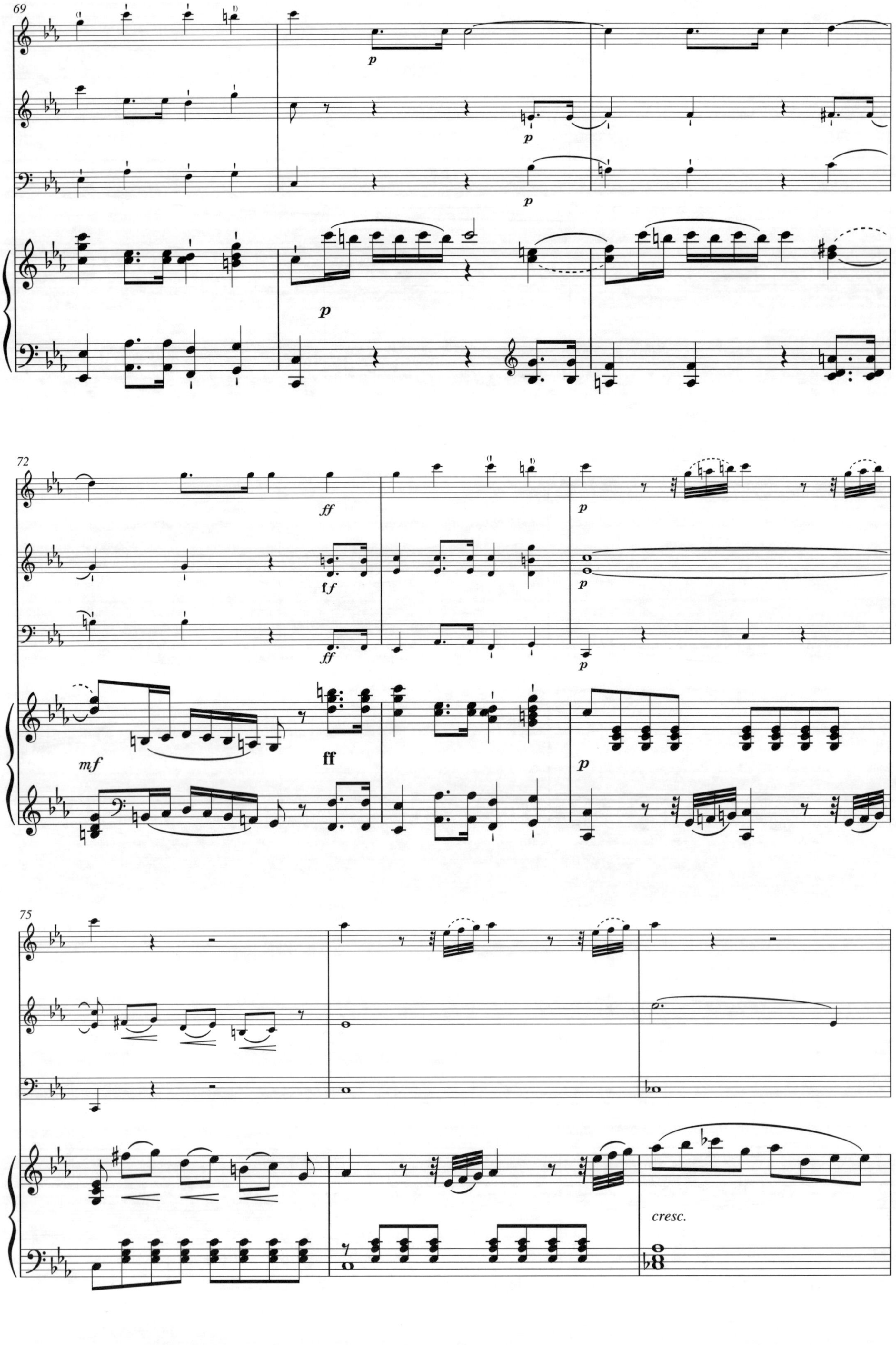
69
p
p
p
p
72
ff
ff
ff
mf
ff
p
p
p
p
75
cresc.

115

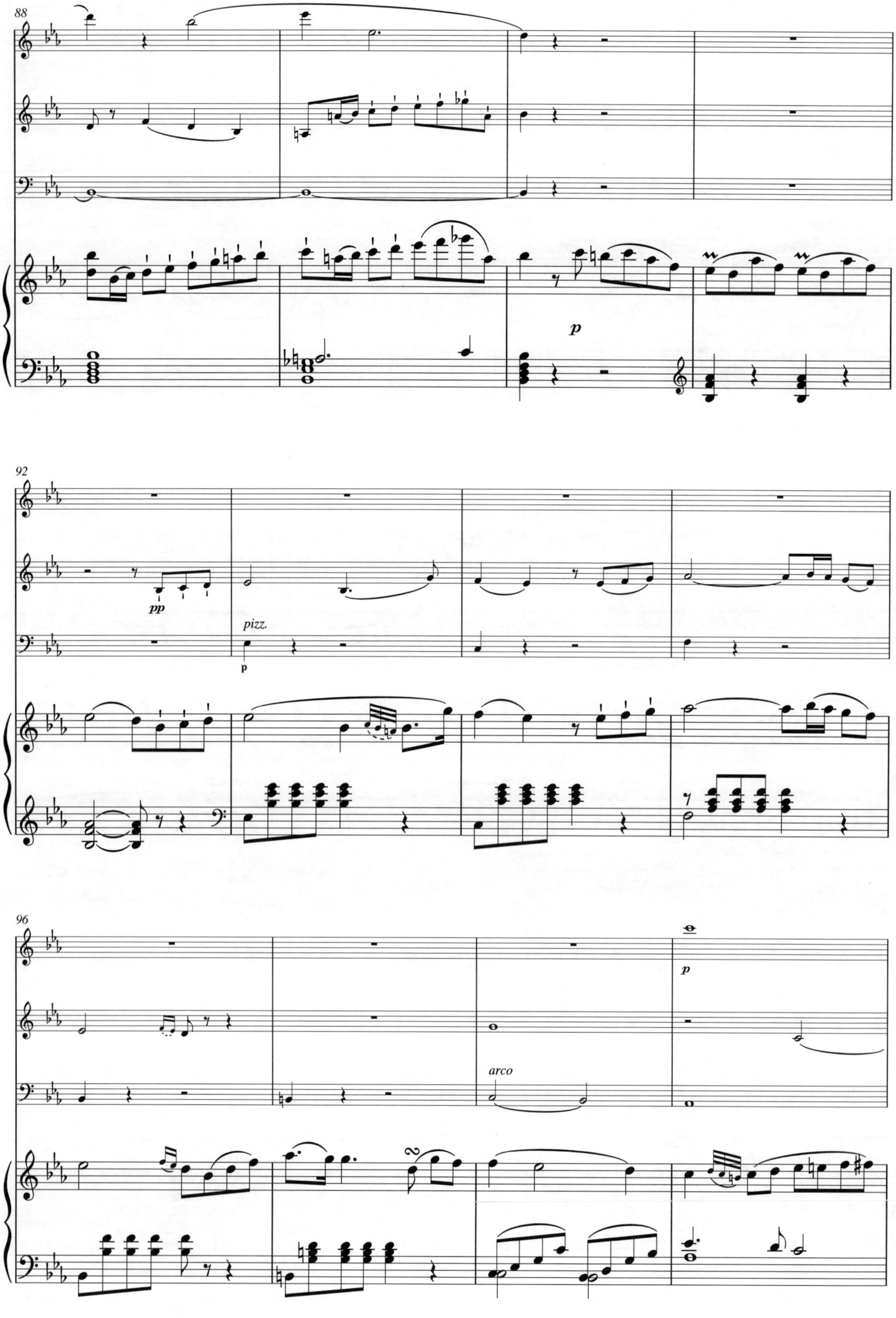
88
p
92
pp
pizz.
p
96
p
arco

117

110
cresc.
cresc.
cresc.
sf
cresc.
f
113
f
sf
sf
f p
fz
fz
p
sf
sf
ff
sf
sf
116
sf
sf
f
fz
fz
p
sf
sf
sf
sf
sf

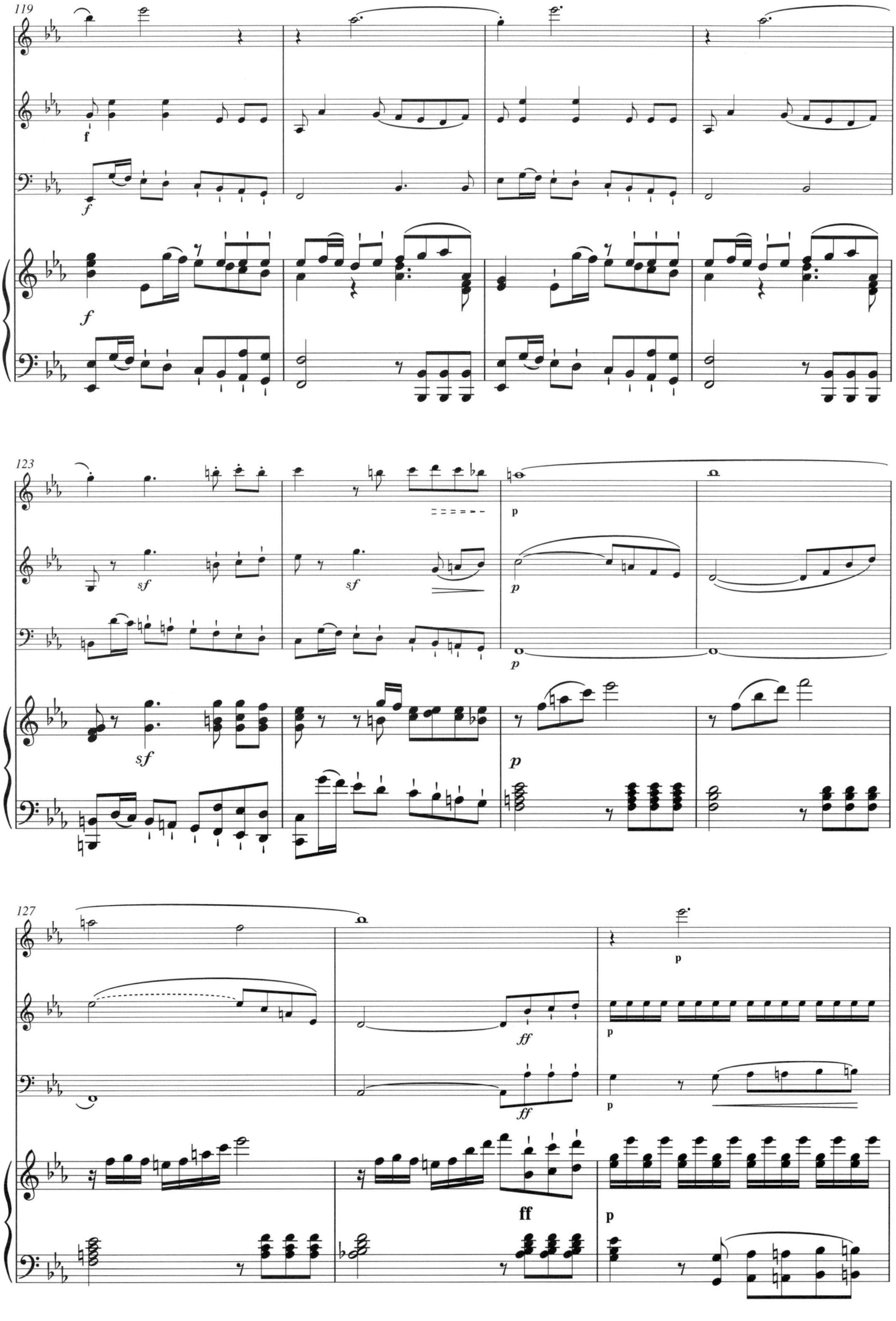
119
f
f
f
123
sf
sf
sf
p
p
p
p
127
p
ff
ff
p
p
ff
p
p

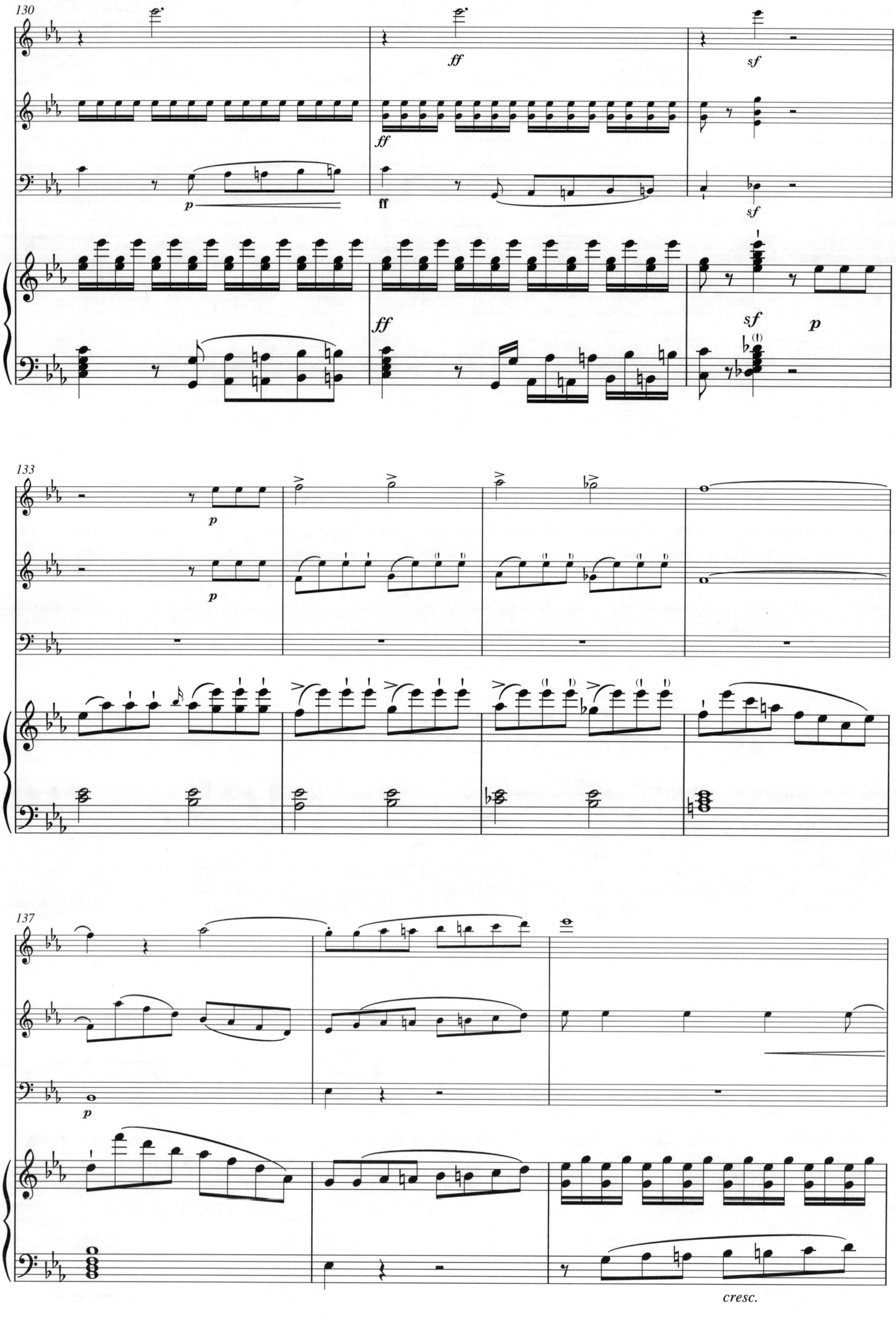
130
ff
sf
p
ff
sf
ff
sf
p
133
p
p
137
p
cresc.

121

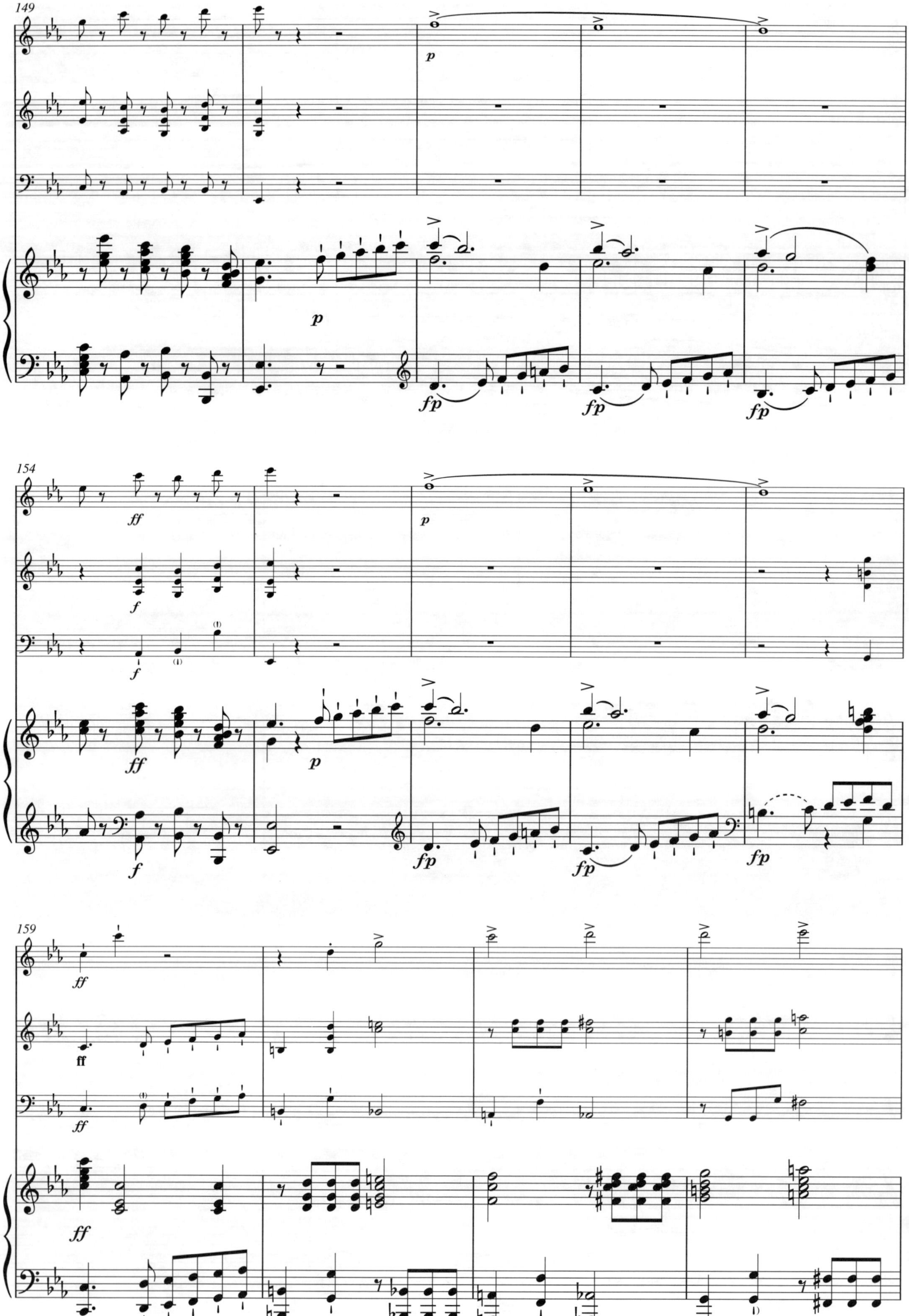
149
154
159

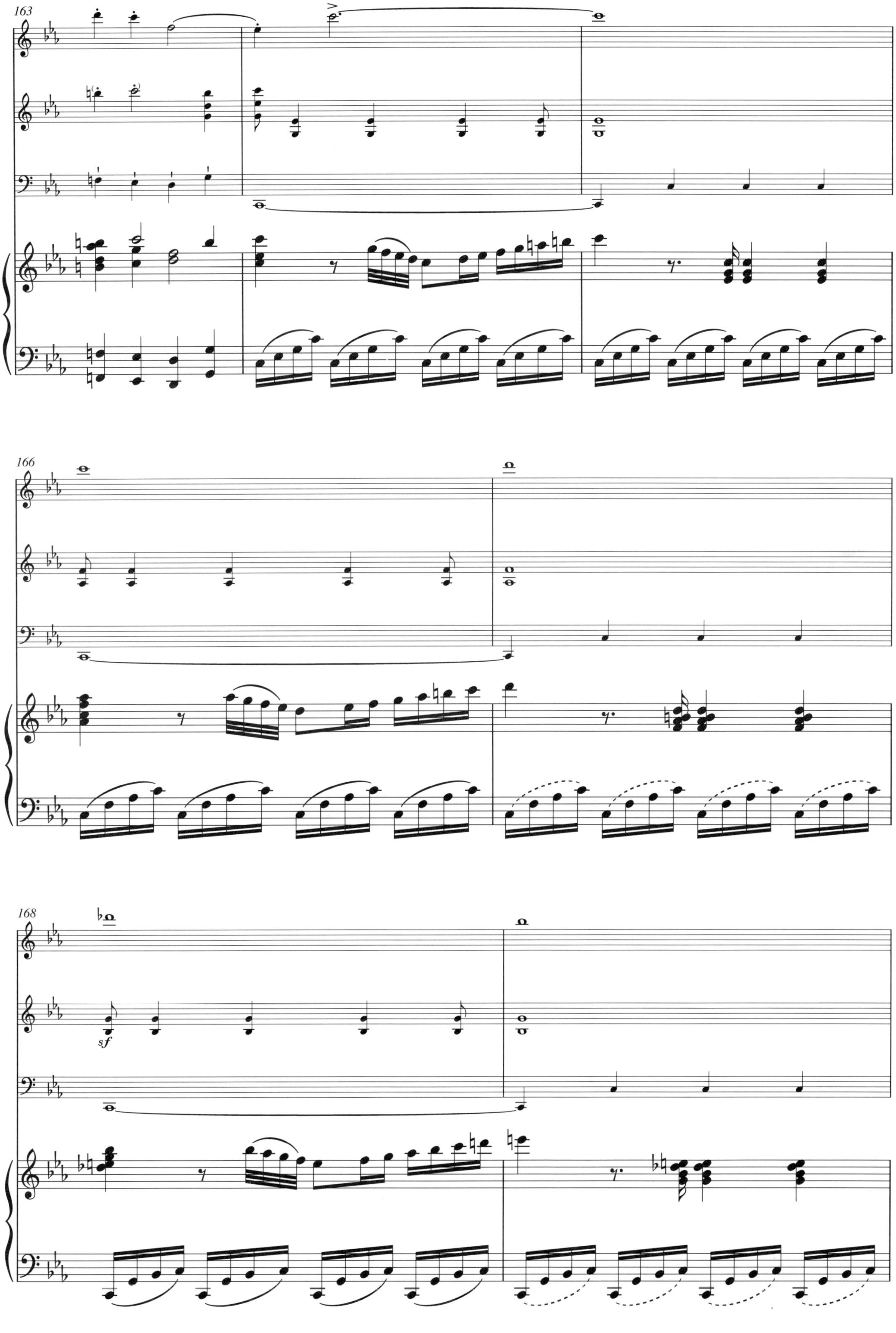
163
166
168
sf

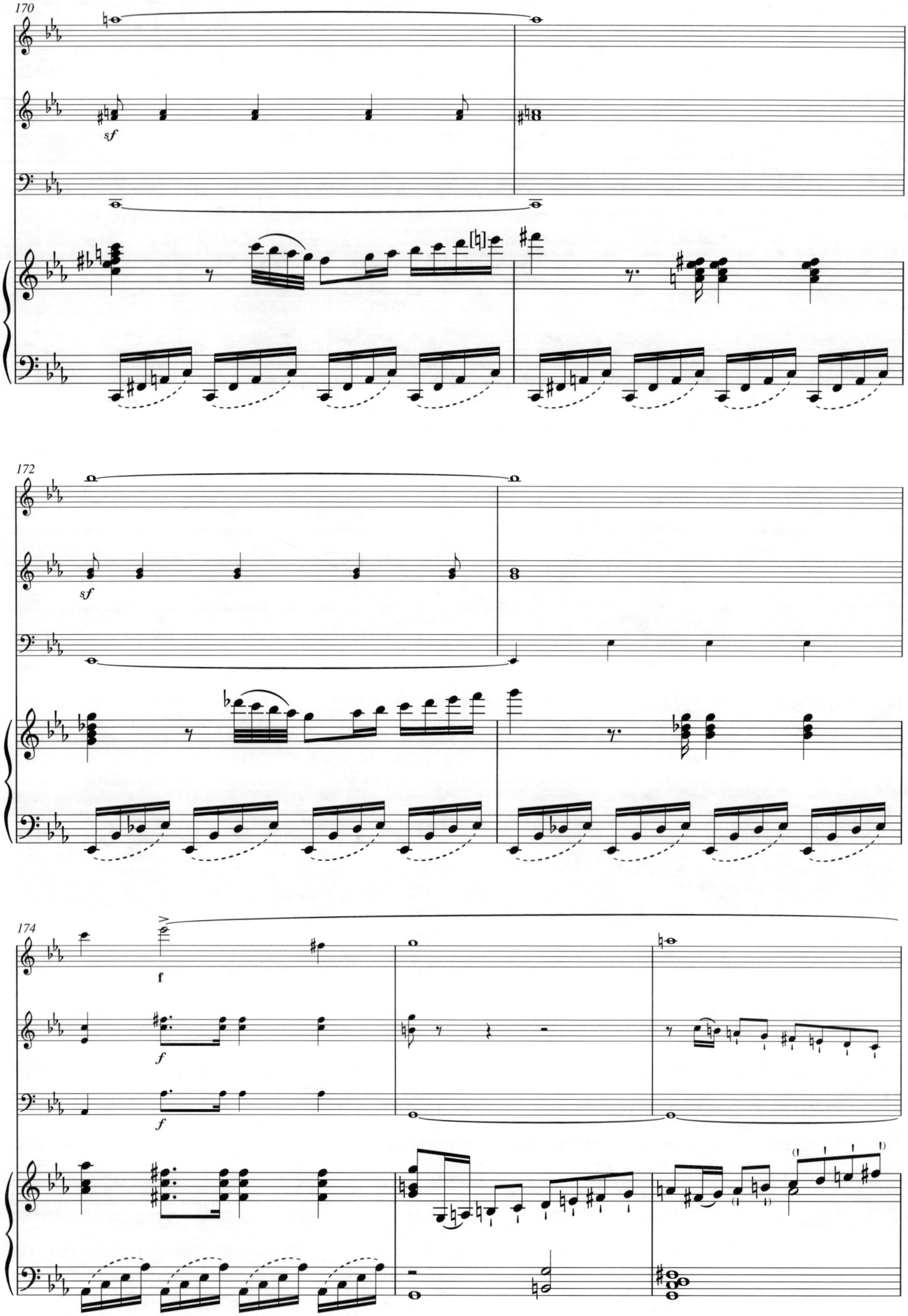
170
sf
172
sf
174
f
f
f

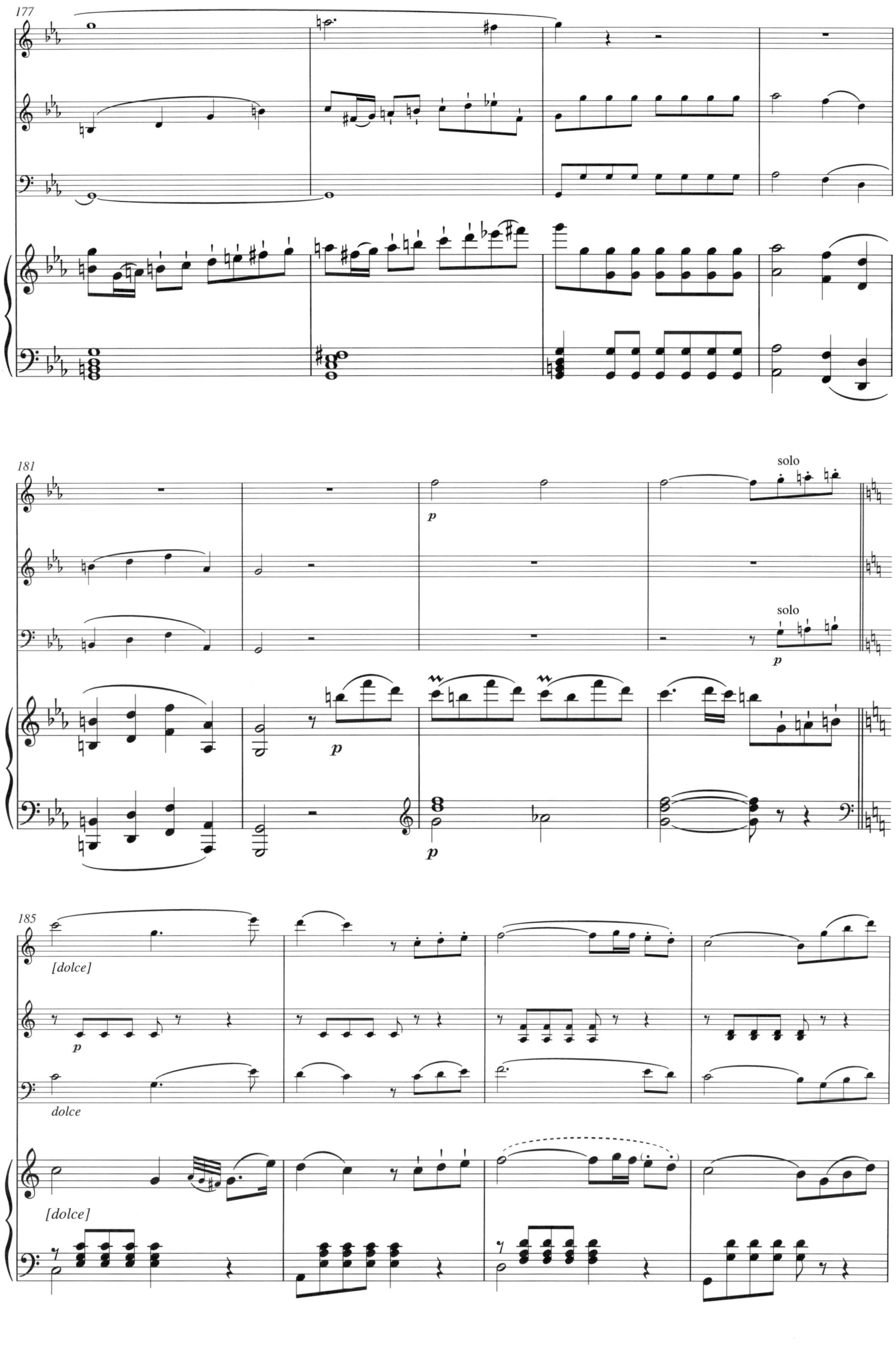
177
181
solo
p
solo
p
p
p
185
[dolce]
p
dolce
[dolce]

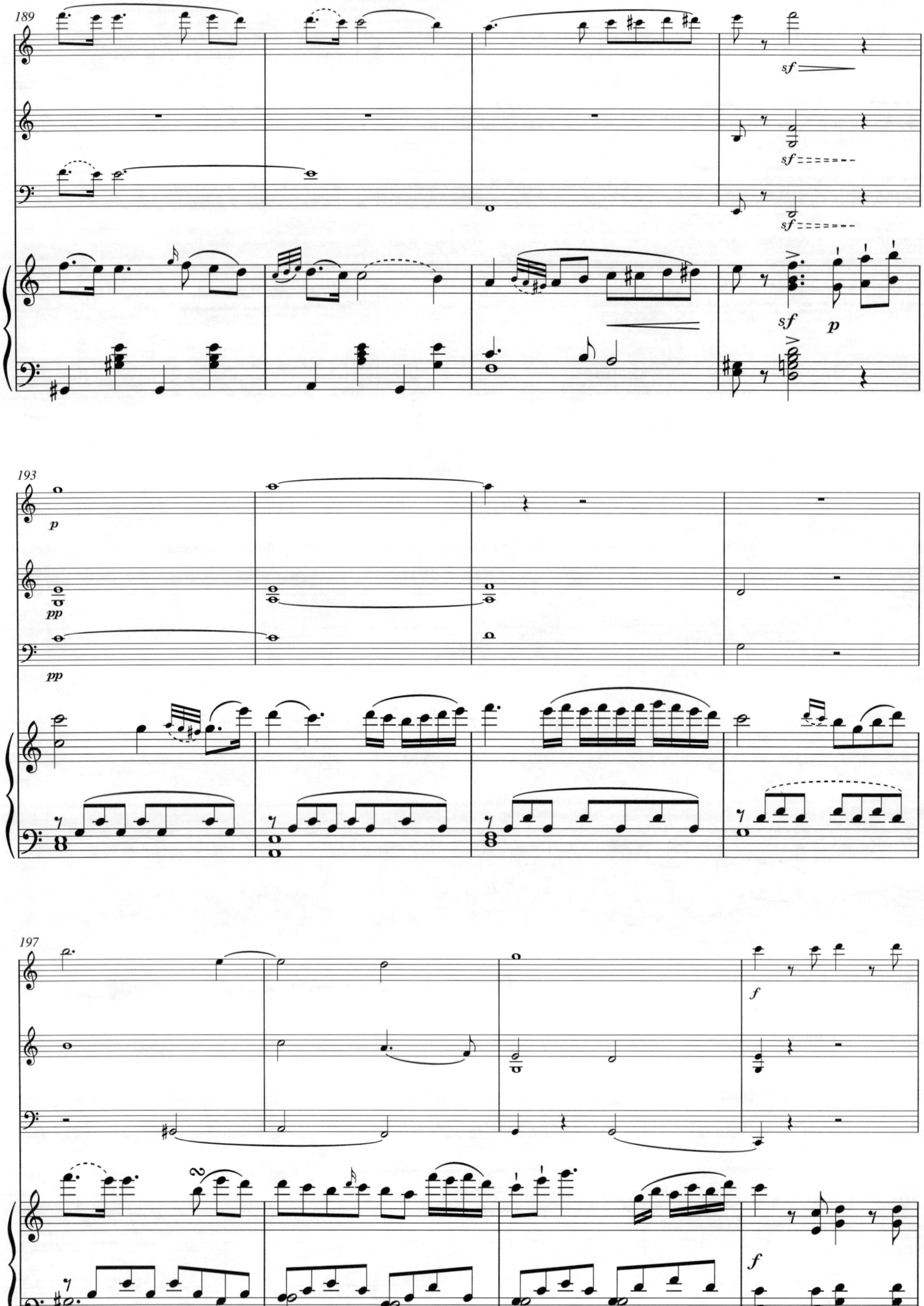
189
sf
sf
sf
sf
p
193
p
pp
pp
197
f
f

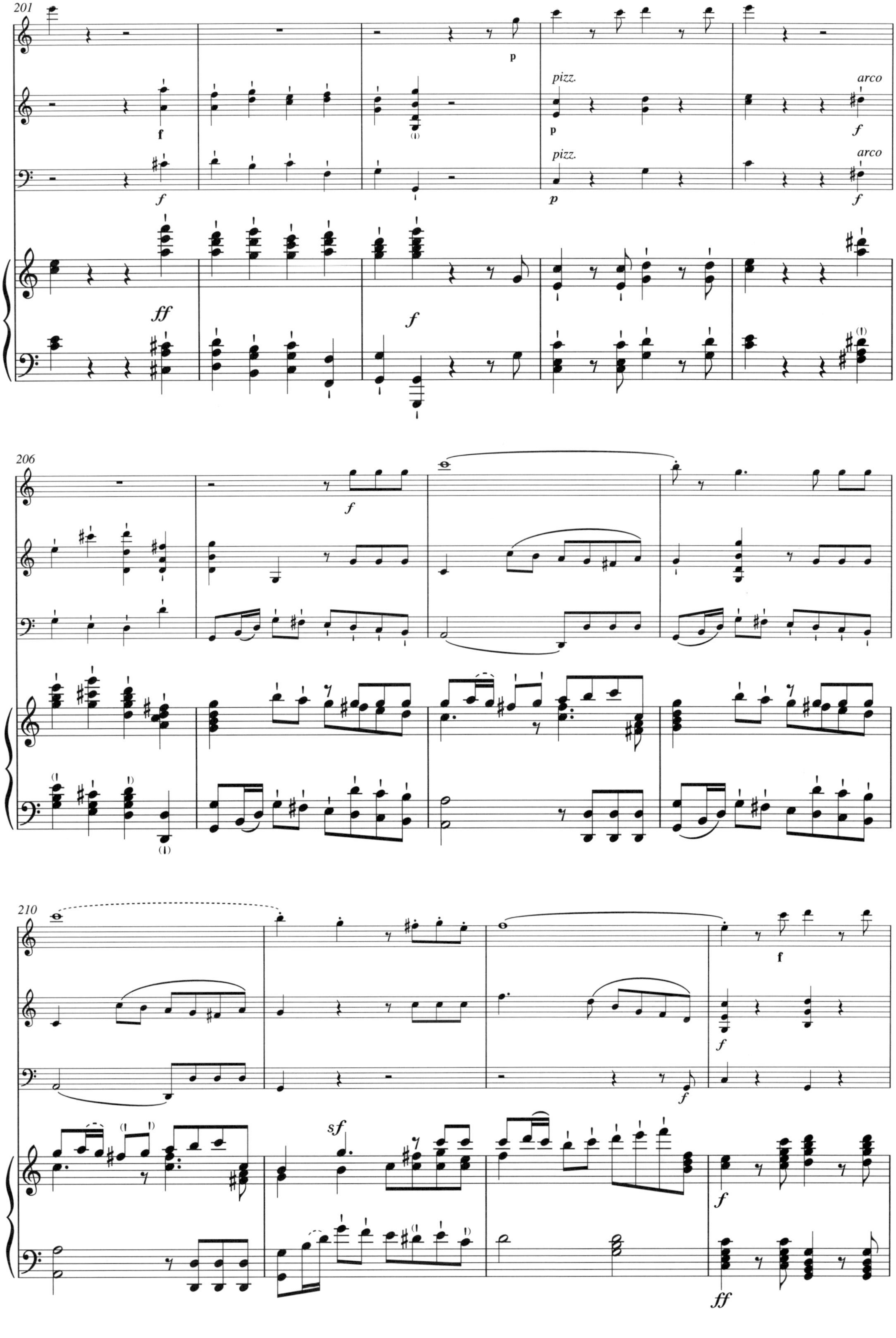
201
pizz.
arco
pizz.
arco
206
210

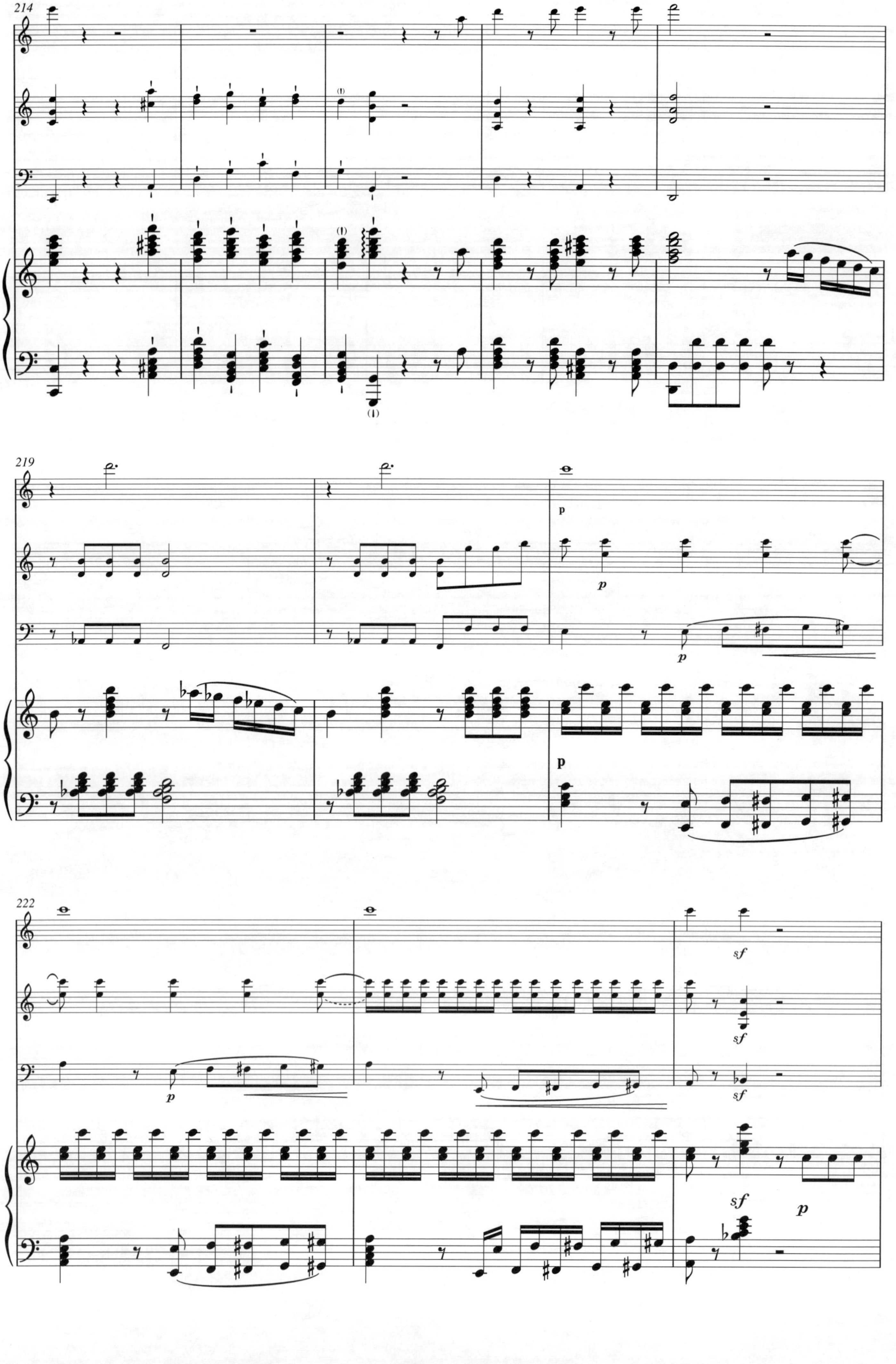
214
219
222
p
sf

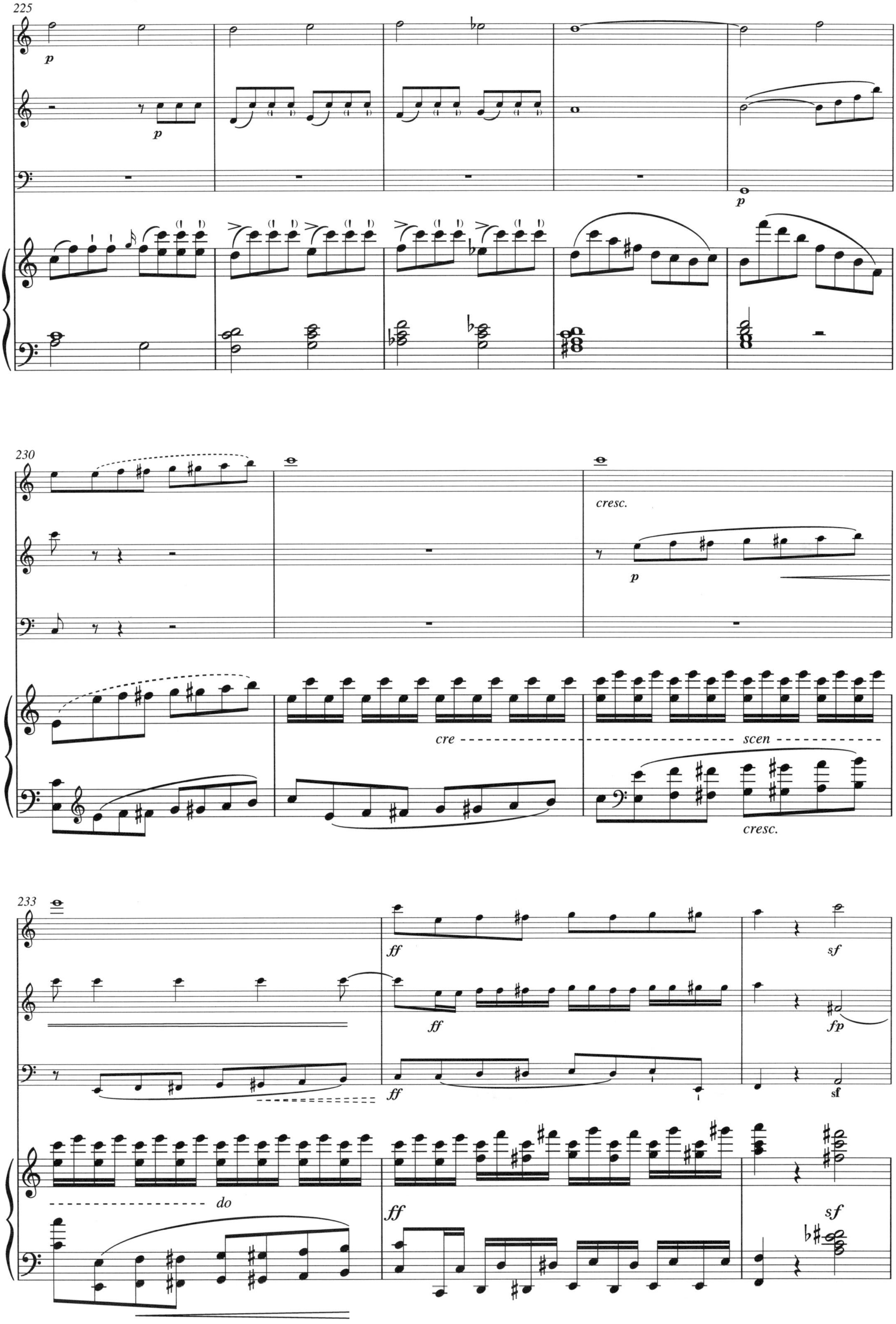
225
p
p
p
230
cresc.
p
cre
scen
cresc.
233
do
ff
ff
ff
ff
sf
fp
sf
sf

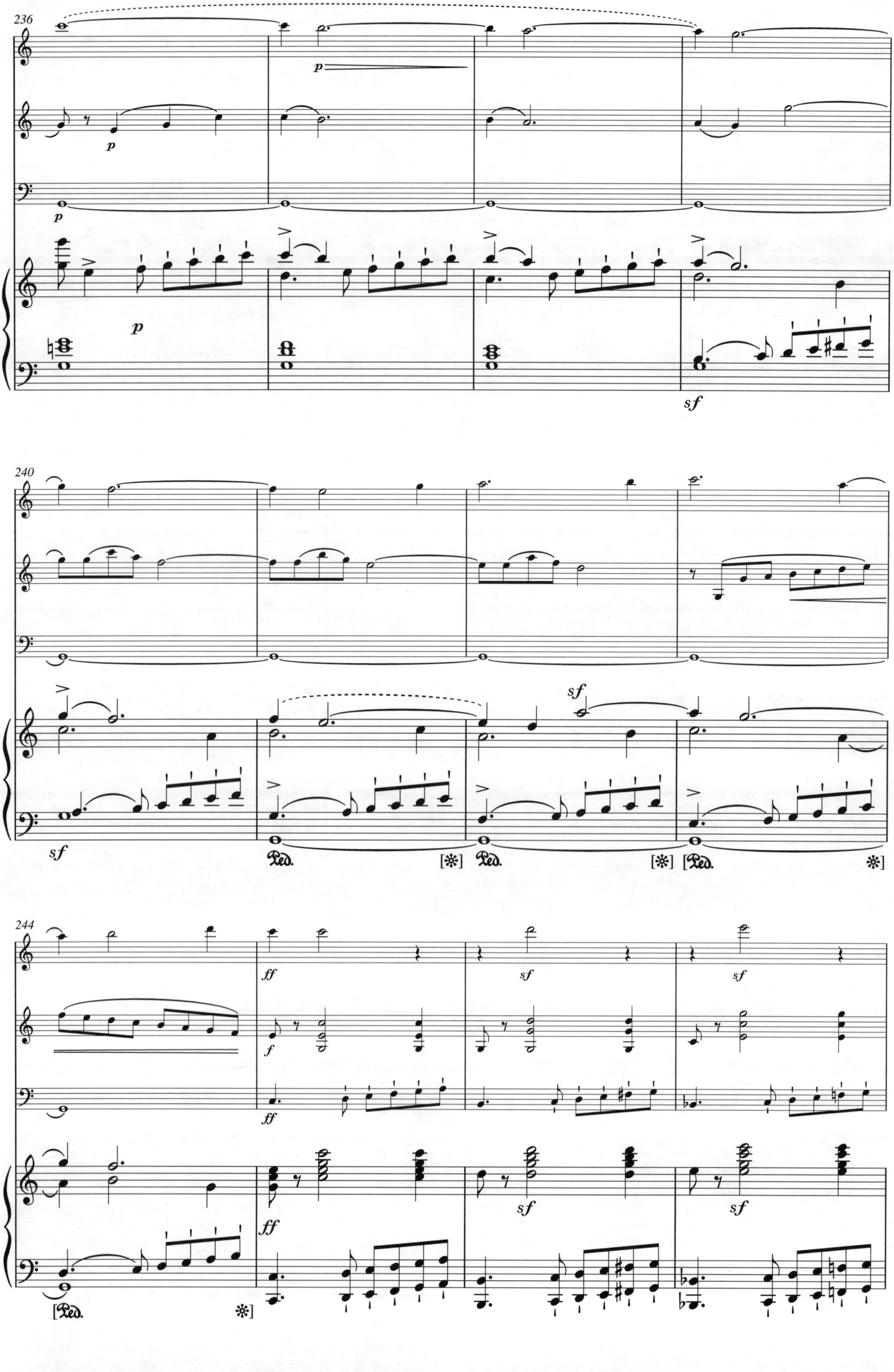
236
p
p
p
sf
240
sf
sf
Ped.
[*]
Ped.
[*]
[Ped.
*]
244
ff
sf
sf
f
ff
ff
sf
sf
[Ped.
*]

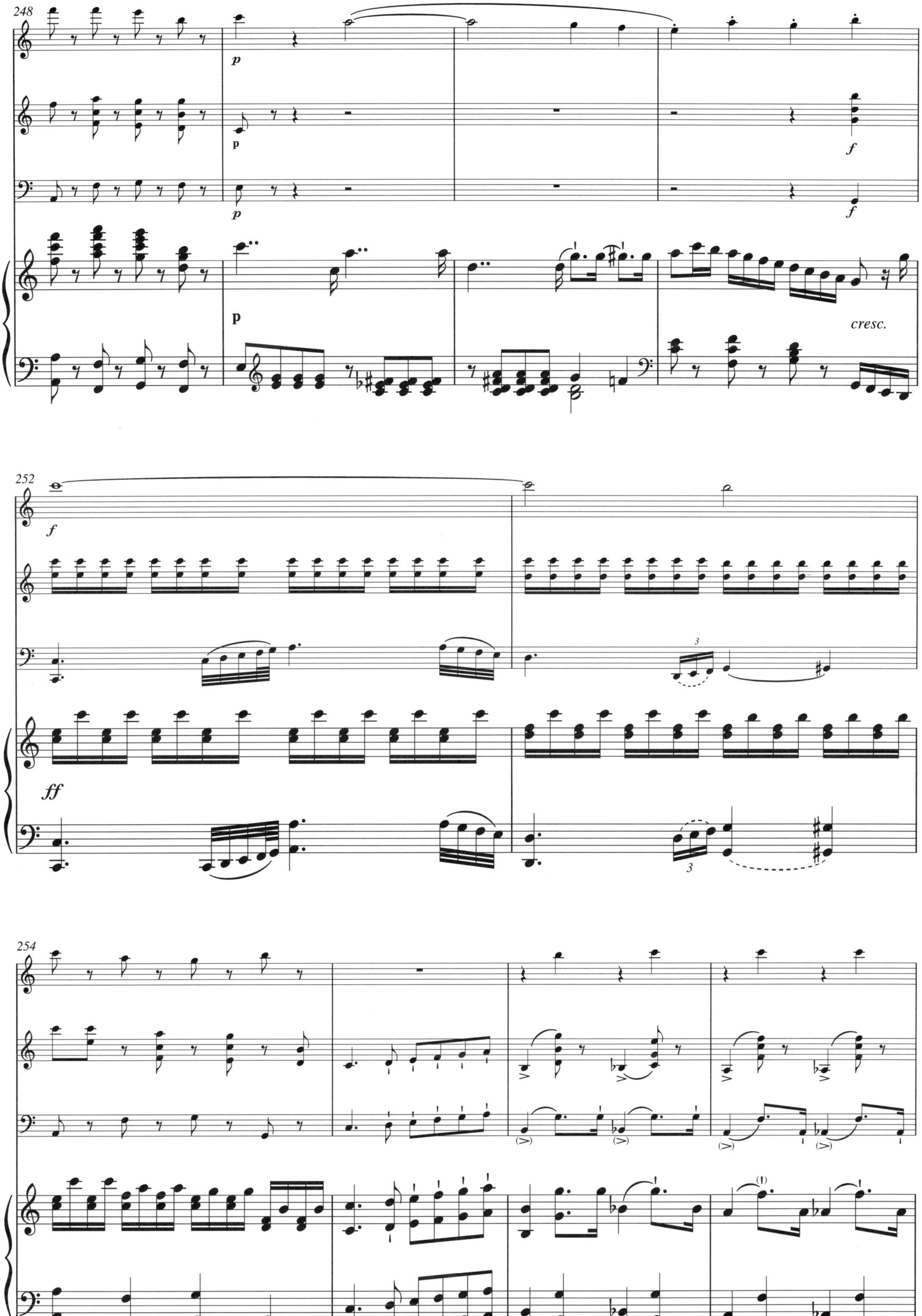
248
p
p
p
f
f
p
cresc.
252
f
3
ff
3
254
(>)
(>)
(>)
(>)
(!)

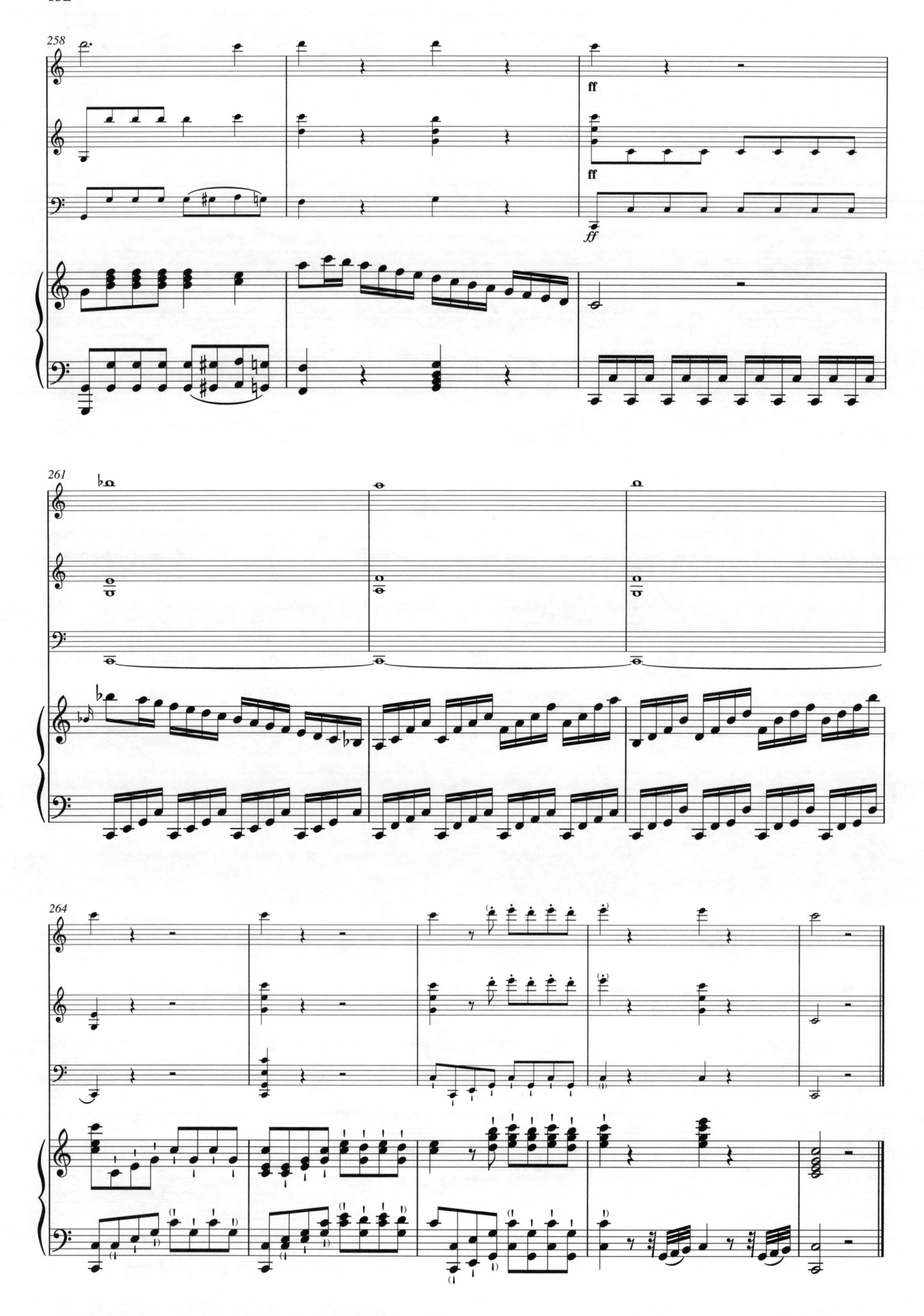
258
ff
ff
ff
261
264

7. Overture to Sargino

Ferdinando Paer

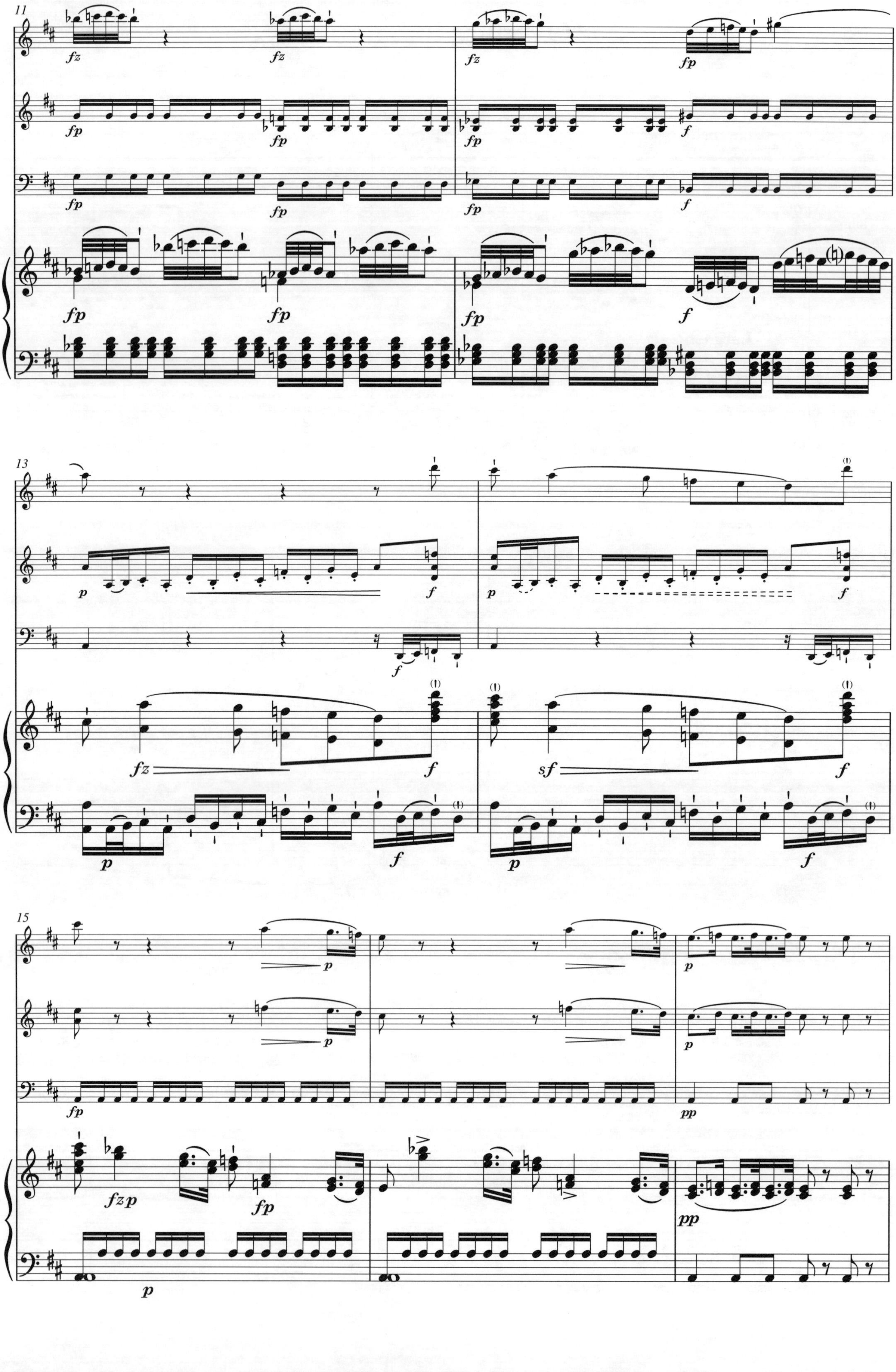

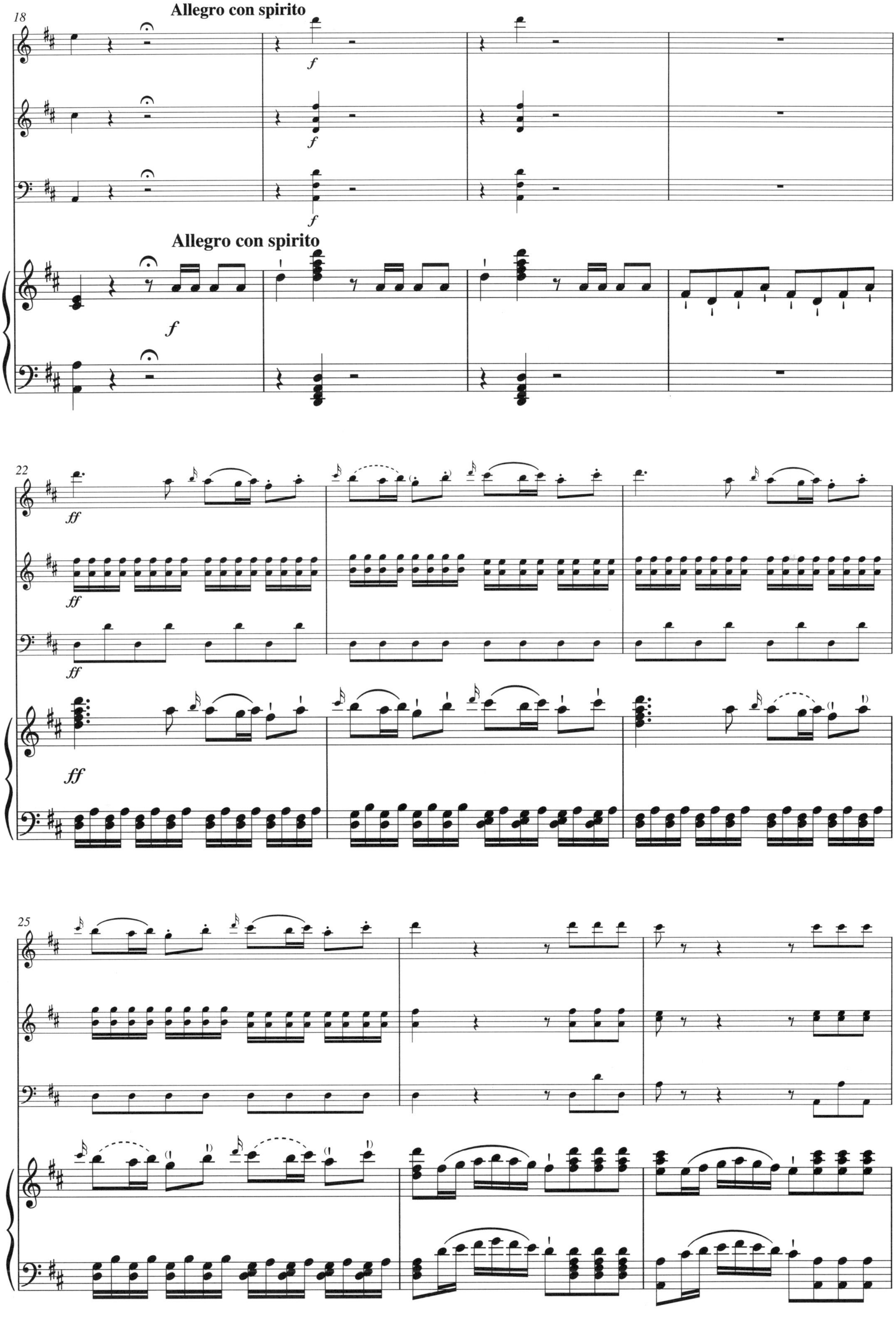
18
Allegro con spirito
Allegro con spirito
22
25

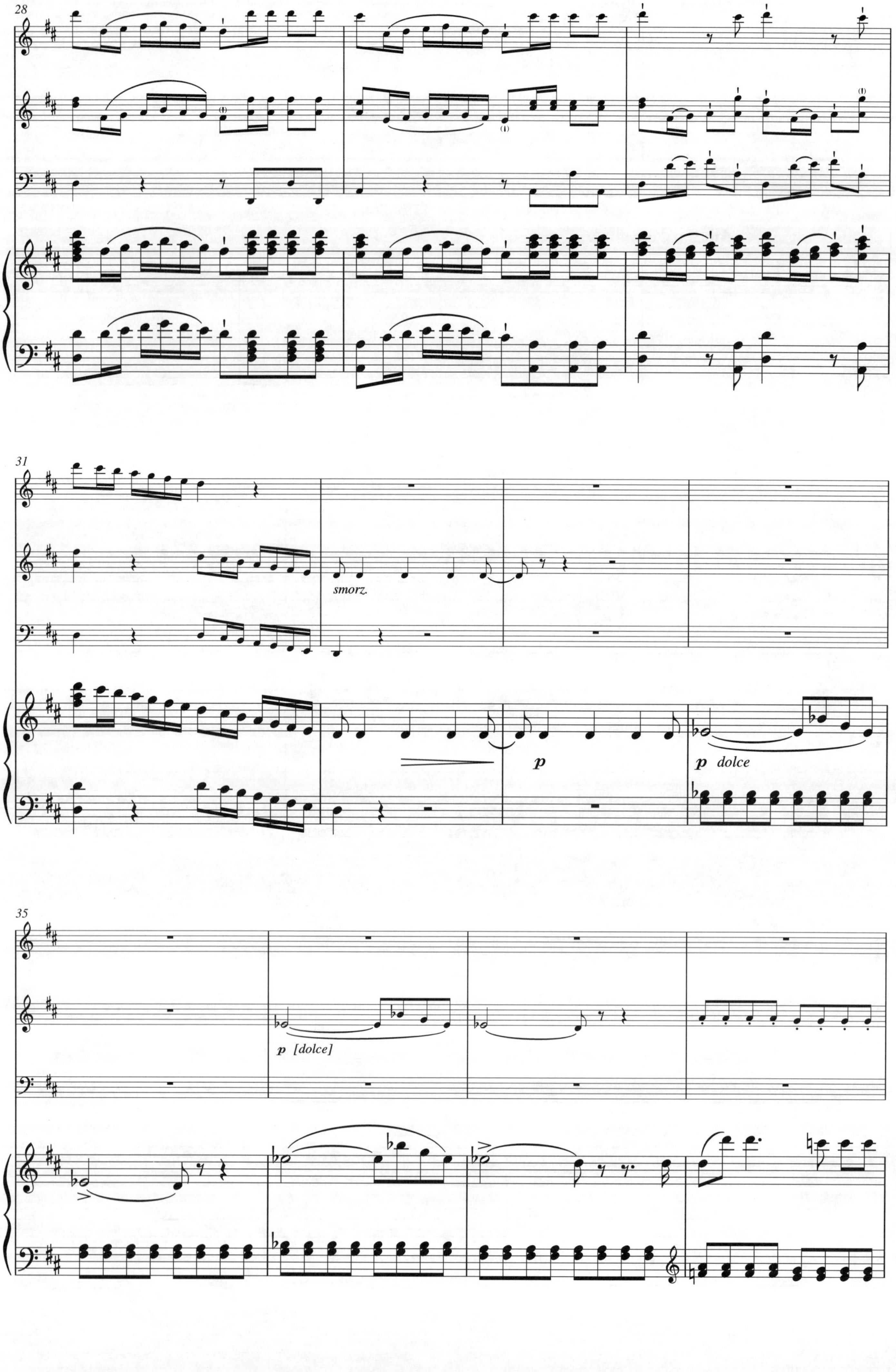
28
31
smorz.
p
p dolce
35
p [dolce]

137

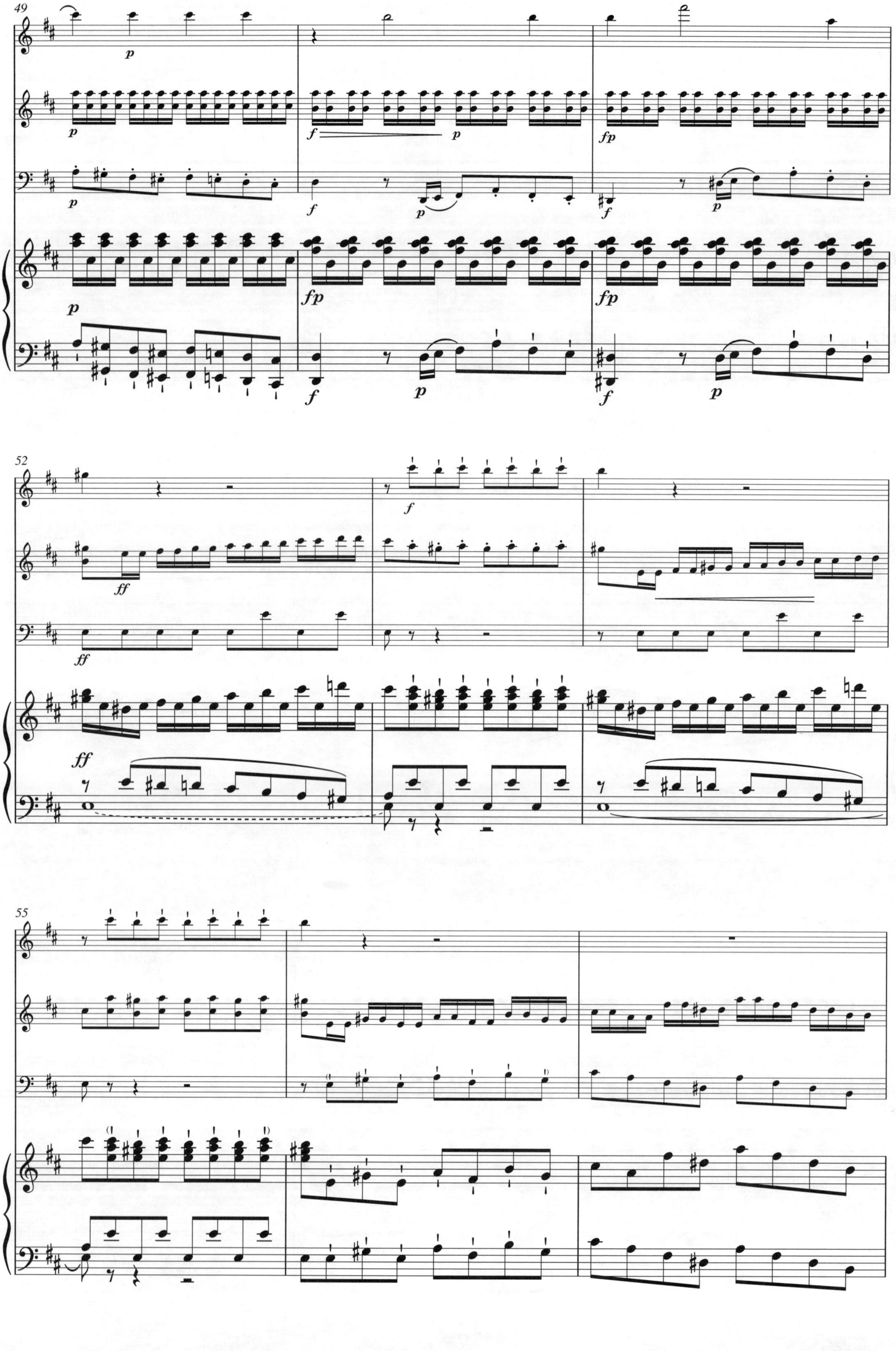

139

140

141

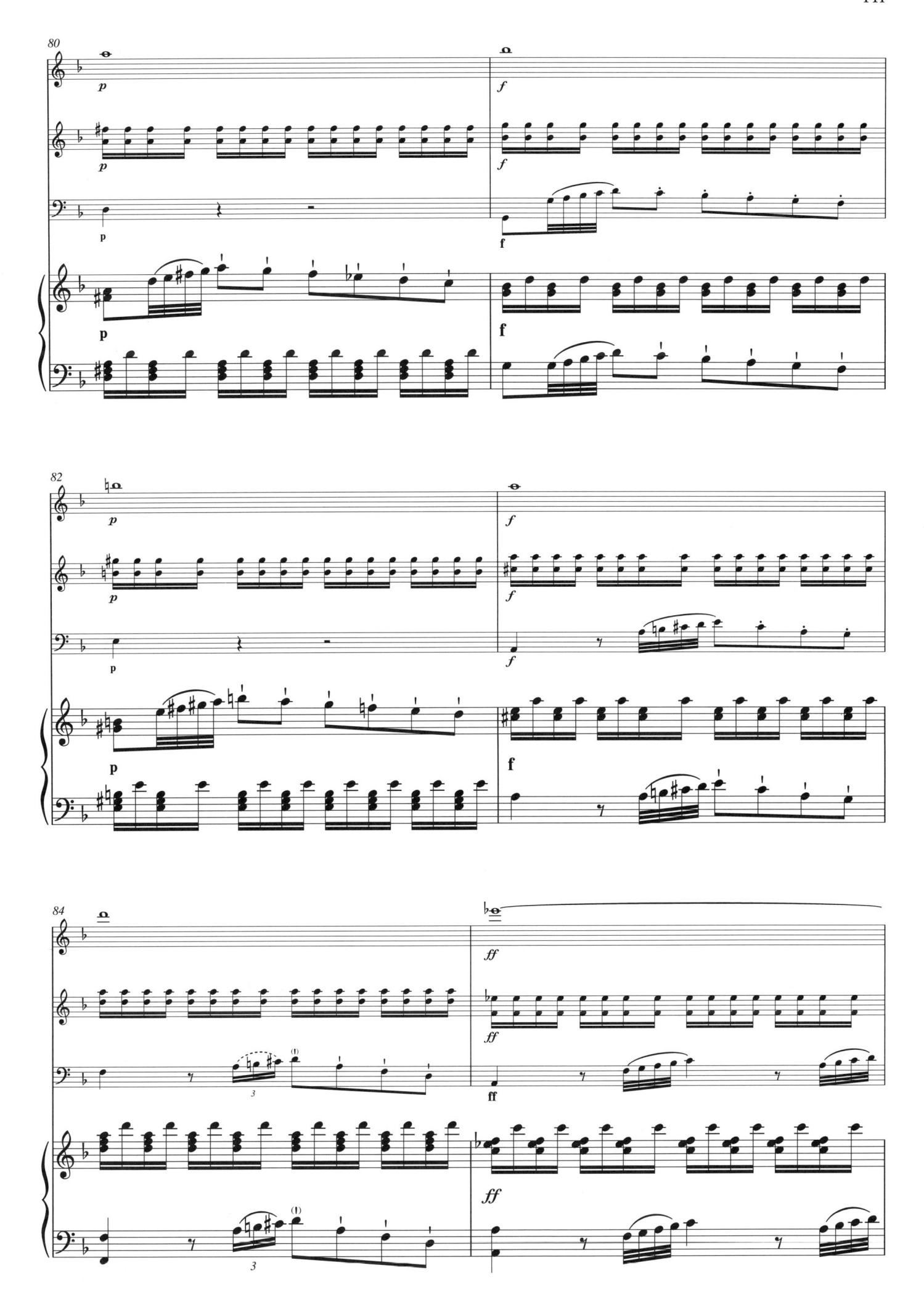

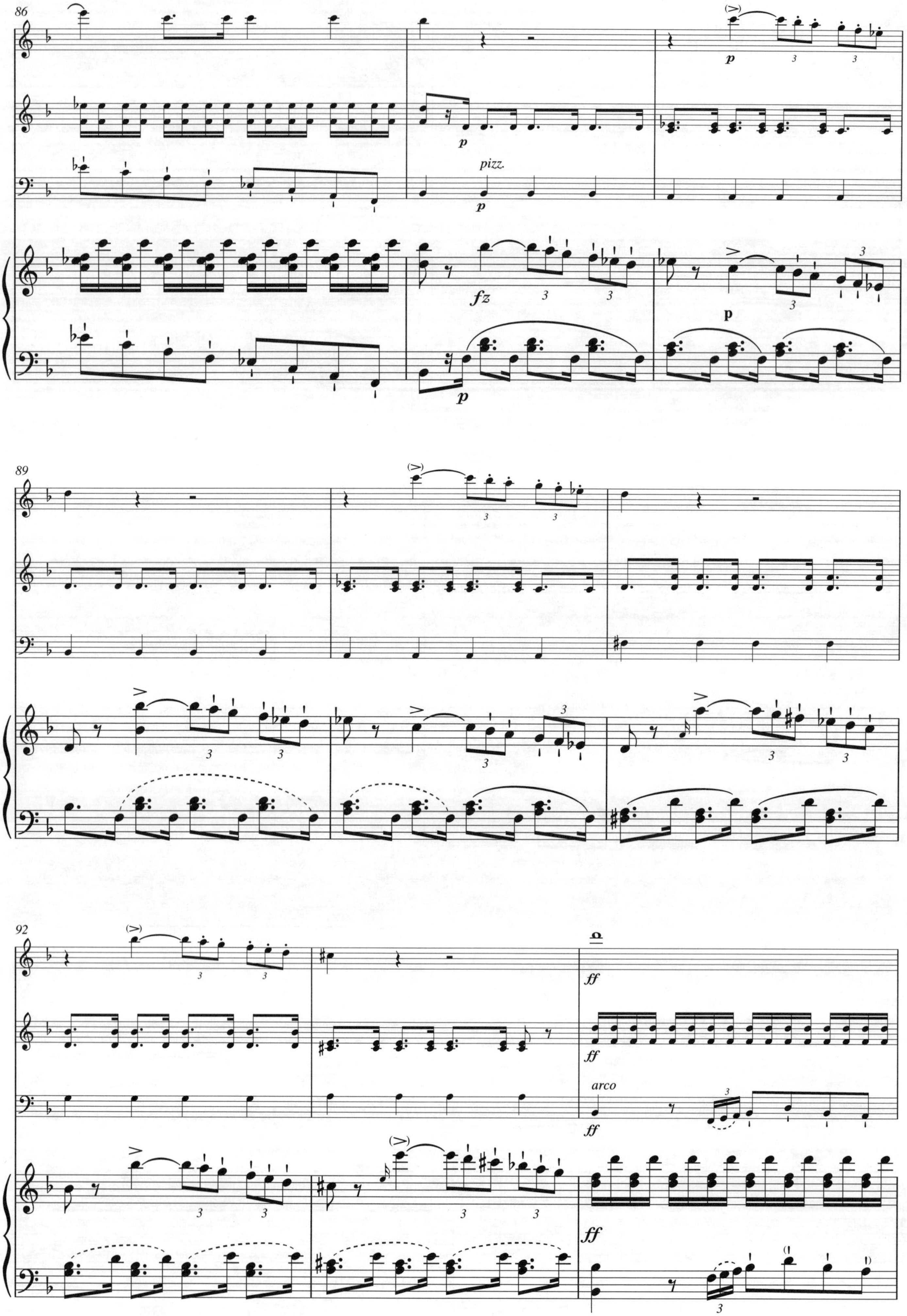
86
pizz.
fz
89
92
arco
ff

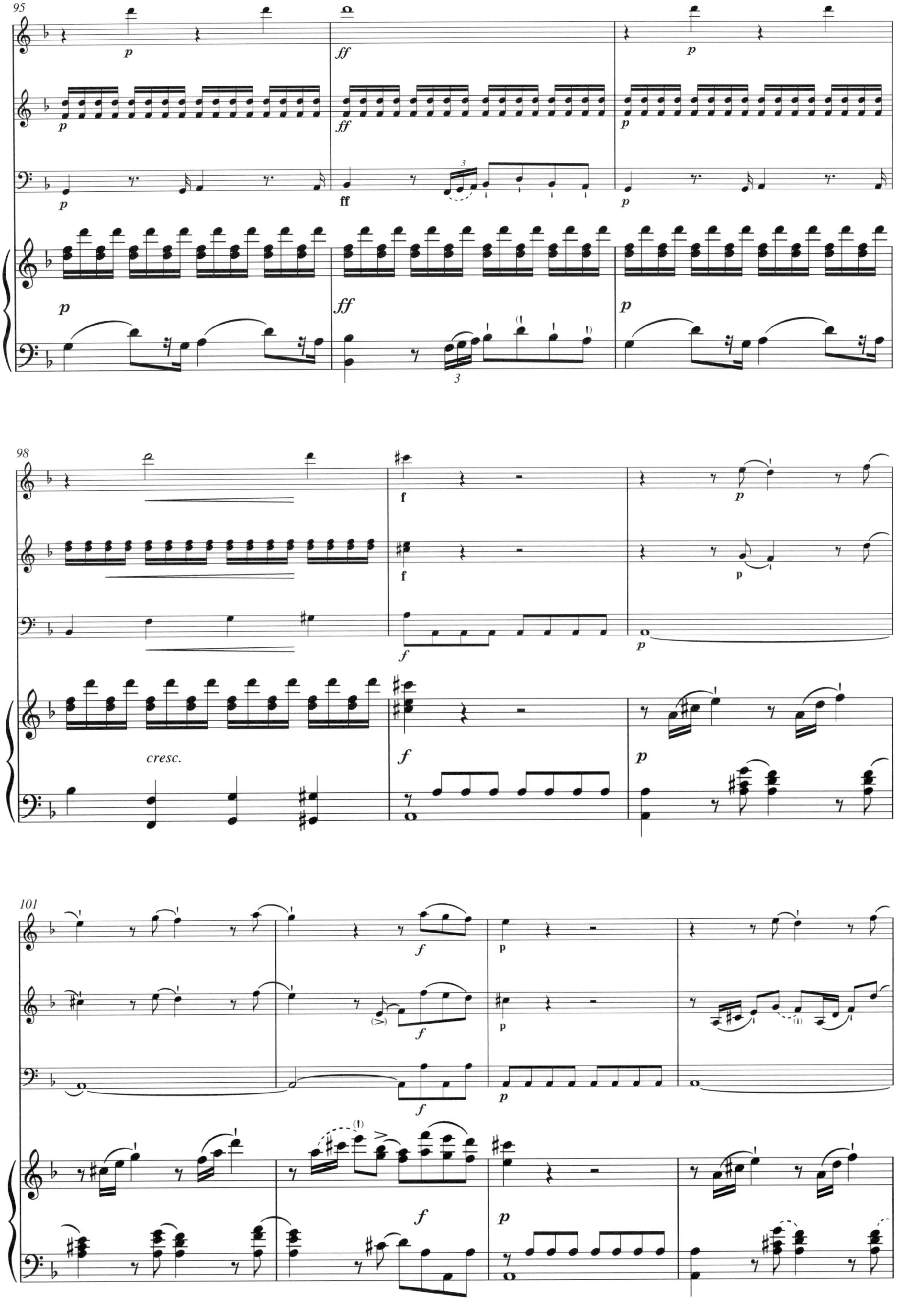
95
98
101
cresc.

144

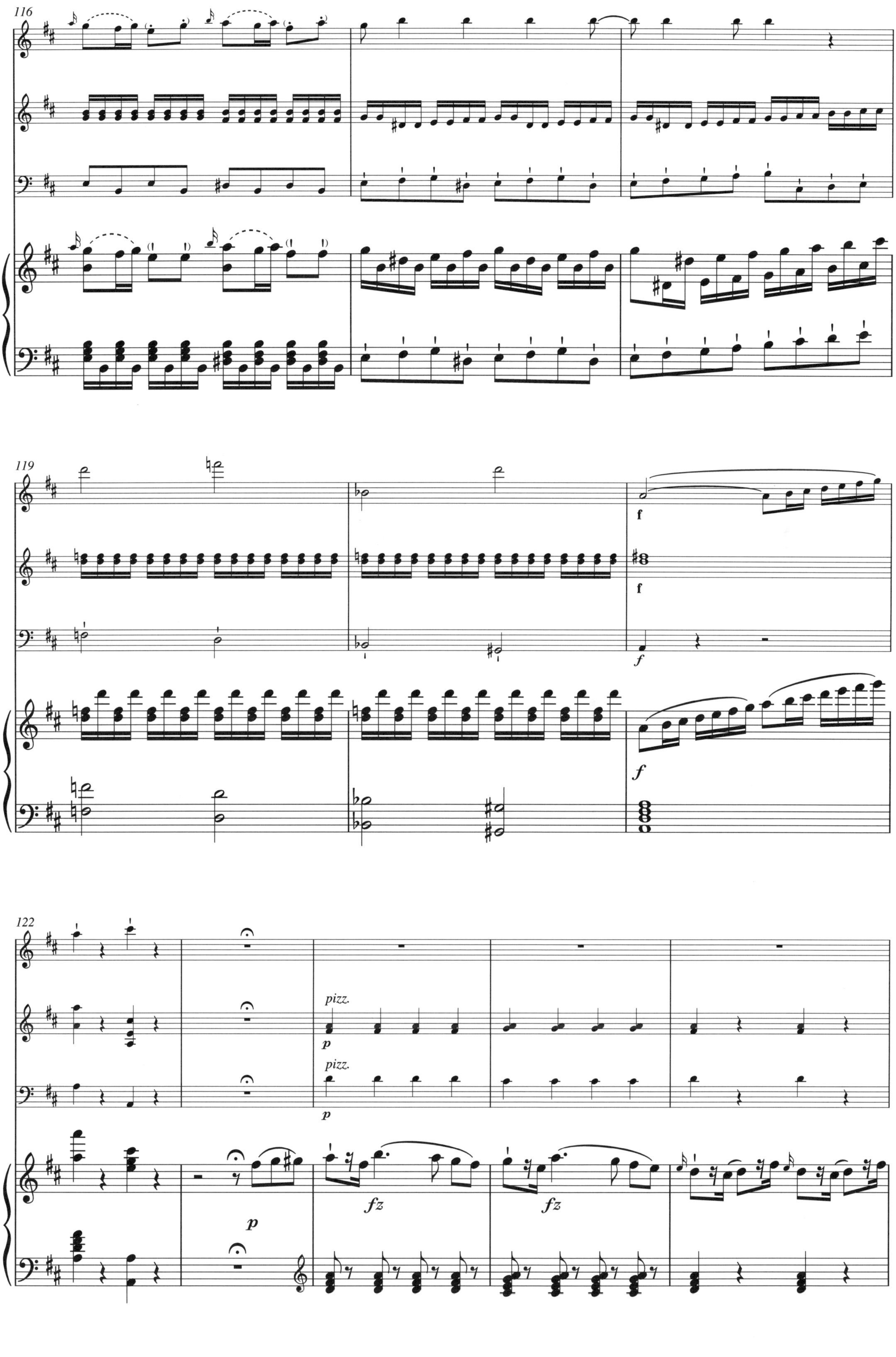
116
119
f
f
f
f
122
pizz.
p
pizz.
p
p
fz
fz

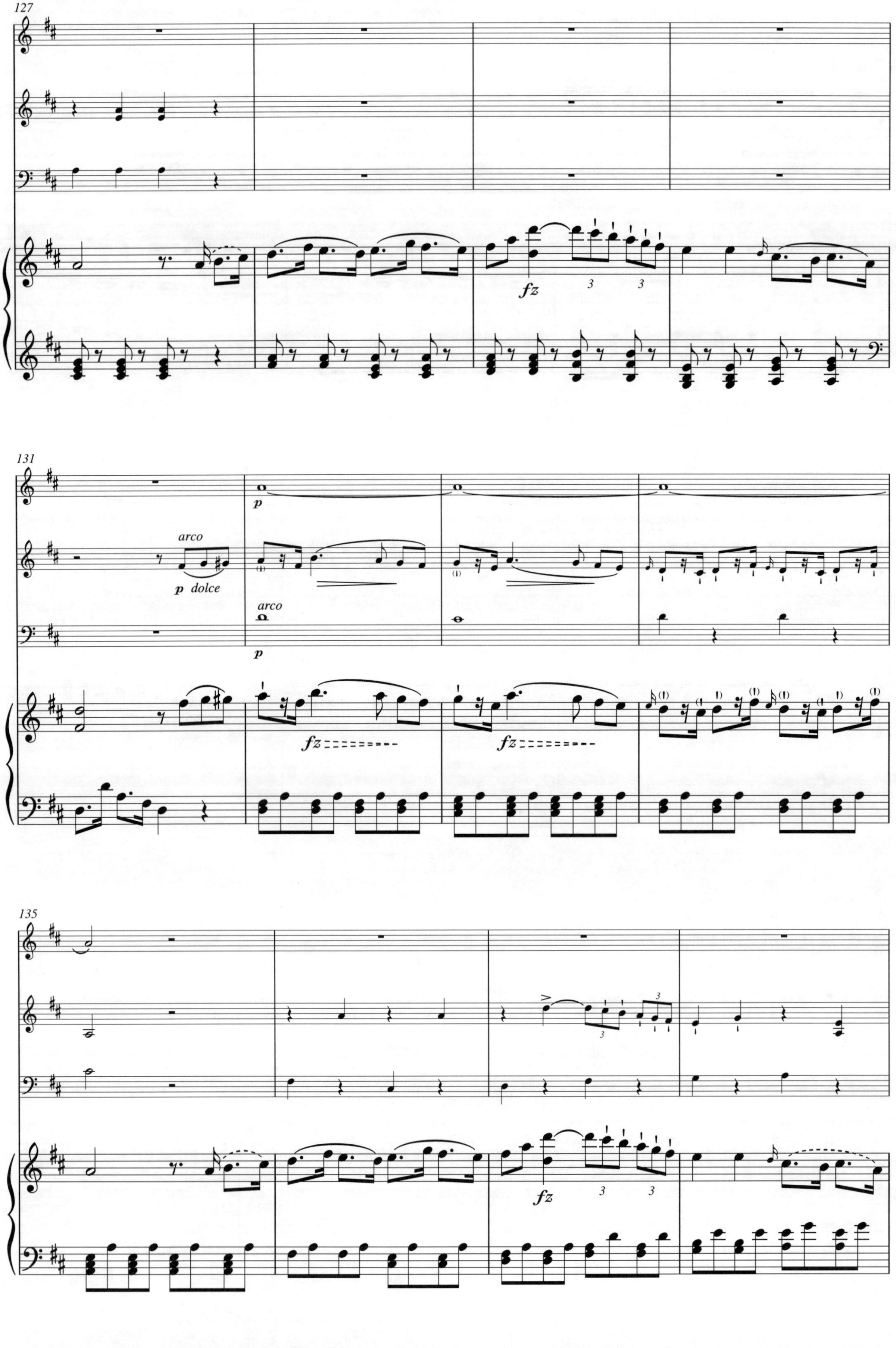
127
fz
3
3
131
arco
p dolce
p
arco
p
fz
fz
135
3
3
fz
3
3

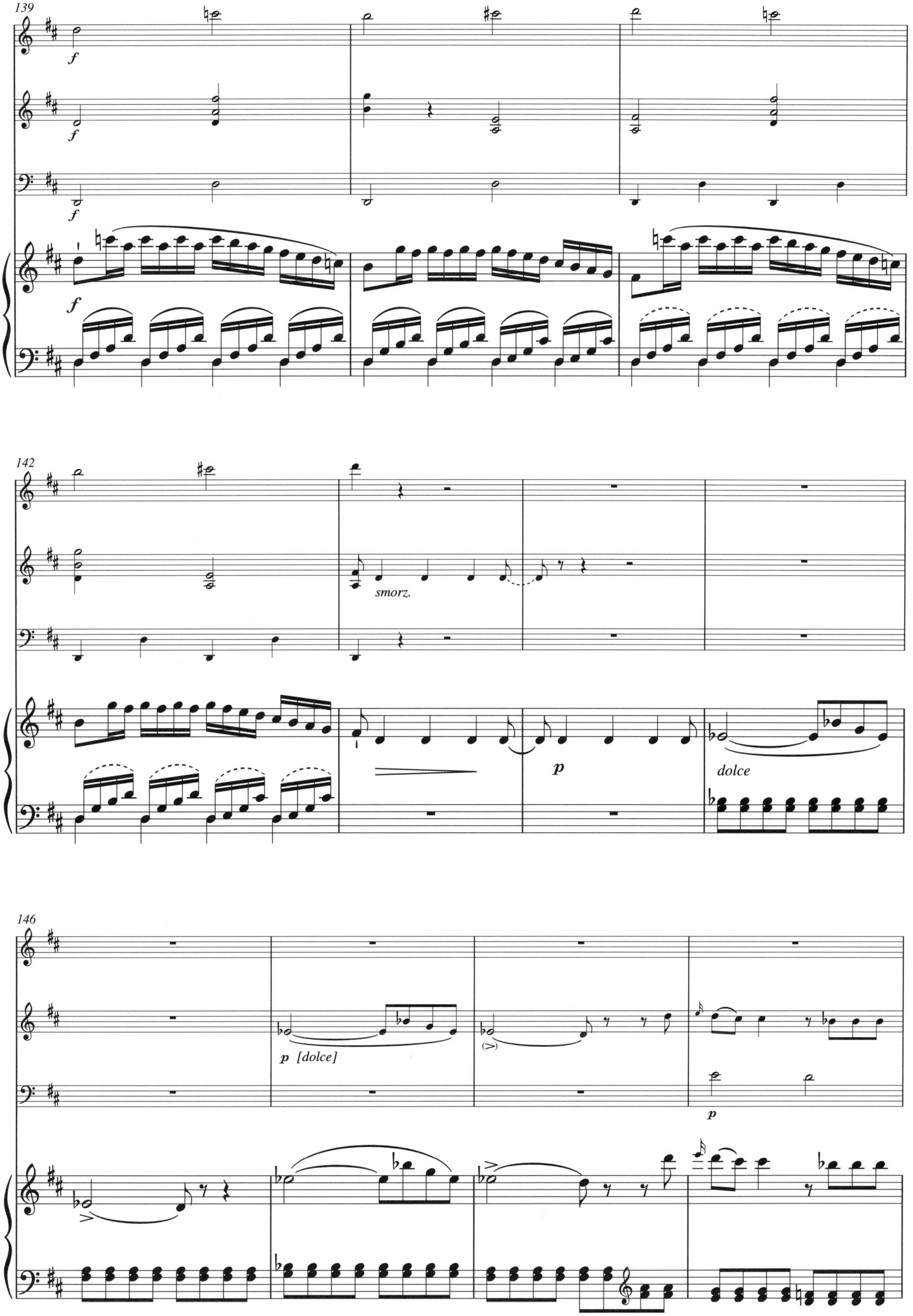
139
f
f
f
f
142
smorz.
p
dolce
146
p [dolce]
(>)
p

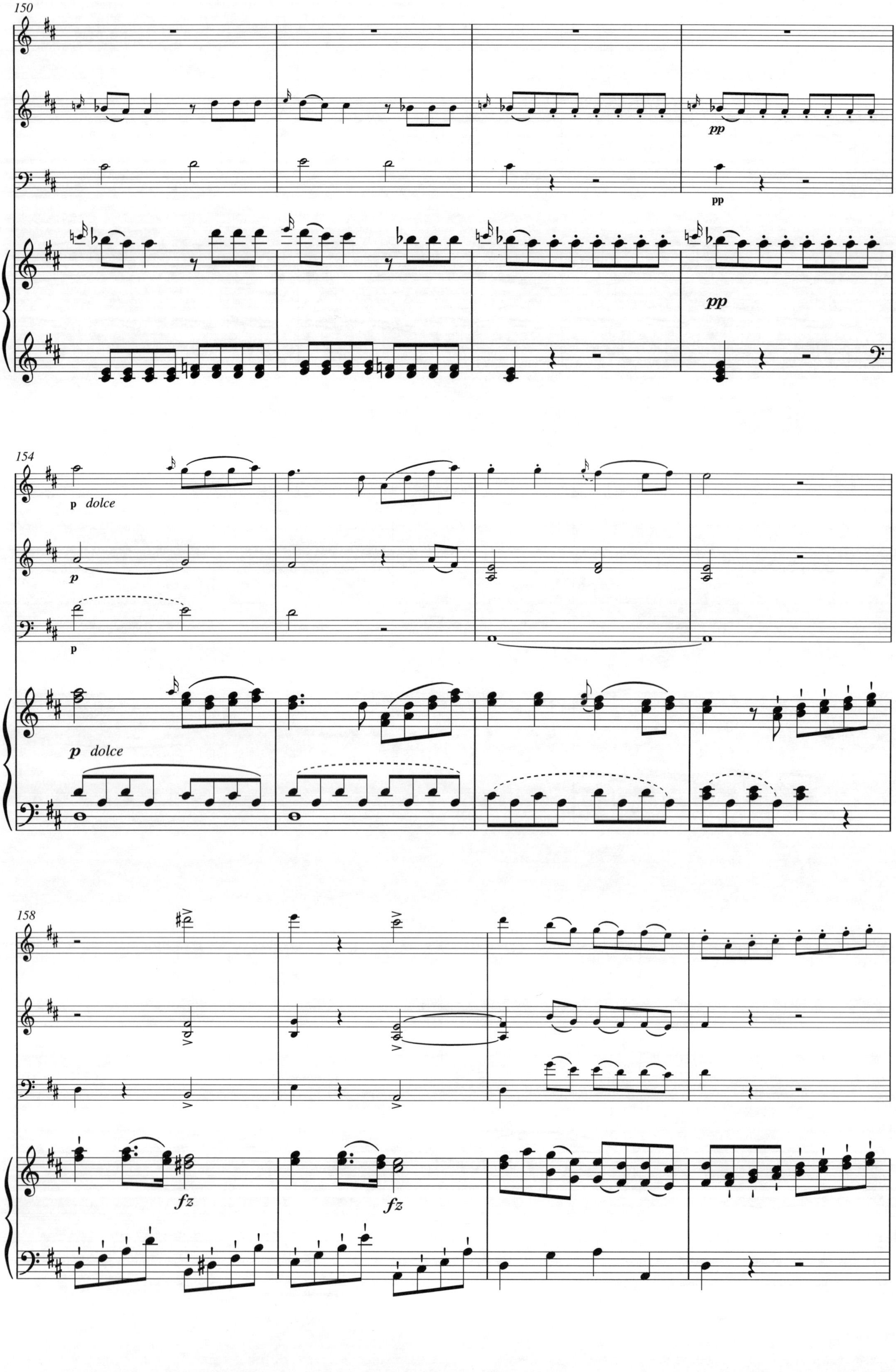
150
pp
pp
pp
154
p dolce
p
p
p dolce
158
fz
fz

162
p
pizz.
p
pizz.
p
p
166
arco
arco
sf
fz
fz
p
p
p
170
cresc.
cresc.
cresc.
cresc.

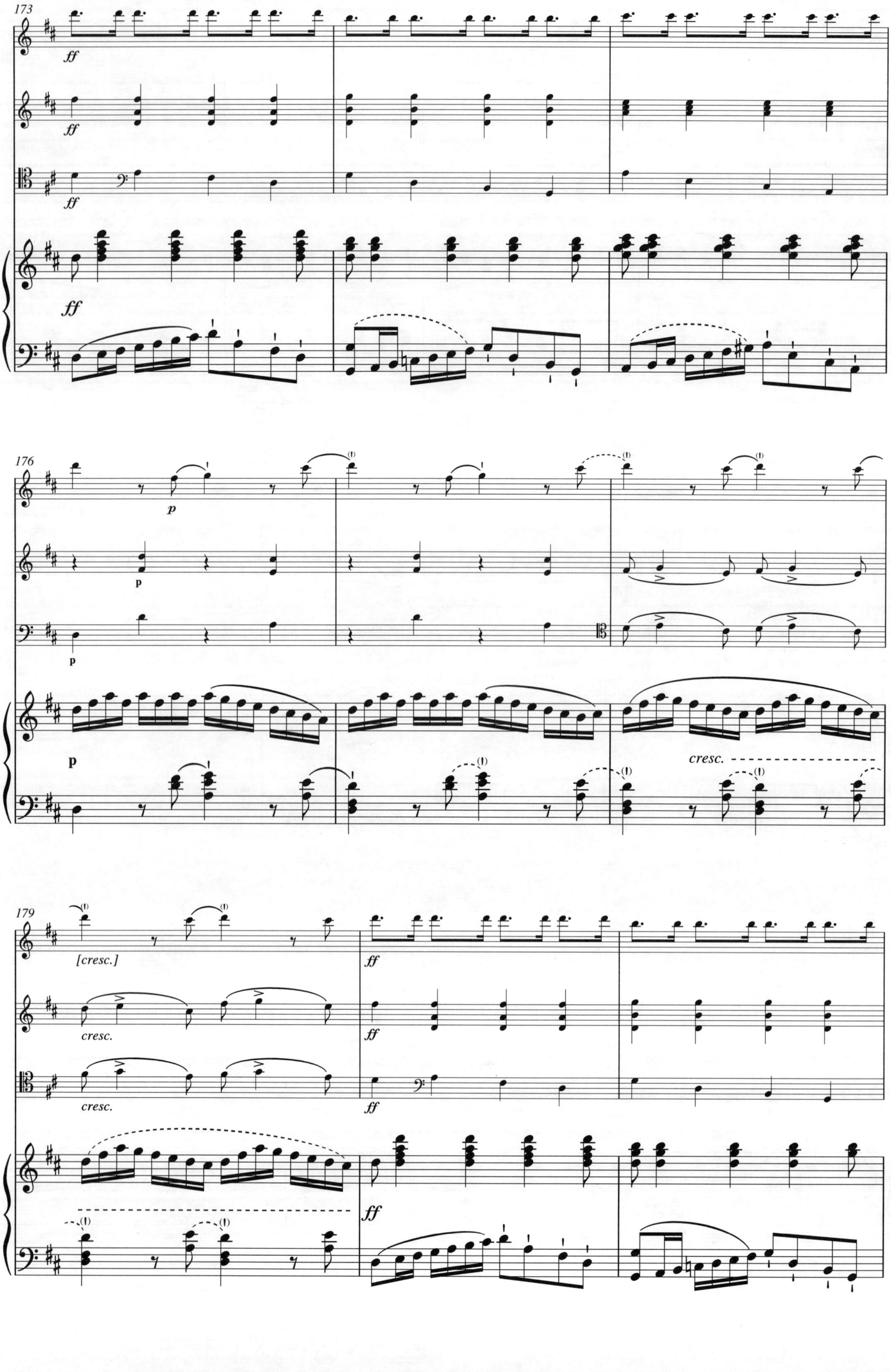
173
ff
ff
ff
ff
176
p
p
p
p
cresc.
179
[cresc.]
cresc.
cresc.
ff
ff
ff
ff

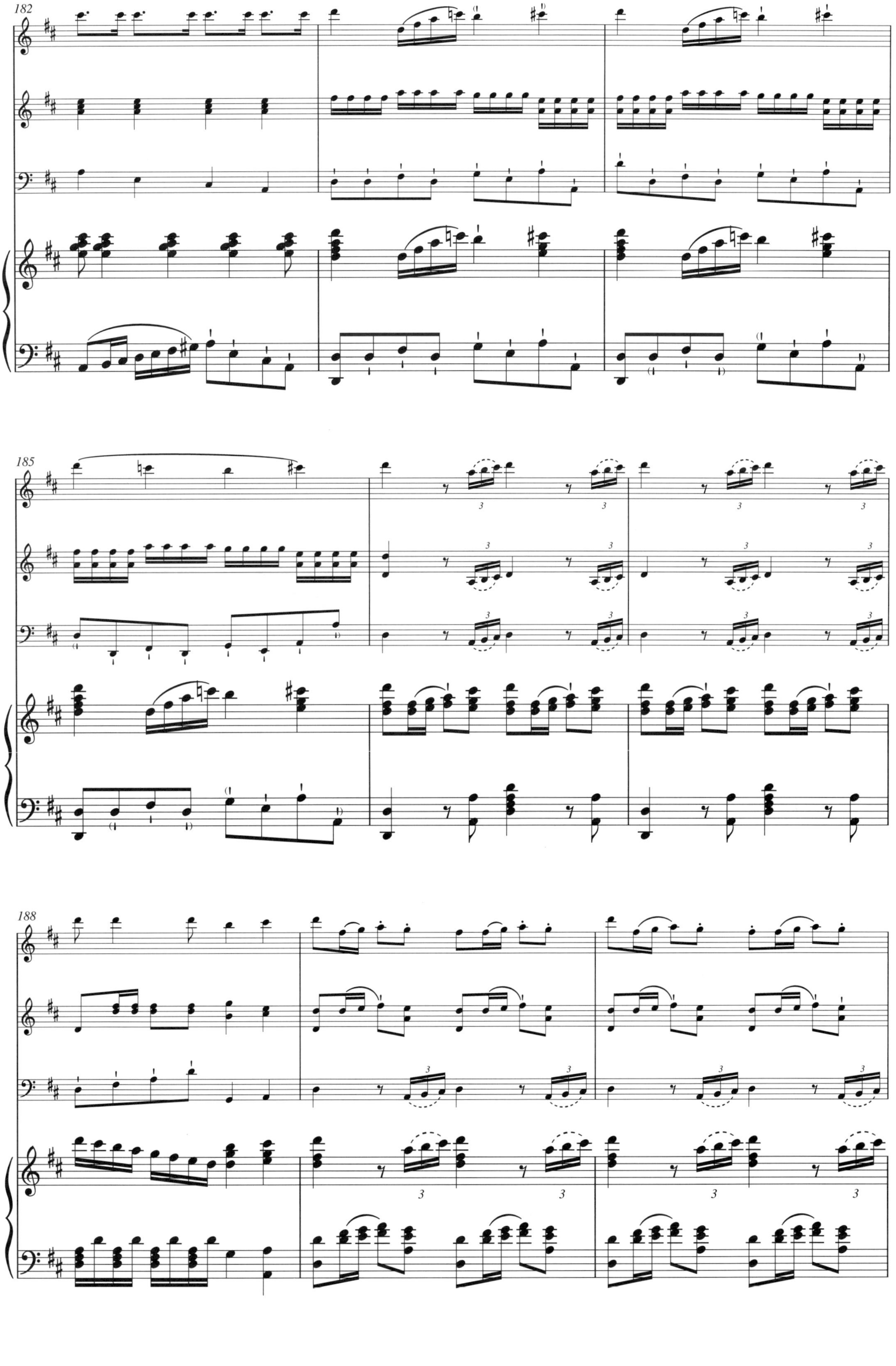
182
185
188

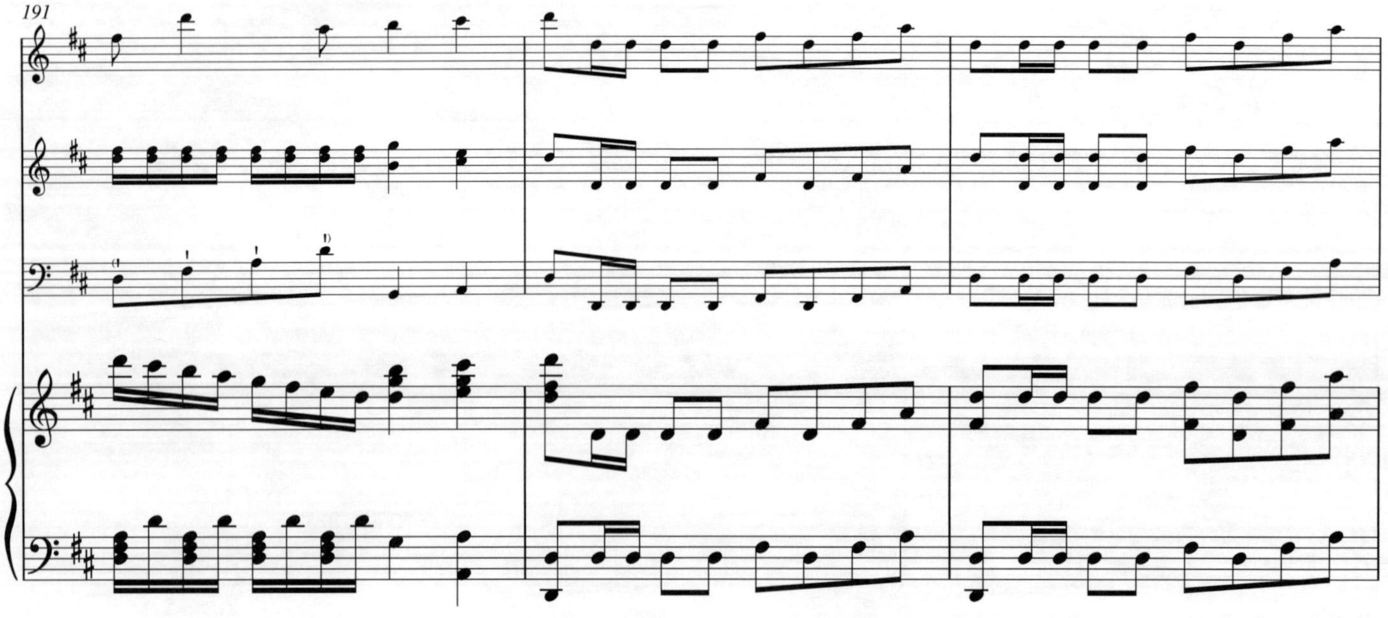
191

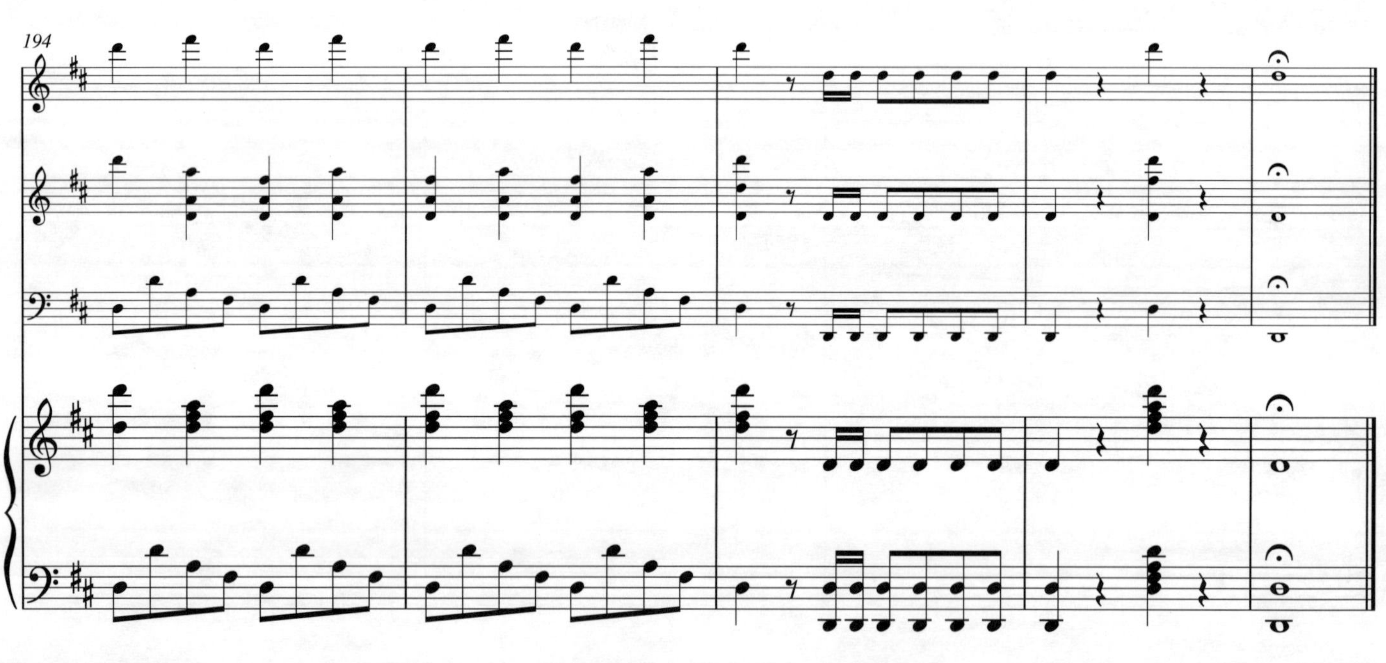
194

8. Overture

Andreas Jakob Romberg

154

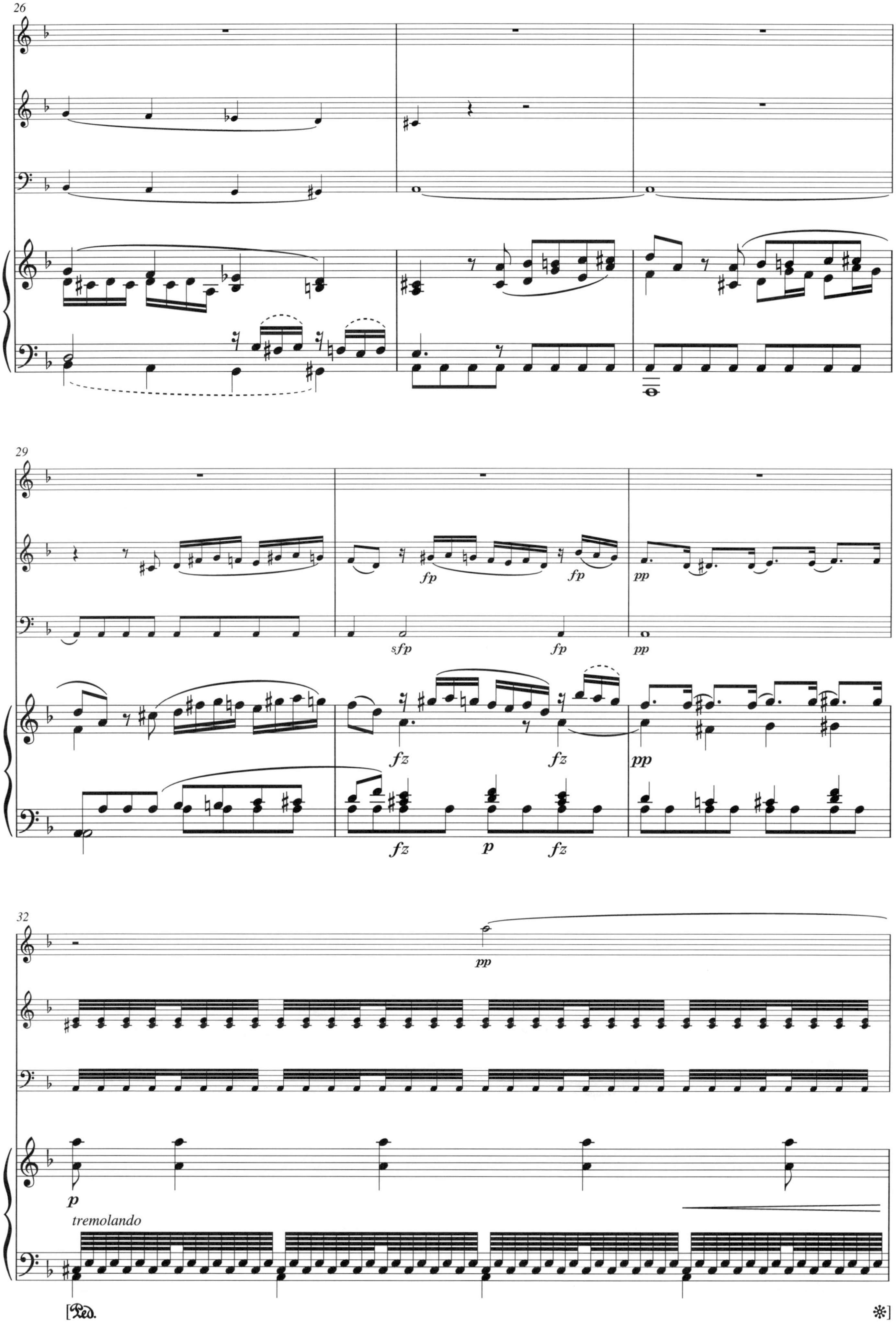
26
29
fp
fp
pp
sfp
fp
pp
fz
fz
pp
fz
p
fz
32
pp
p
tremolando
[Ped.
*]

33
[cresc.]
cre - - - - - - - - - - - - - scen - - - - - - - - - - - - - do
[Ped.
*]
Allegro vivace
34
ff
ff
ff
Allegro vivace
ff
38
p

157

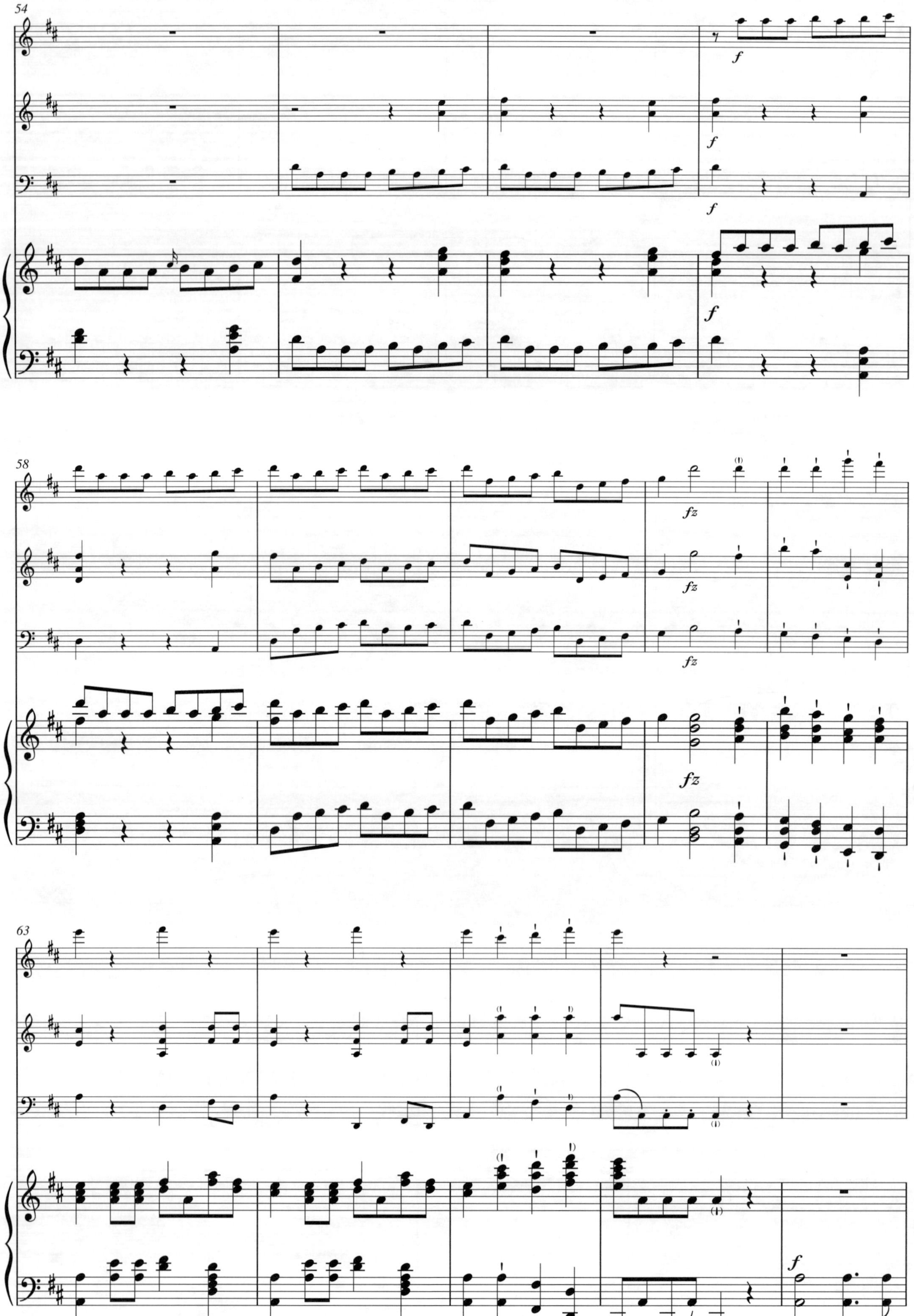

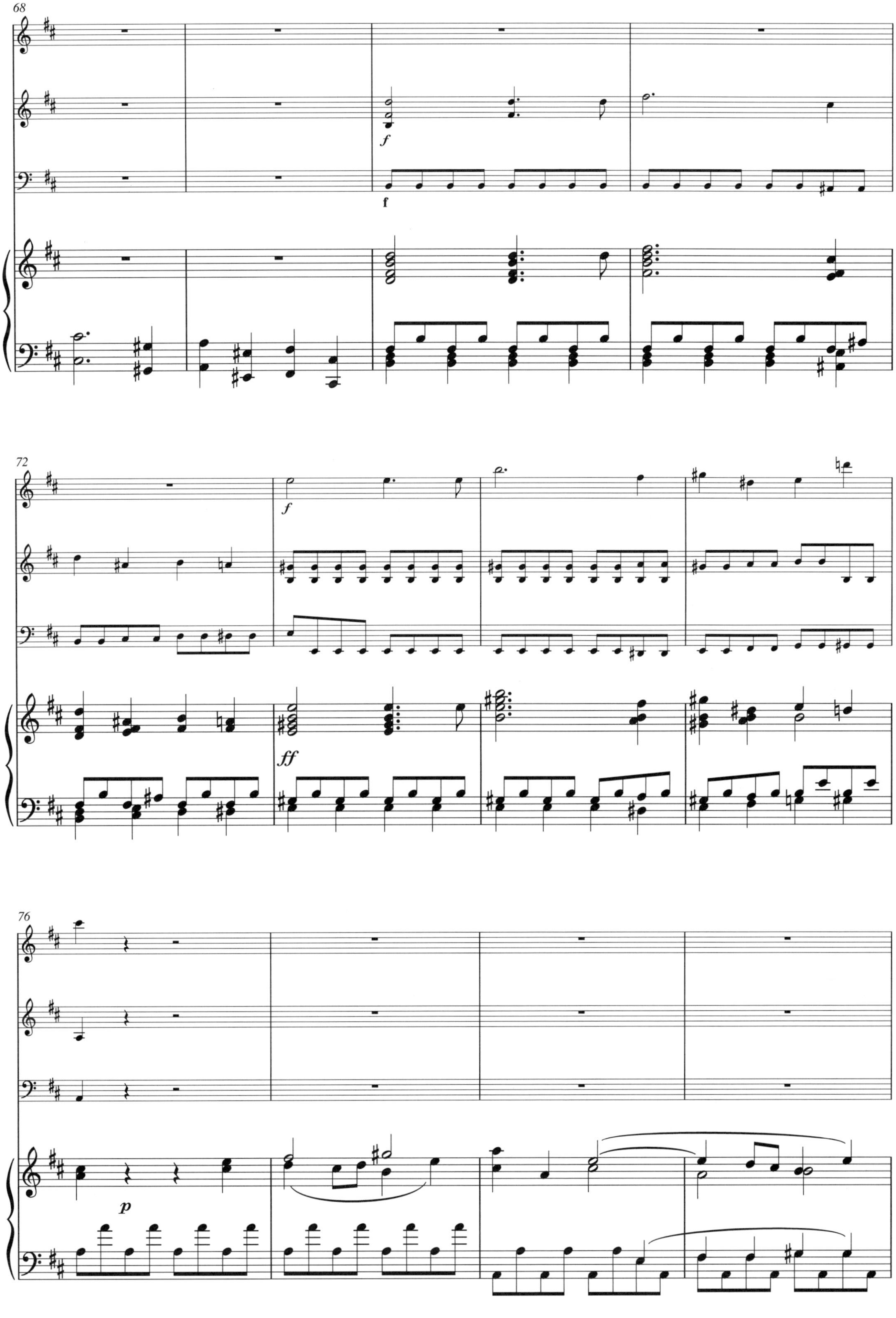
68
f
f
72
f
ff
76
p

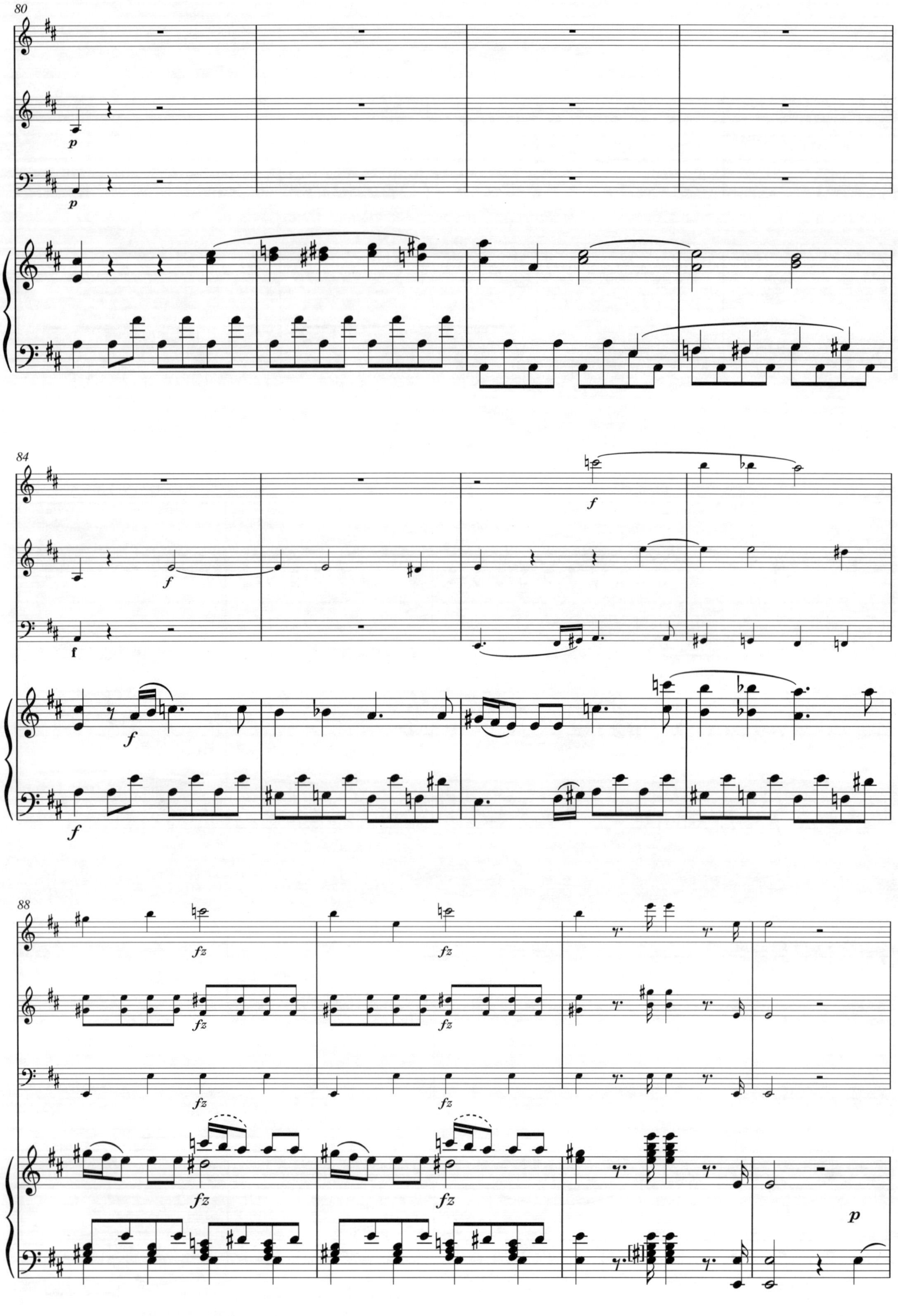
80
84
88

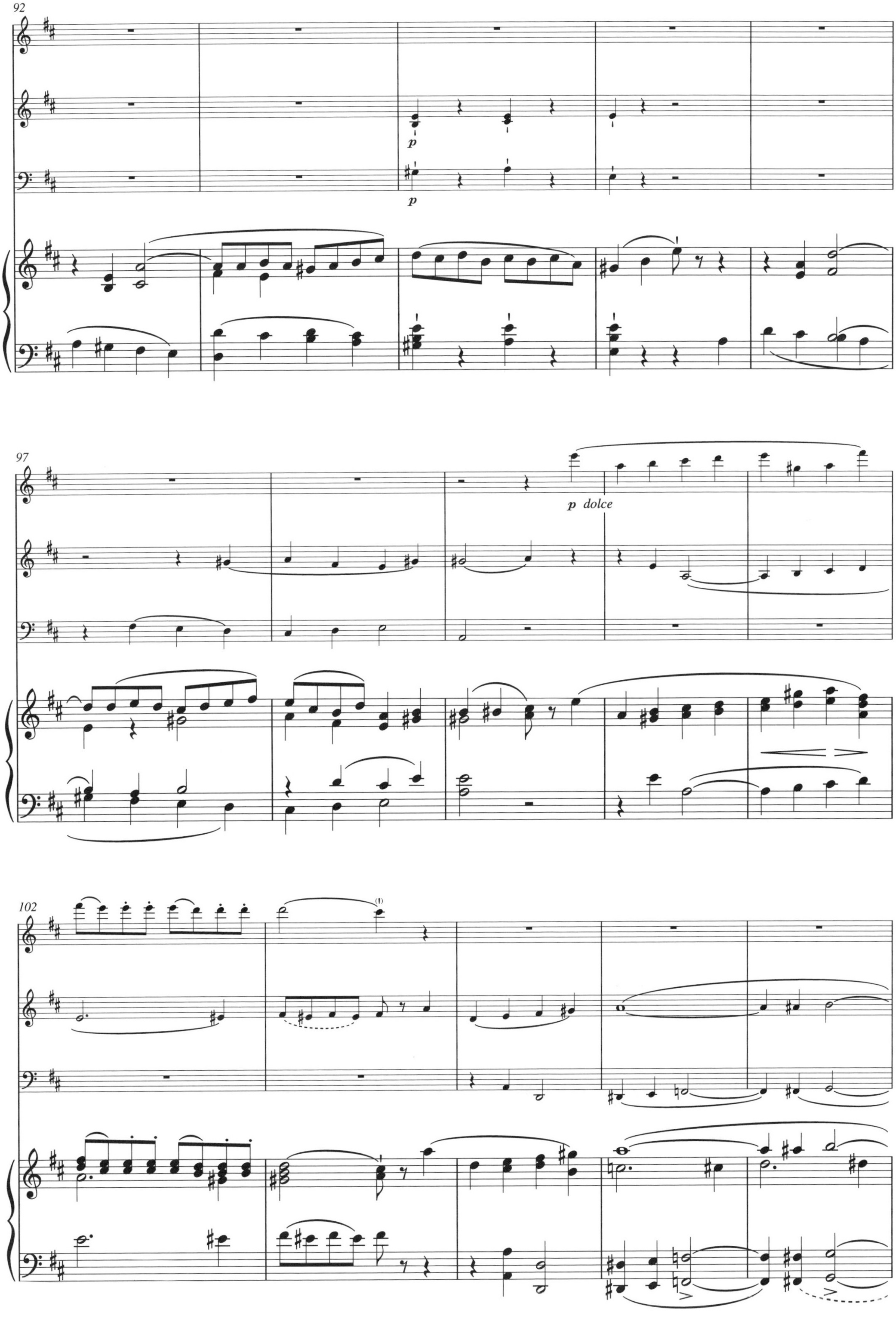
92
p
p
97
p dolce
102
(!)

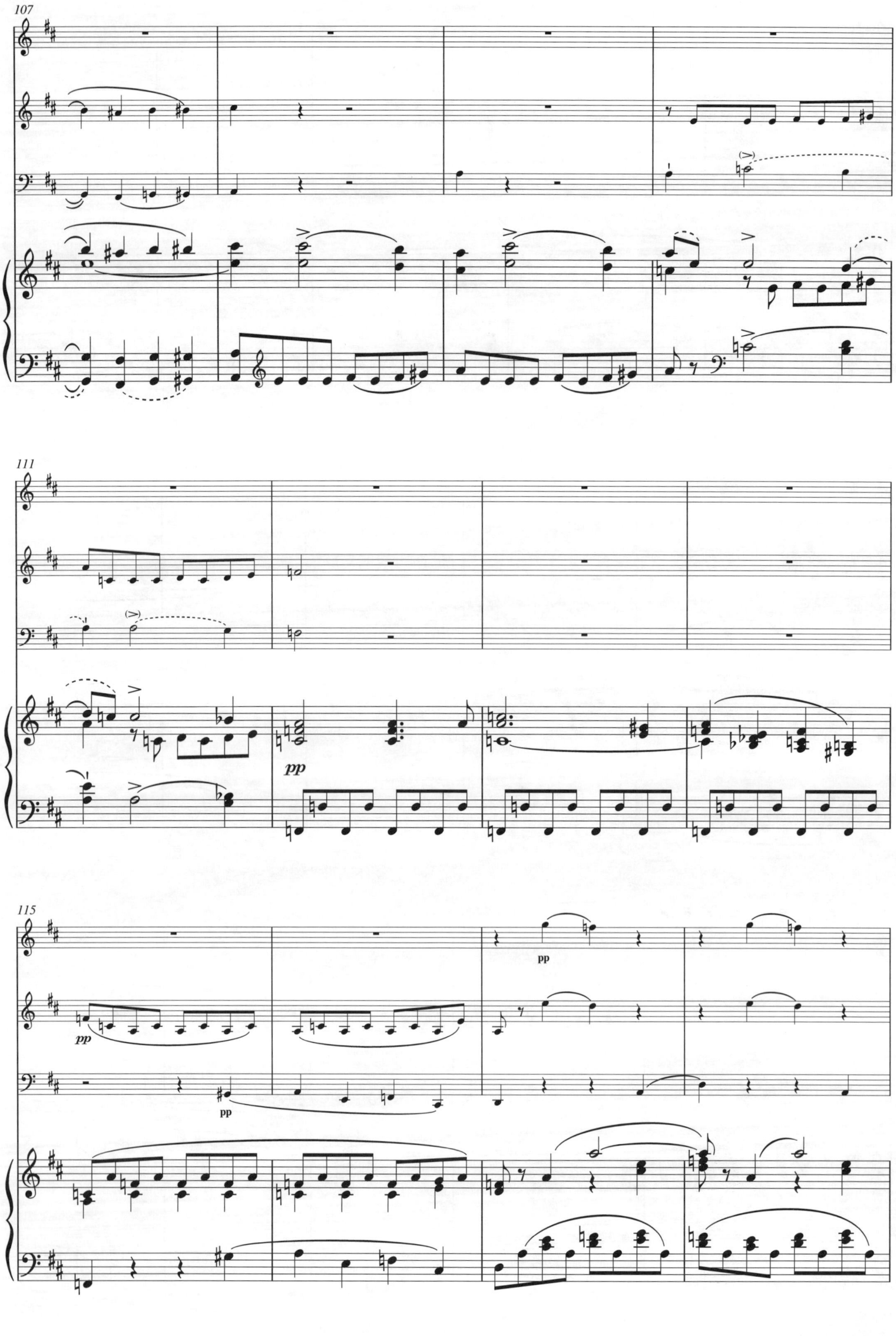
107
111
pp
115
pp
pp
pp

119
cresc.
cresc.
f
ff
f
f
123
fz
fz
fz
fz
(1)
fz
fz
fz
fz
fz
128
fz
fz
ff
ff

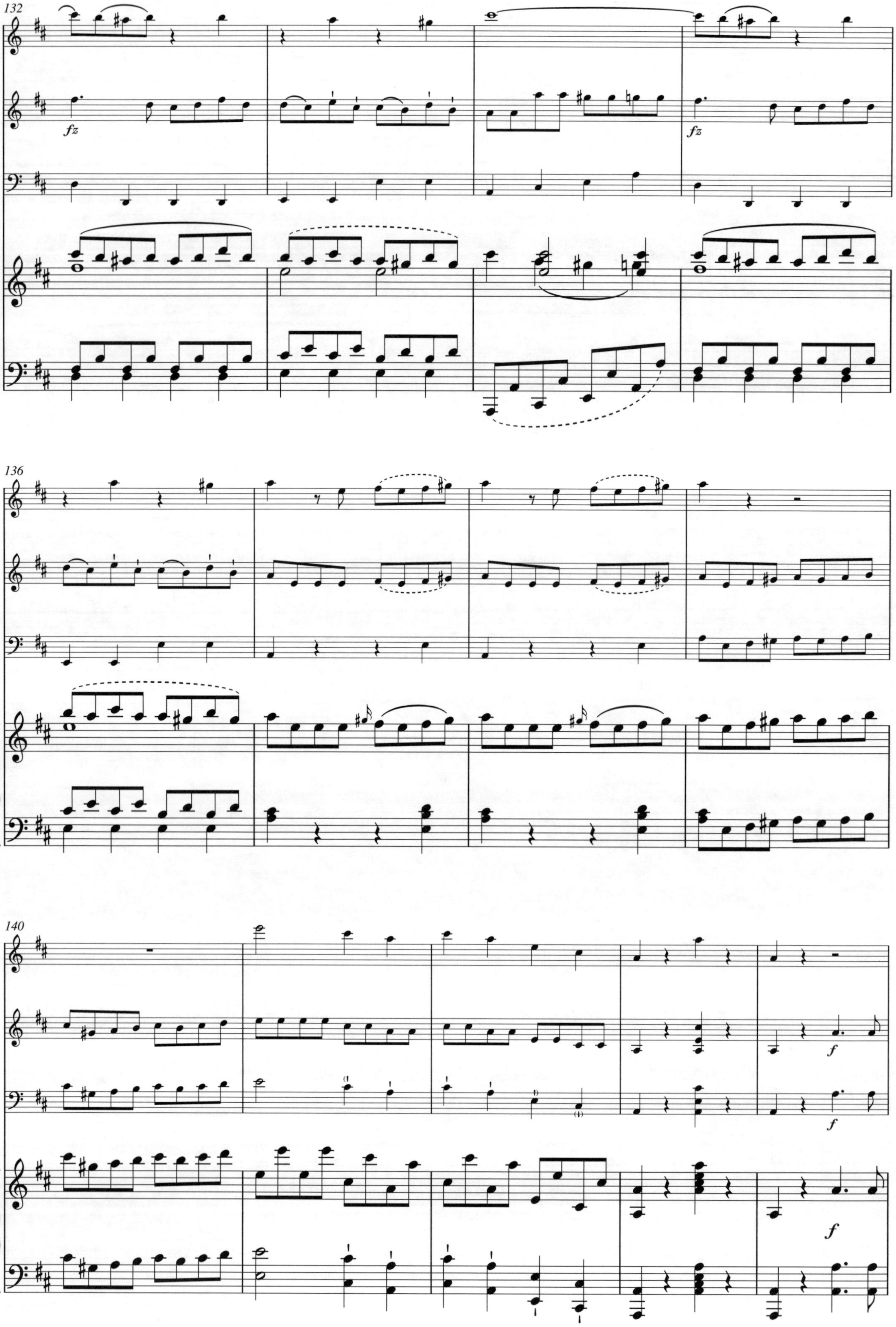
132
fz
fz
136
140
f
f
f

165

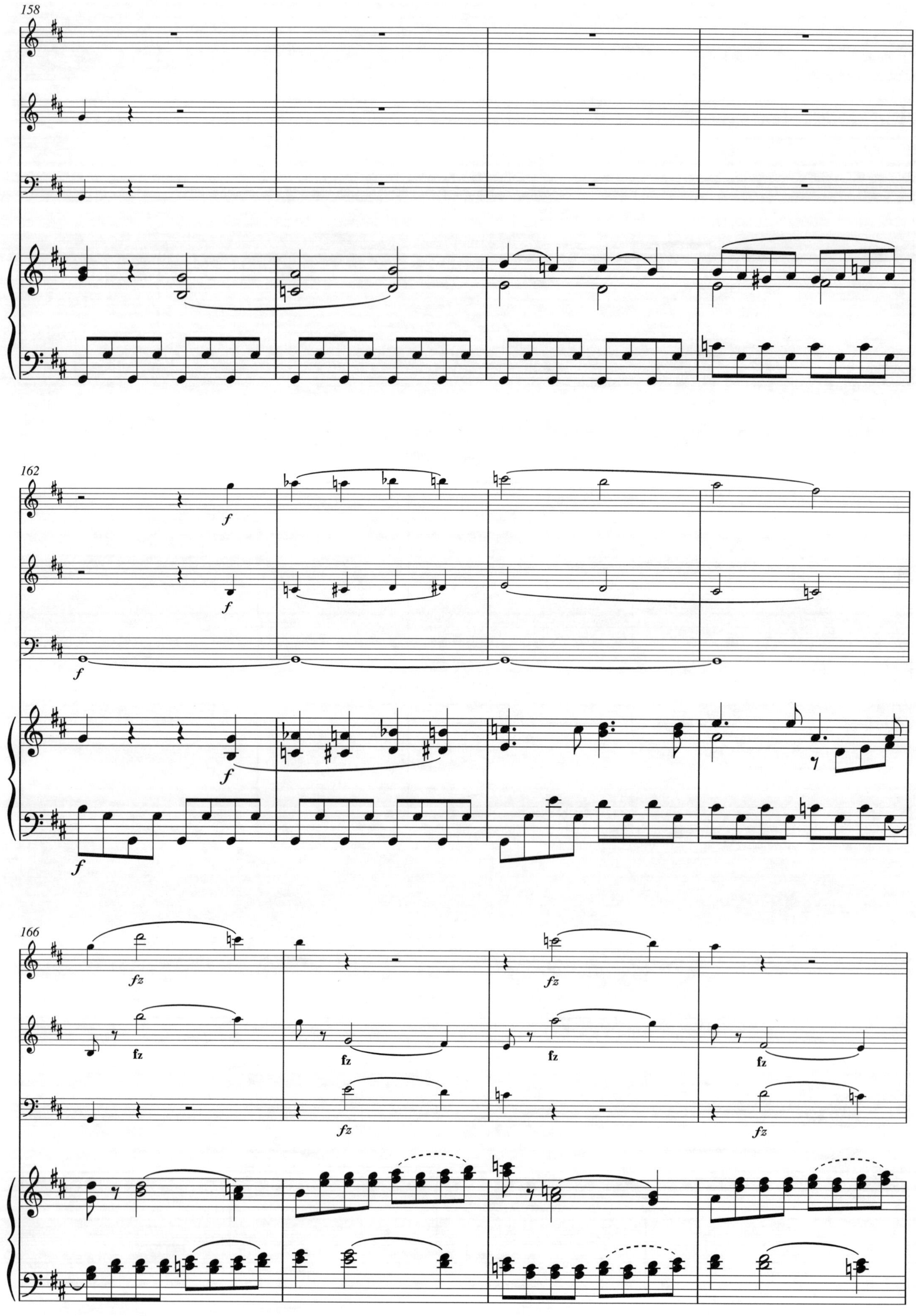
158
162
f
f
f
f
f
166
fz
fz
fz
fz
fz
fz
fz

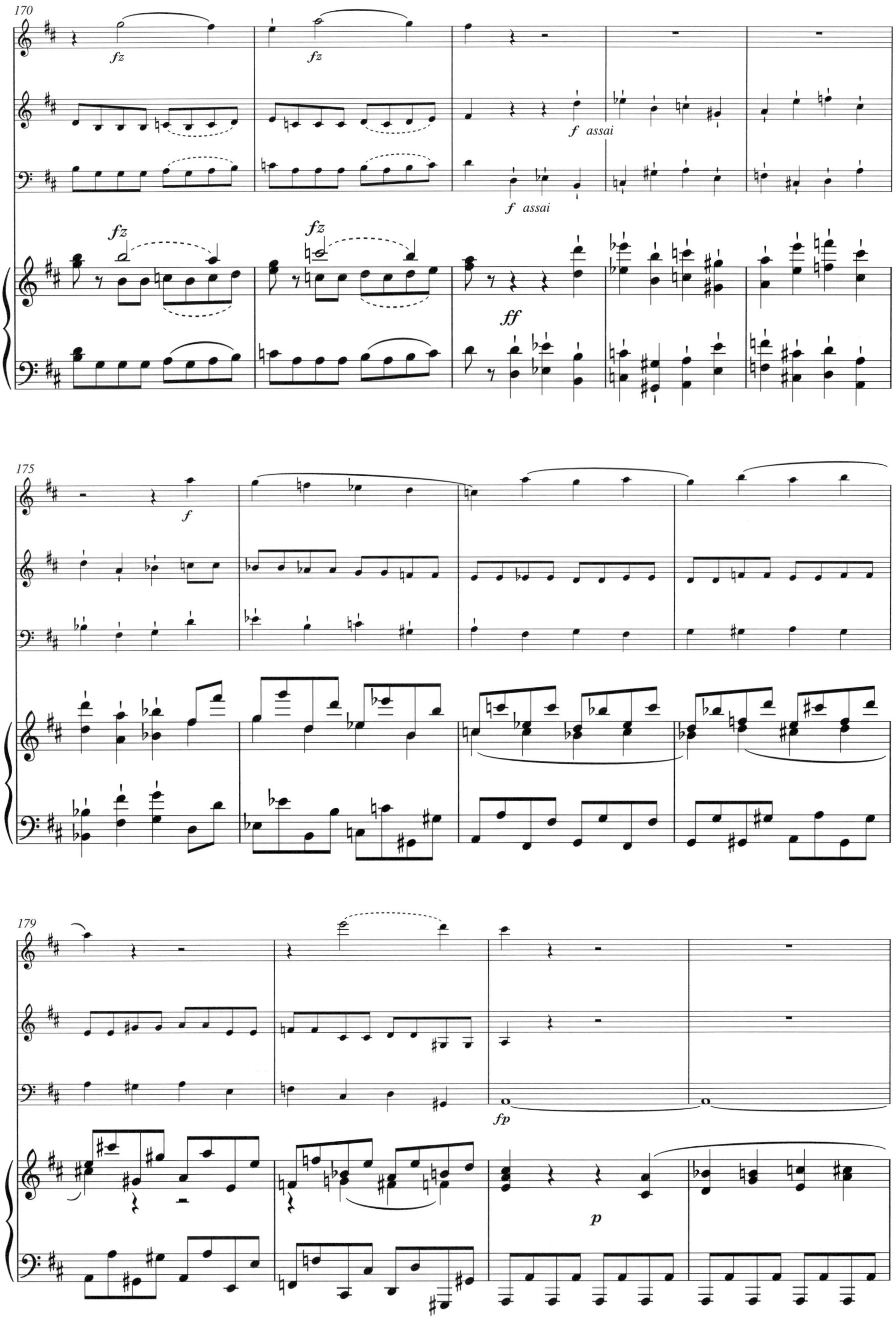
170
fz
fz
f assai
f assai
fz
fz
ff
175
f
179
fp
p

183
fp
fp
fp
fp
pp
rf
p
rf
p
rf
p
rf
pp
188
pp
192
pp
cresc.
cresc.
cre - scen - - - - - - - - - - -do
[3]
[3]

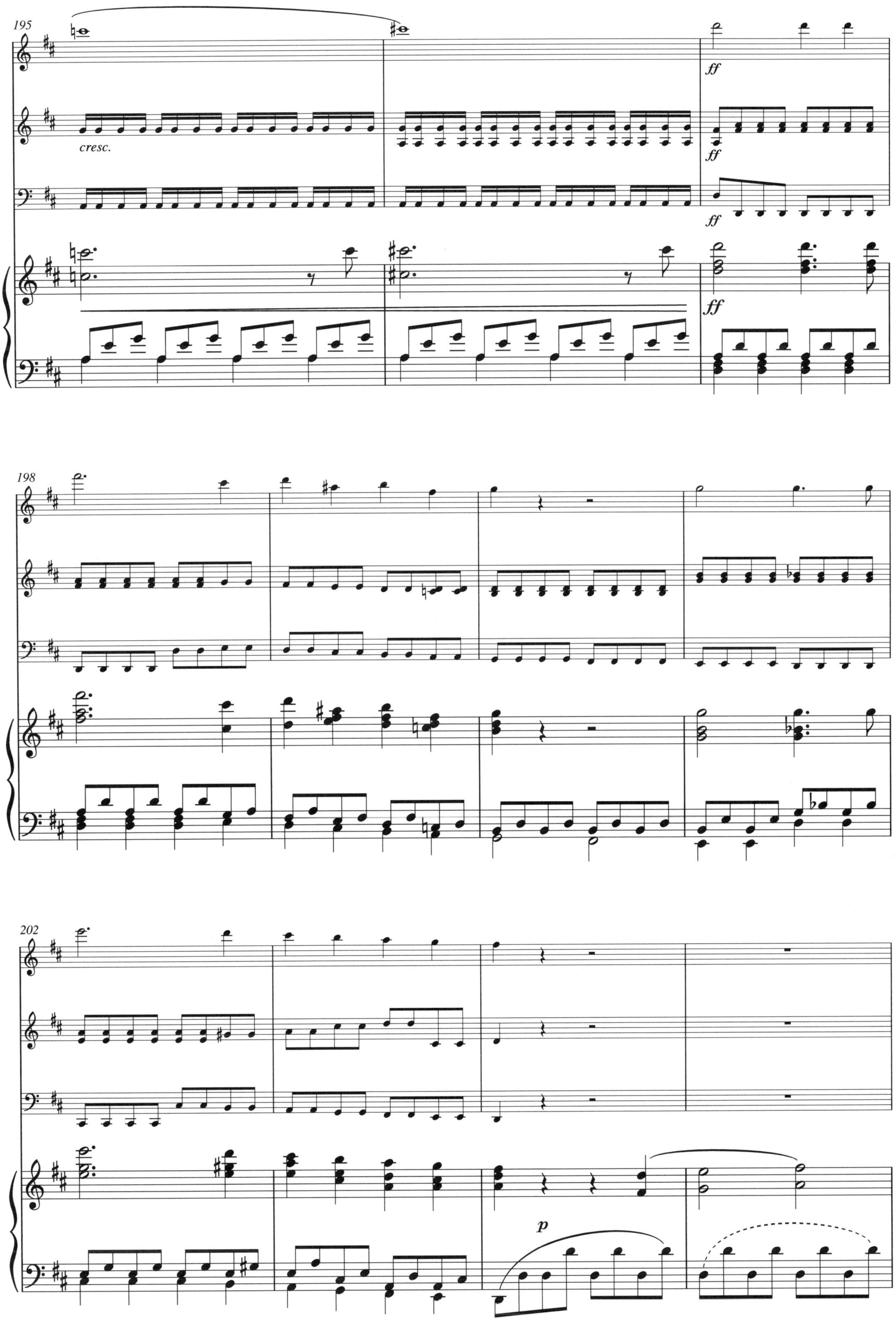
195
cresc.
ff
ff
ff
ff
198
202
p

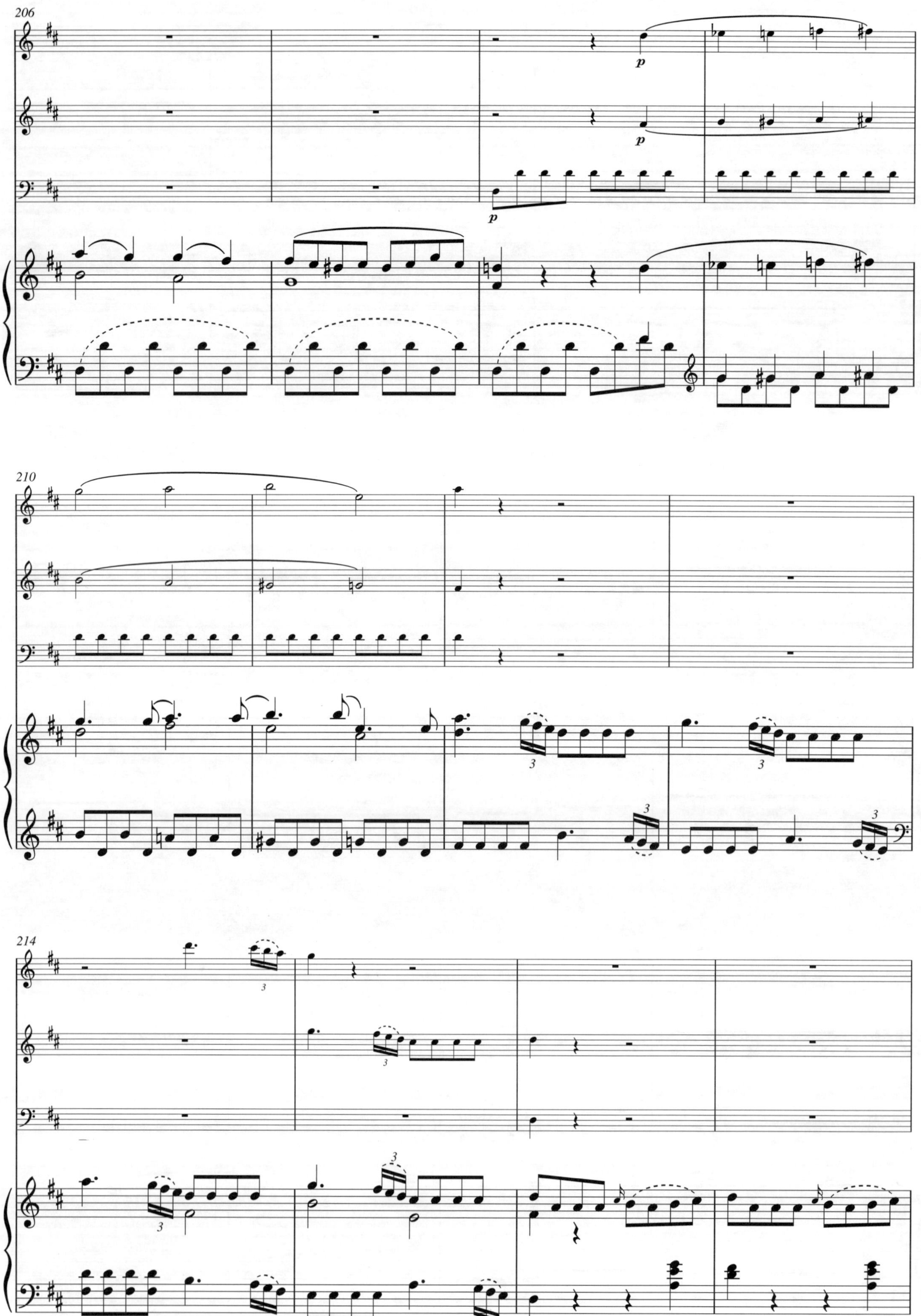
206
p
p
p
210
214

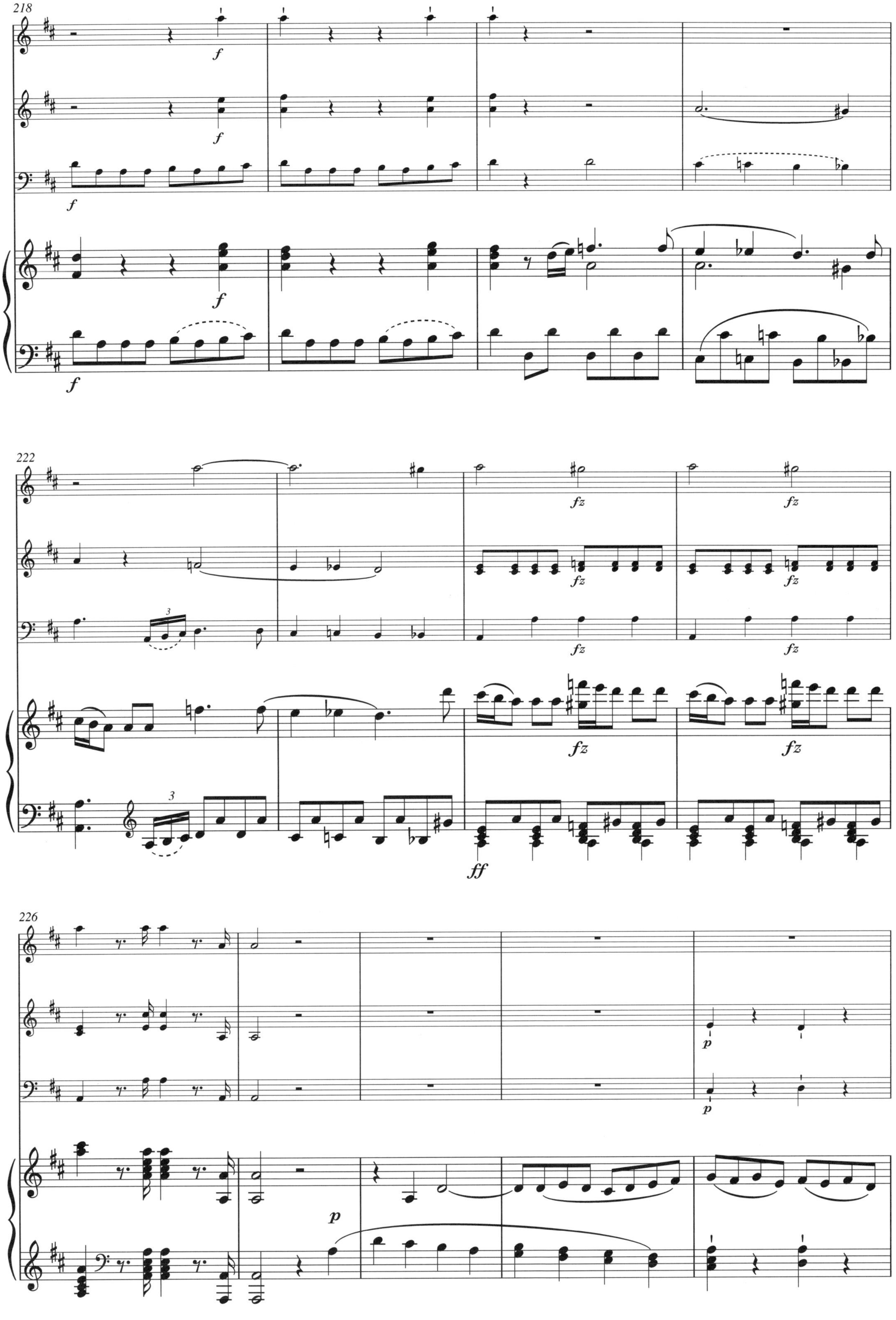
218
f
f
f
f
f
222
3
fz
fz
fz
fz
fz
fz
fz
fz
3
ff
226
p
p
p

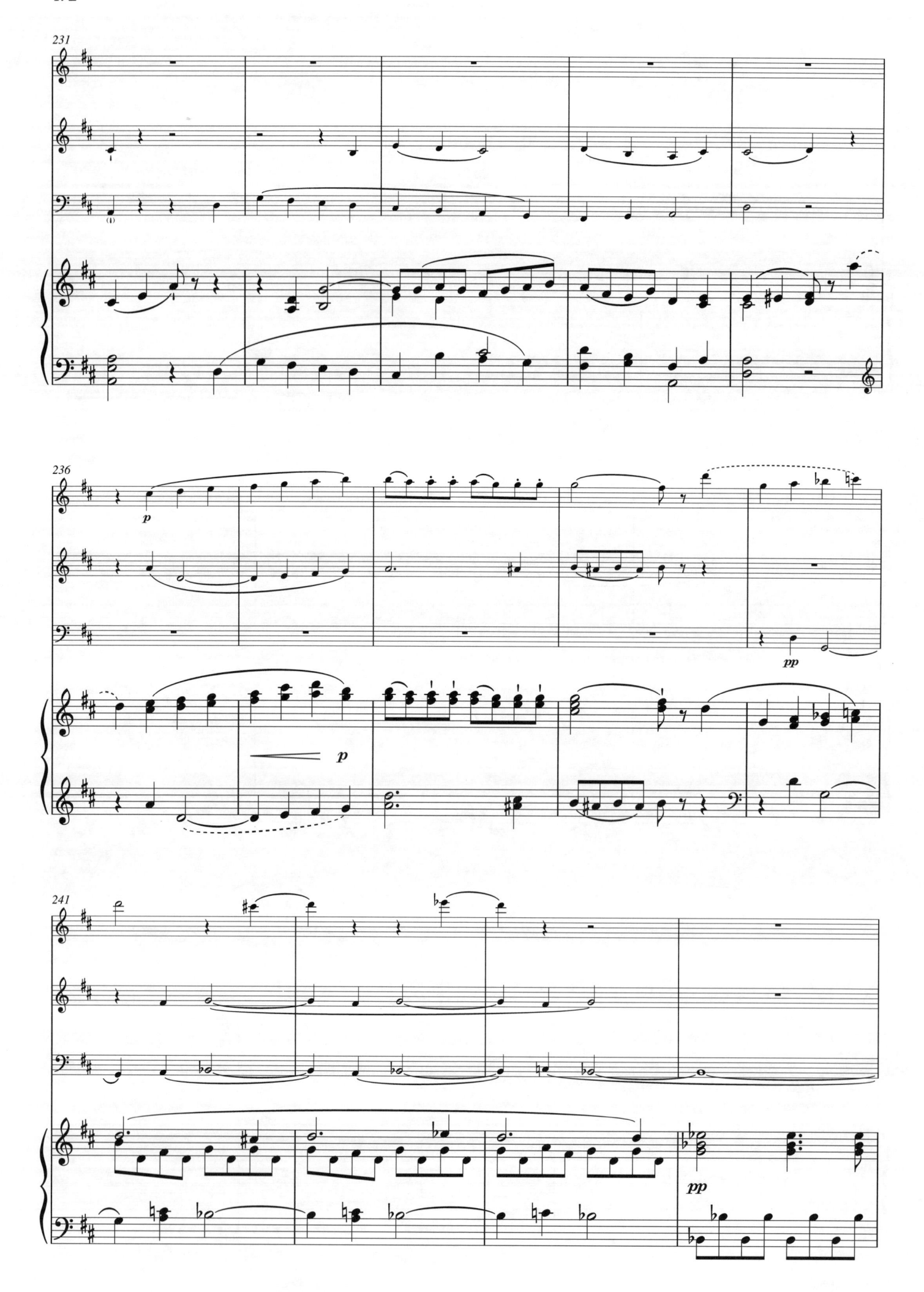
231
236
p
pp
p
241
pp

173

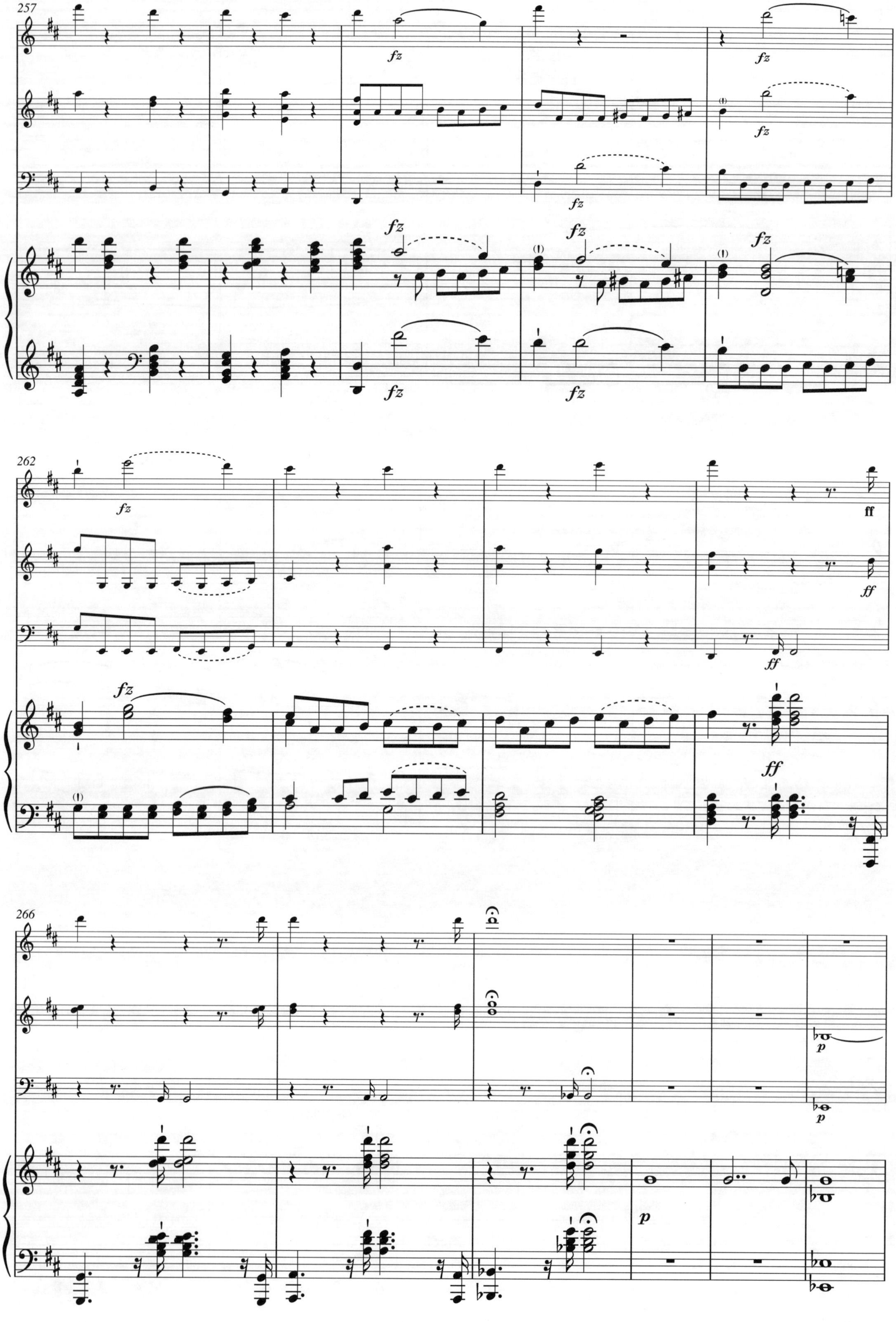
257
fz
fz
fz
fz
fz
fz
fz
fz
262
fz
ff
ff
ff
fz
ff
266
p
p
p

272
marcato
278
Pn.
283
288
Fl.
p dolce
Vn.
p sotto voce
pizz.
Vc.
p [dolce]
Pn.

176

177

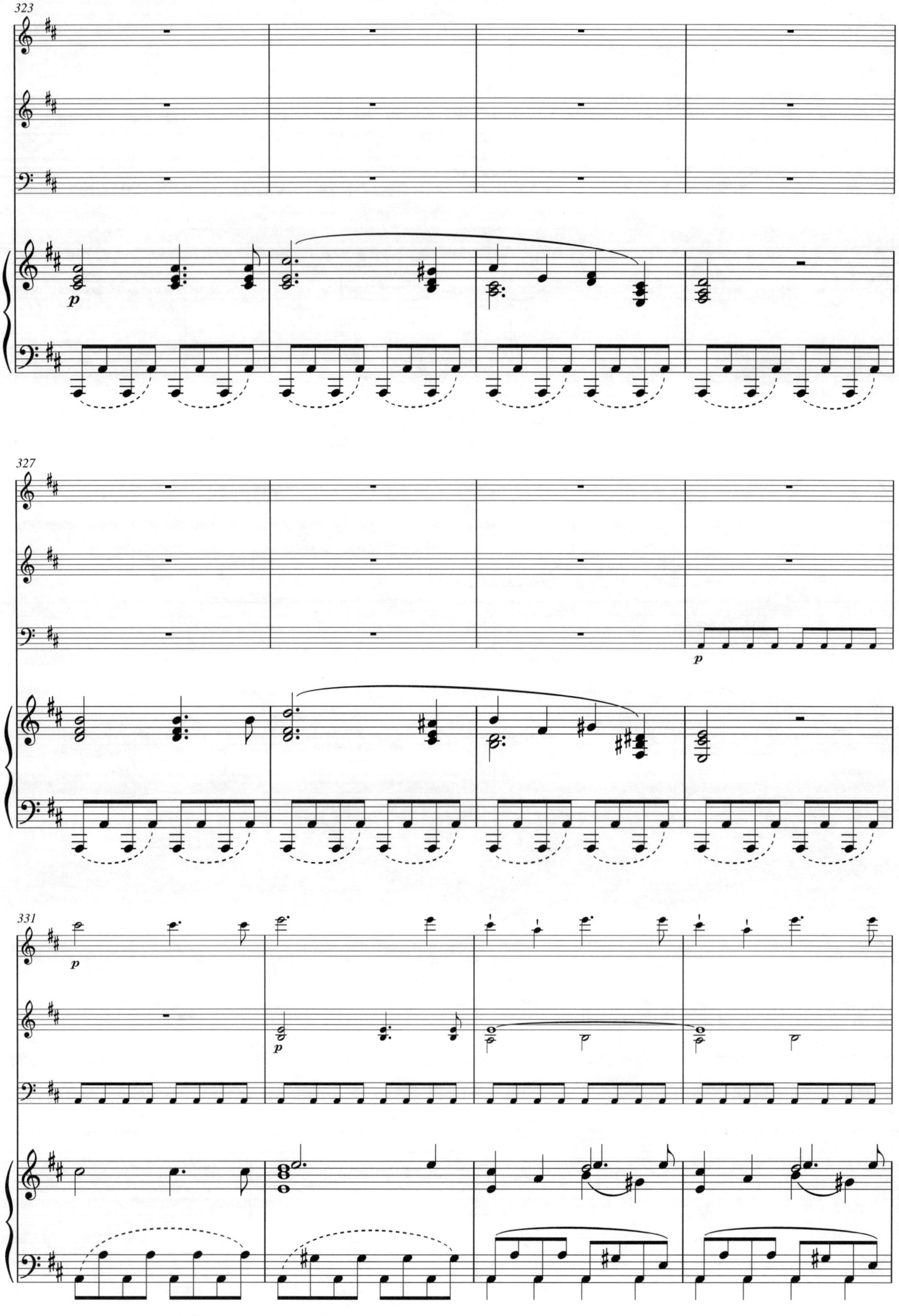
323
p
327
p
331
p
p

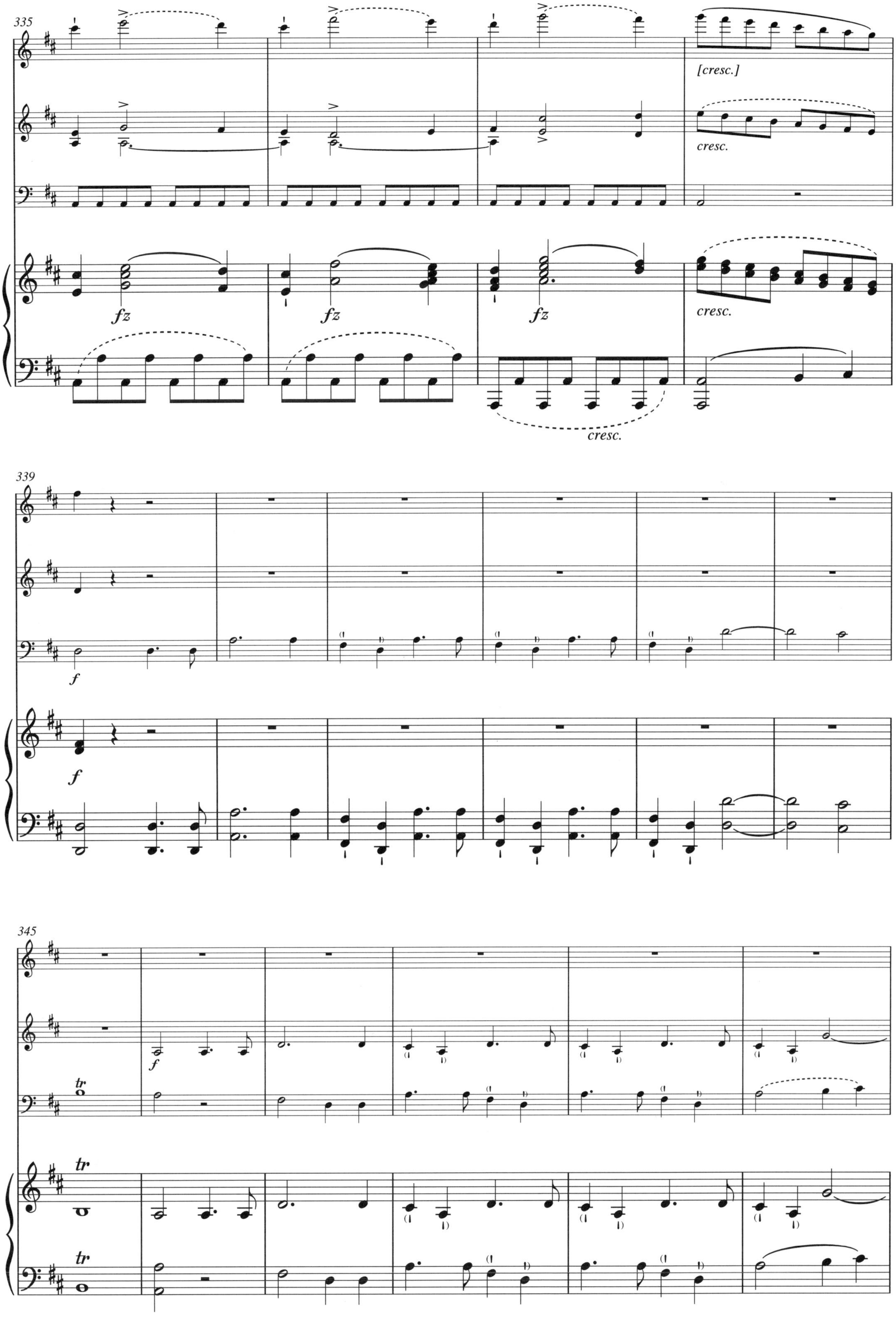
335
[cresc.]
cresc.
fz
fz
fz
cresc.
cresc.
339
f
f
345
tr
f
tr
tr

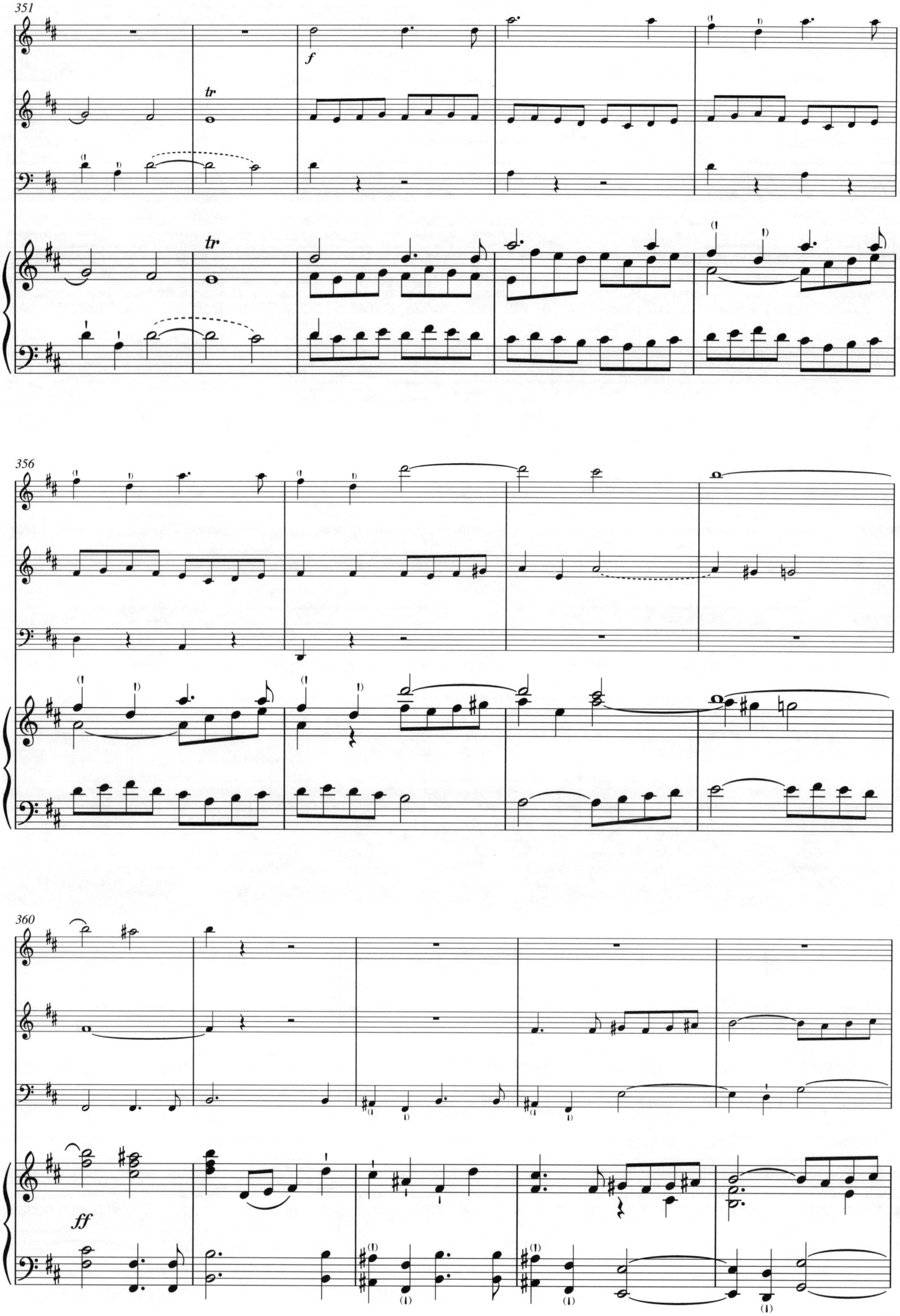
351
tr
f
tr
356
360
ff

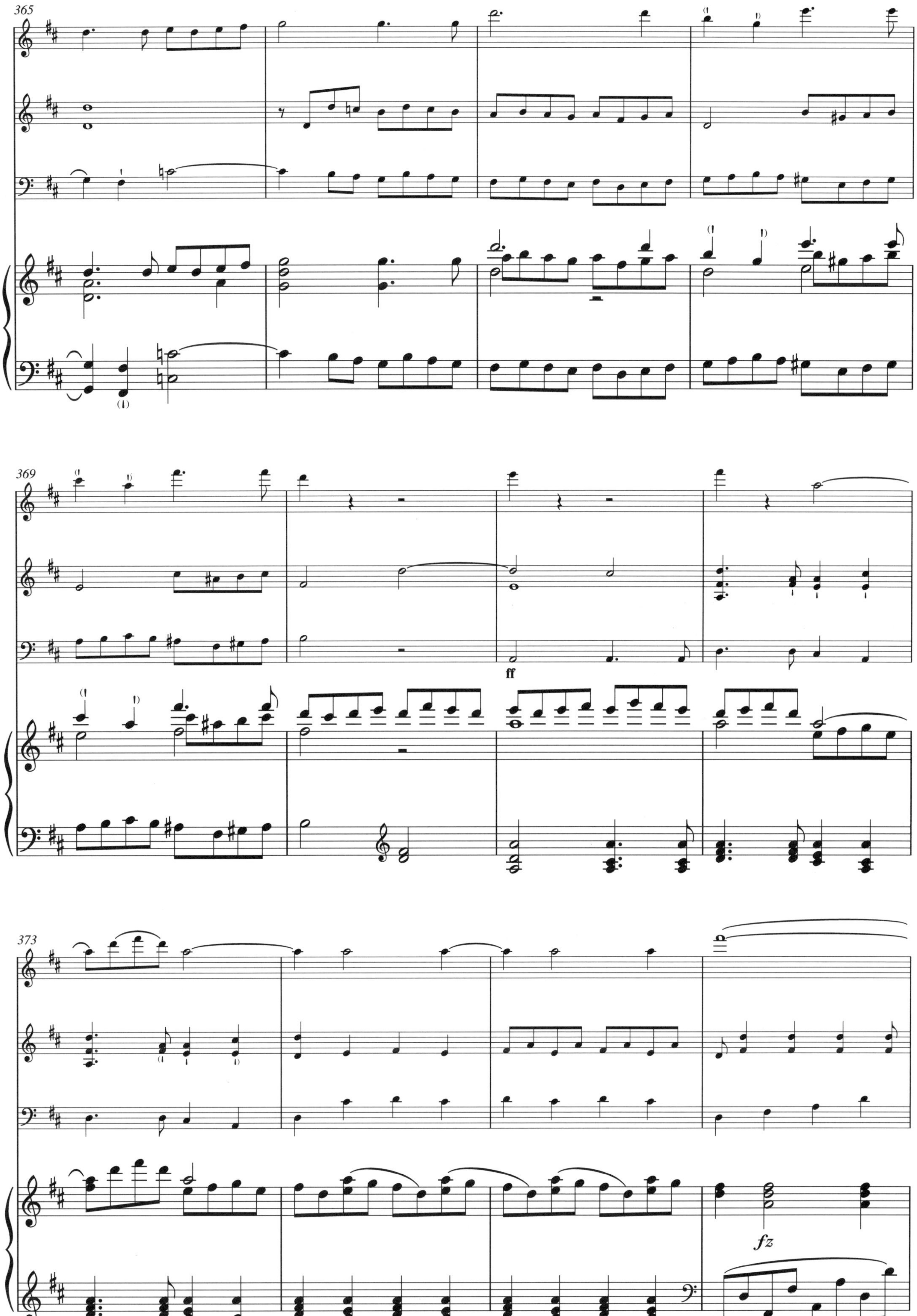
365
369
ff
373
fz

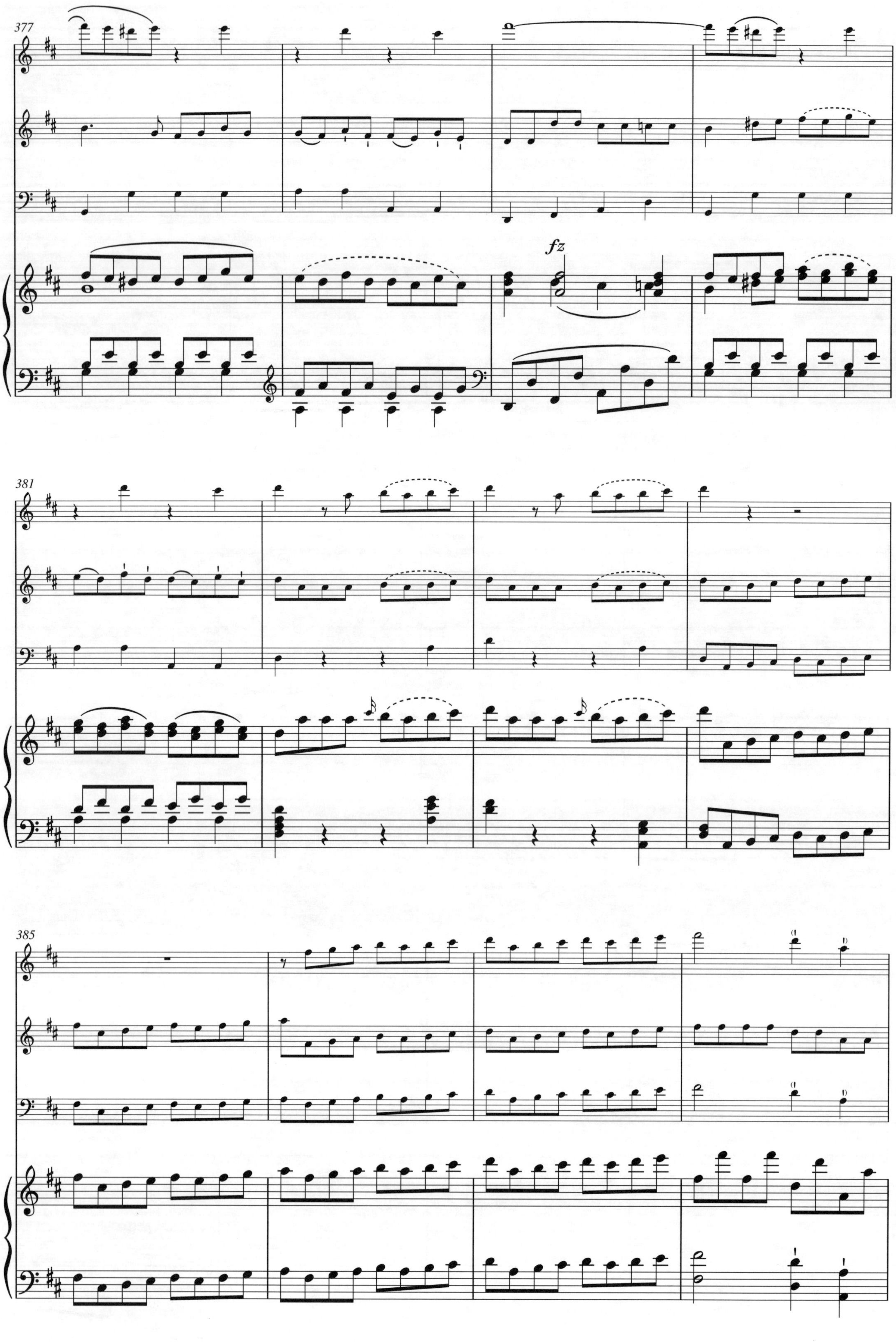
377
fz
381
385

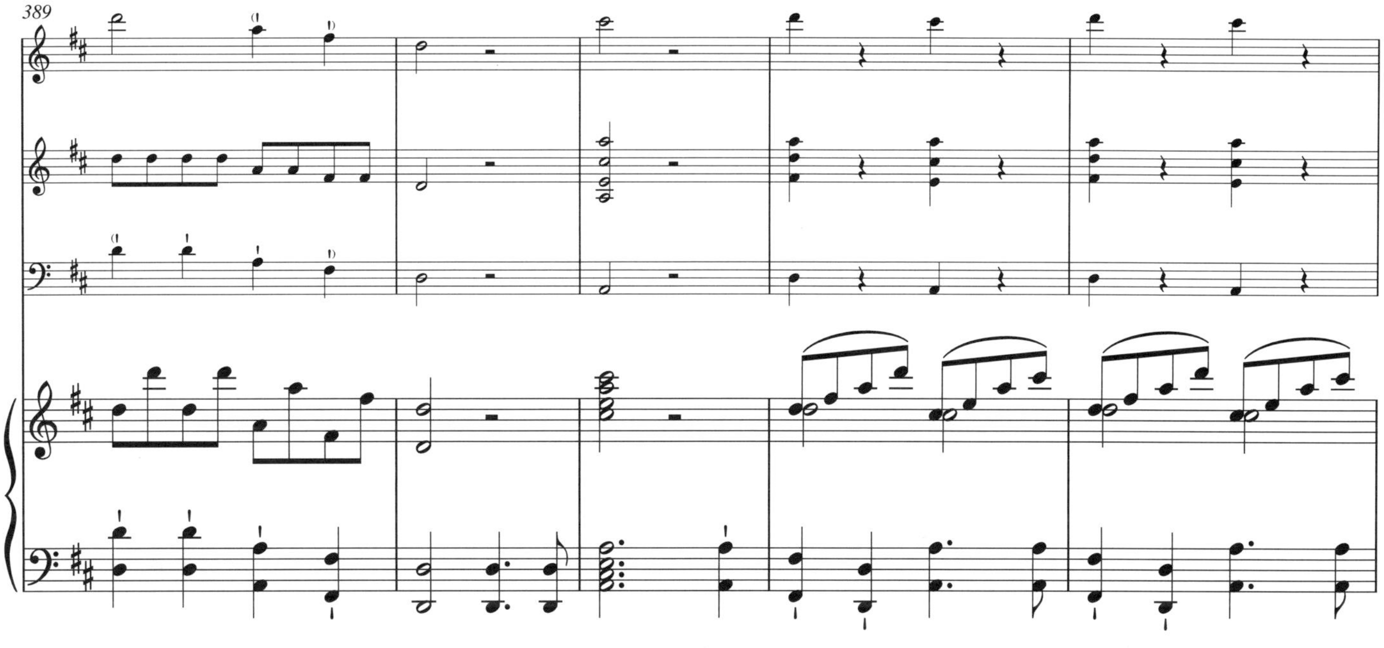
389

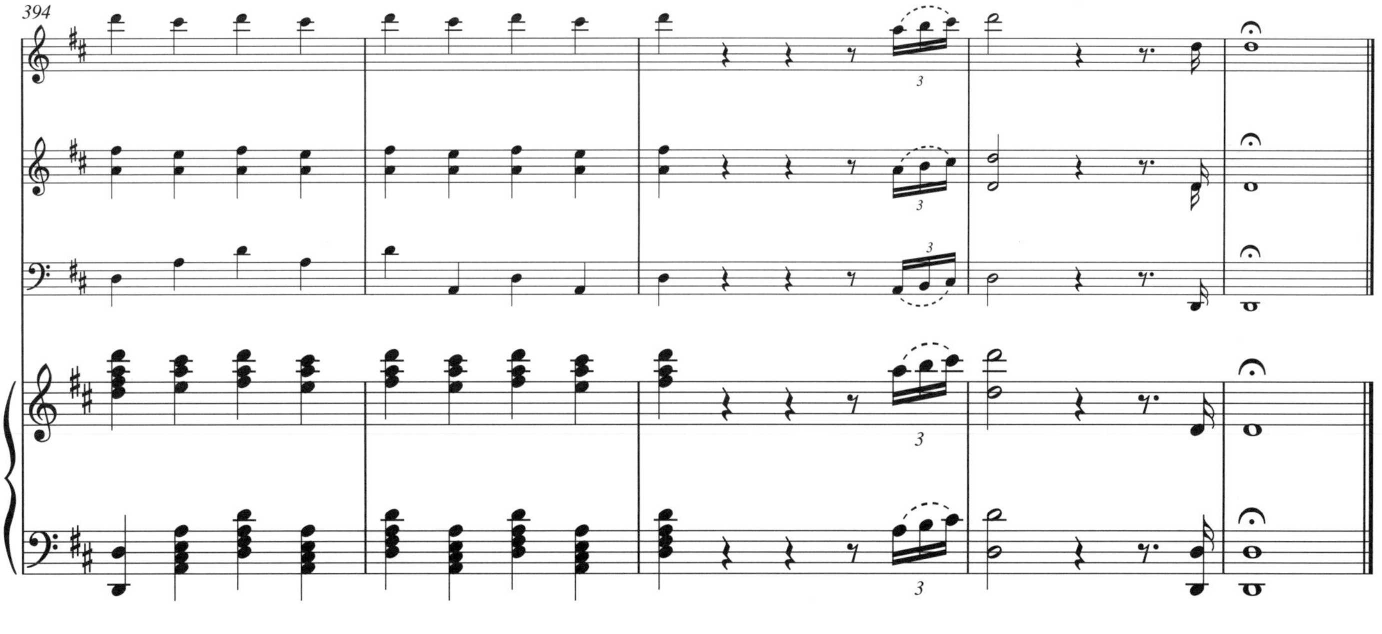
394

9. Overture to Der Freischütz

Carl Maria von Weber

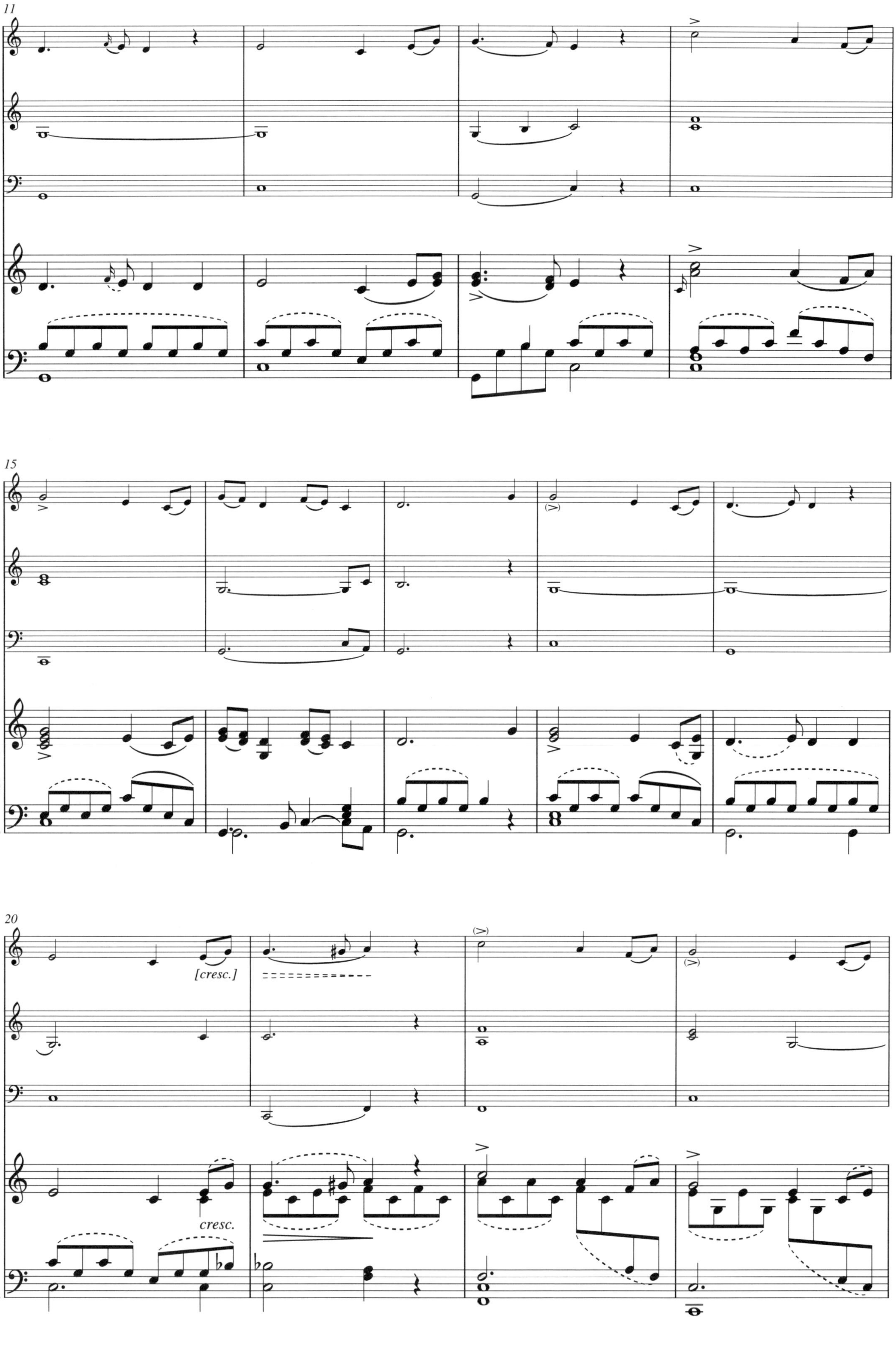
11
15
20
[cresc.]
cresc.

186

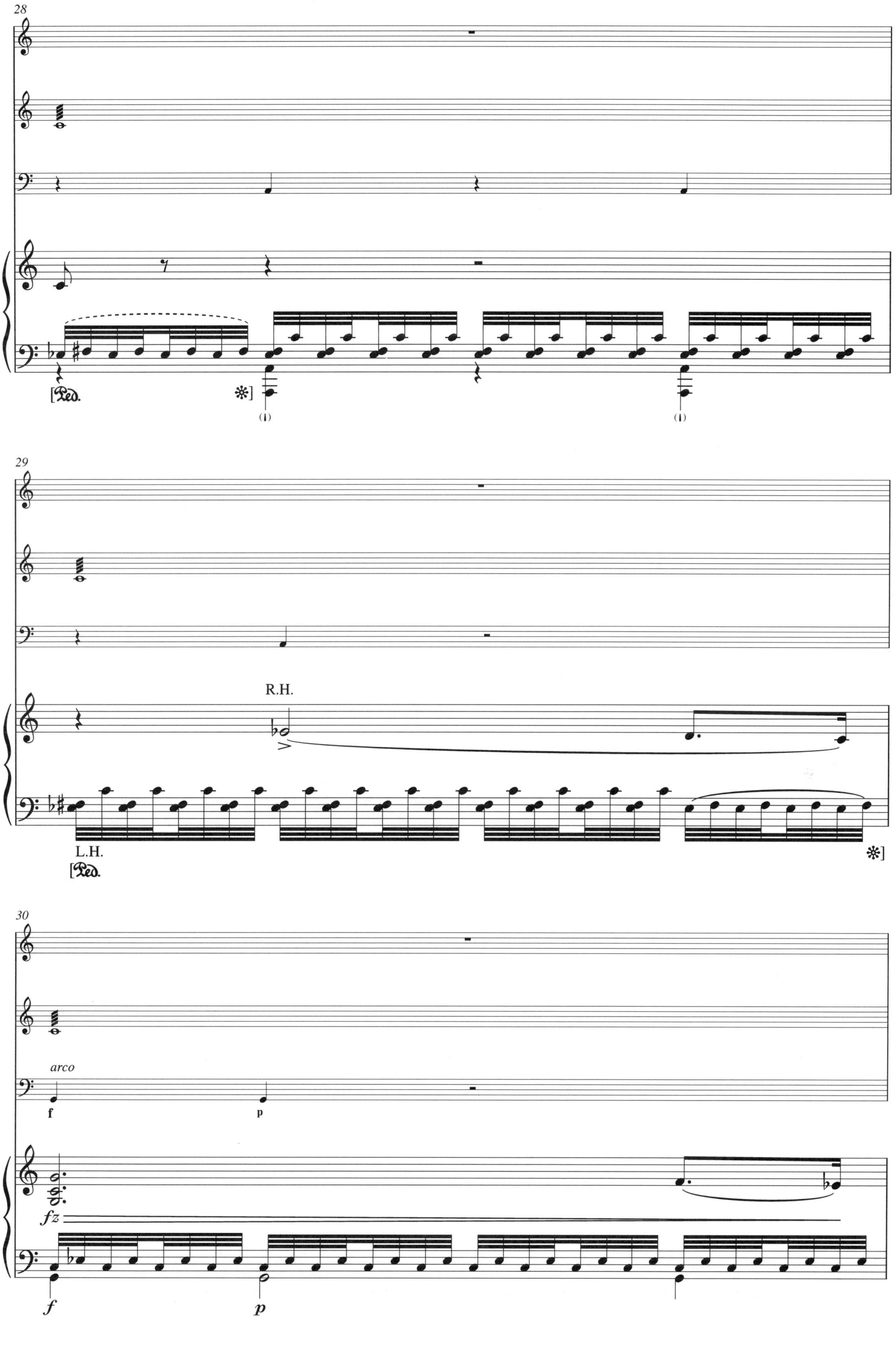
28
[Ped.
29
R.H.
L.H.
[Ped.
30
arco
f
p
fz
f
p

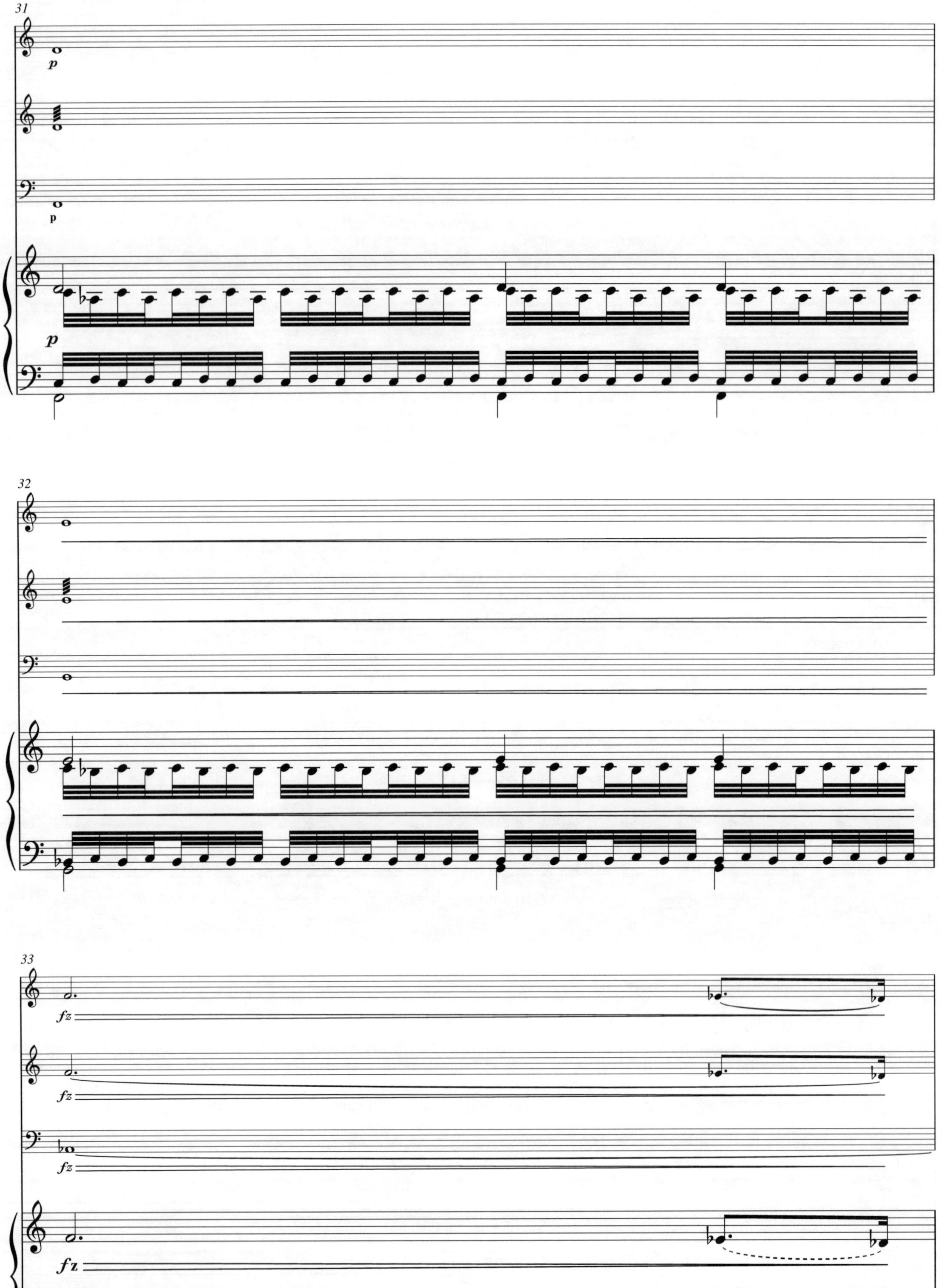
31
p
p
p
32
33
fz
fz
fz
fz
fp

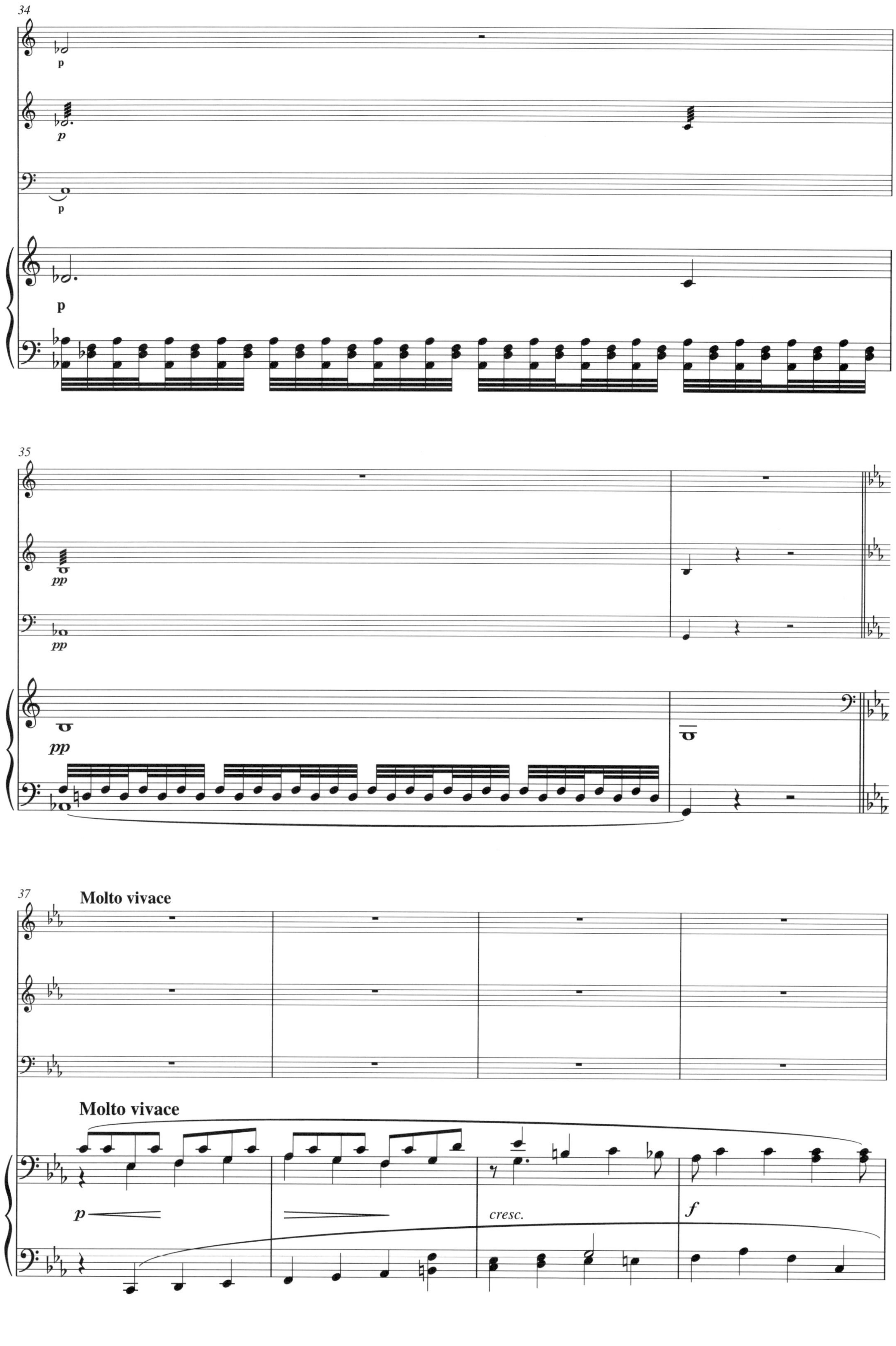
34
p
p
p
p
35
pp
pp
pp
37
Molto vivace
Molto vivace
p
cresc.
f

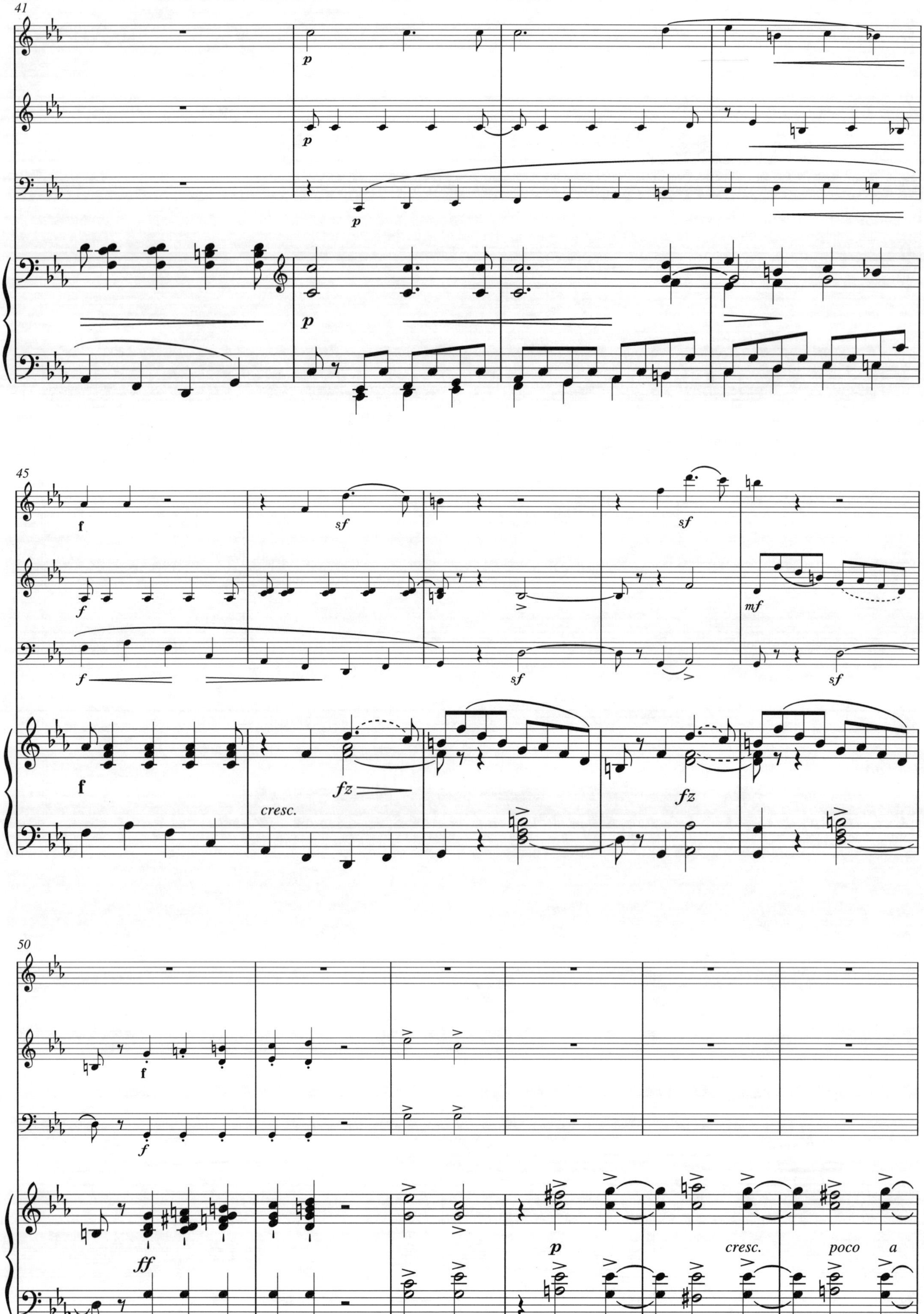
41
45
50
cresc.
cresc.
poco
a

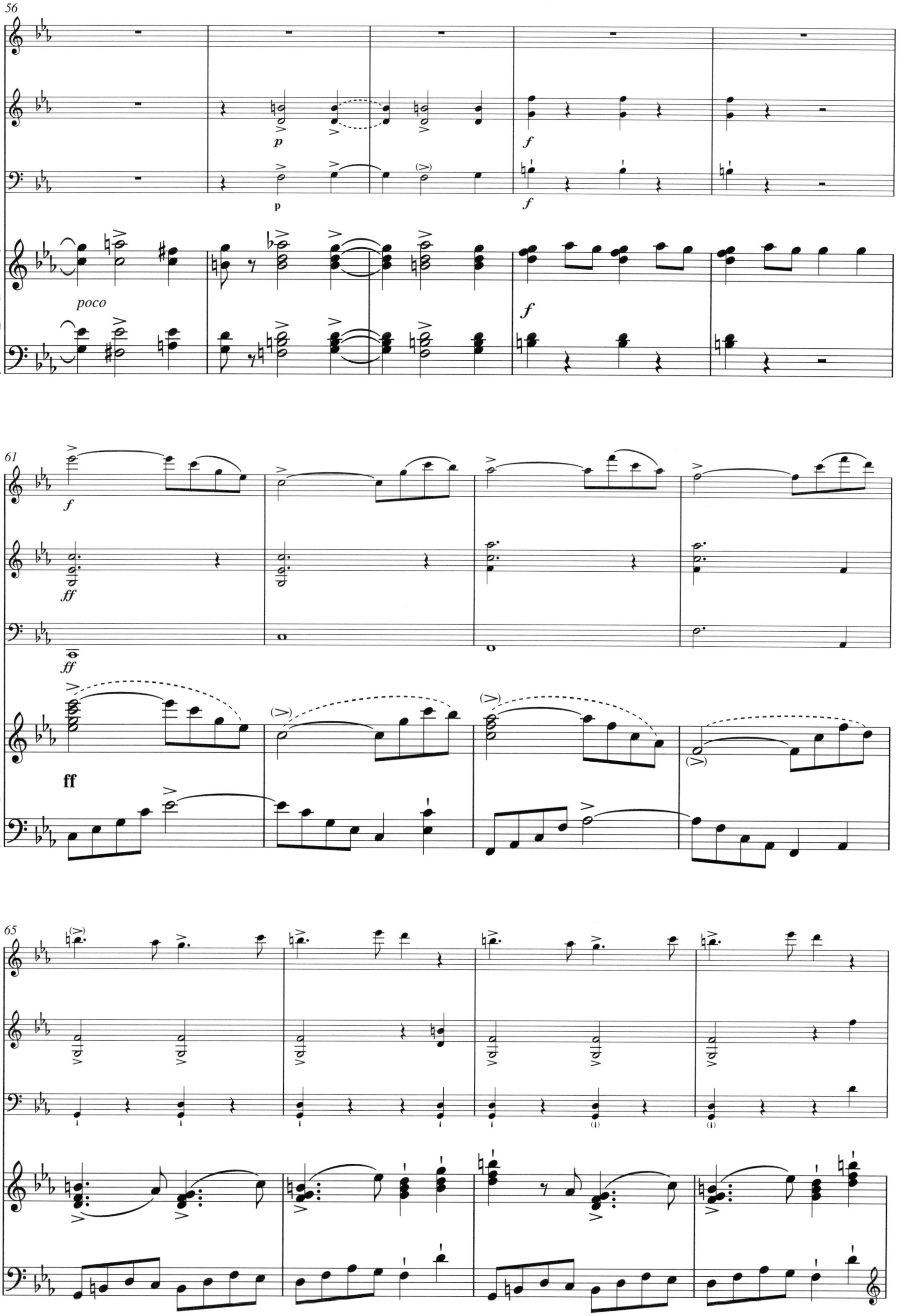
56
p
p
f
f
poco
f
61
f
ff
ff
ff
65

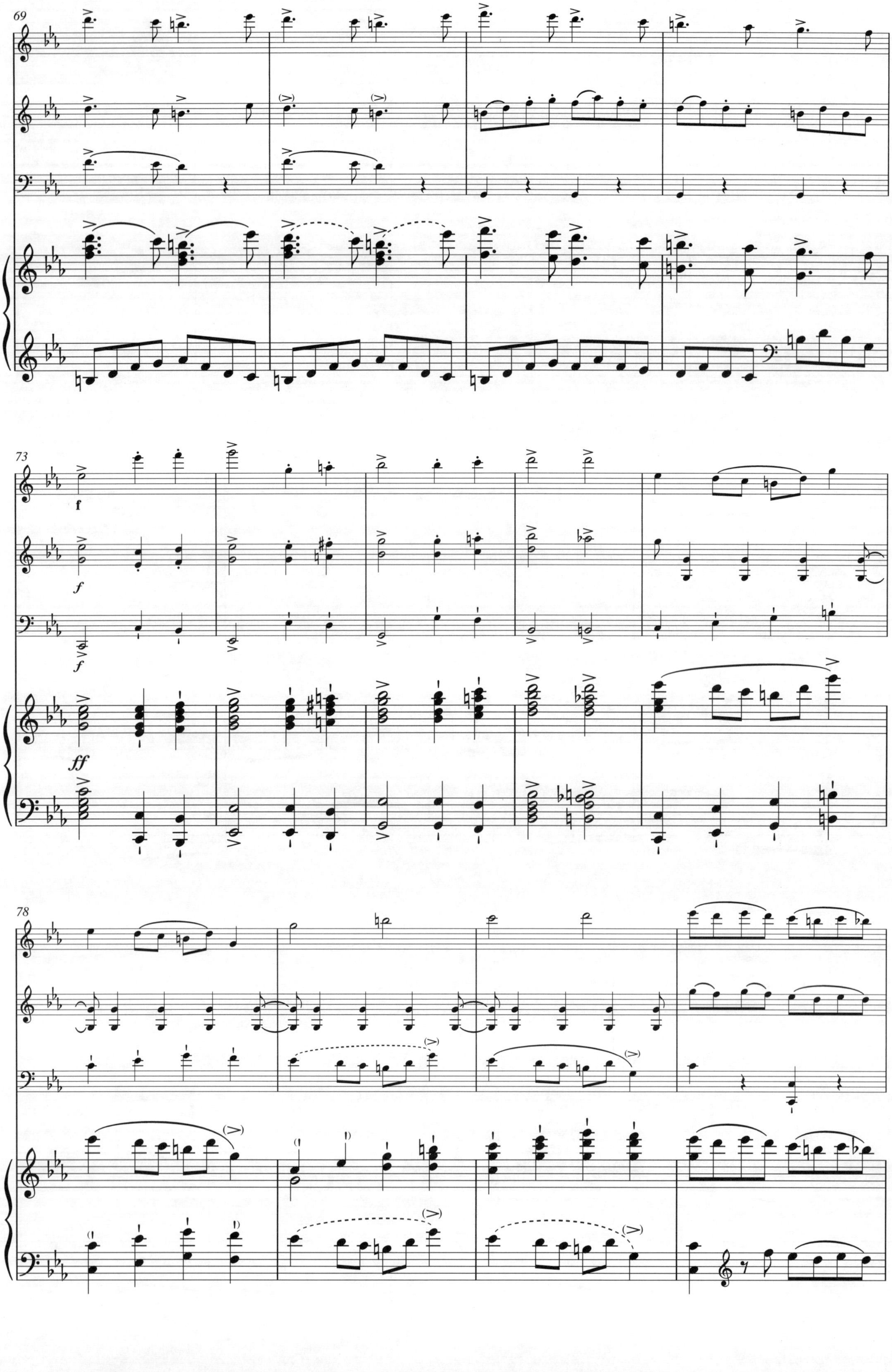
69
73
f
f
f
ff
78

82
p
p
p
86
f
f
f
f
f
cresc.
[cresc.]
[cresc.]
[cresc.]
89
sf
sf
sf
sf
fz
ff
ff
[Ped.

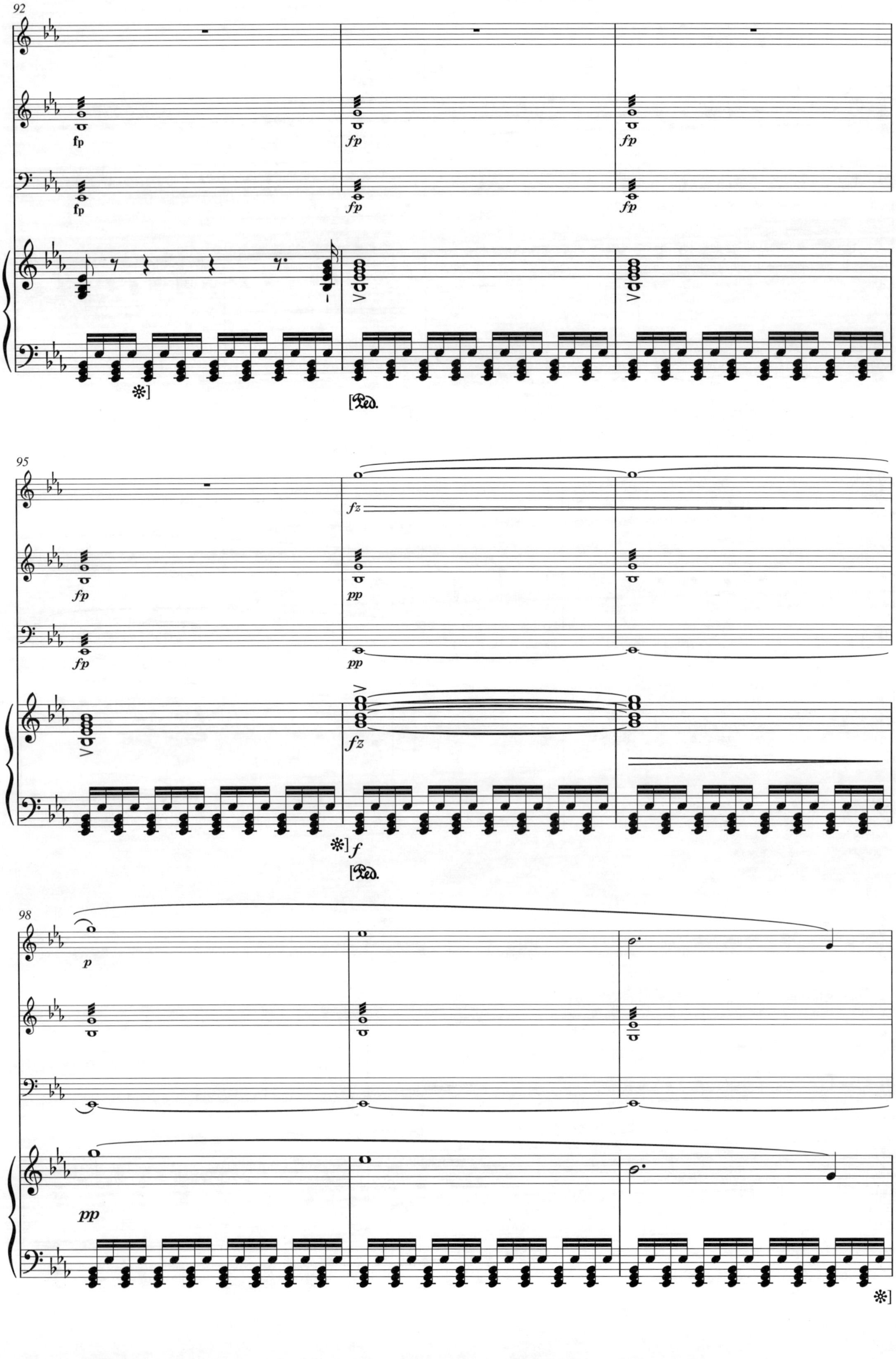
92
fp
fp
fp
fp
fp
fp
[Ped.
95
fz
fp
pp
fp
pp
fz
f
[Ped.
98
p
pp

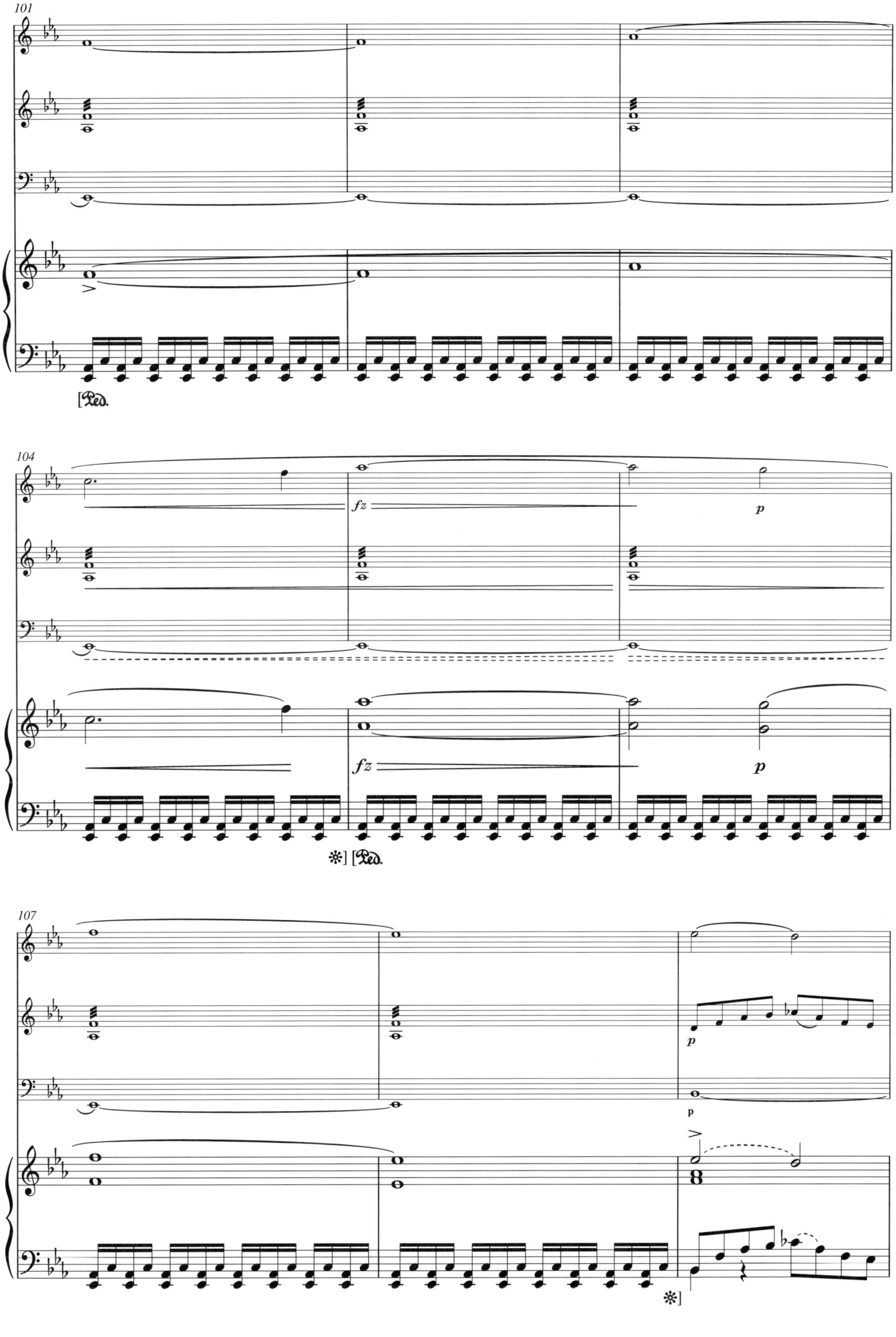
101
[Ped.
104
fz
p
fz
p
※] [Ped.
107
p
p
p
※]

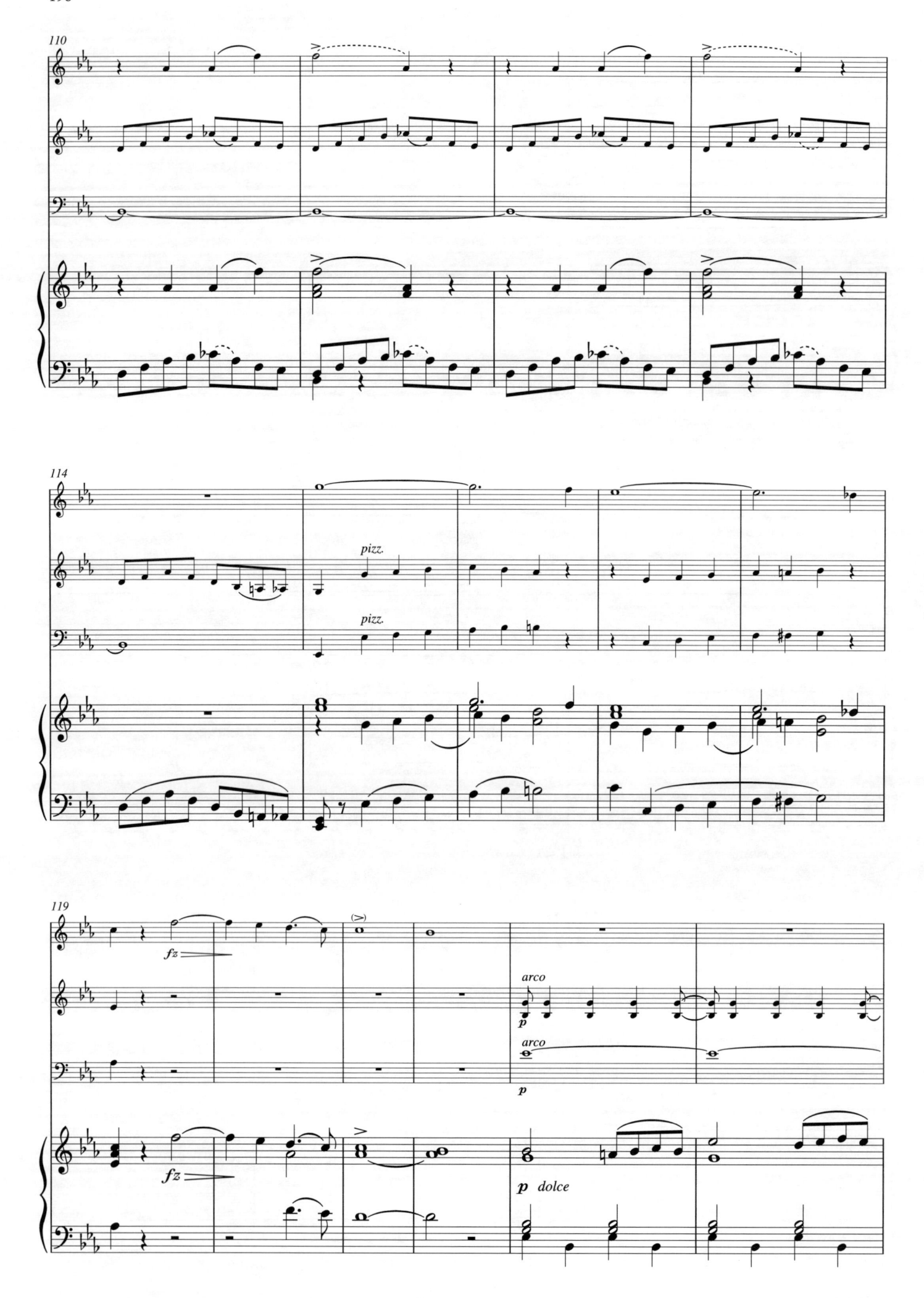
110
114
pizz.
pizz.
119
fz
(>)
arco
p
arco
p
fz
p dolce

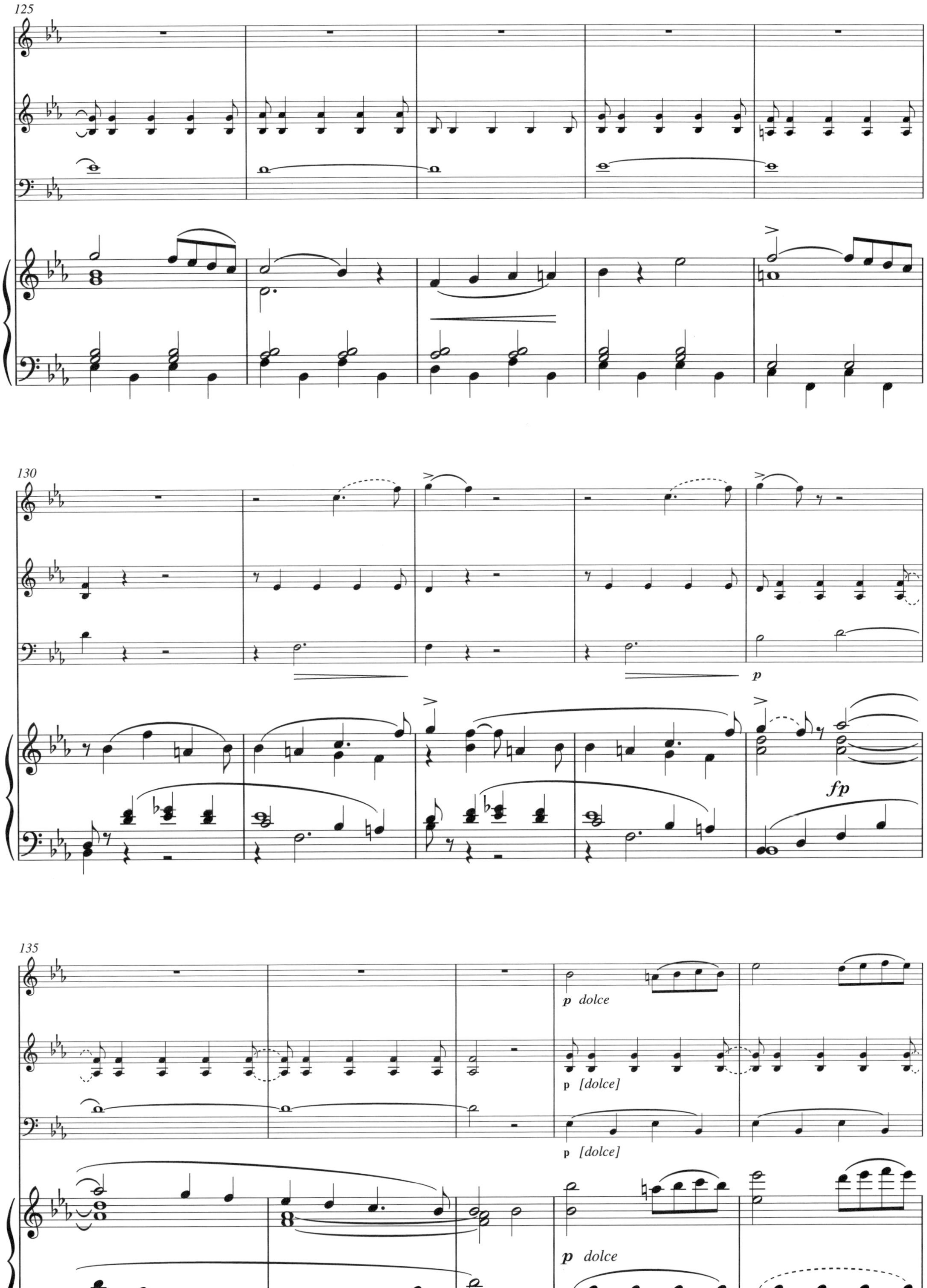
125
130
p
fp
135
p dolce
p [dolce]
p [dolce]
p dolce

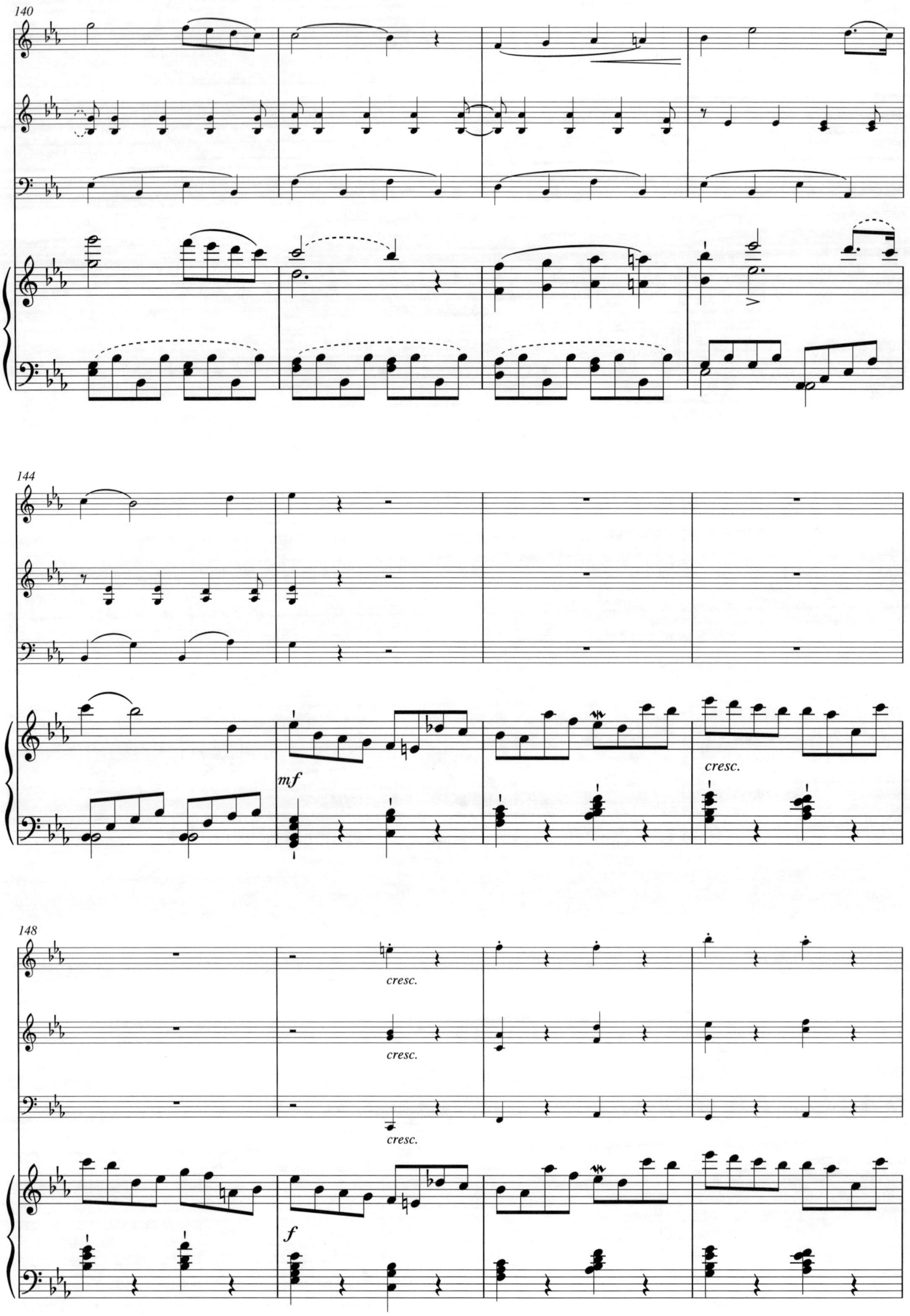
140
144
mf
cresc.
148
cresc.
cresc.
cresc.
f

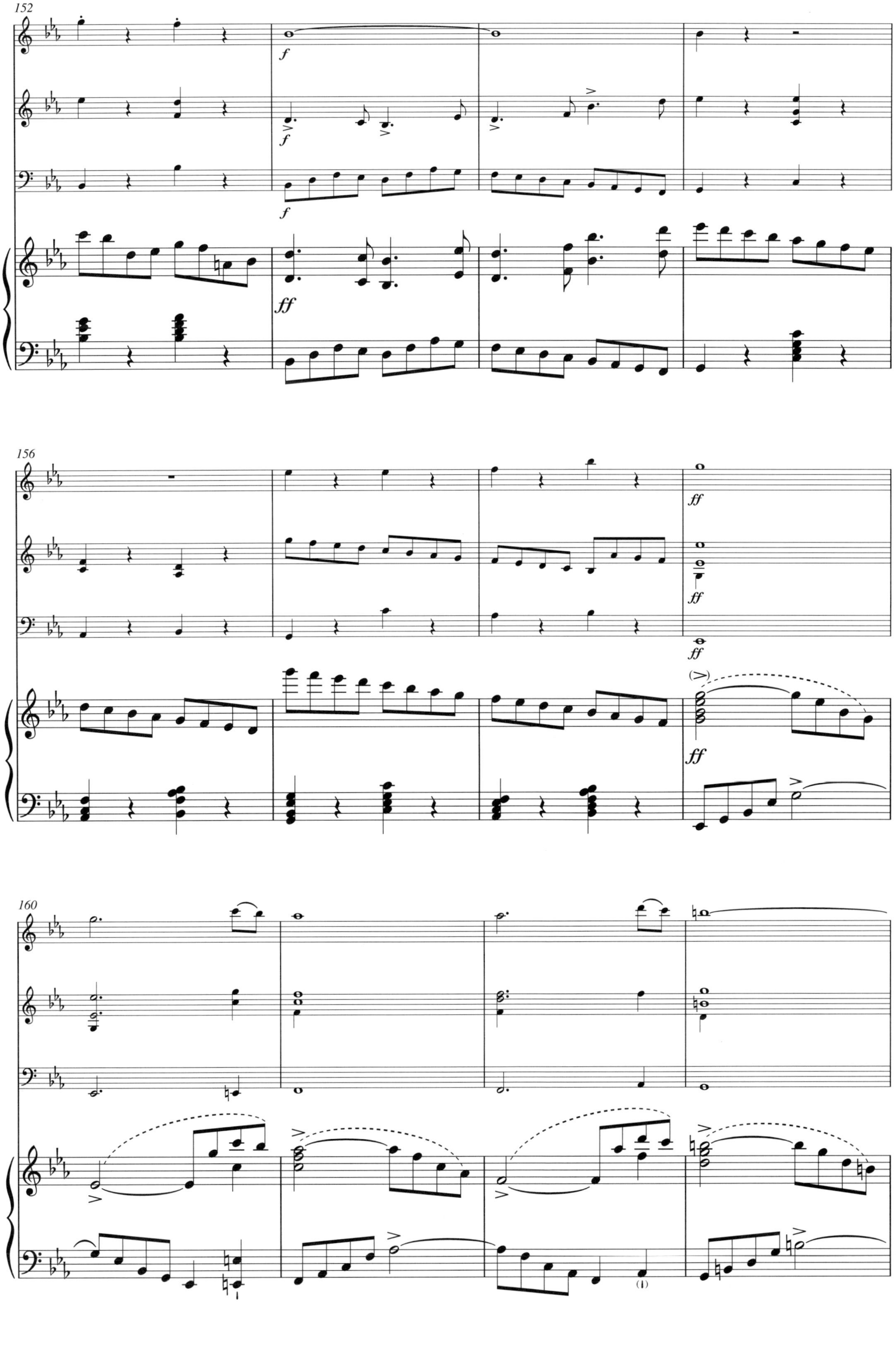
152
f
f
f
ff
156
ff
ff
ff
(>)
ff
160
(1)

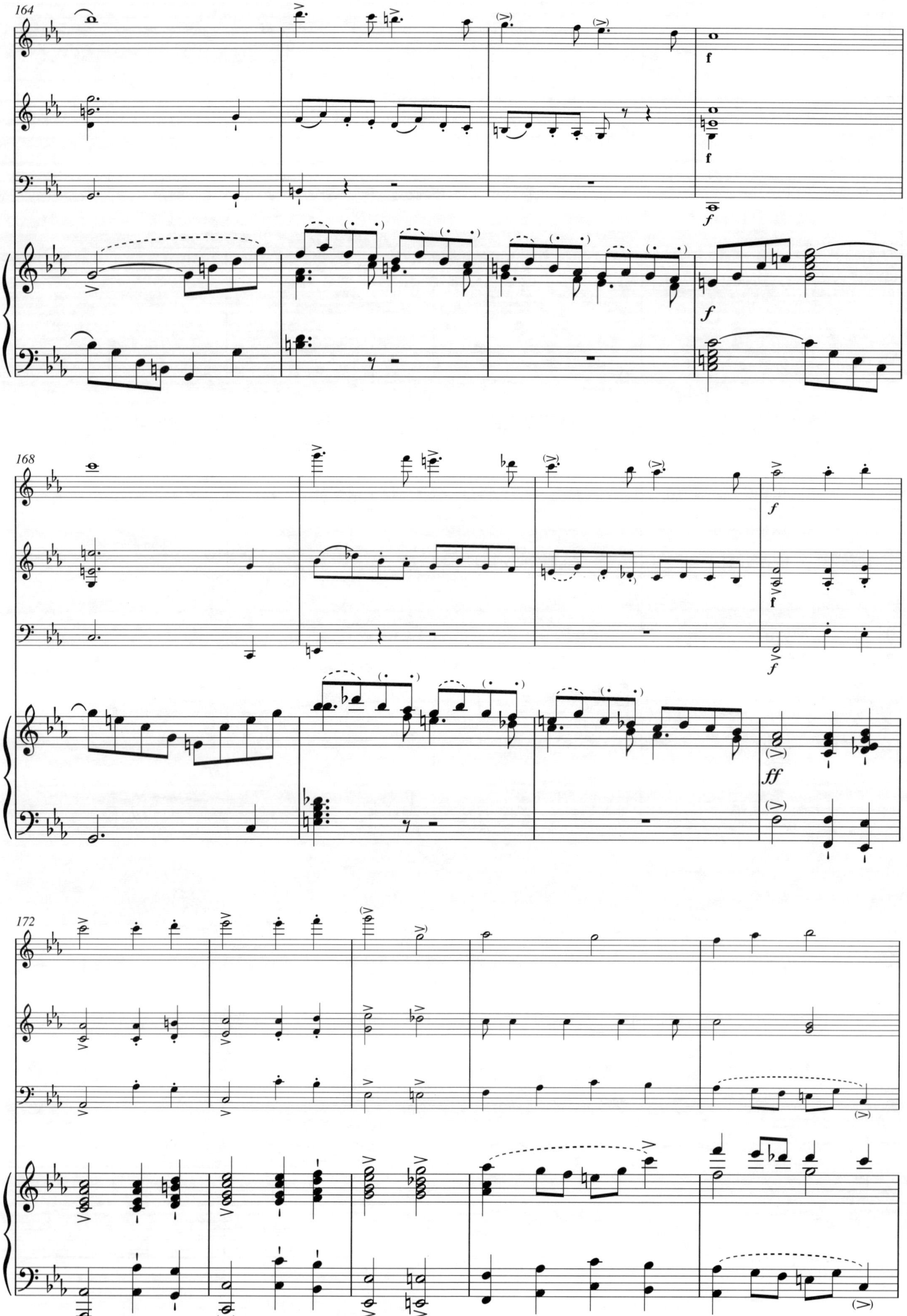
164
f
f
f
f
168
f
f
f
ff
172

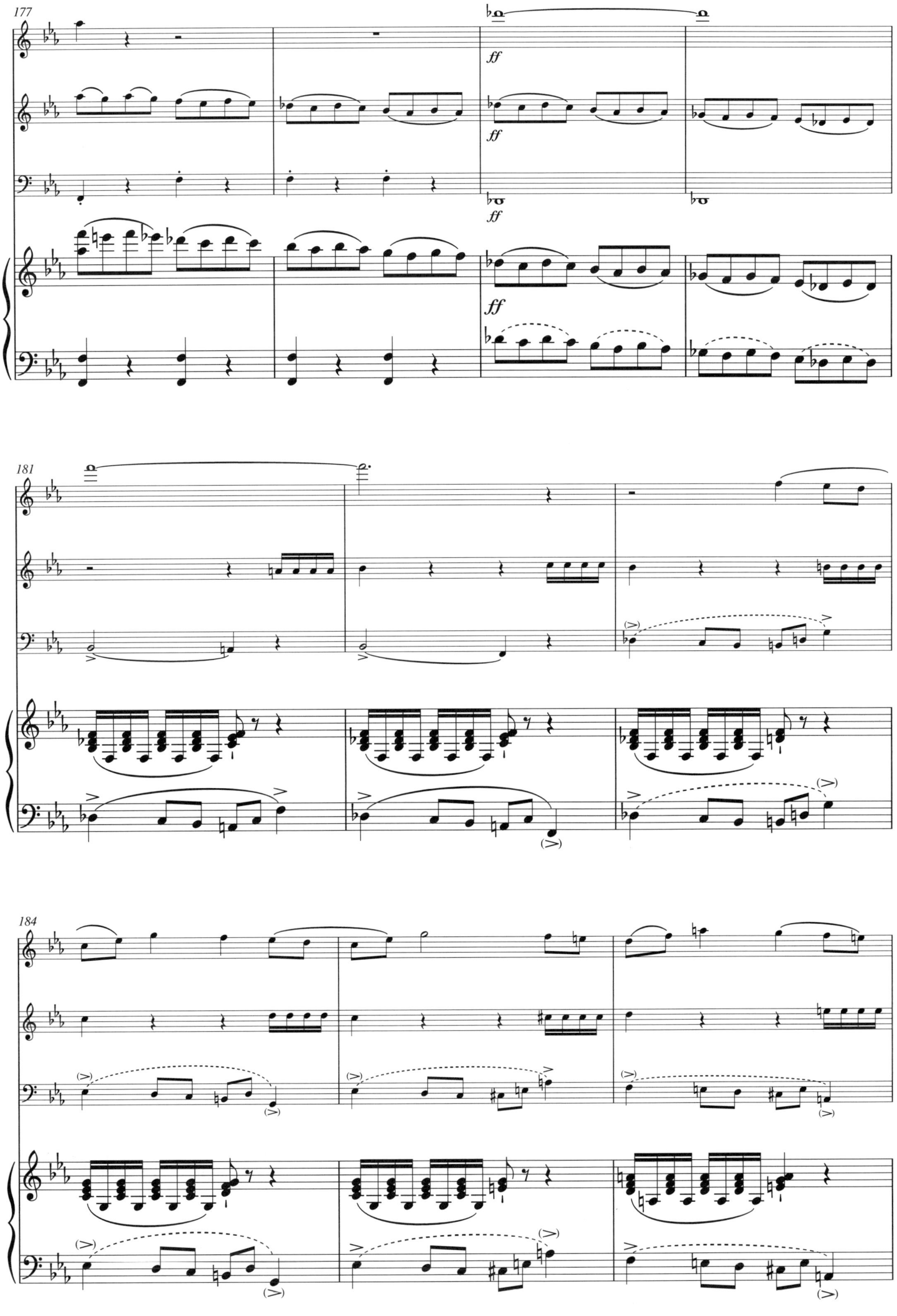
177
ff
ff
ff
ff
181
184

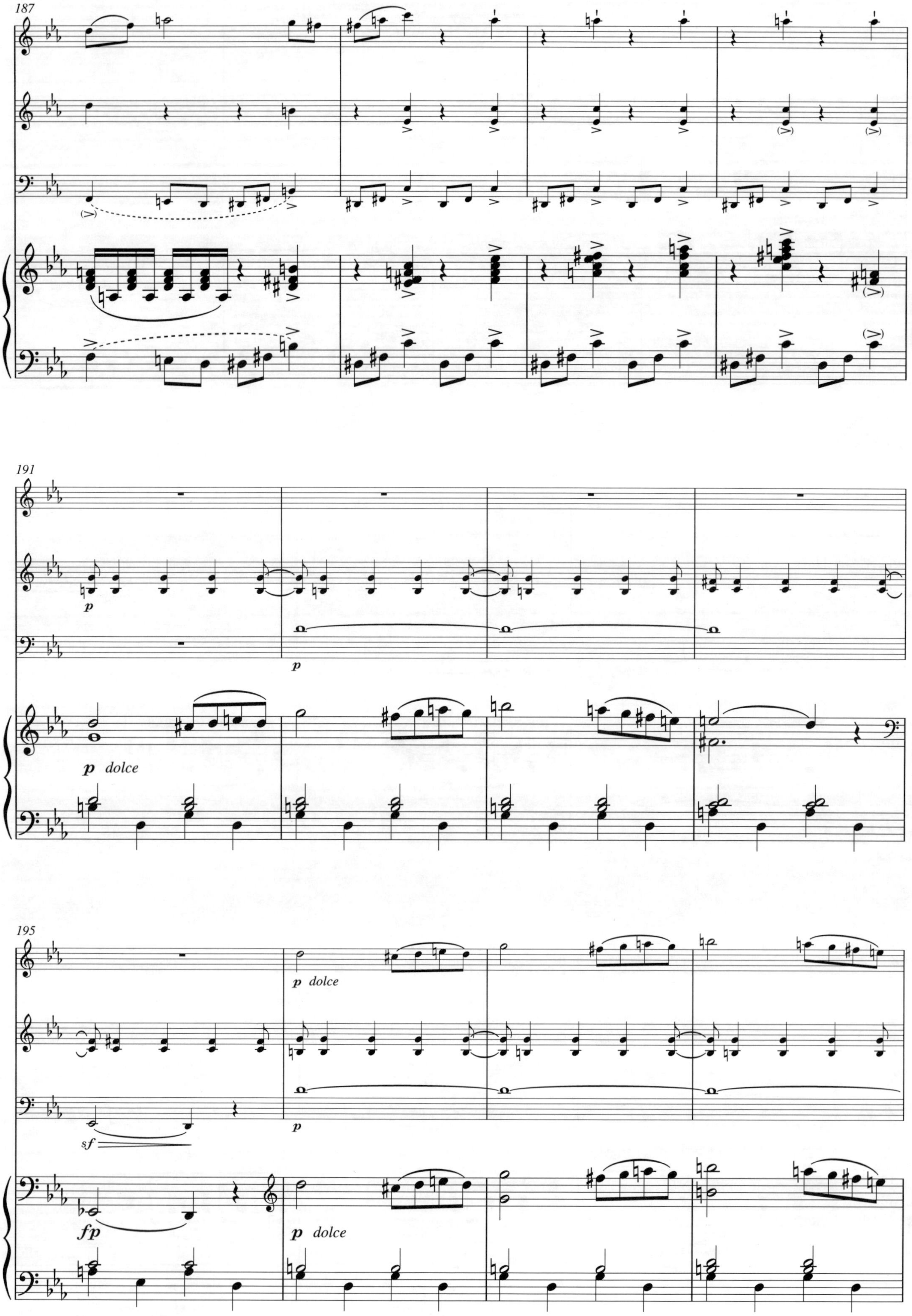
187
191
p
p
p dolce
195
p dolce
sf
p
fp
p dolce

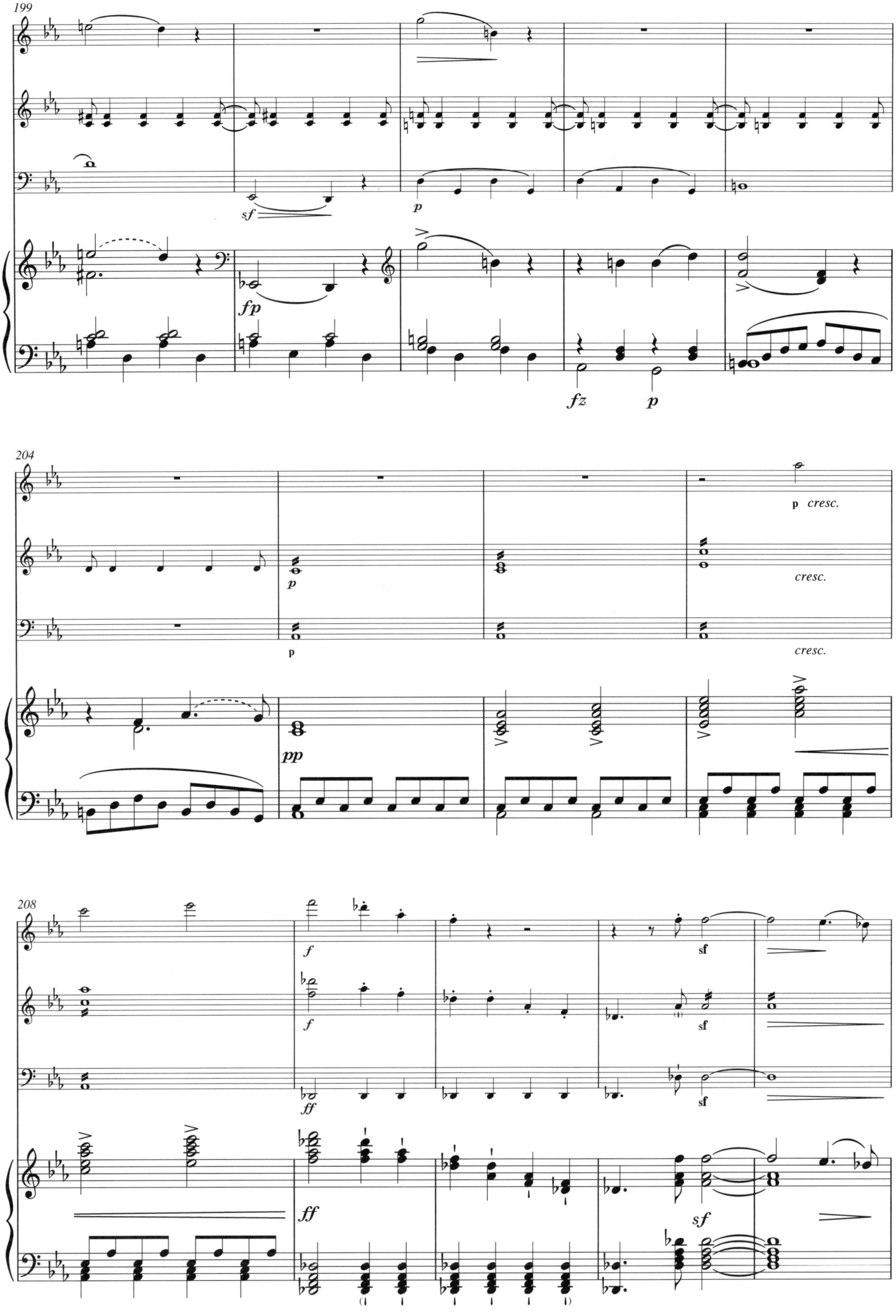
199
204
p cresc.
cresc.
cresc.
208

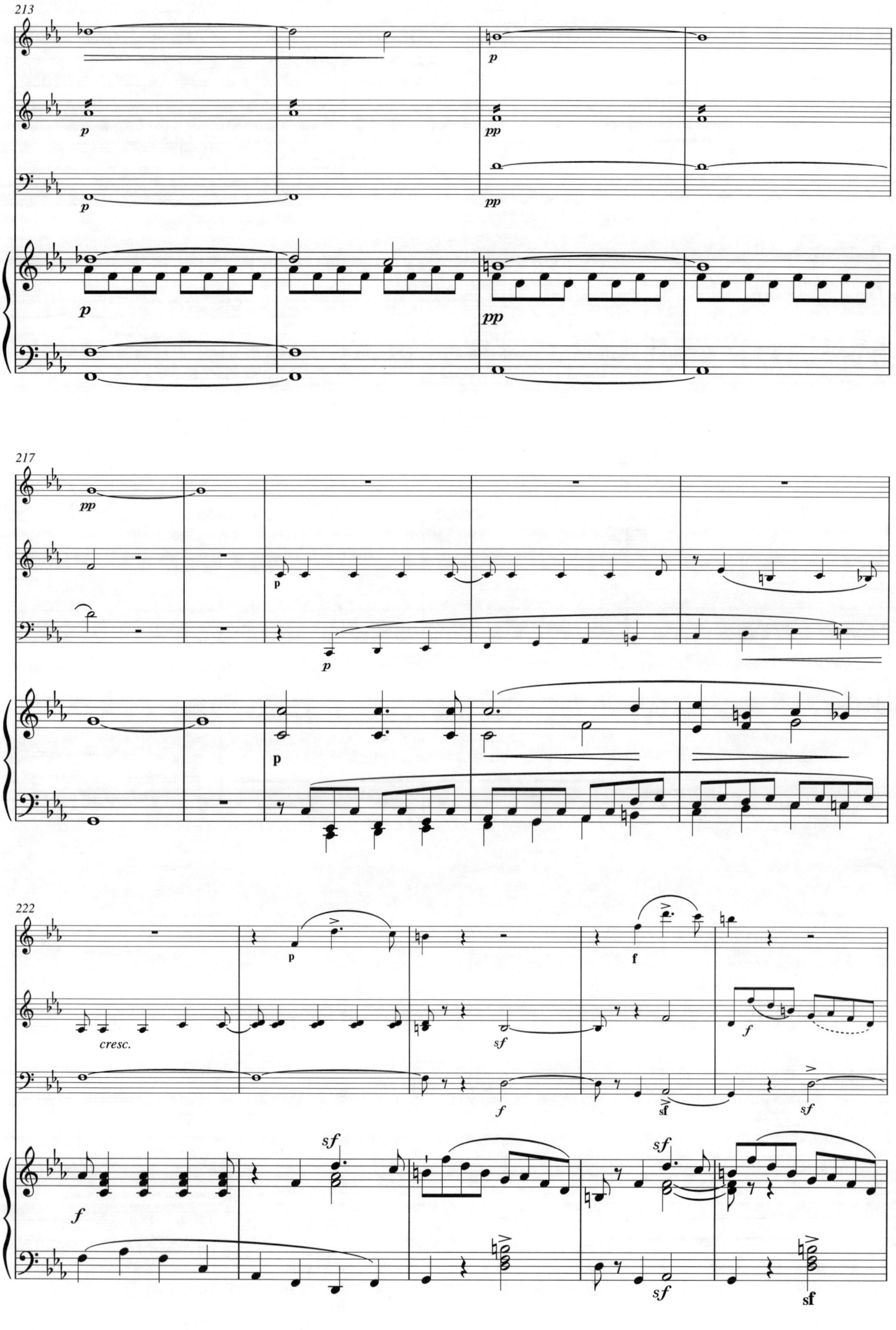
213
217
222
cresc.

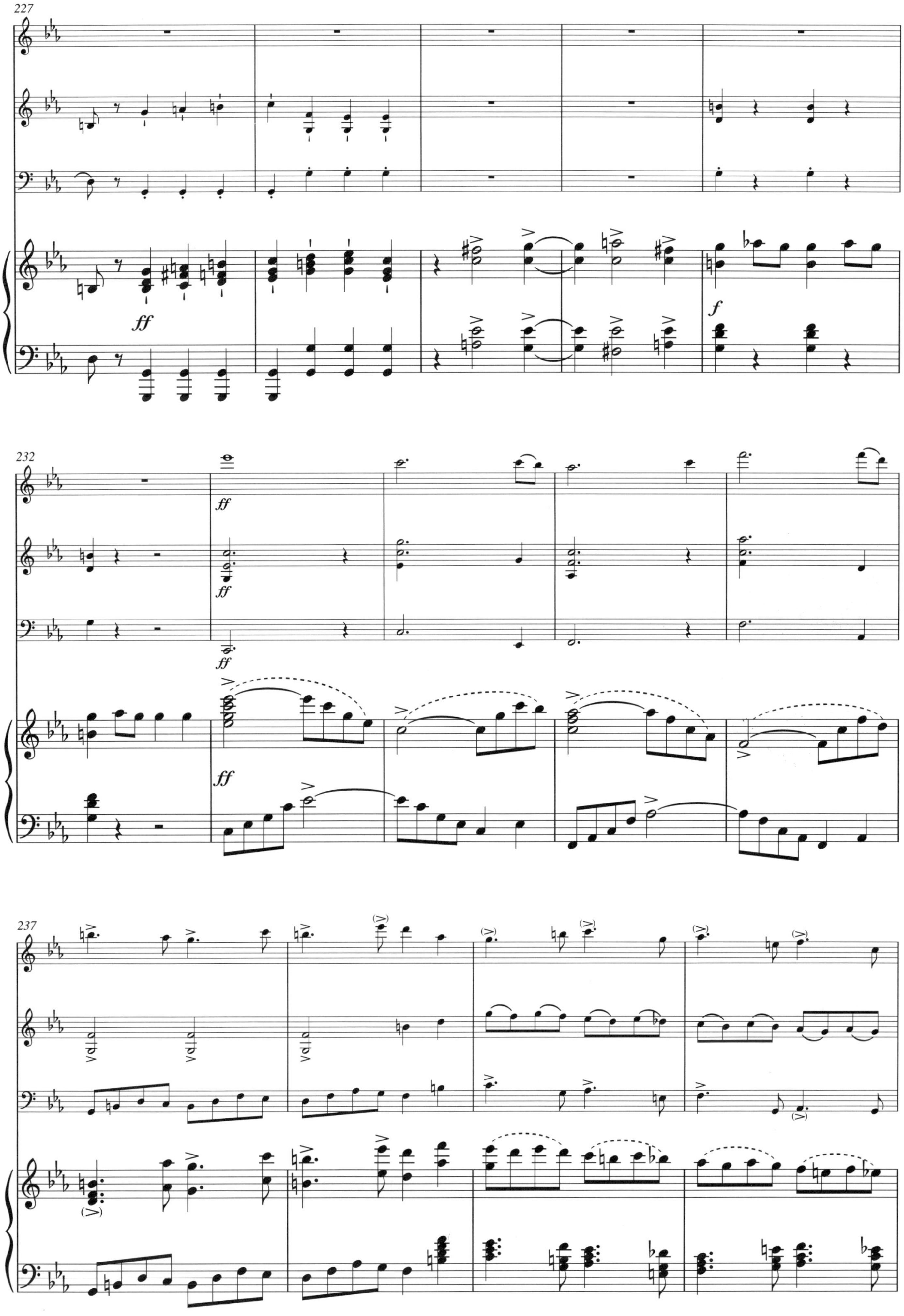
227
ff
f
232
ff
ff
ff
ff
237

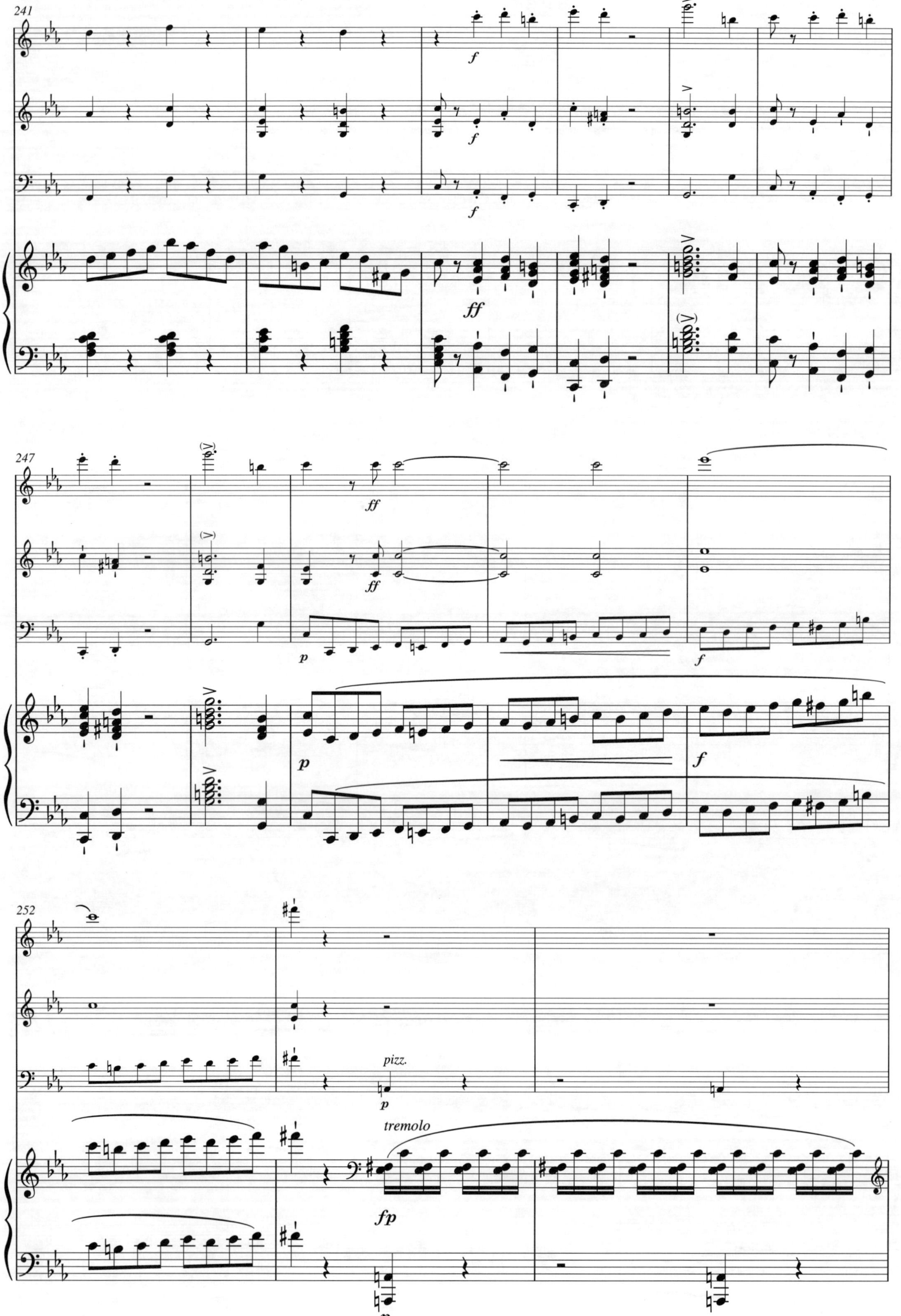
241
f
ff
247
ff
p
f
252
pizz.
p
tremolo
fp

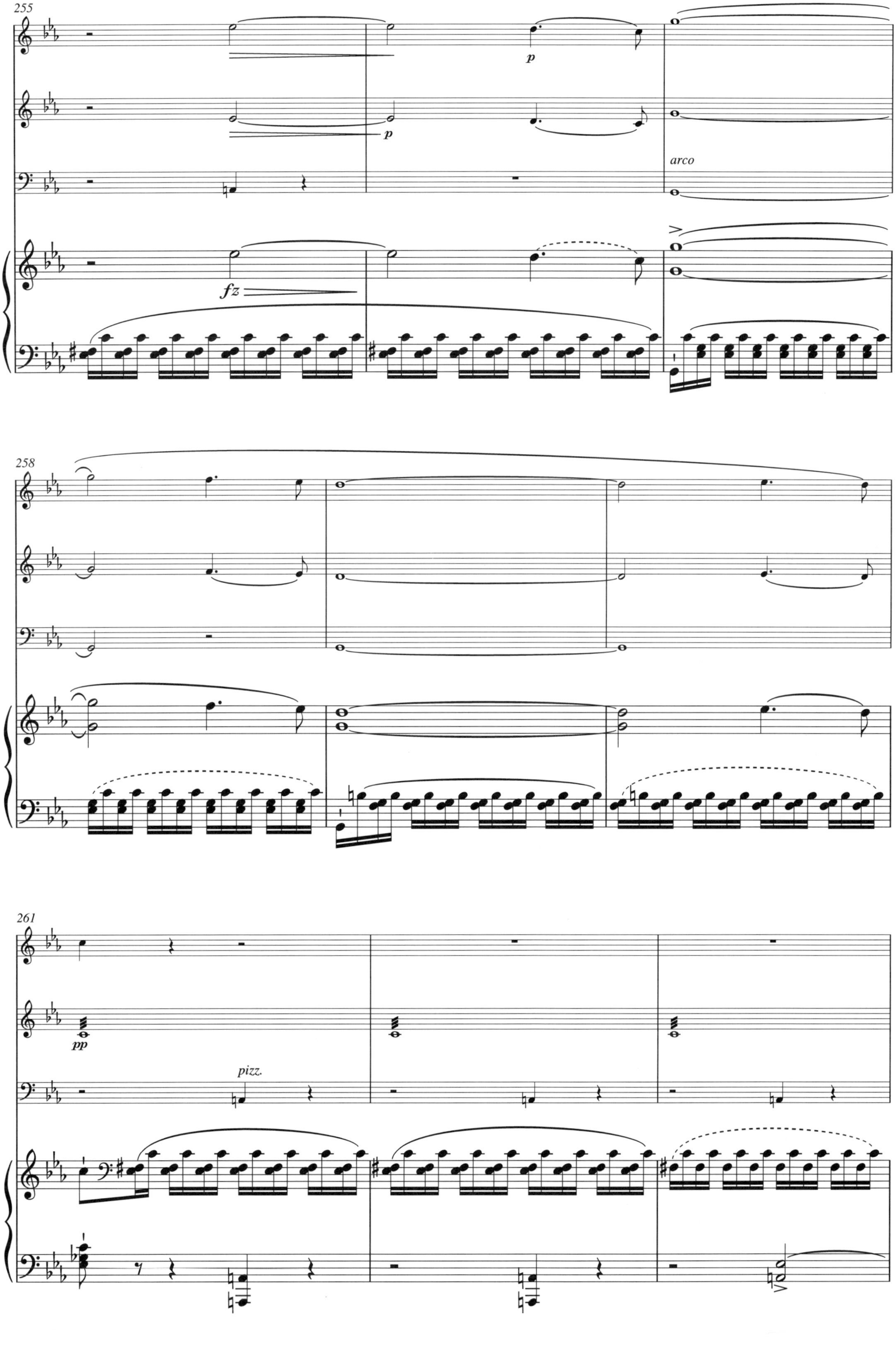
255
p
p
arco
fz
258
261
pp
pizz.

208

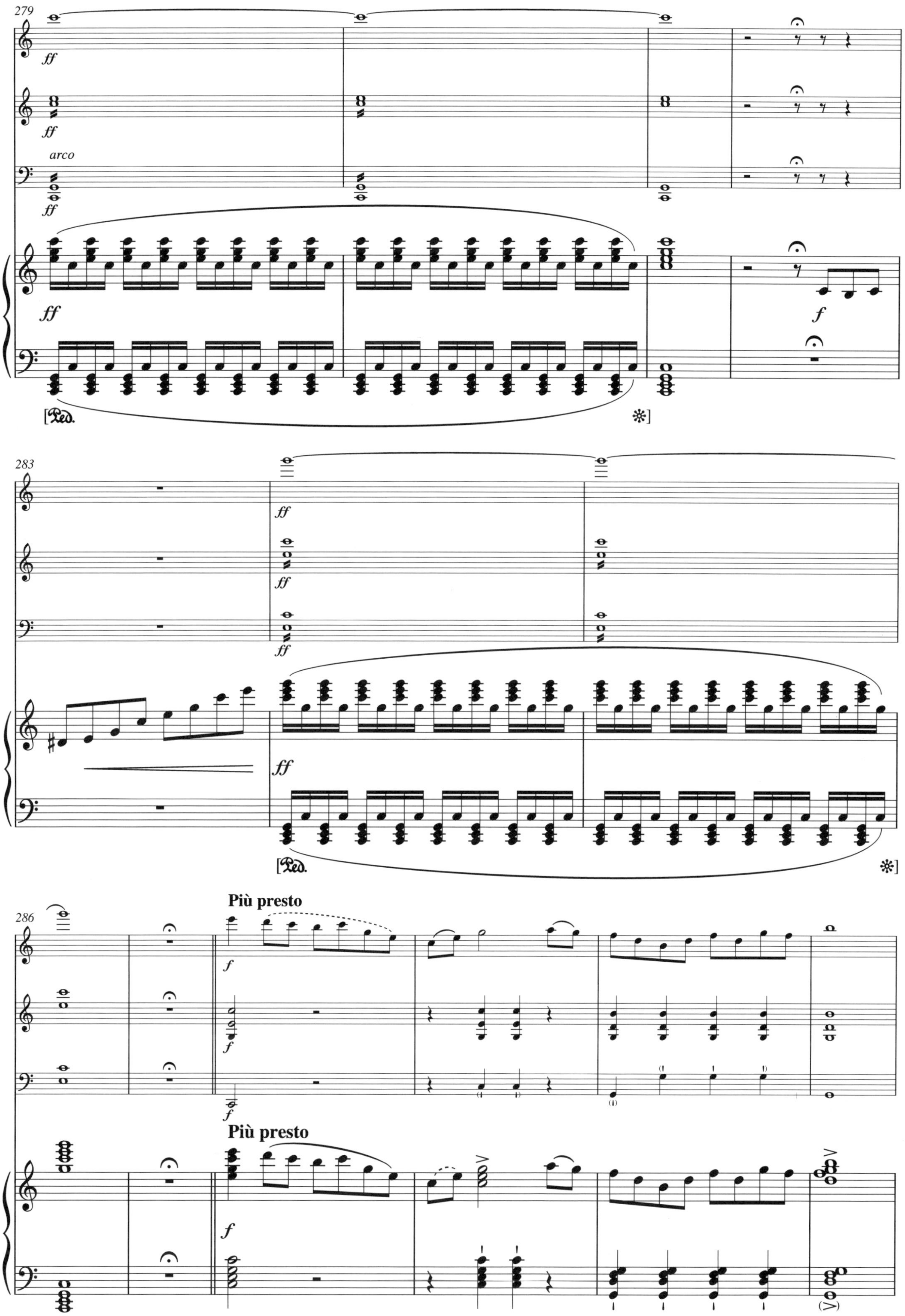
279
arco
283
286
Più presto
Più presto

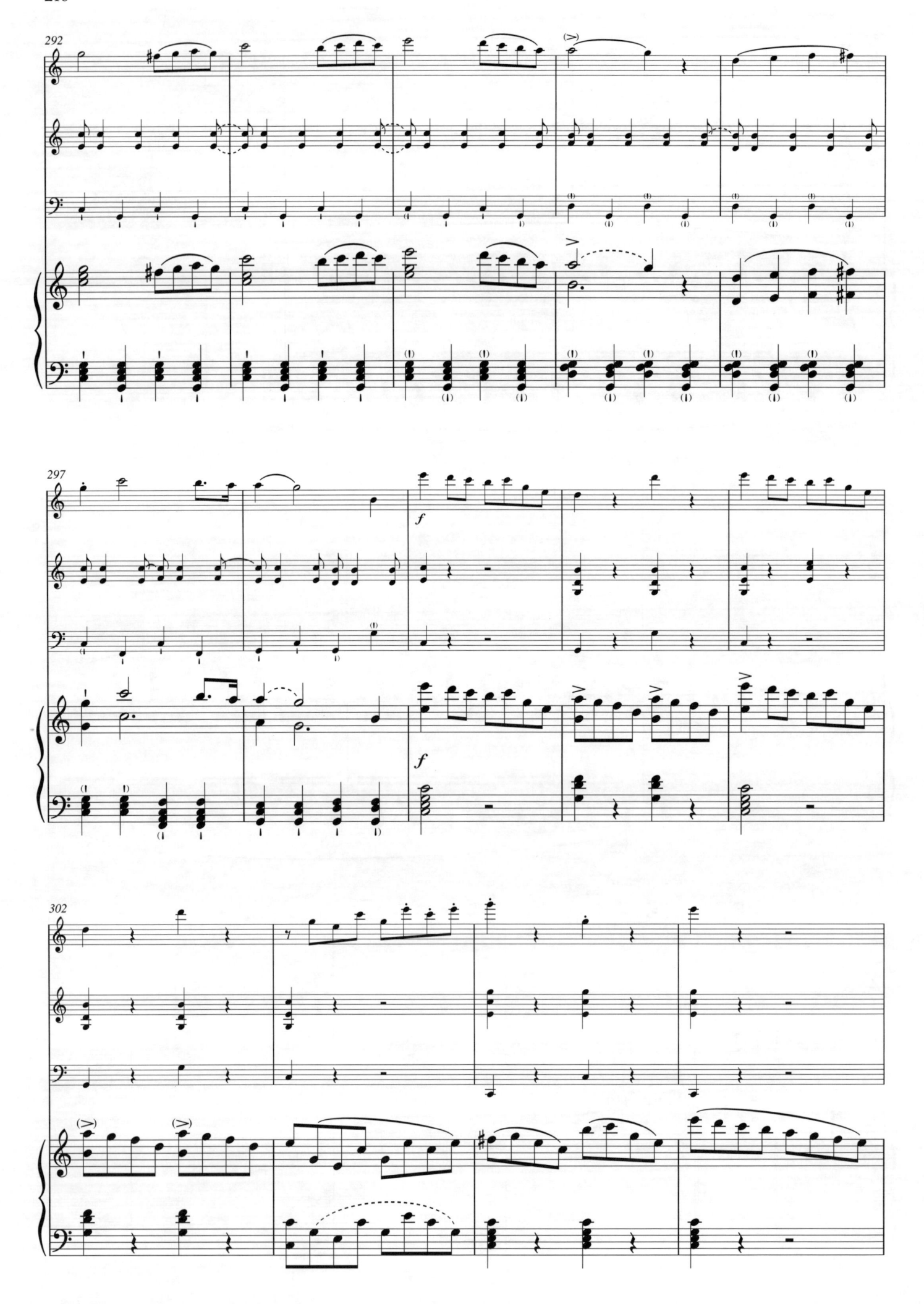
292
297
f
f
302

306
312
Ancora più stringendo
Ancora più stringendo
316
8va

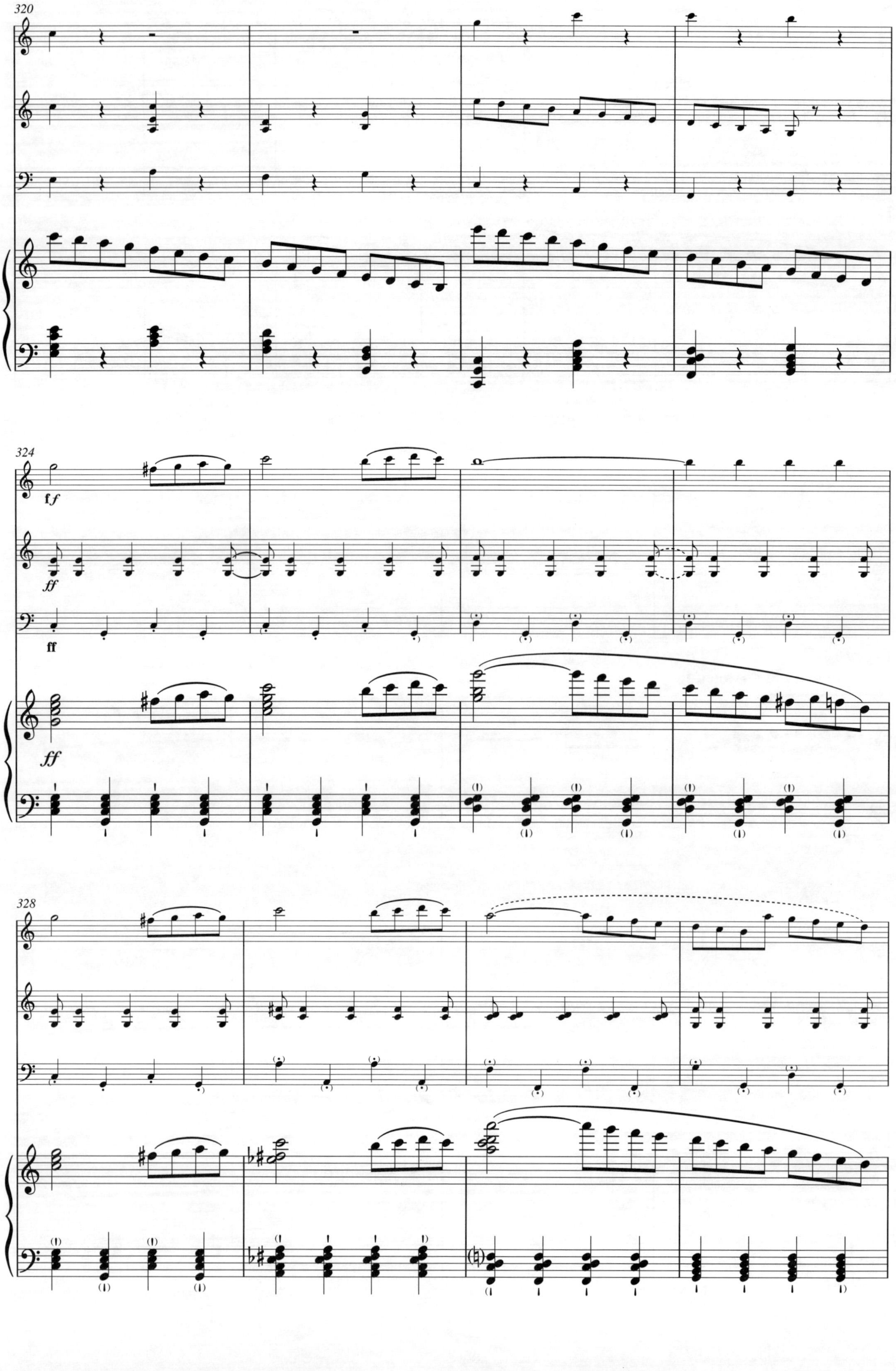
320
324
fƒ
ff
ff
ff
328

213

10. Overture to Euryanthe

Carl Maria von Weber

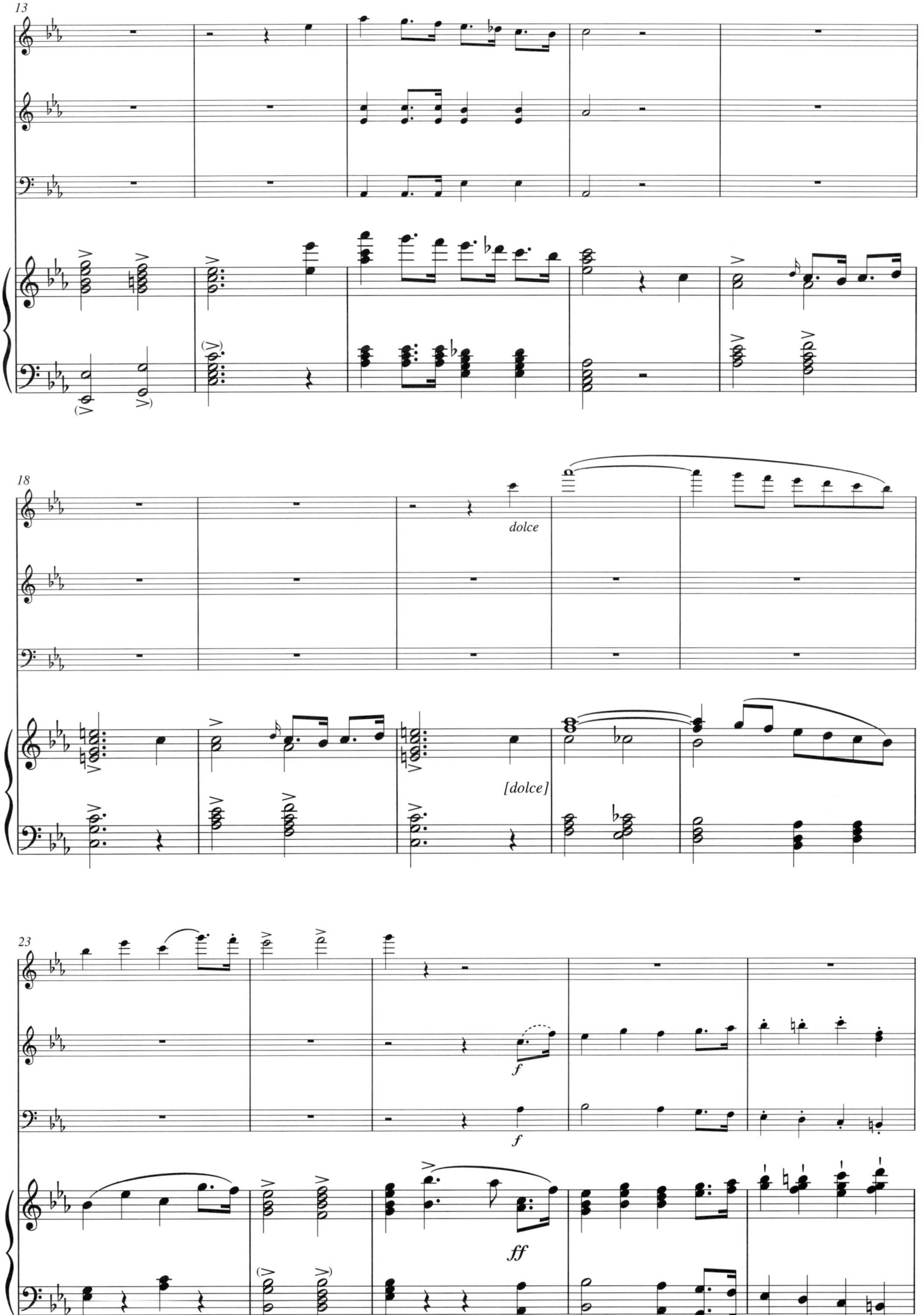
13
18
dolce
[dolce]
23
f
f
ff

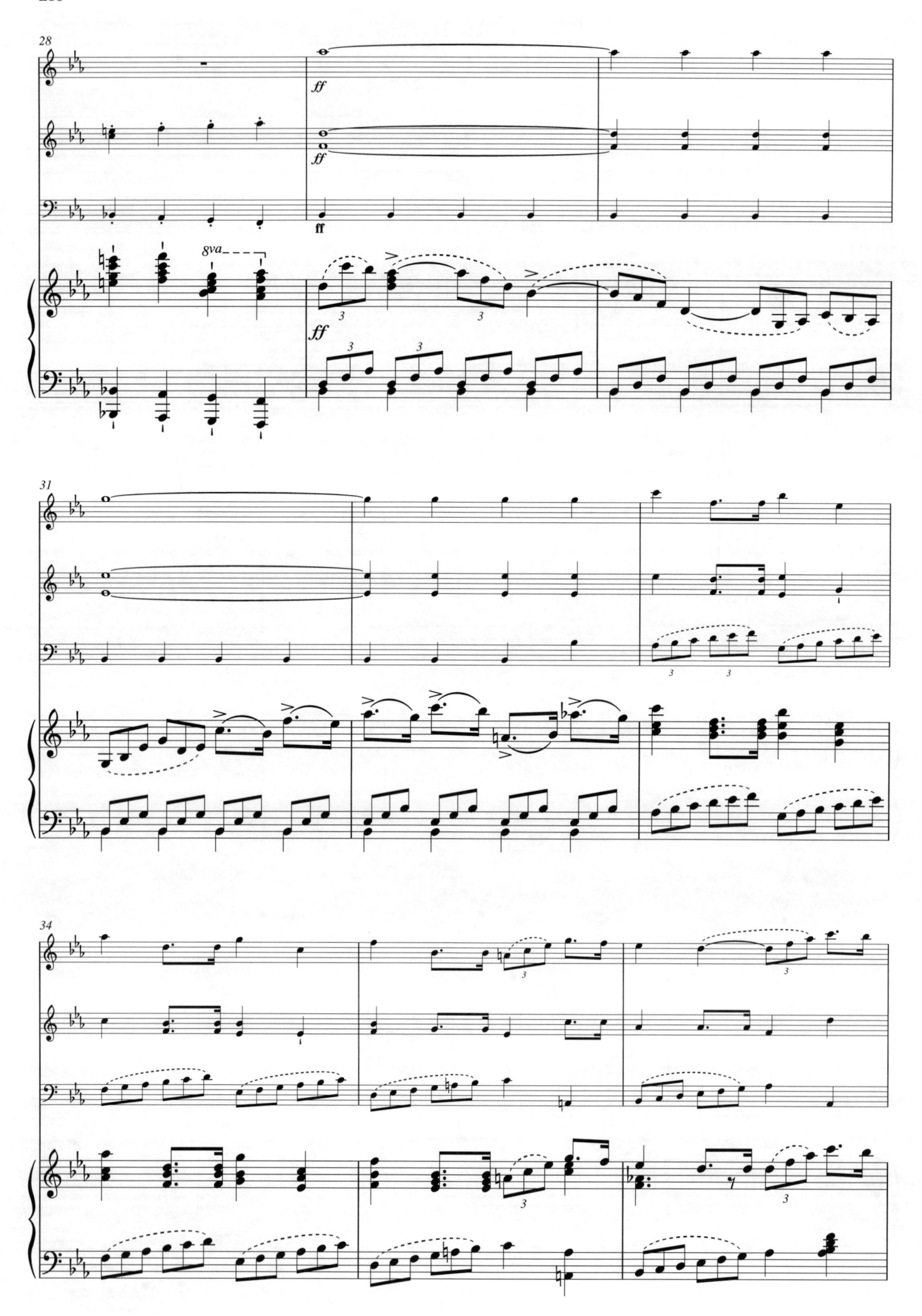
28
ff
ff
ff
8va
ff
31
34

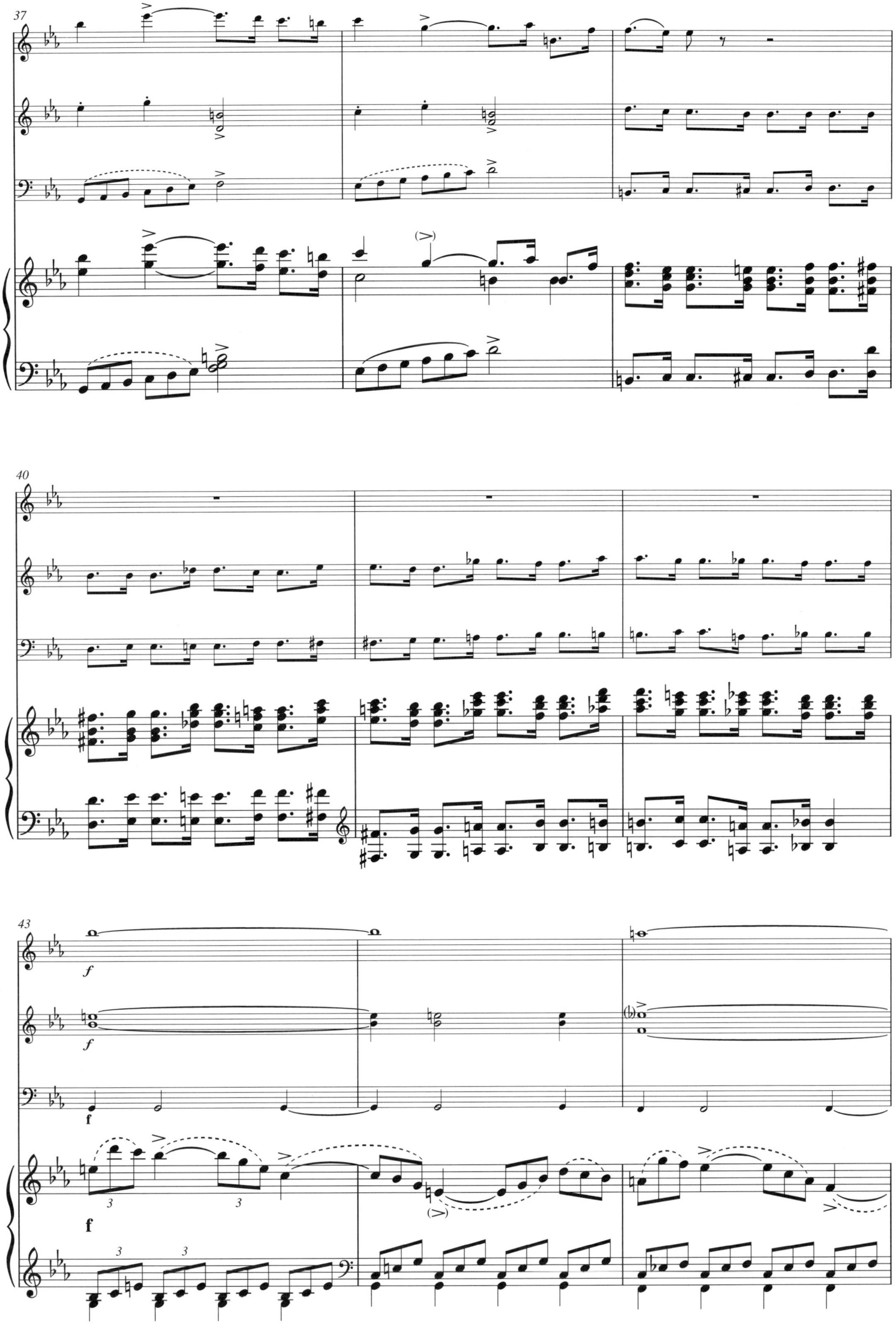
37
40
43

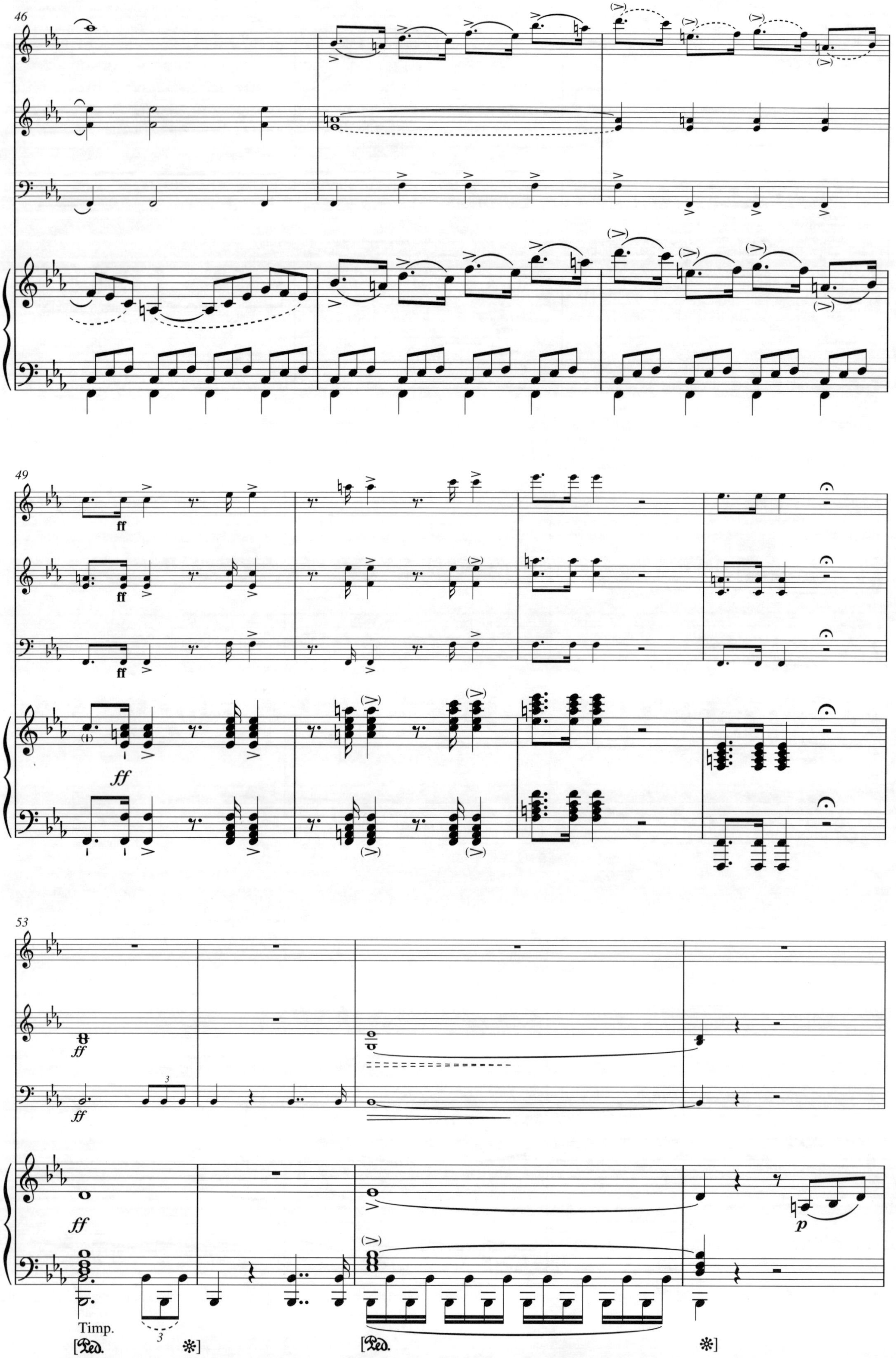
46
49
ff
53
ff
p
Timp.
[Ped.
*]

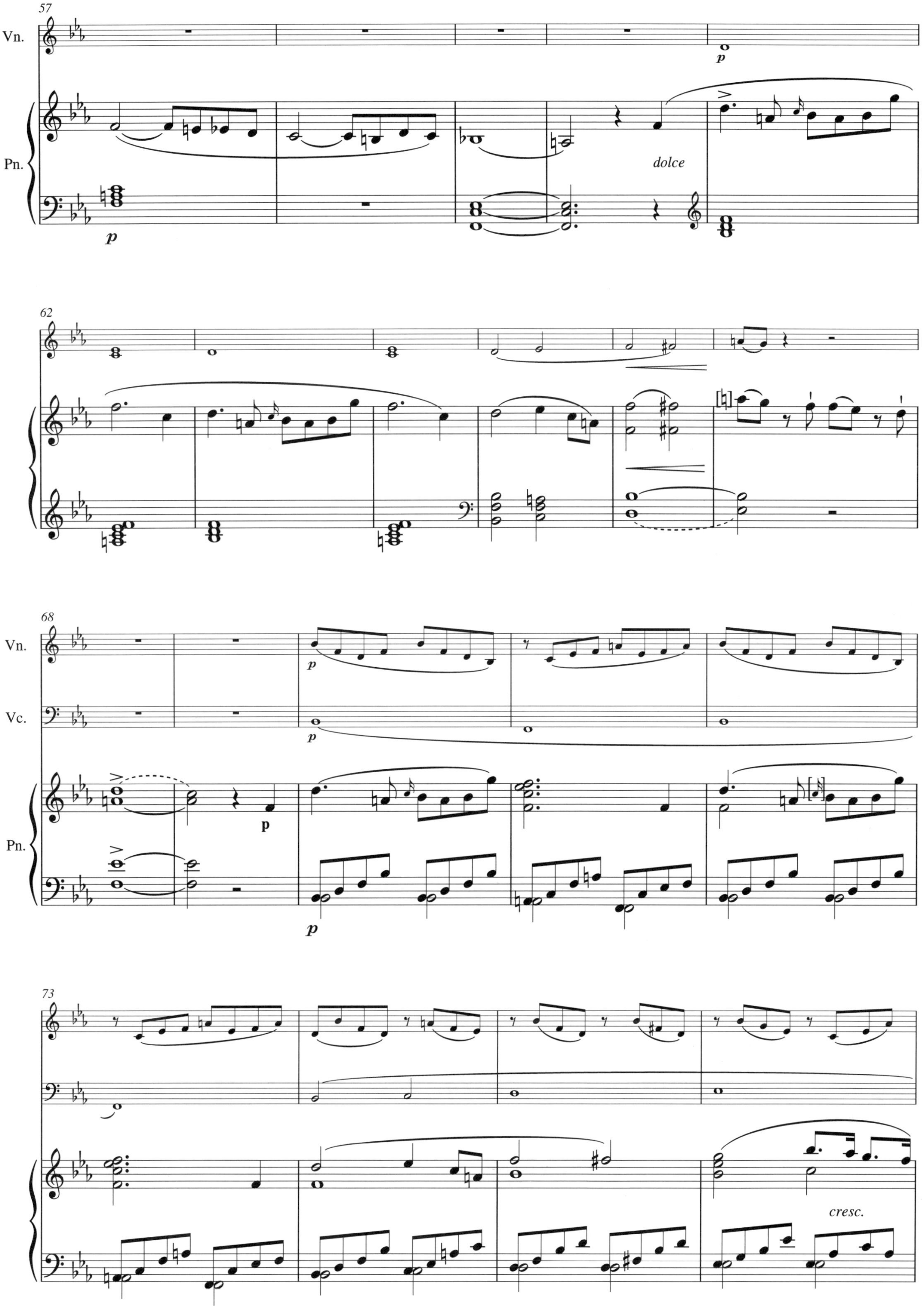
57
Vn.
Pn.
dolce
62
68
Vn.
Vc.
Pn.
73
cresc.

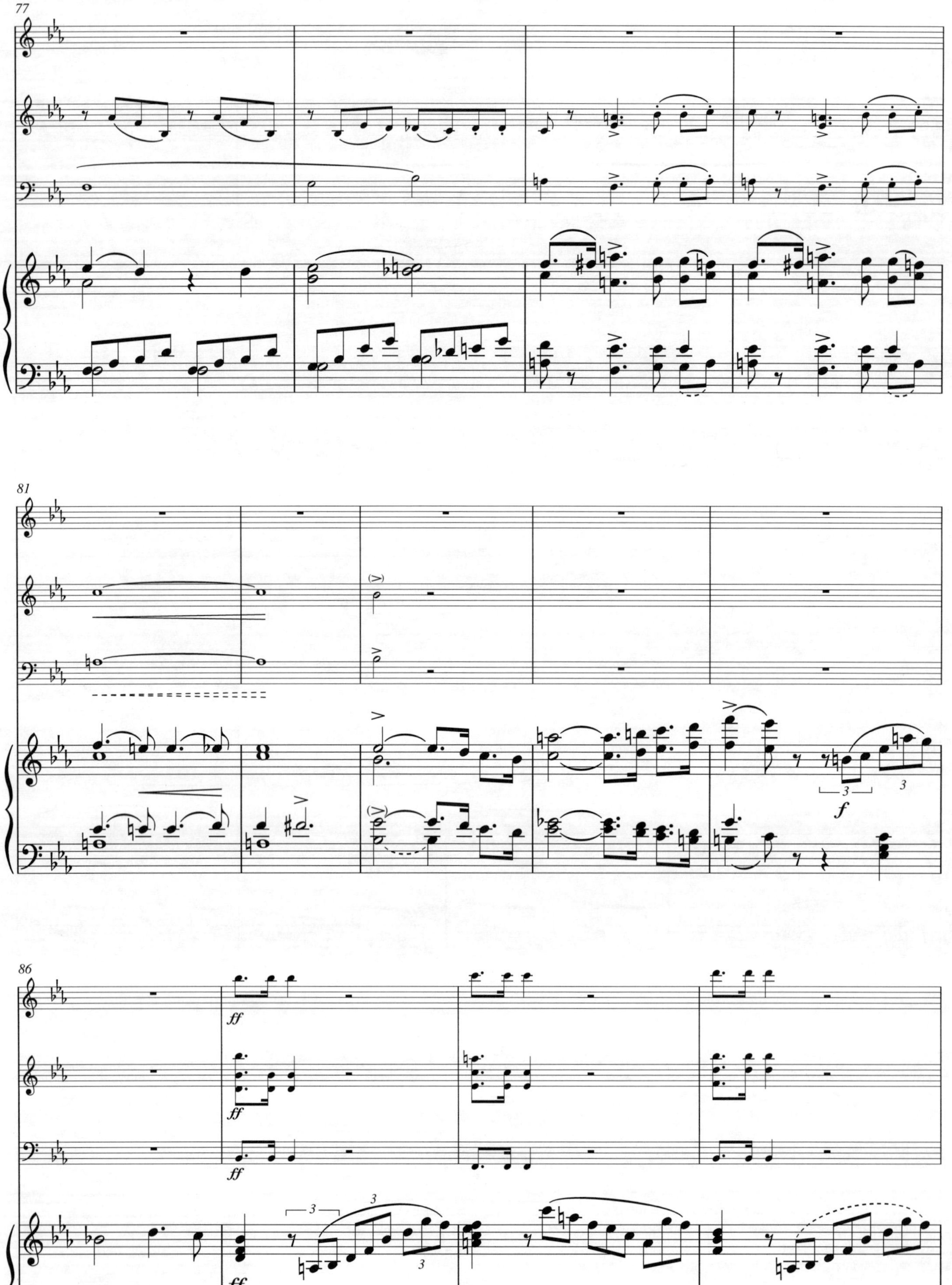
77
Fl.
Vn.
Vc.
Pn.
81
f
86
ff
ff
ff
ff

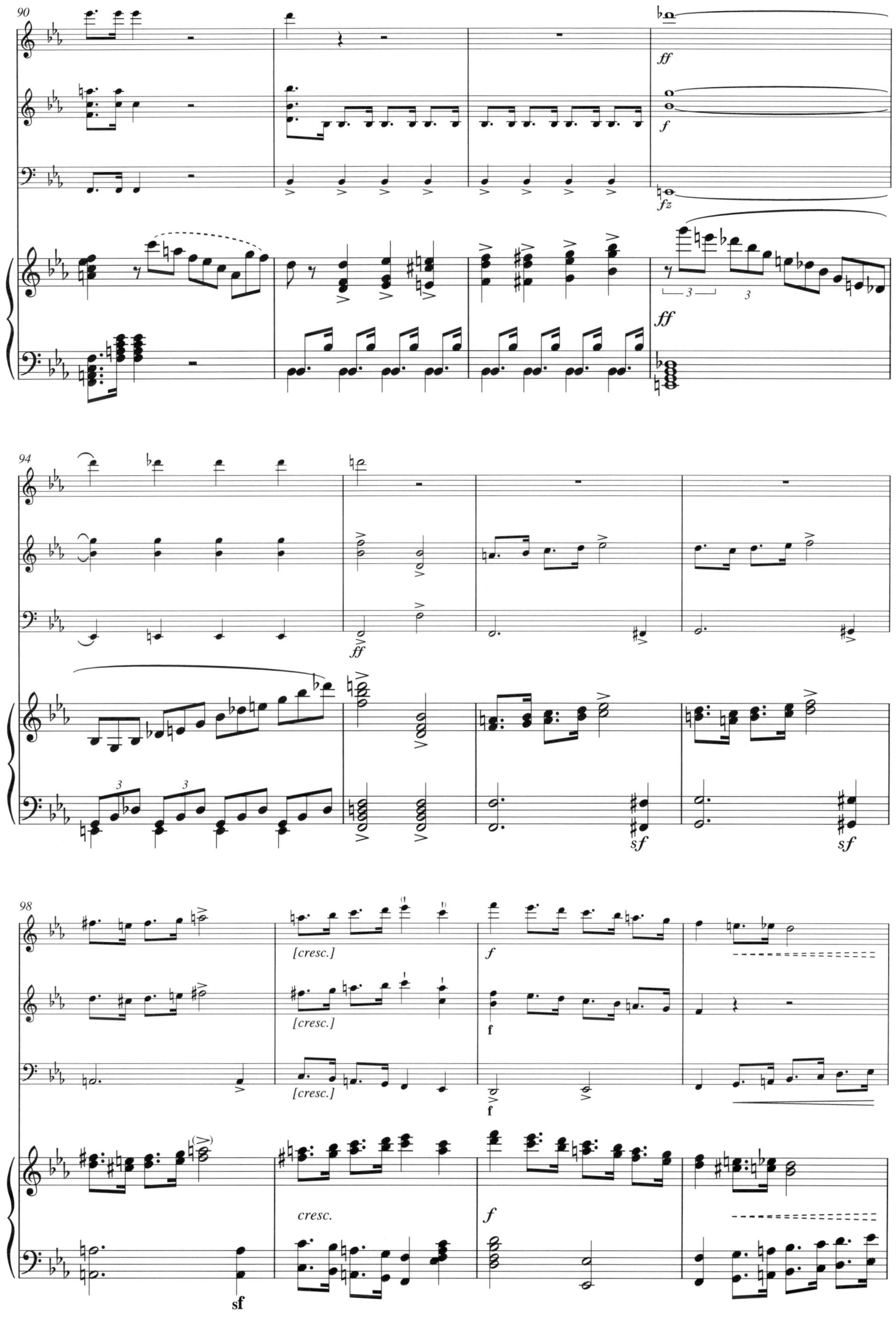
90
ff
f
fz
ff
94
ff
sf
sf
98
[cresc.]
f
[cresc.]
f
[cresc.]
f
sf
cresc.
f

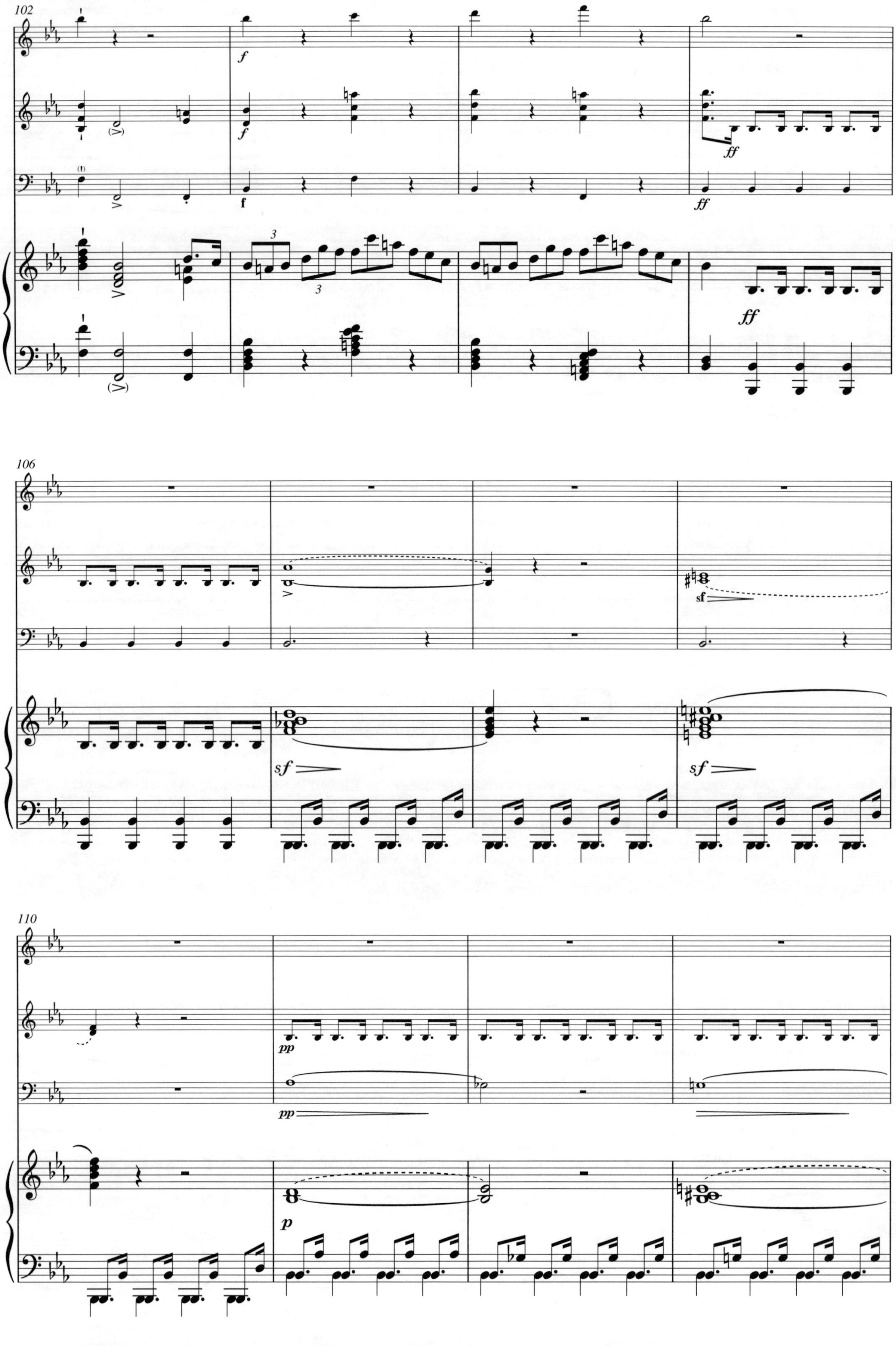
102
106
110

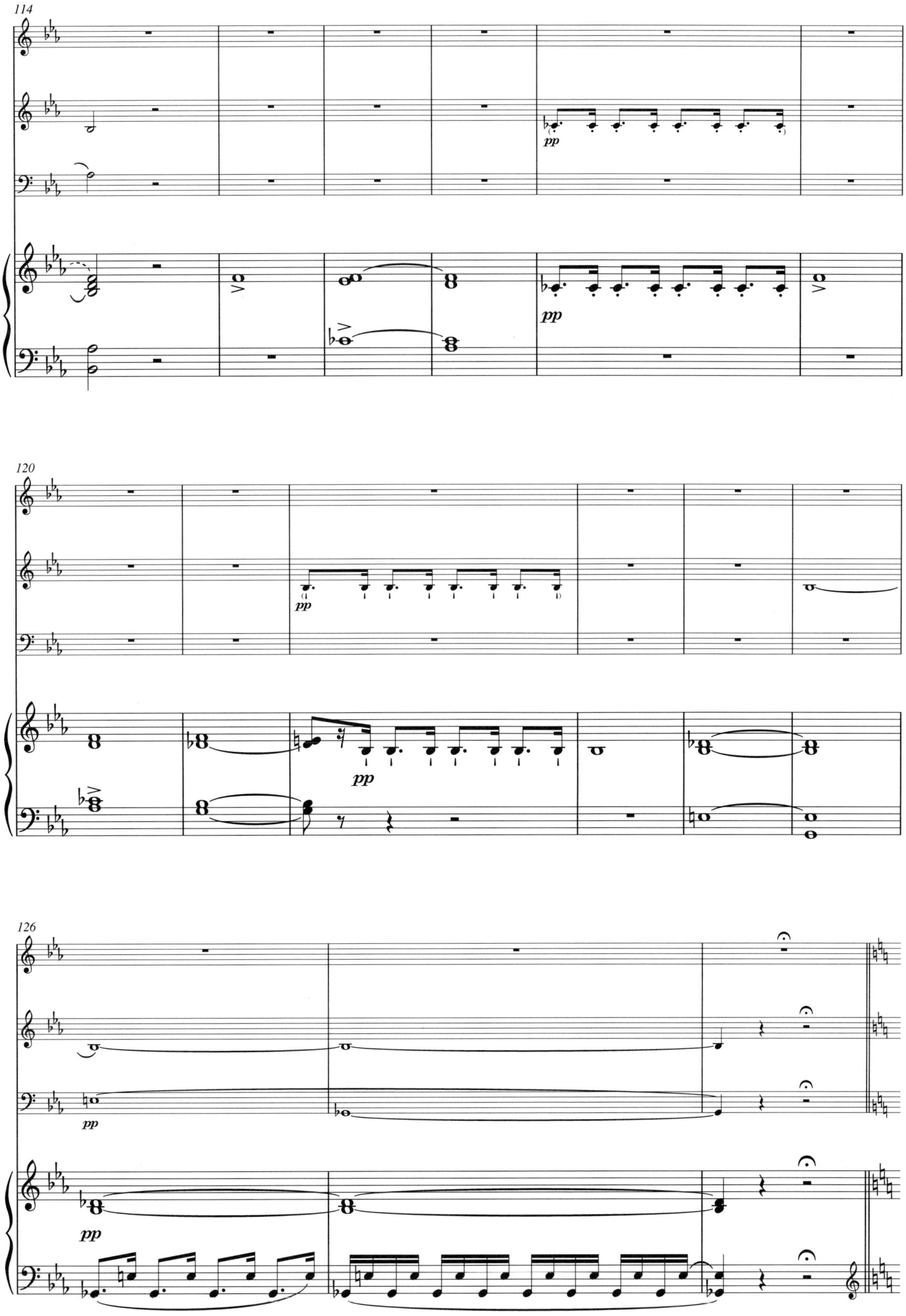
114
pp
pp
120
pp
pp
126
pp
pp

224

139
pp
pp
p
142
Tempo 1 assai moderato
pp
Tempo 1 assai moderato
p
147
3
3
3

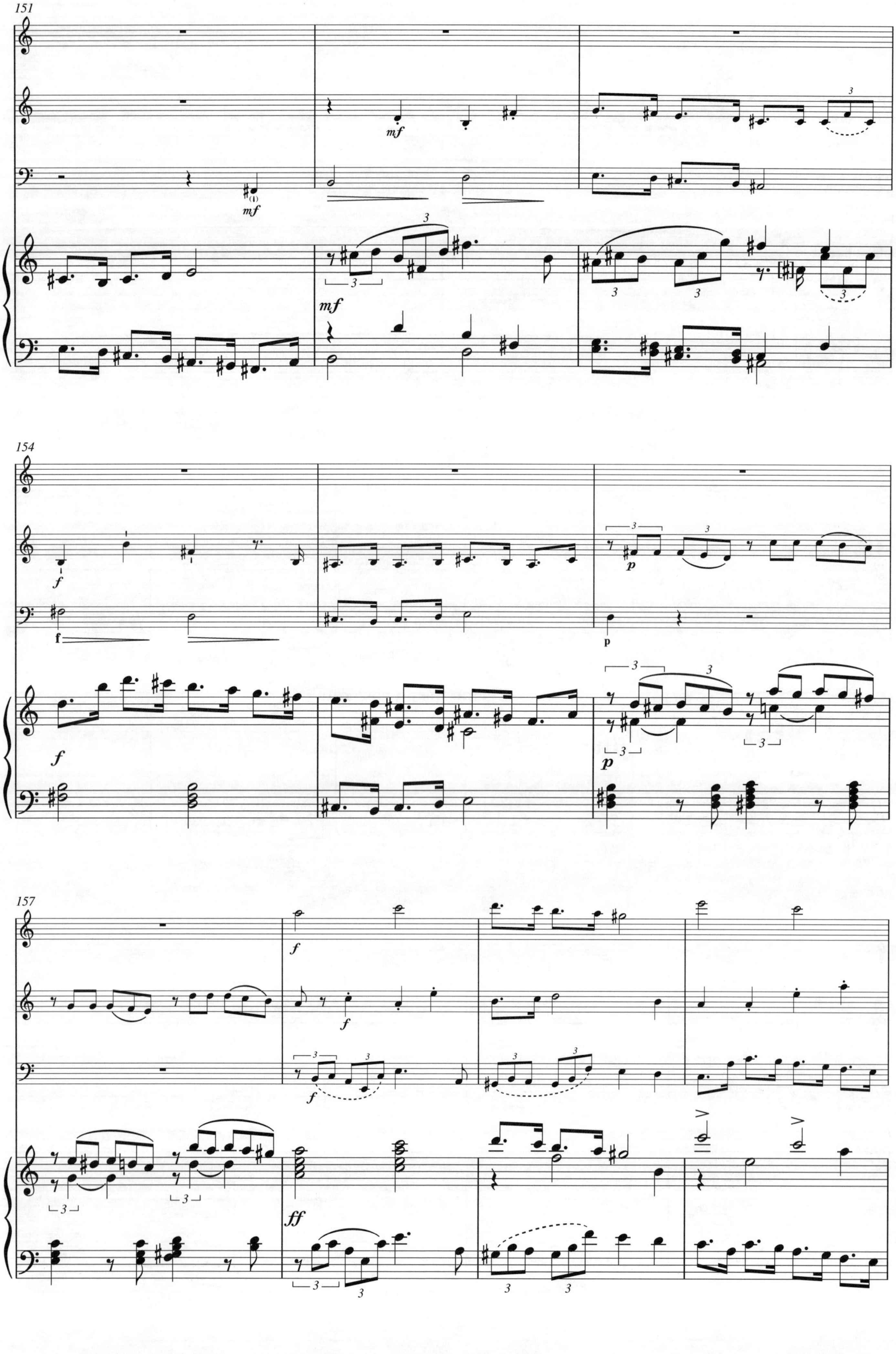
151
mf
mf
mf
154
f
f
f
p
p
p
157
f
f
f
ff

227

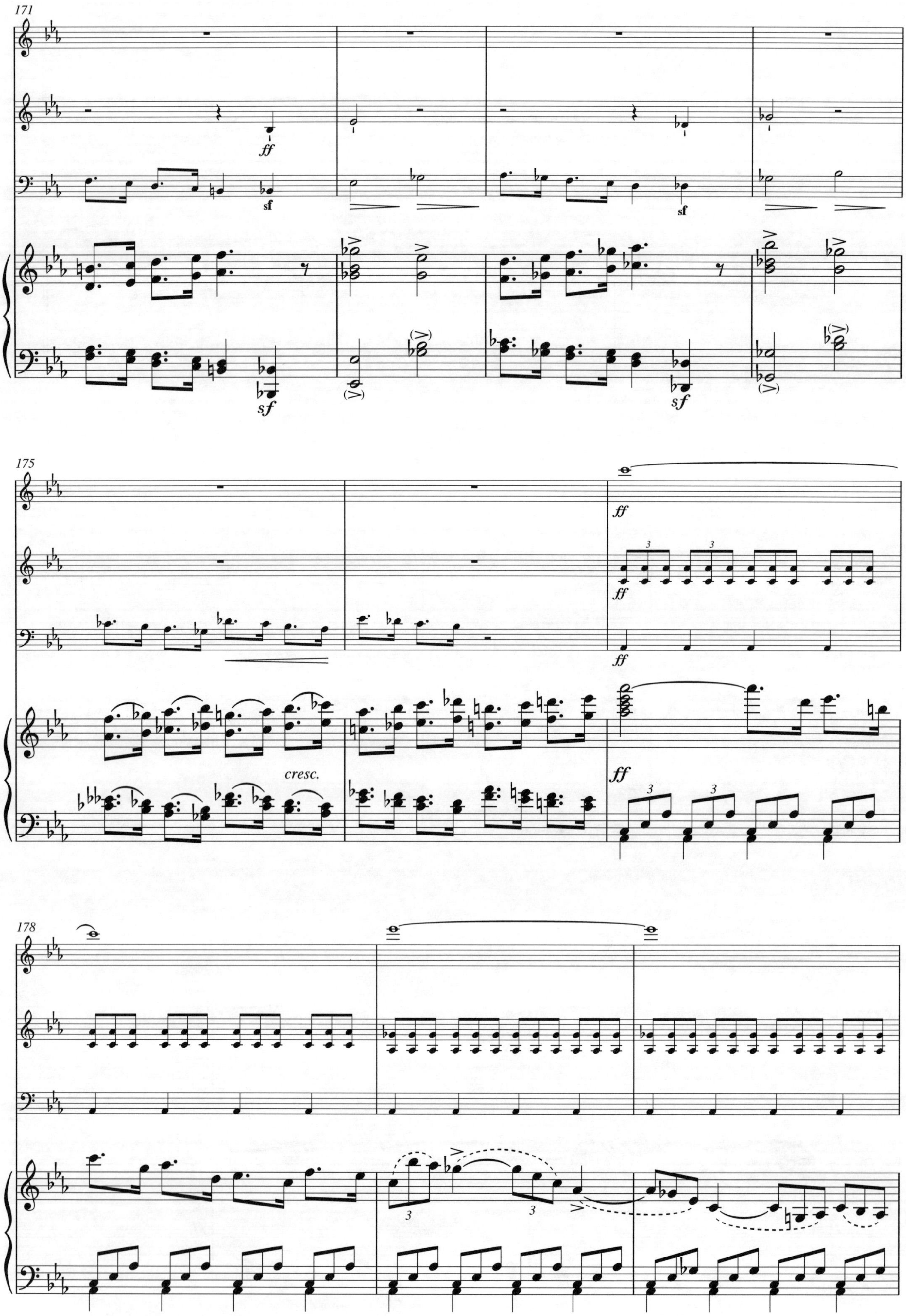
171
ff
sf
sf
sf
sf
175
ff
ff
ff
cresc.
ff
178
3
3

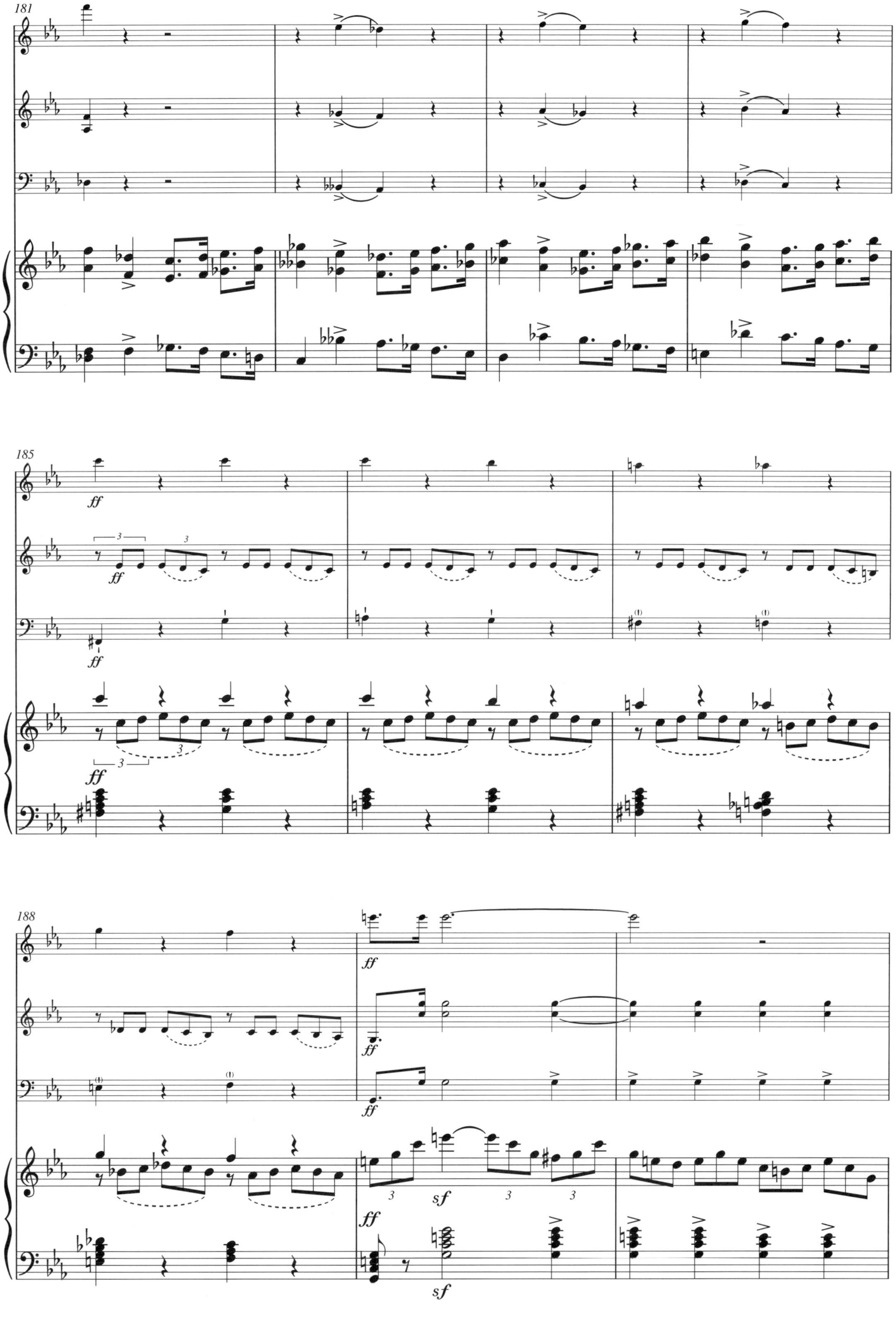
181
185
ff
188
sf

191
sf
sf
194
p
197
ff
ff
ff
ff
[accelerando]
accelerando
accelerando
accelerando
ff più mosso sf
ff più mosso sf
ff [più mosso]
sf
ff più mosso
sf

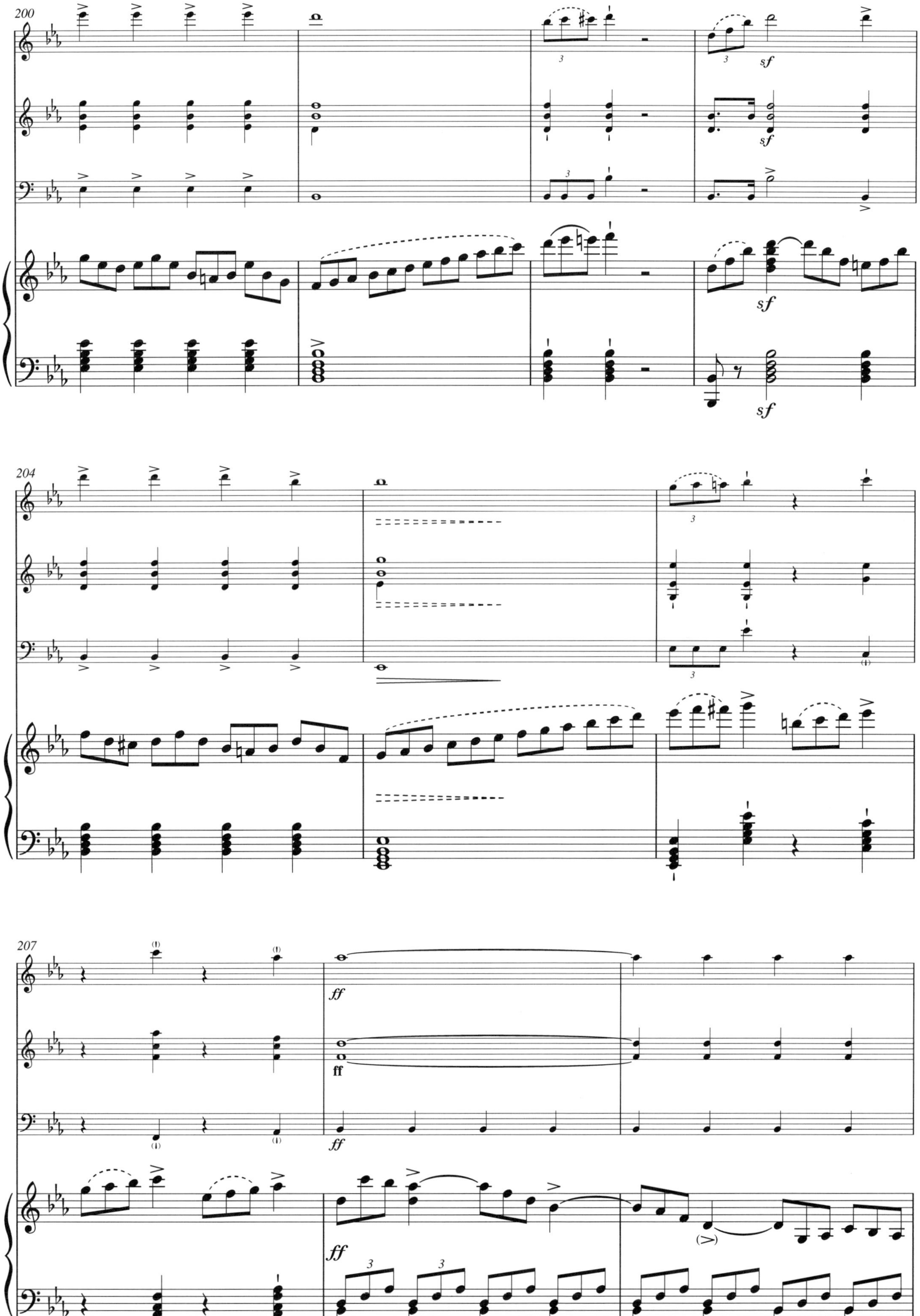
200
sf
204
207
ff

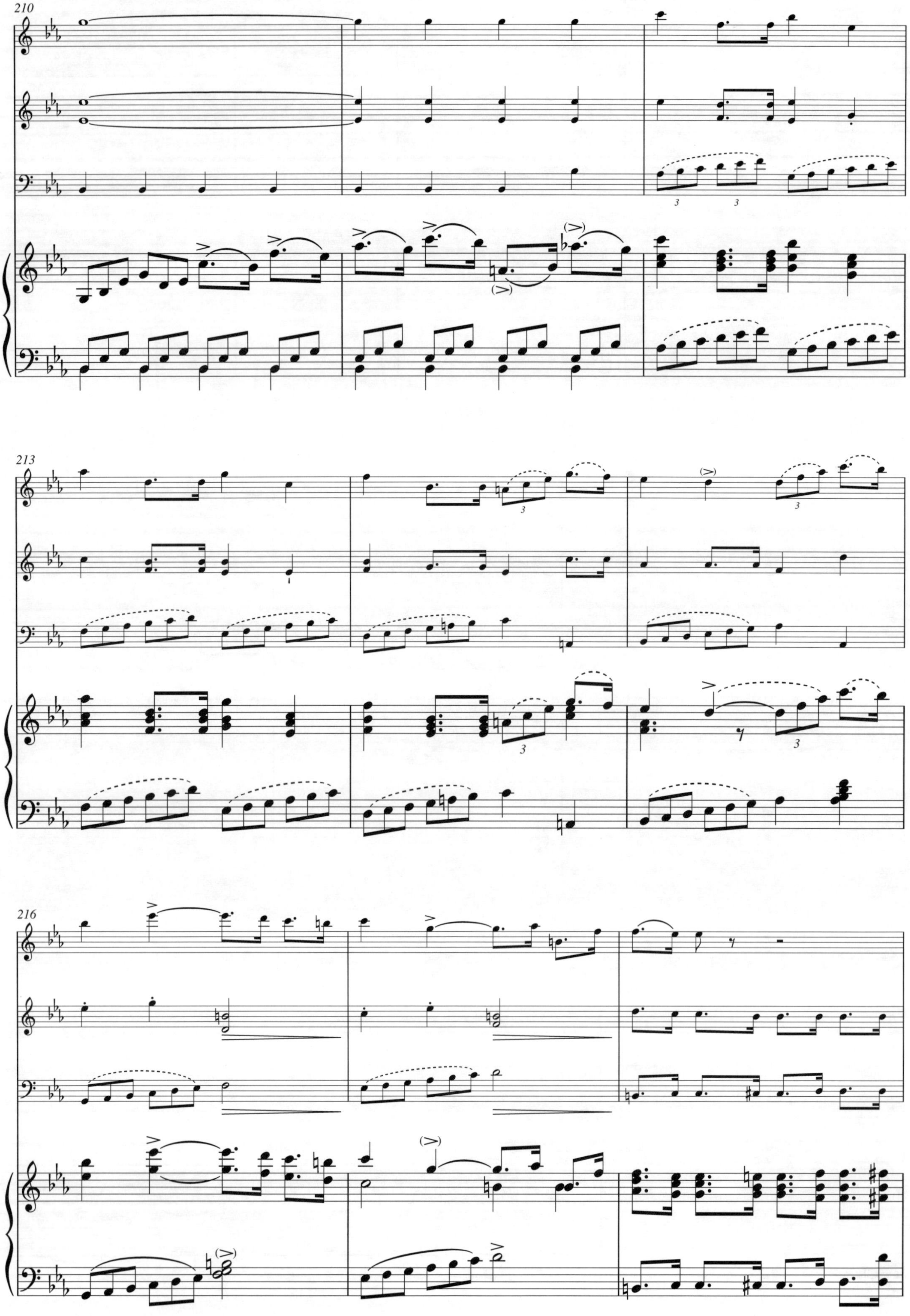

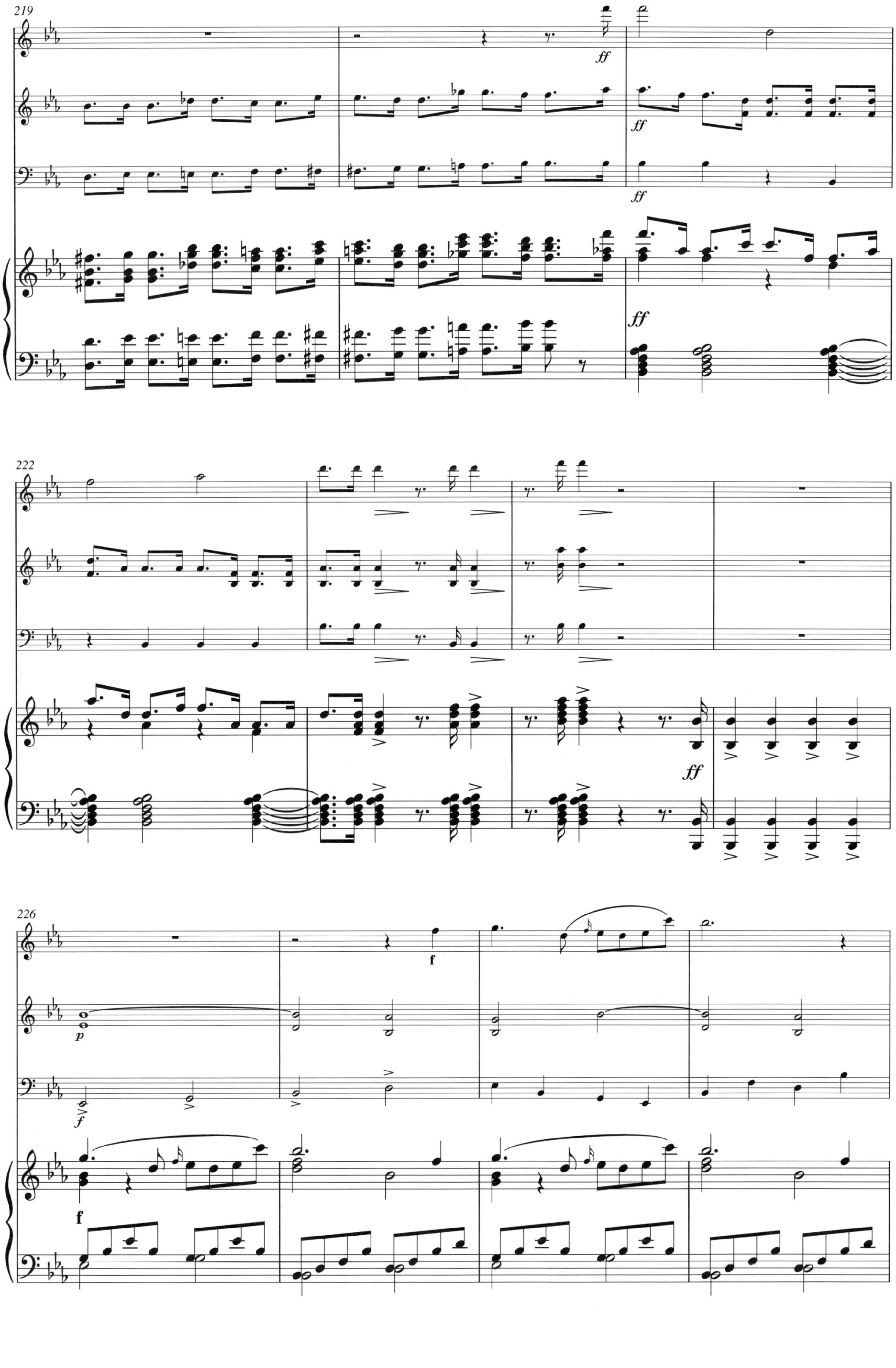
219
ff
ff
ff
ff
222
ff
226
f
p
f
f

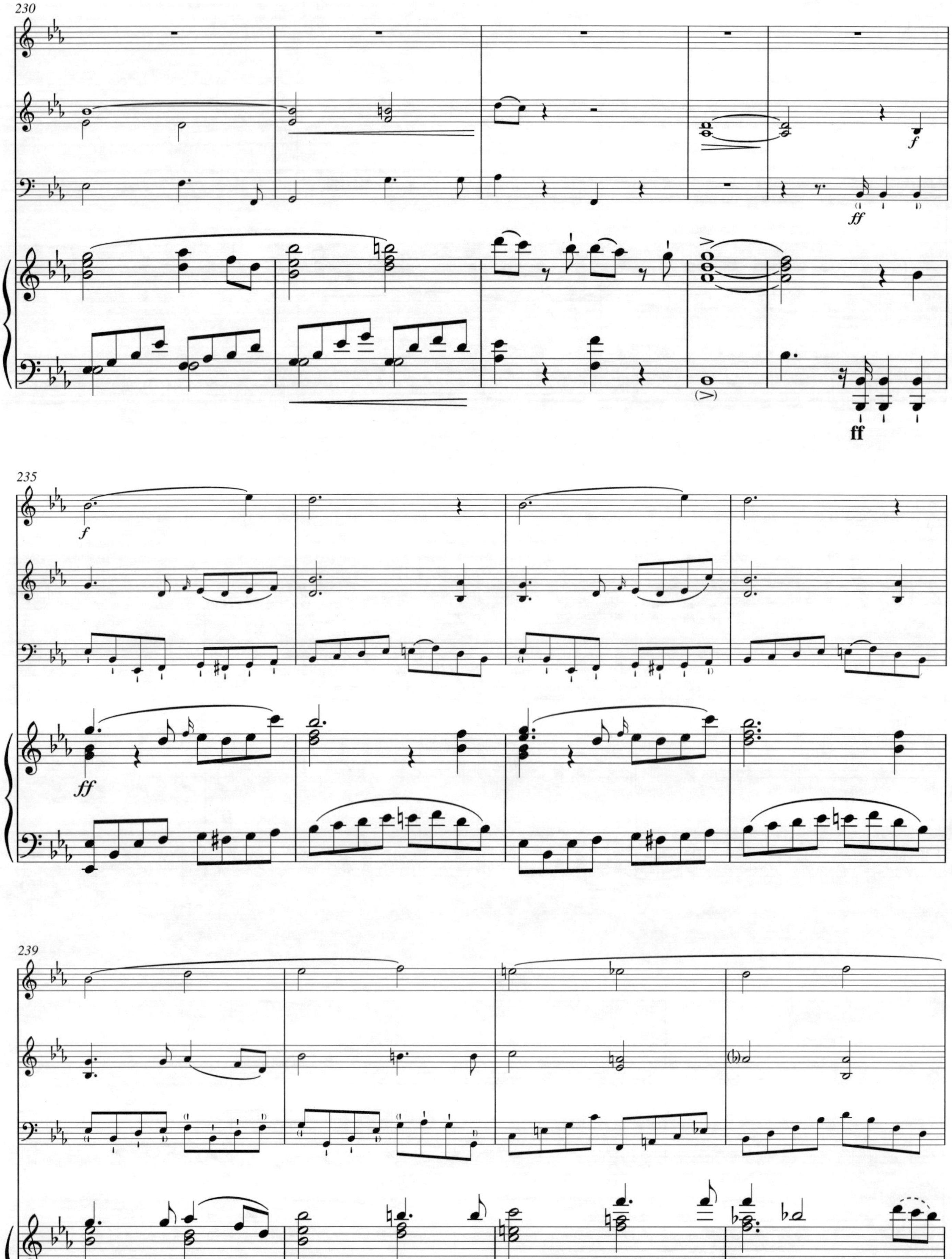

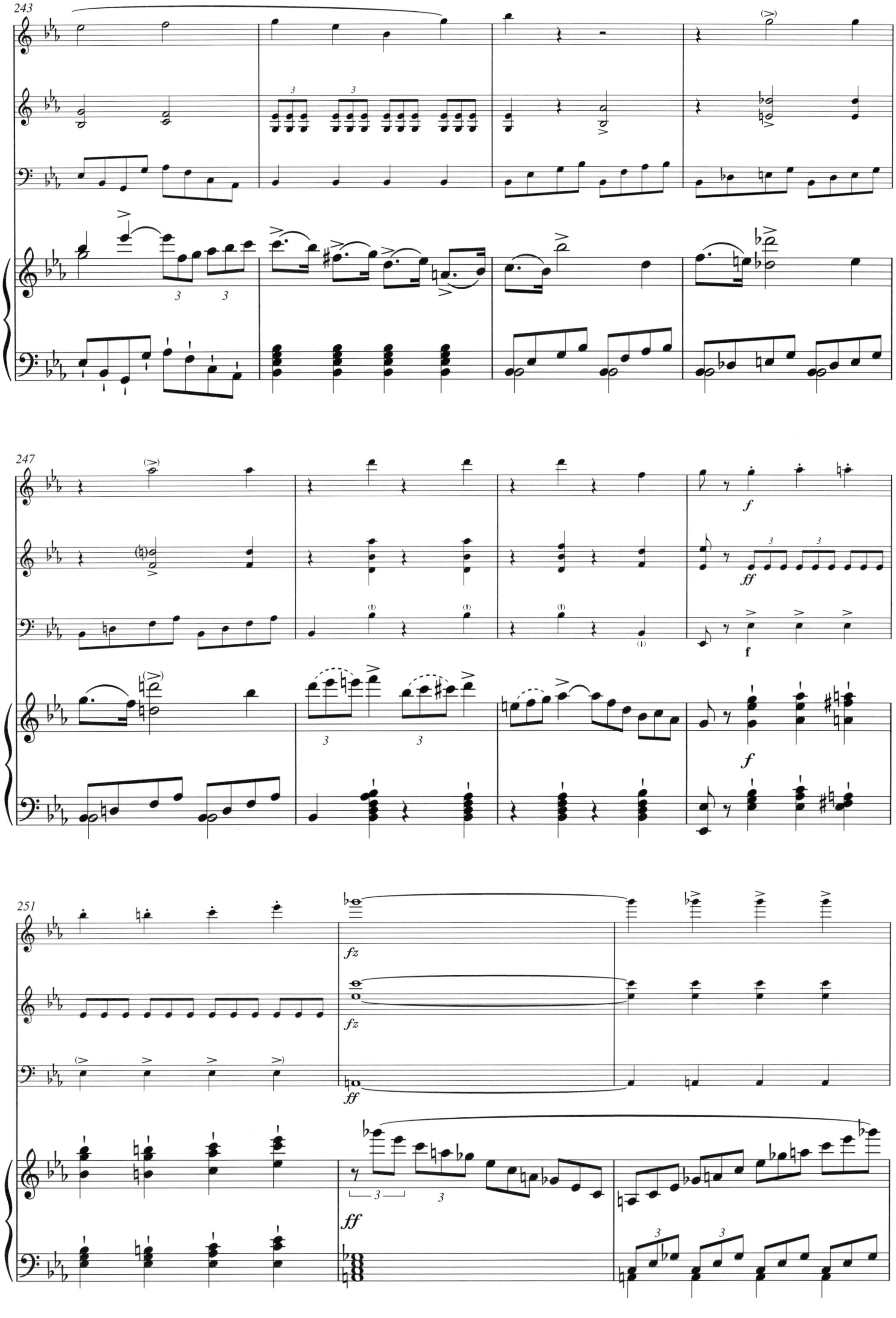
243
247
f
ff
f
f
251
fz
fz
ff
ff

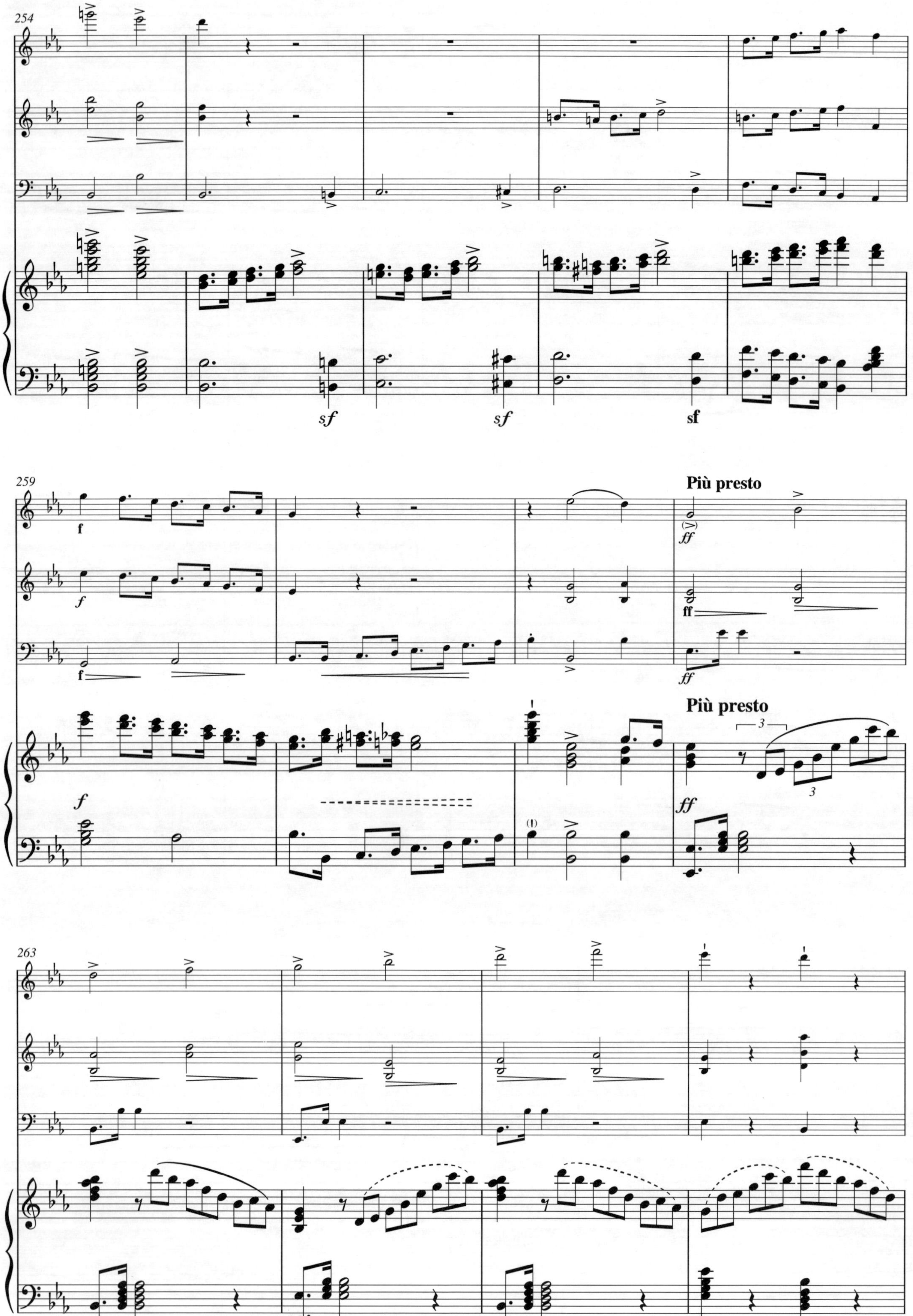
254
sf
sf
sf
259
f
f
f
f
Più presto
ff
ff
ff
Più presto
ff
263

237

11. Overture to Tancredi

Gioachino Rossini

239

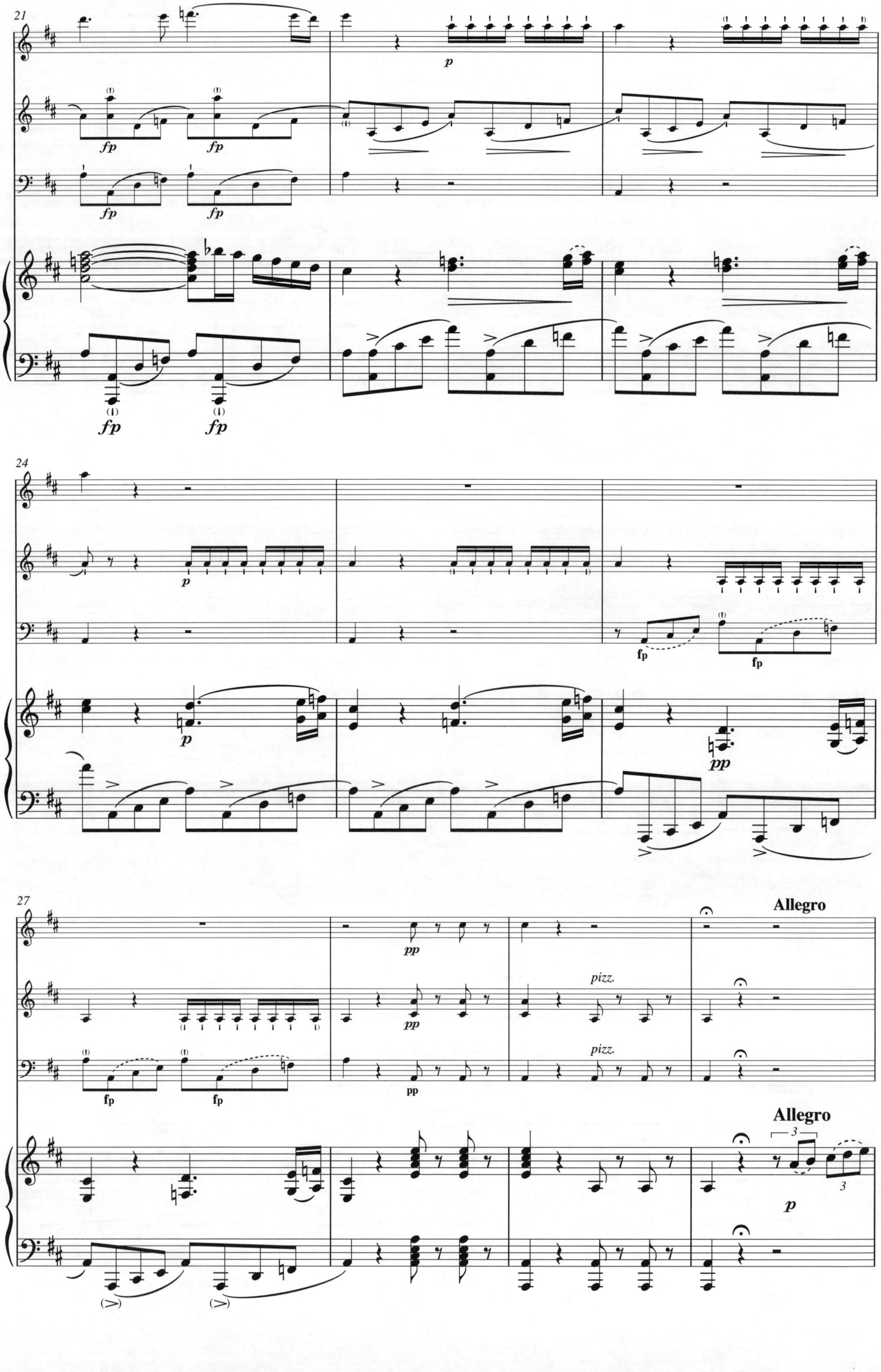
21
24
27
Allegro
pizz.
pizz.
Allegro

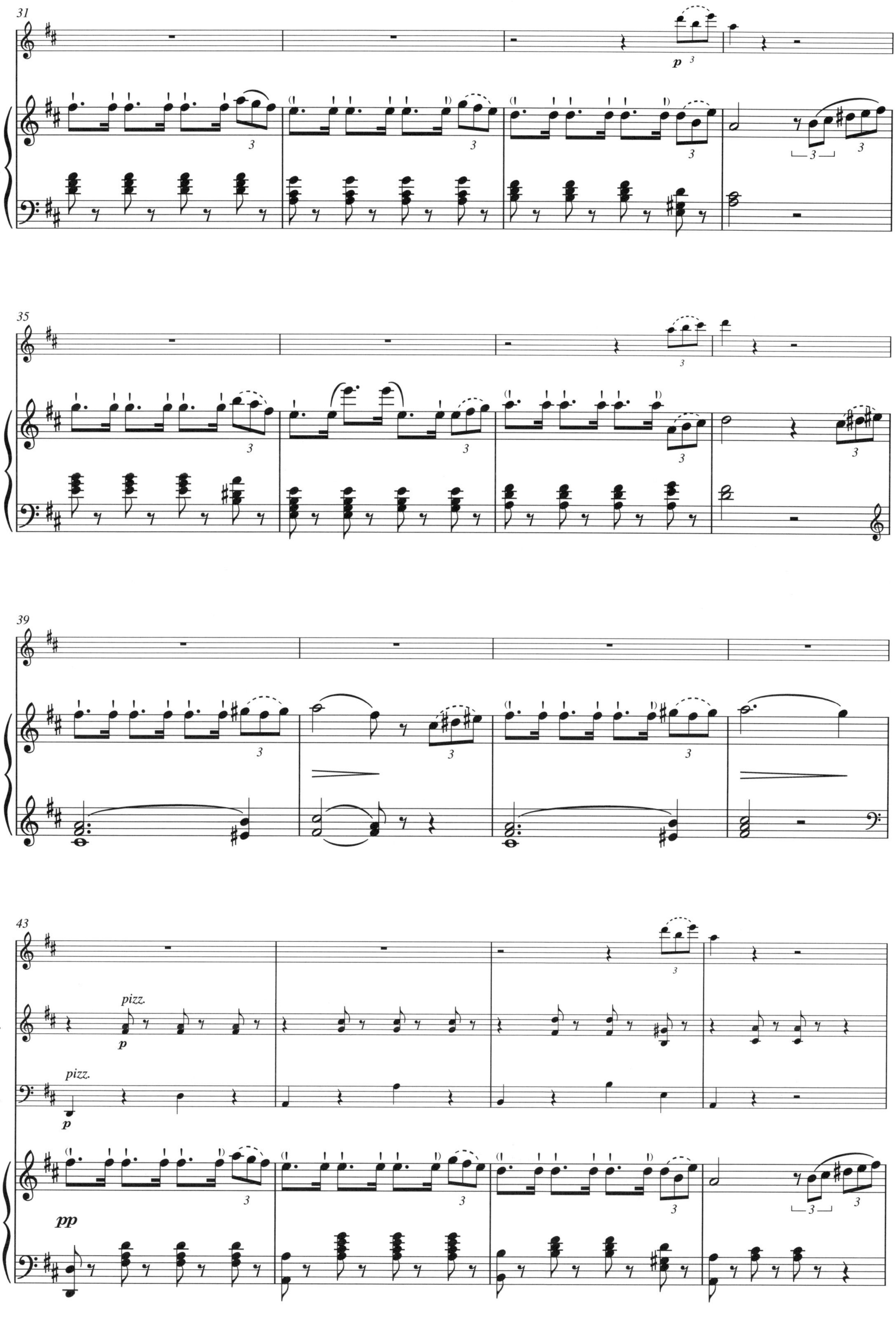
31
Fl.
p
Pn.
35
39
43
Fl.
Vn.
pizz.
p
Vc.
pizz.
p
Pn.
pp

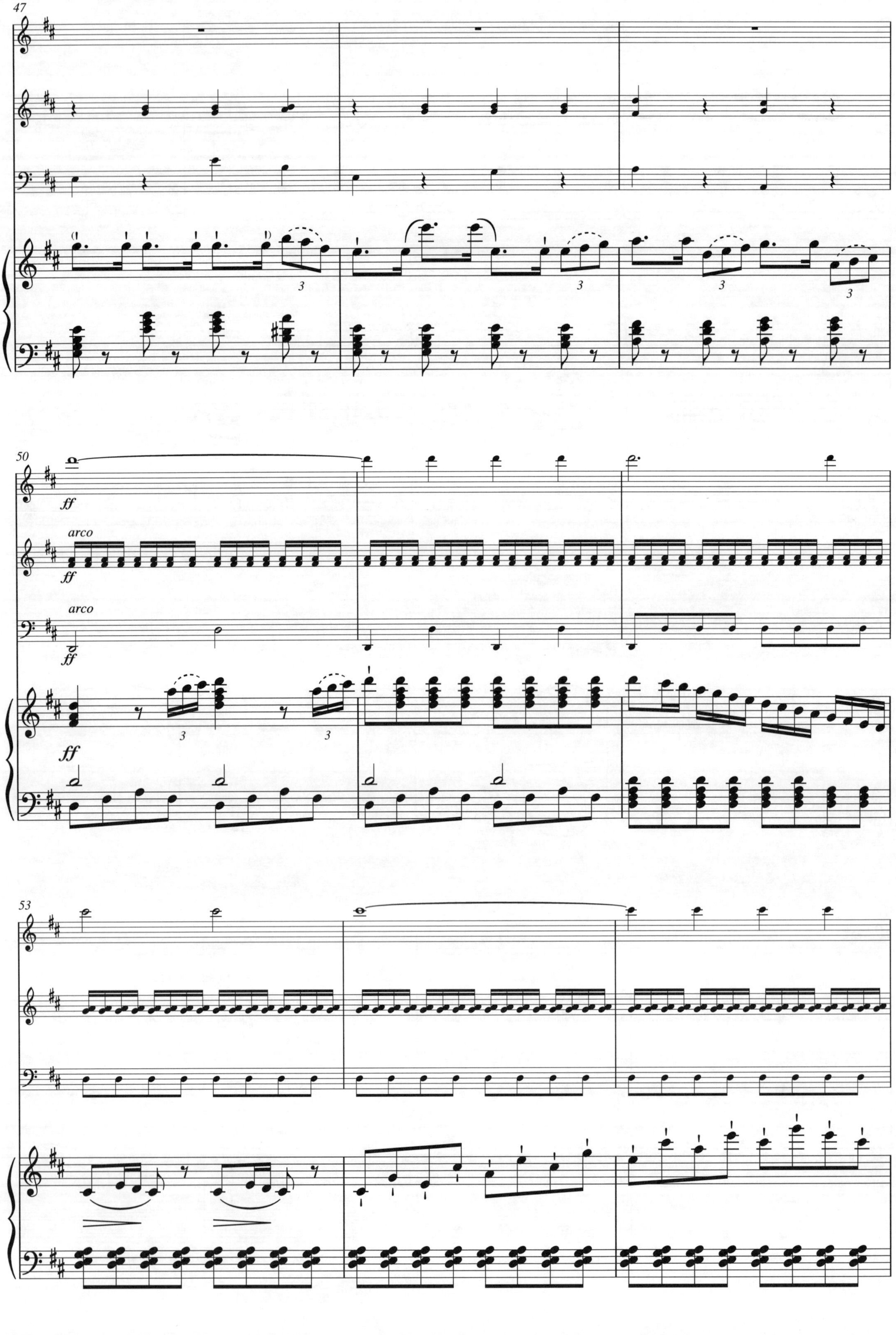
47
50
ff
arco
ff
arco
ff
ff
53

243

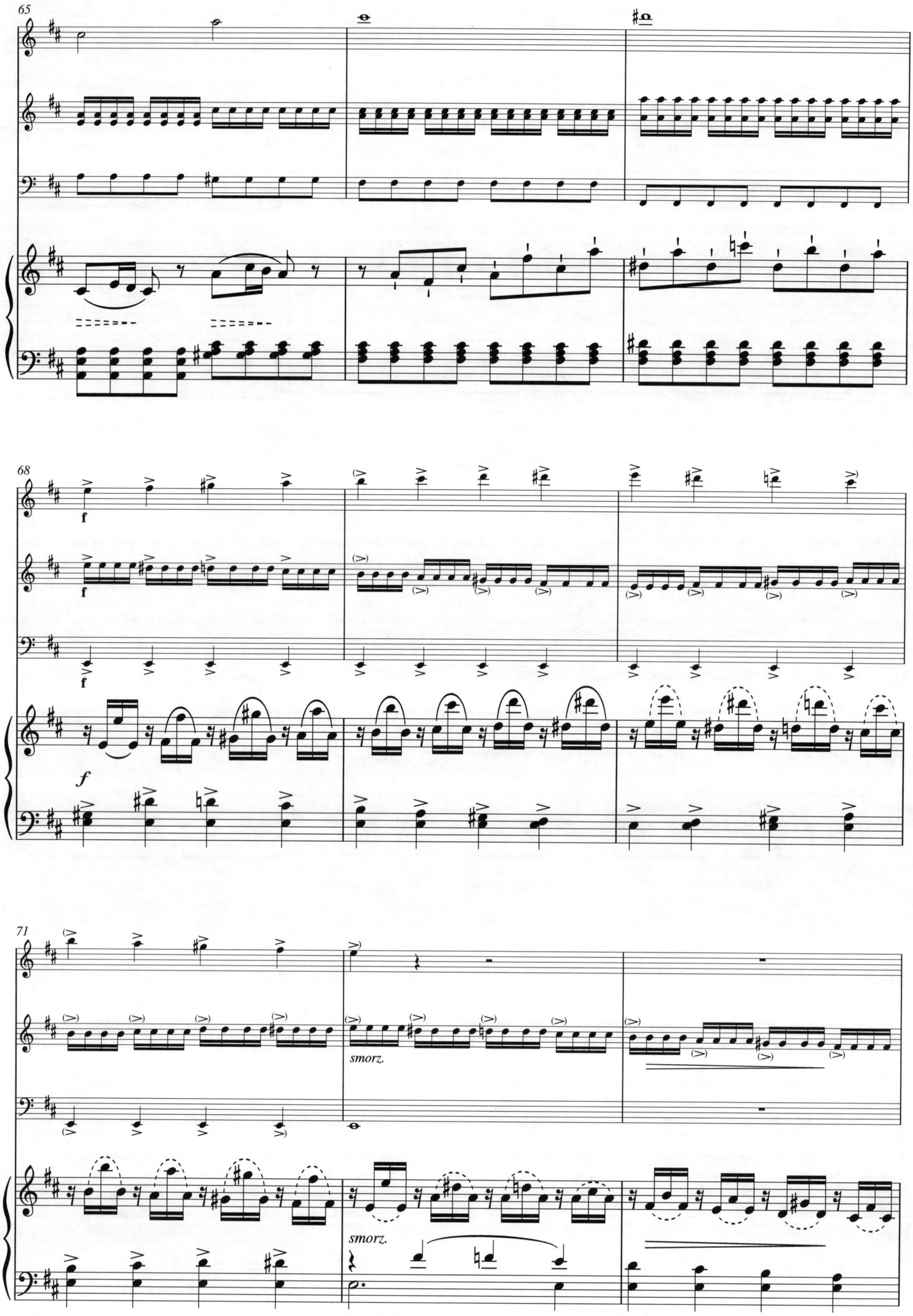
65
68
f
f
f
f
71
smorz.
smorz.

245

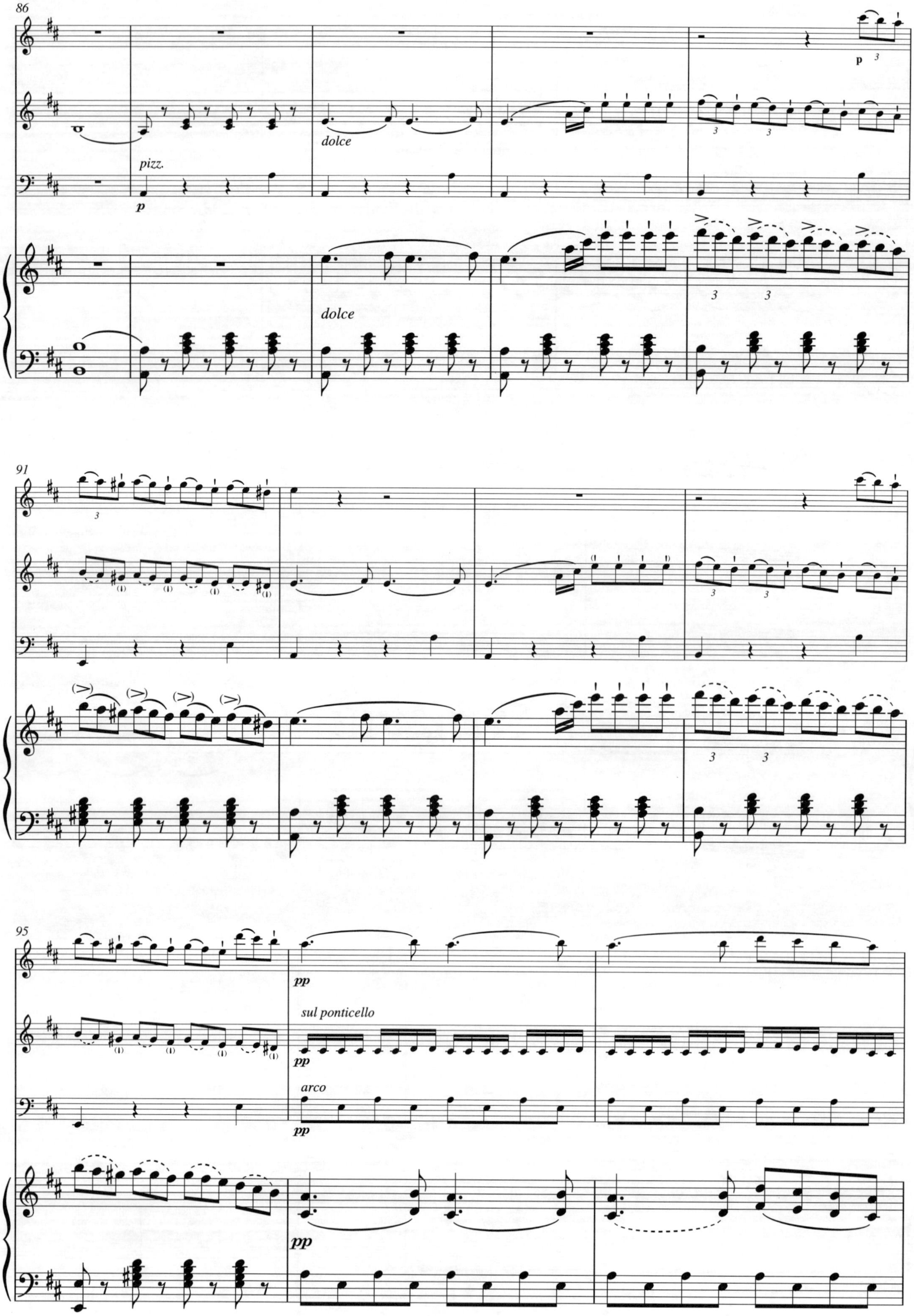
86
pizz.
p
dolce
dolce
p
91
95
pp
sul ponticello
pp
arco
pp
pp

98
cre
scen
cre
cresc.
101
do
poco
a
poco
scen
do
poco
a
poco
104
cre
scen
do
al
poco
a
poco
cresc.

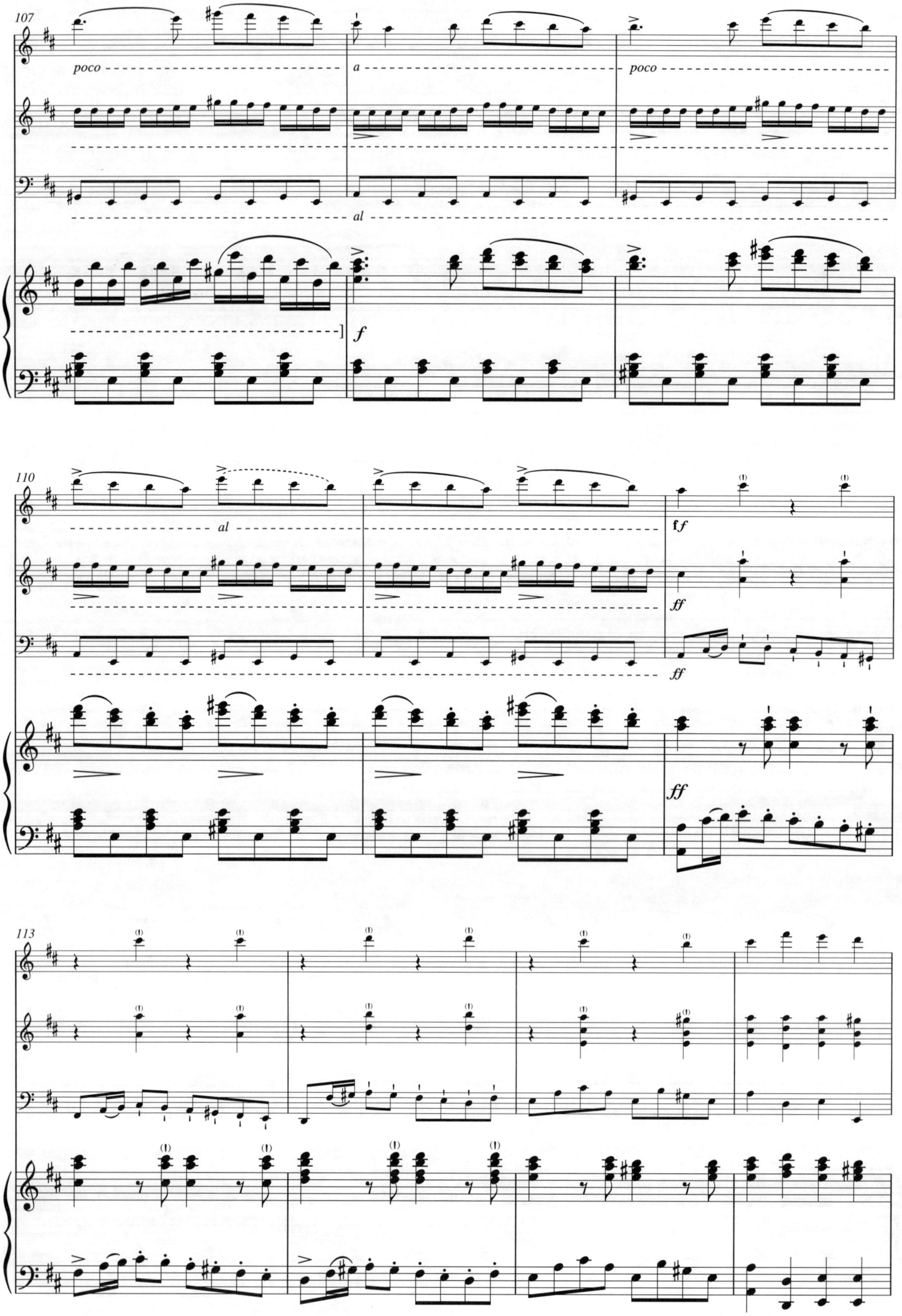
107
poco
a
poco
al
f
110
al
ff
ff
ff
ff
113

249

133
Fl.
Vn.
Vc.
Pn.
dolce
pizz.
p
pizz.
p
dolce
pp
137
8va
141
pp
arco [sul] ponticello
pp
arco
pp
pp

144
cre
cresc. [
147
scen
do
al
cre
scen
do
] poco [
] a [
] poco
150
cre-
scen
do
poco
a
poco
al

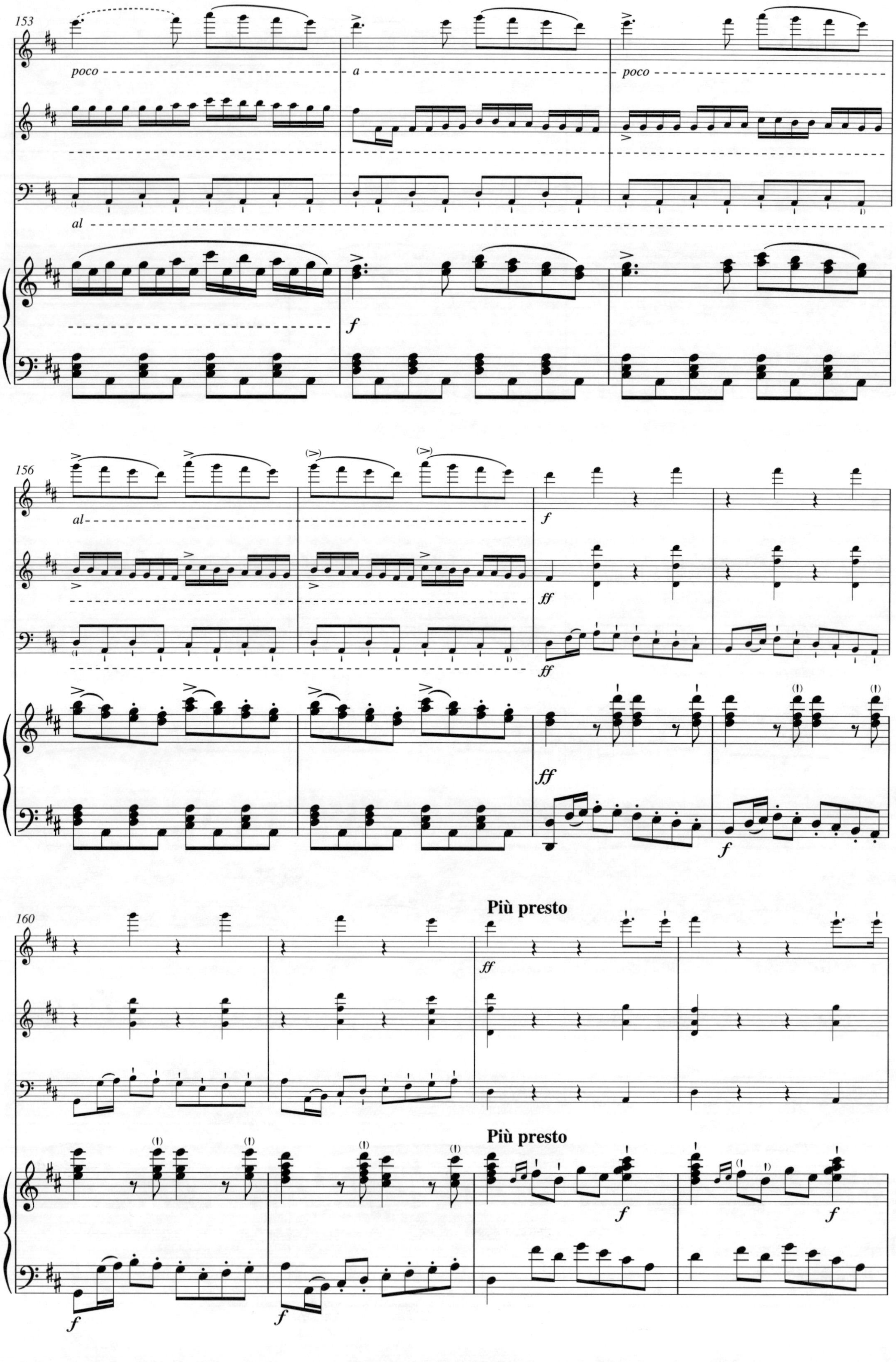
153
poco
a
poco
al
156
al
160
Più presto
Più presto

253

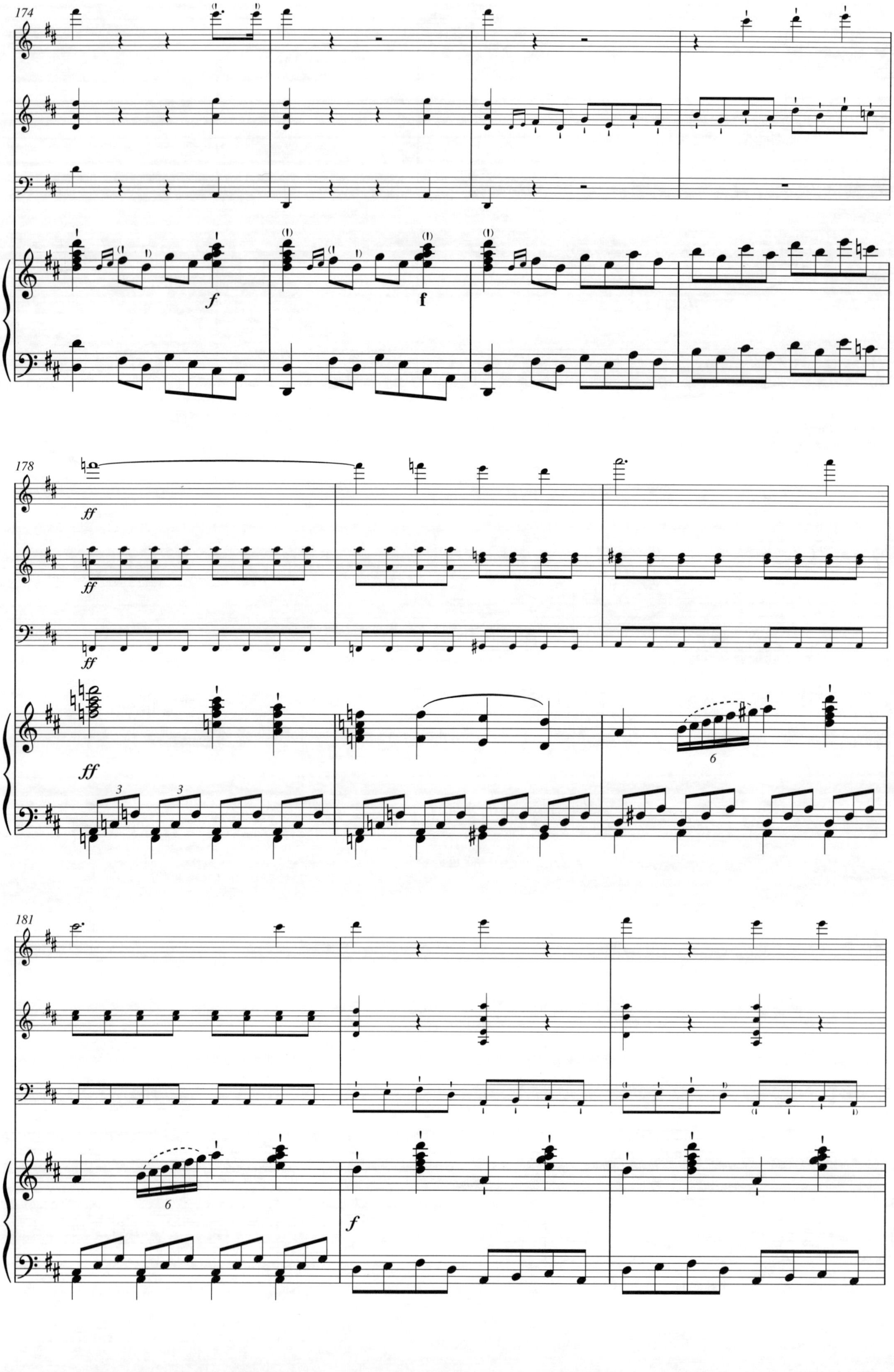
174
178
181

255

12. Overture to Anacreon

Luigi Cherubini

18
pp
pp
22
ppp
ppp
pp
rallentando
26
ff
ff
ff
ff
tremolo
pp sempre
pp sempre
[Ped.
*]

258

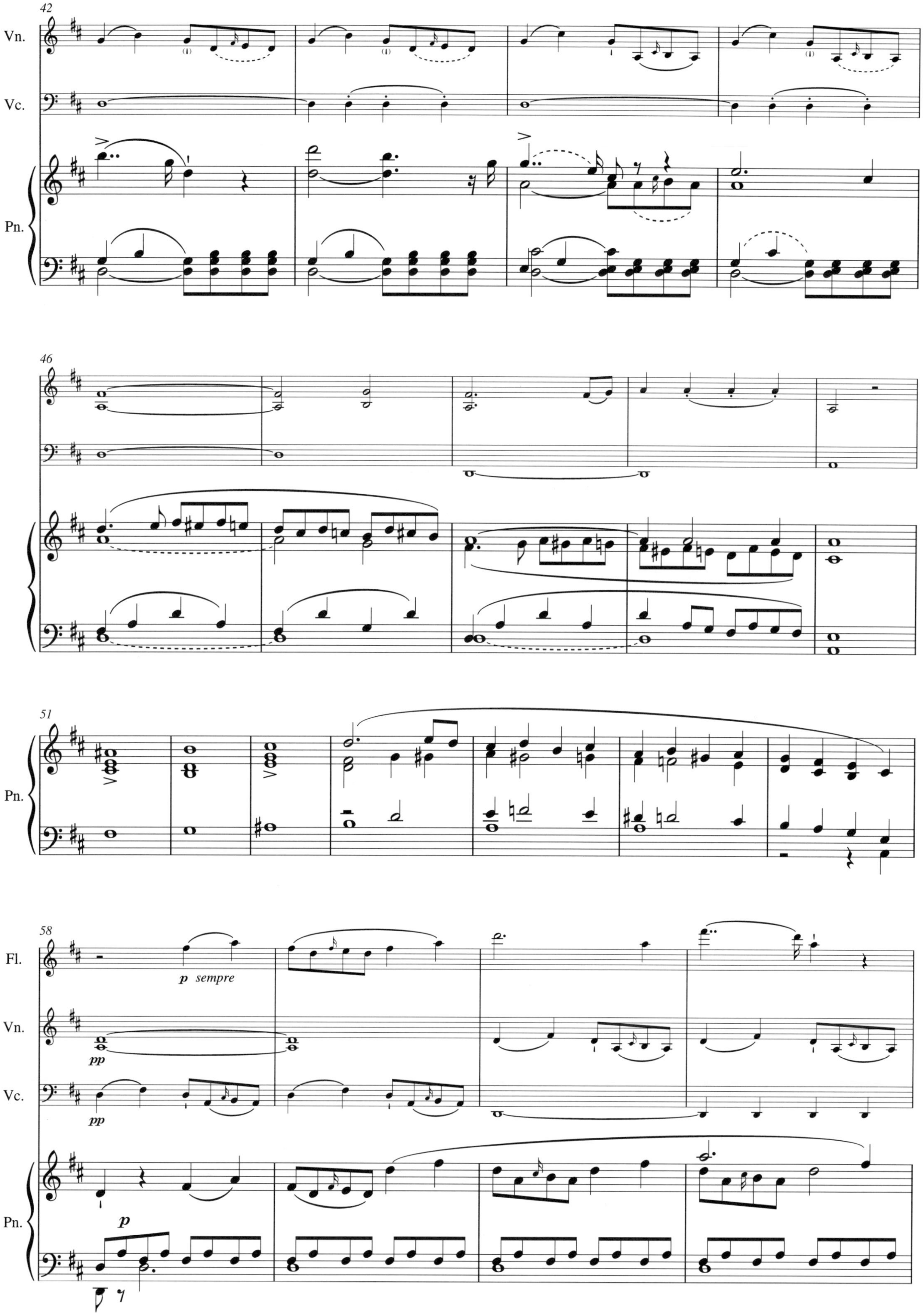
42
Vn.
Vc.
Pn.
46
51
Pn.
58
Fl.
p sempre
Vn.
pp
Vc.
pp
Pn.
p

260

74
tr
cresc.
78
(tr)
cre
scendo
poco [
]
a [
]
82
poco
a
poco
cre
scen
do
poco
a
al [
poco
sempre
di
più

262

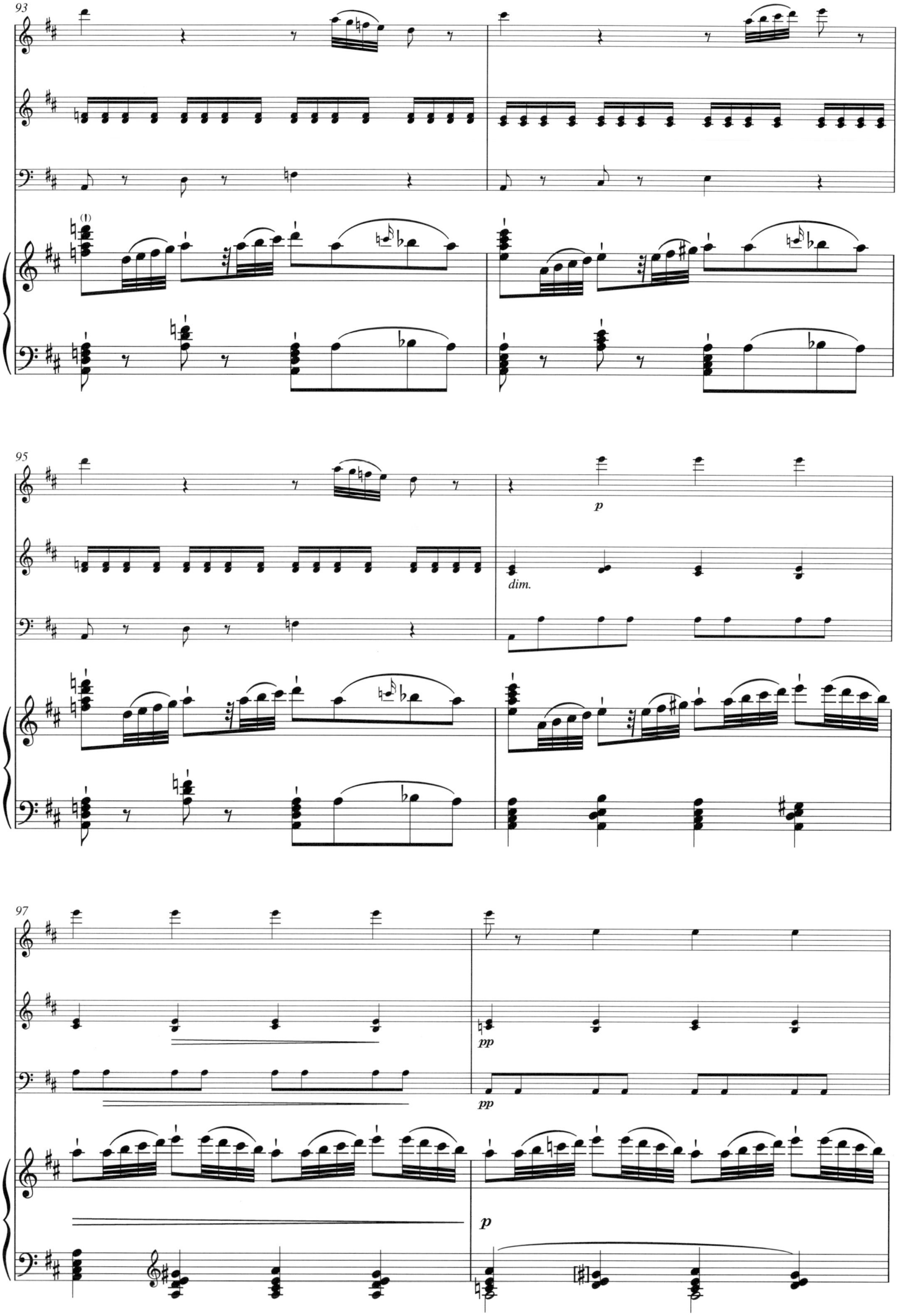
93
95
p
dim.
97
pp
pp
p

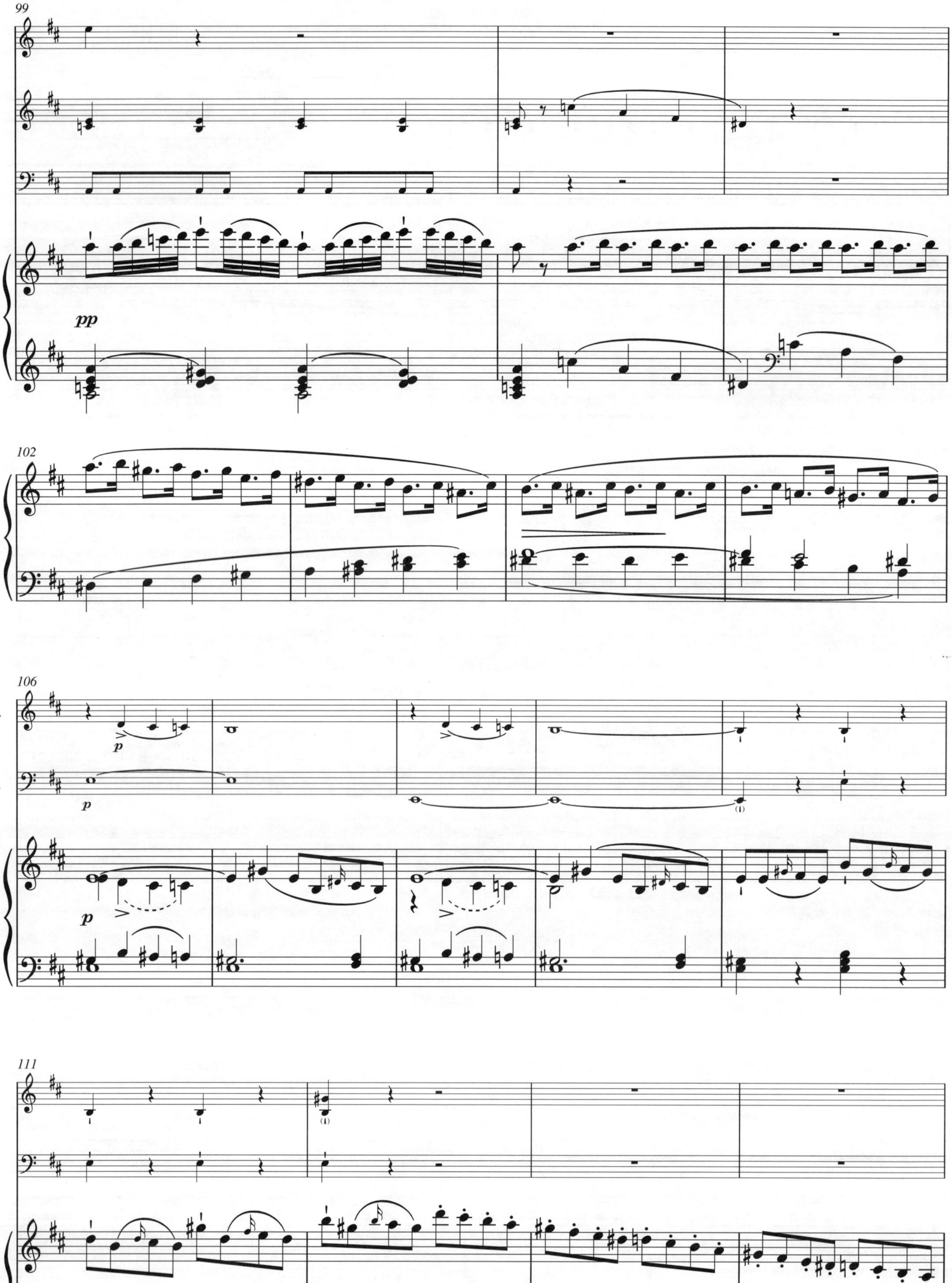

99
pp
102
Pn.
106
Vn.
p
Vc.
p
Pn.
p
111

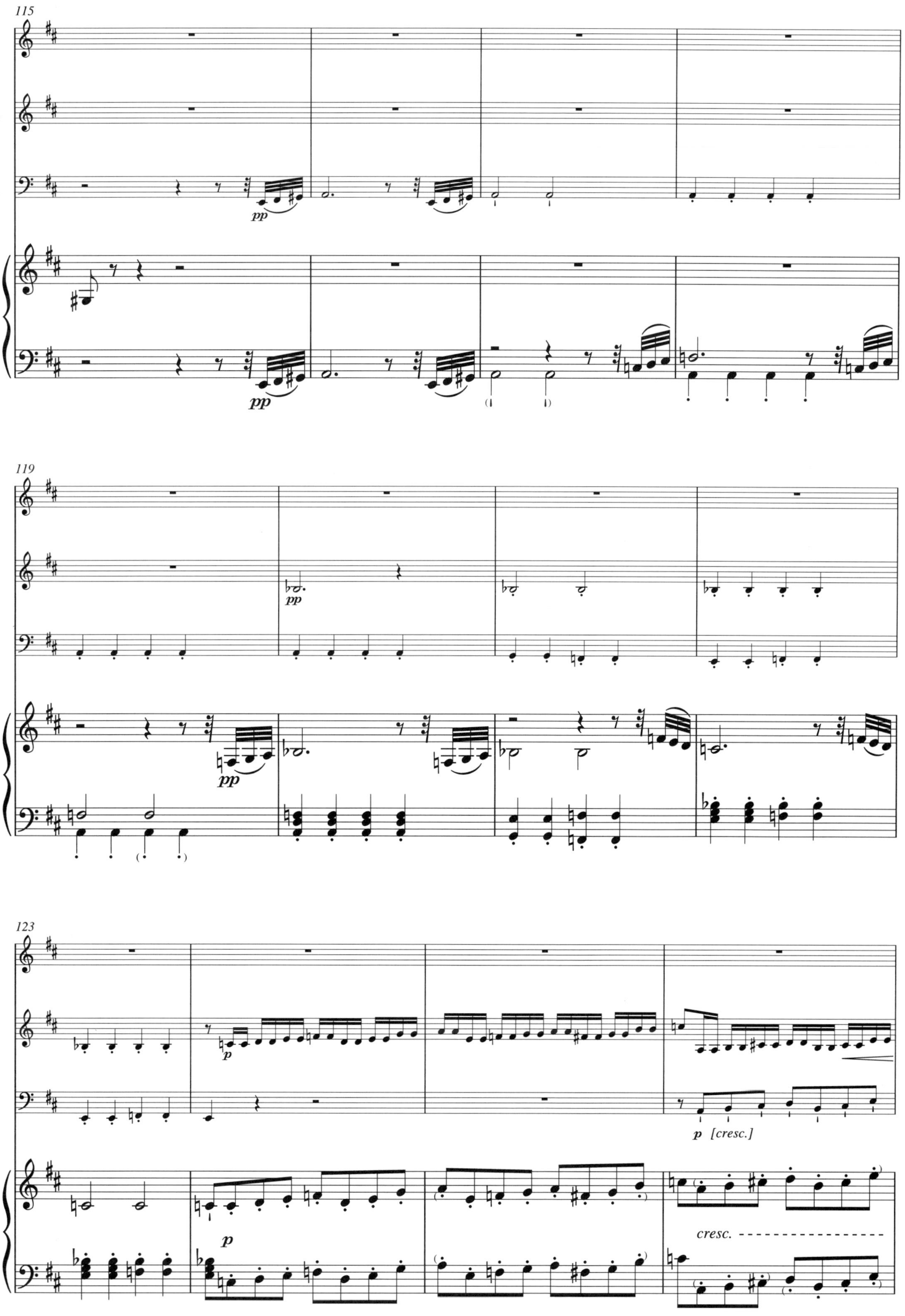
115
Fl.
Vn.
Vc.
Pn.
pp
pp
119
pp
pp
123
p
p [cresc.]
p
cresc.

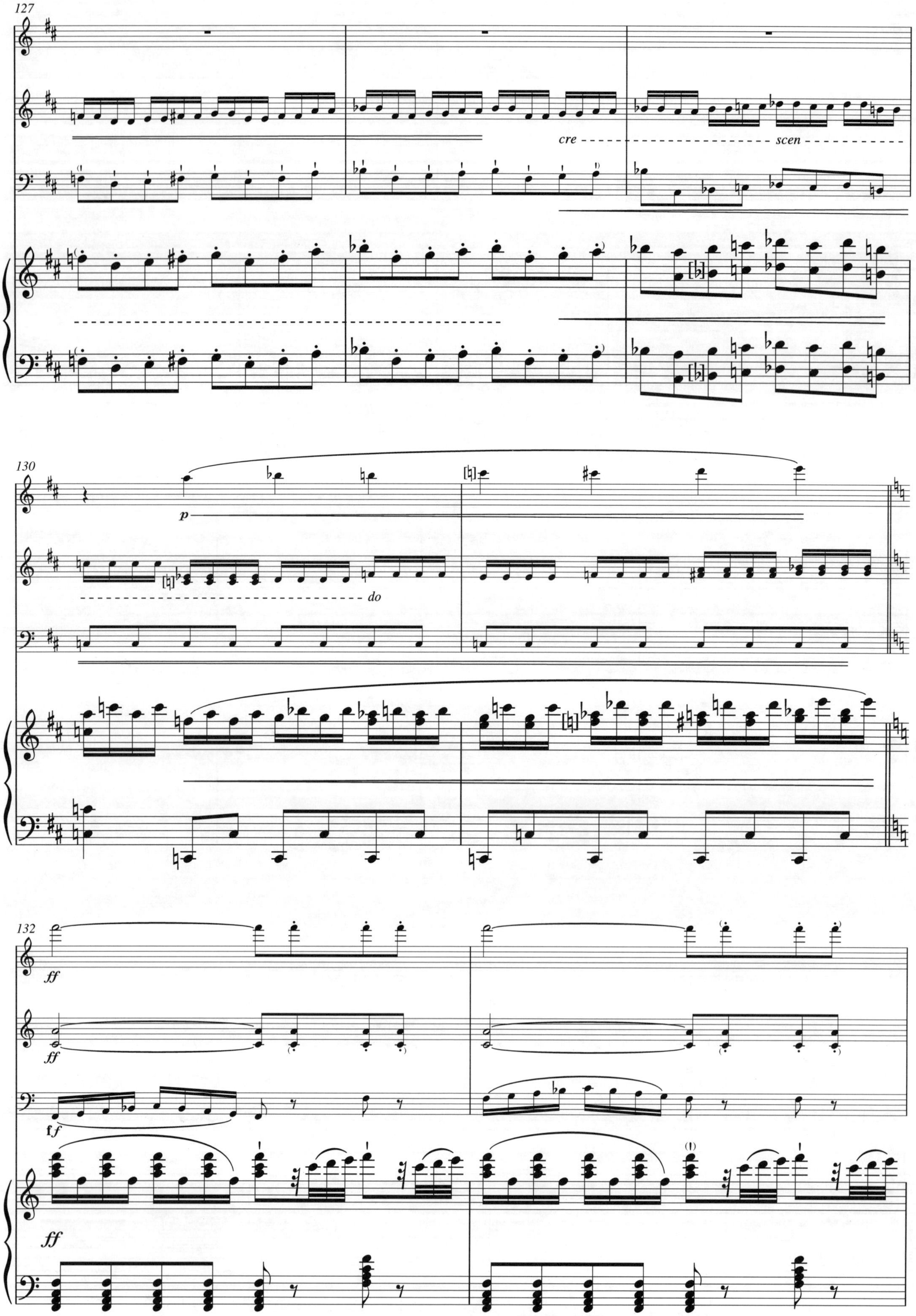
127
cre
scen
130
p
do
132
ff
ff
ff
ff

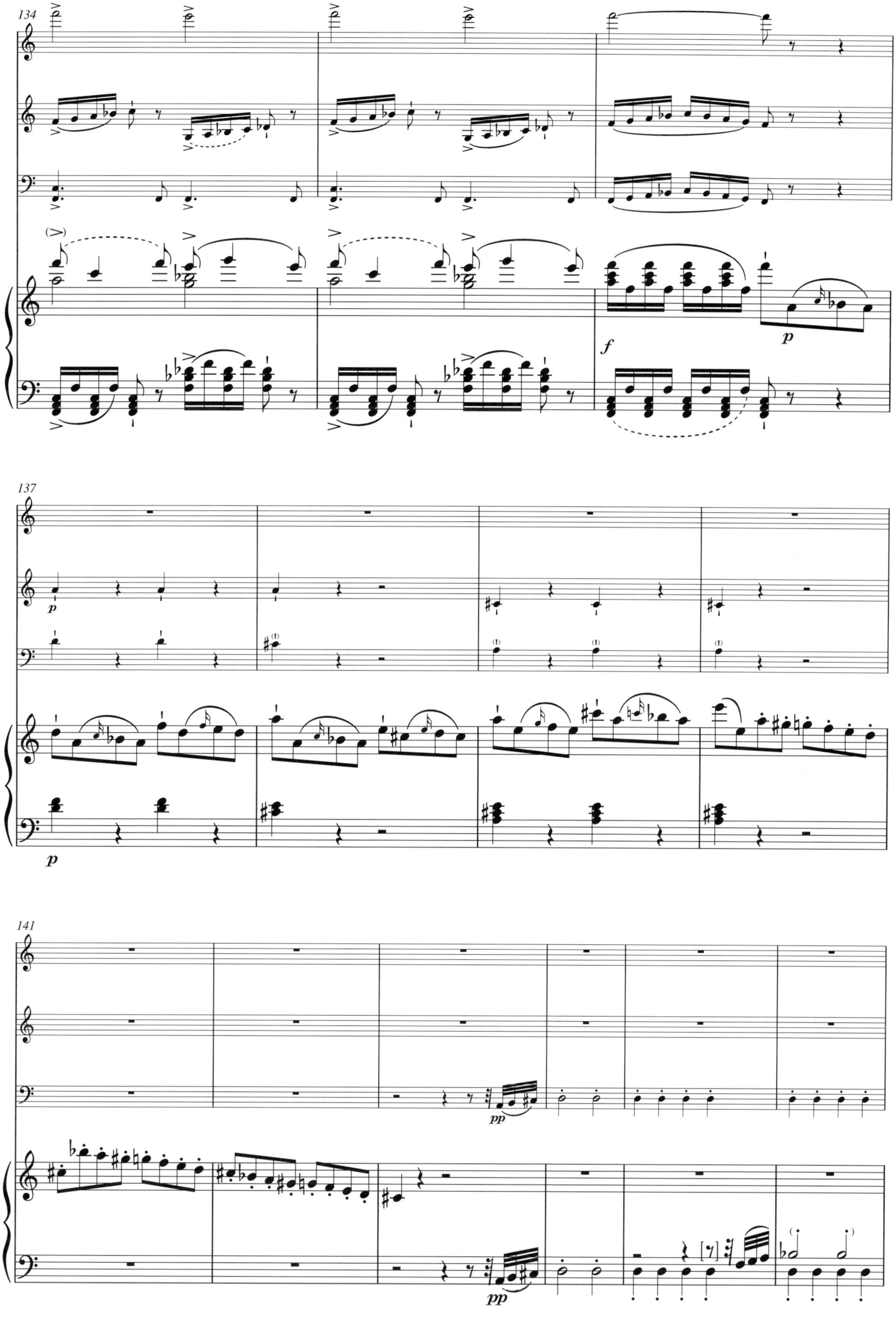
134
(>)
f
p
137
p
p
(!)
141
pp
pp

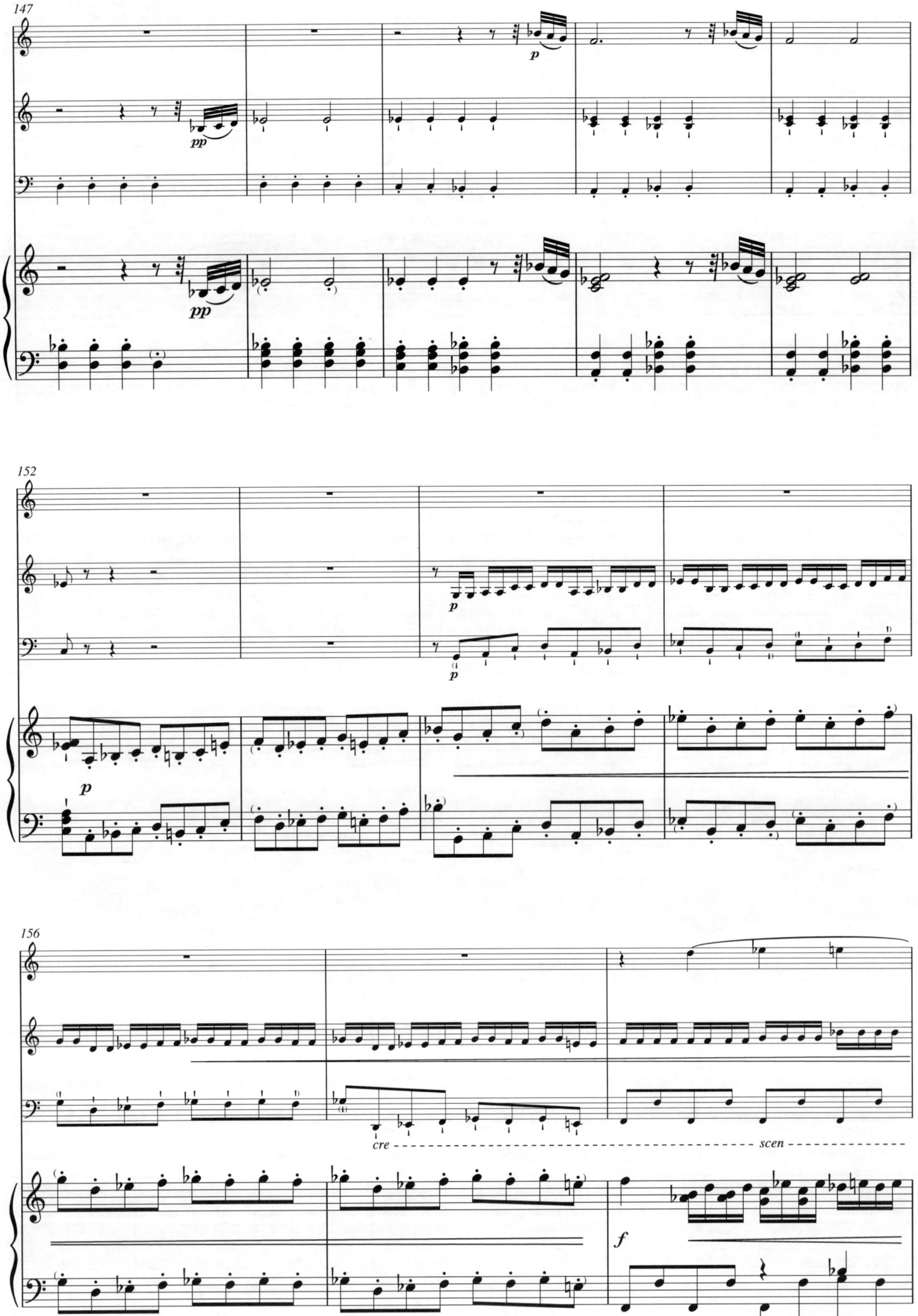
147
pp
p
152
p
156
cre
scen
f

269

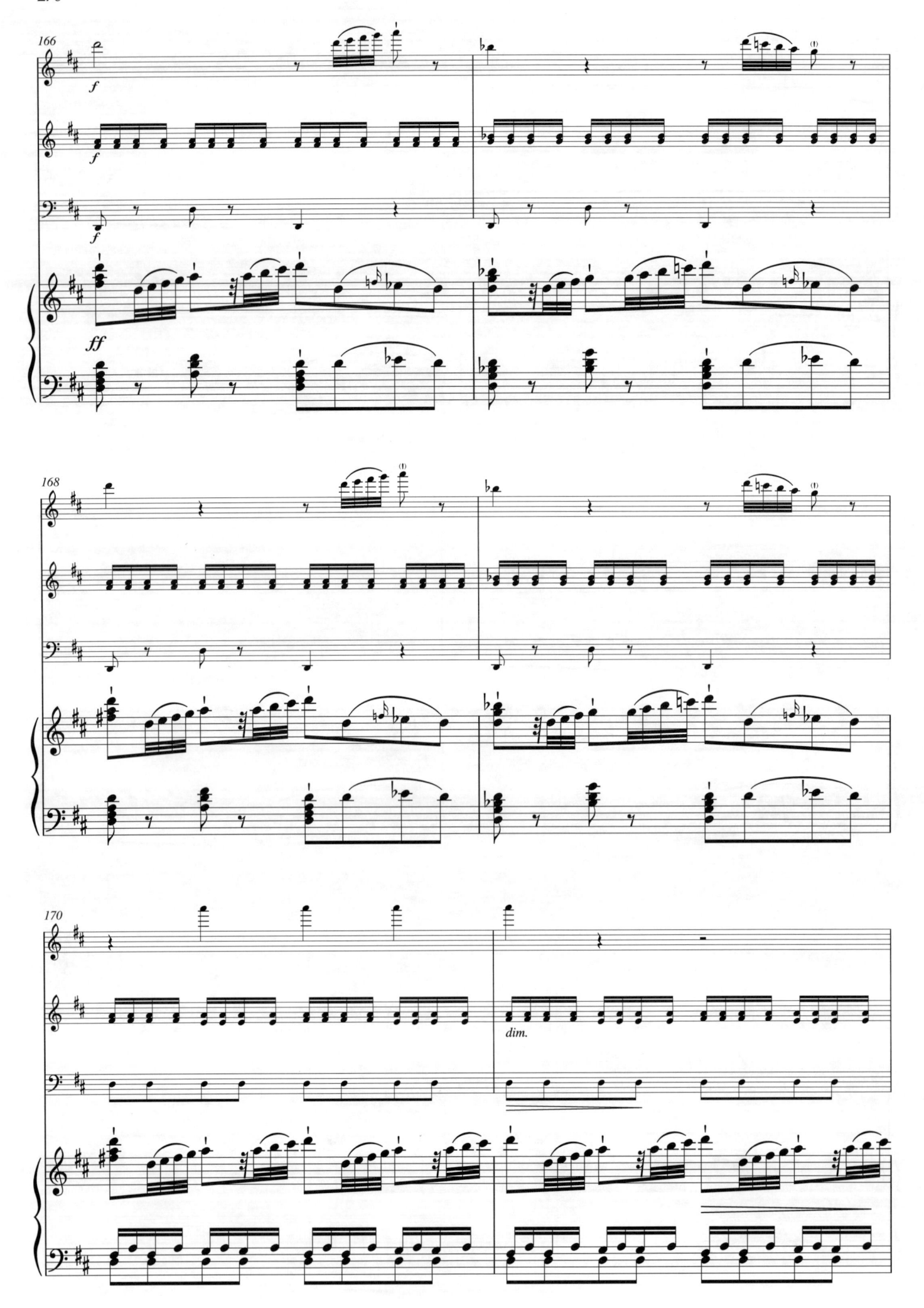
166
f
f
f
ff
168
170
dim.

271

272

273

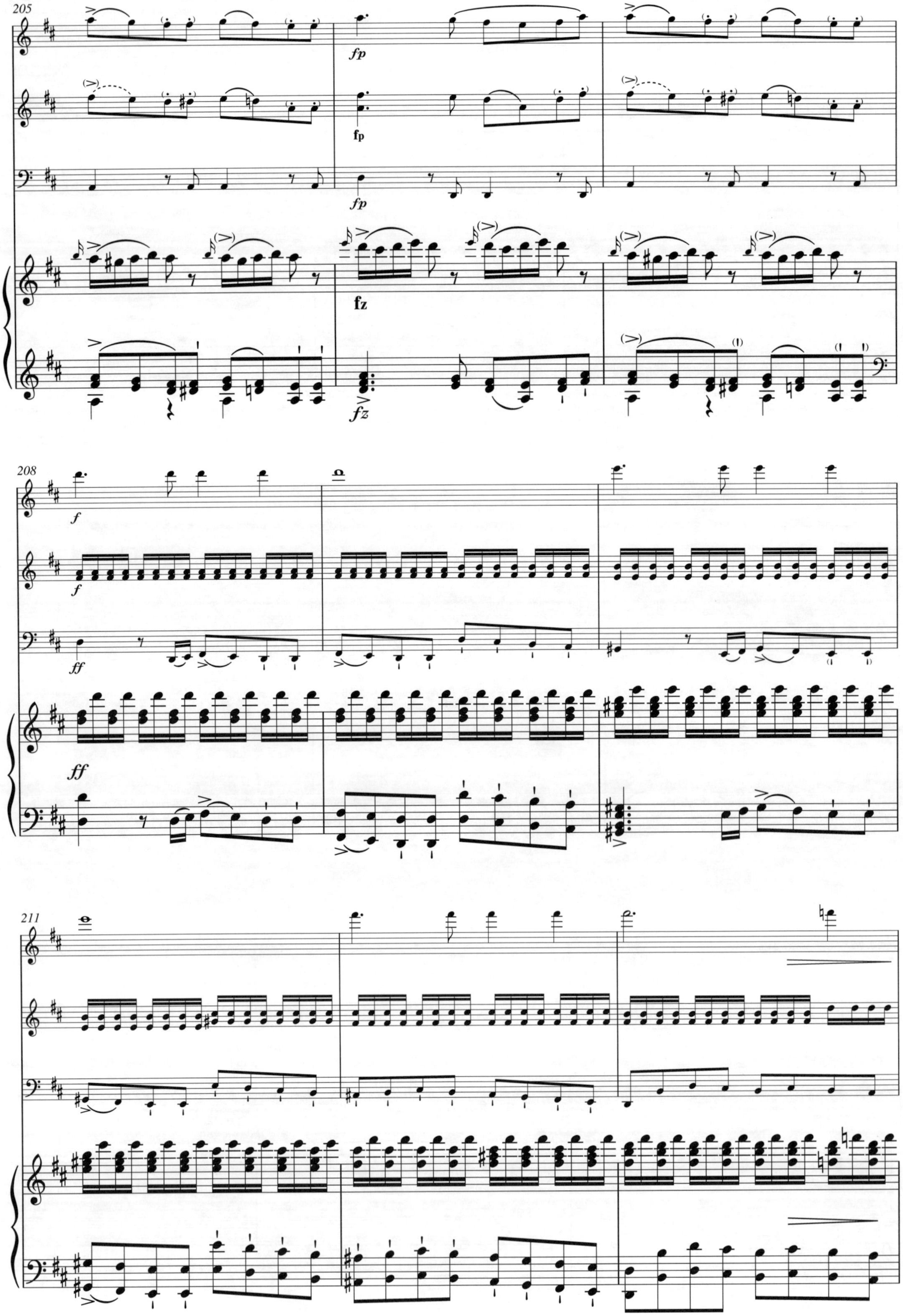
205
fp
fp
fp
fz
fz
208
f
f
ff
ff
211

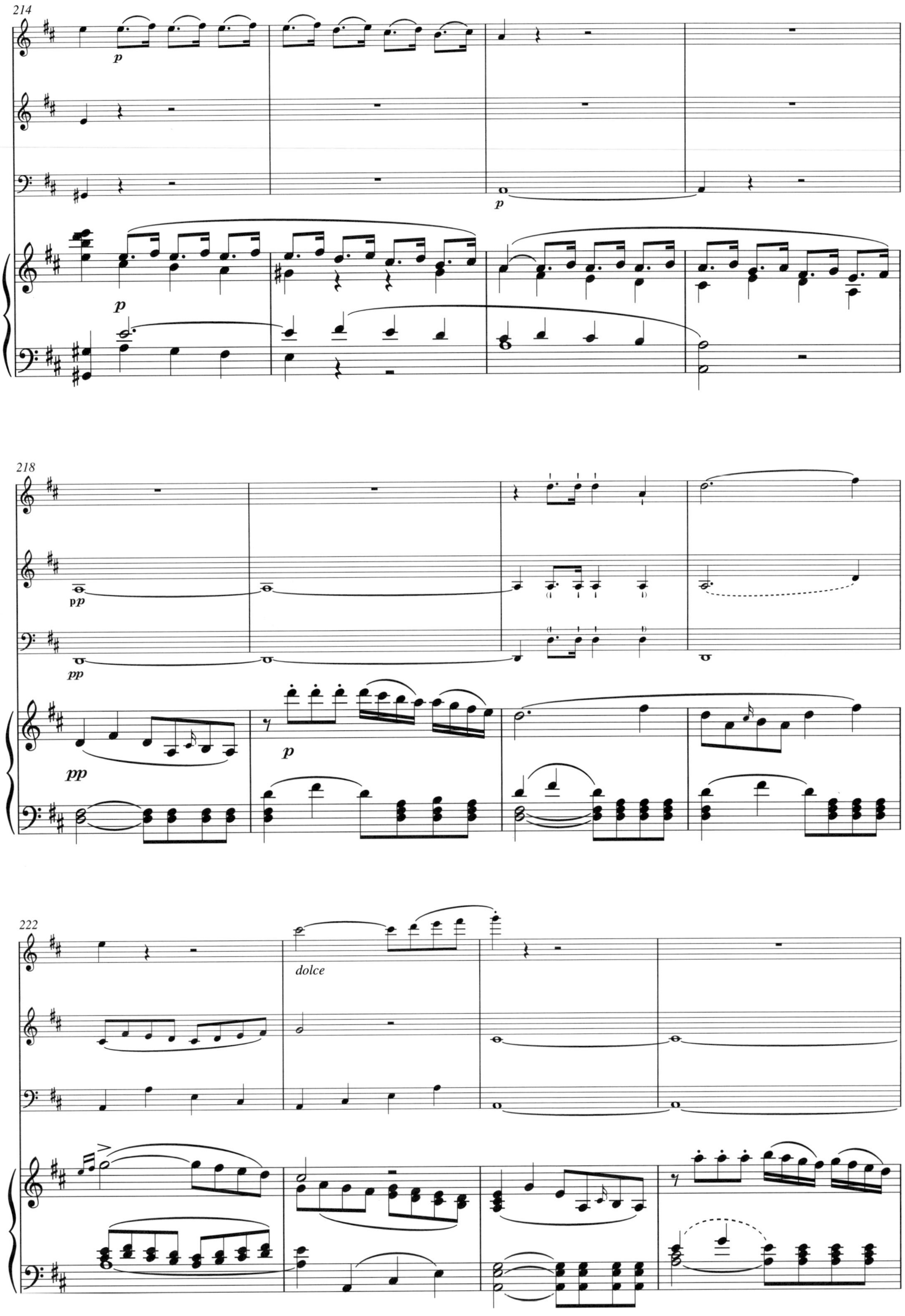
214
218
222
dolce

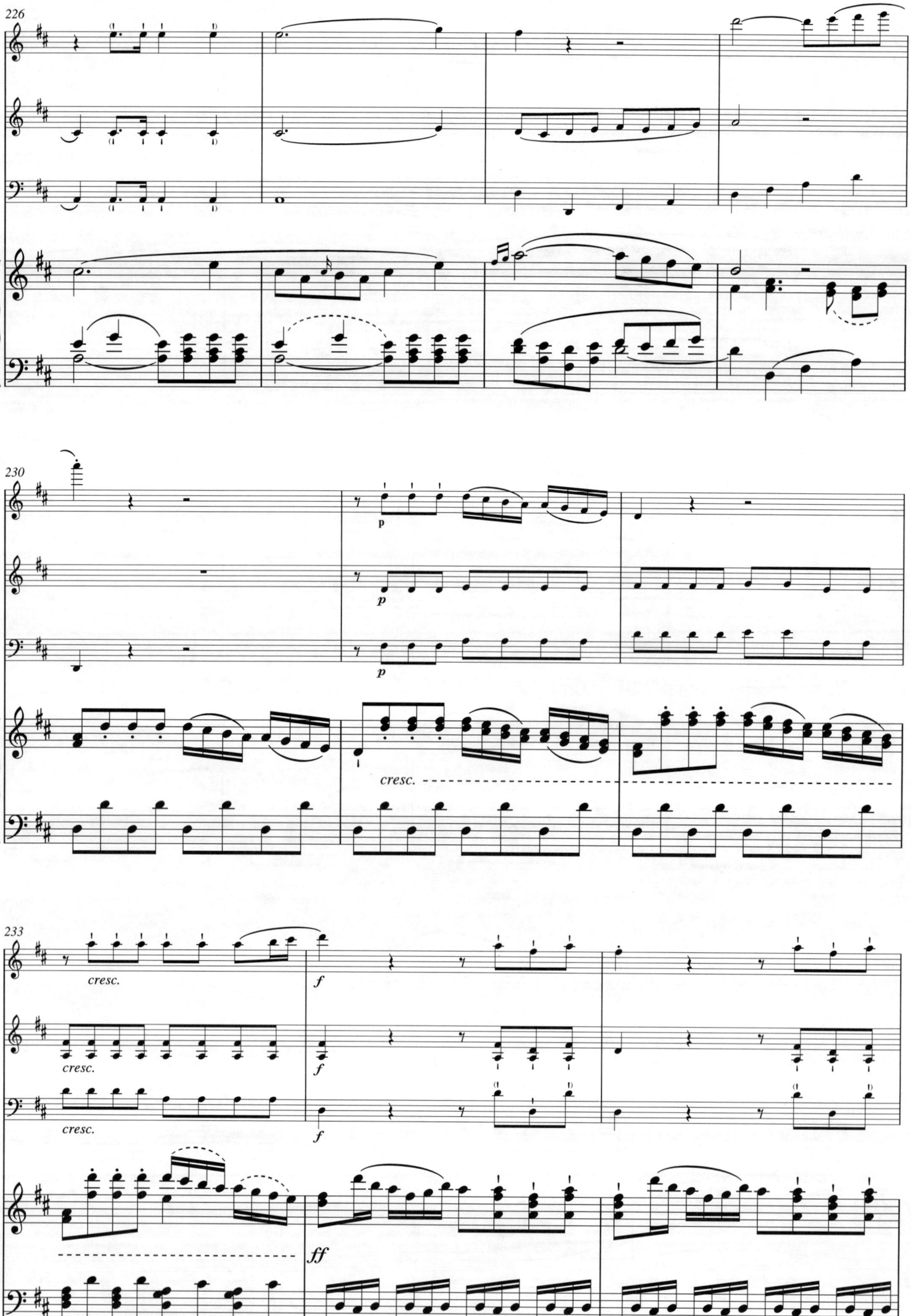
226
230
p
p
p
cresc.
233
cresc.
cresc.
cresc.
f
f
f
ff

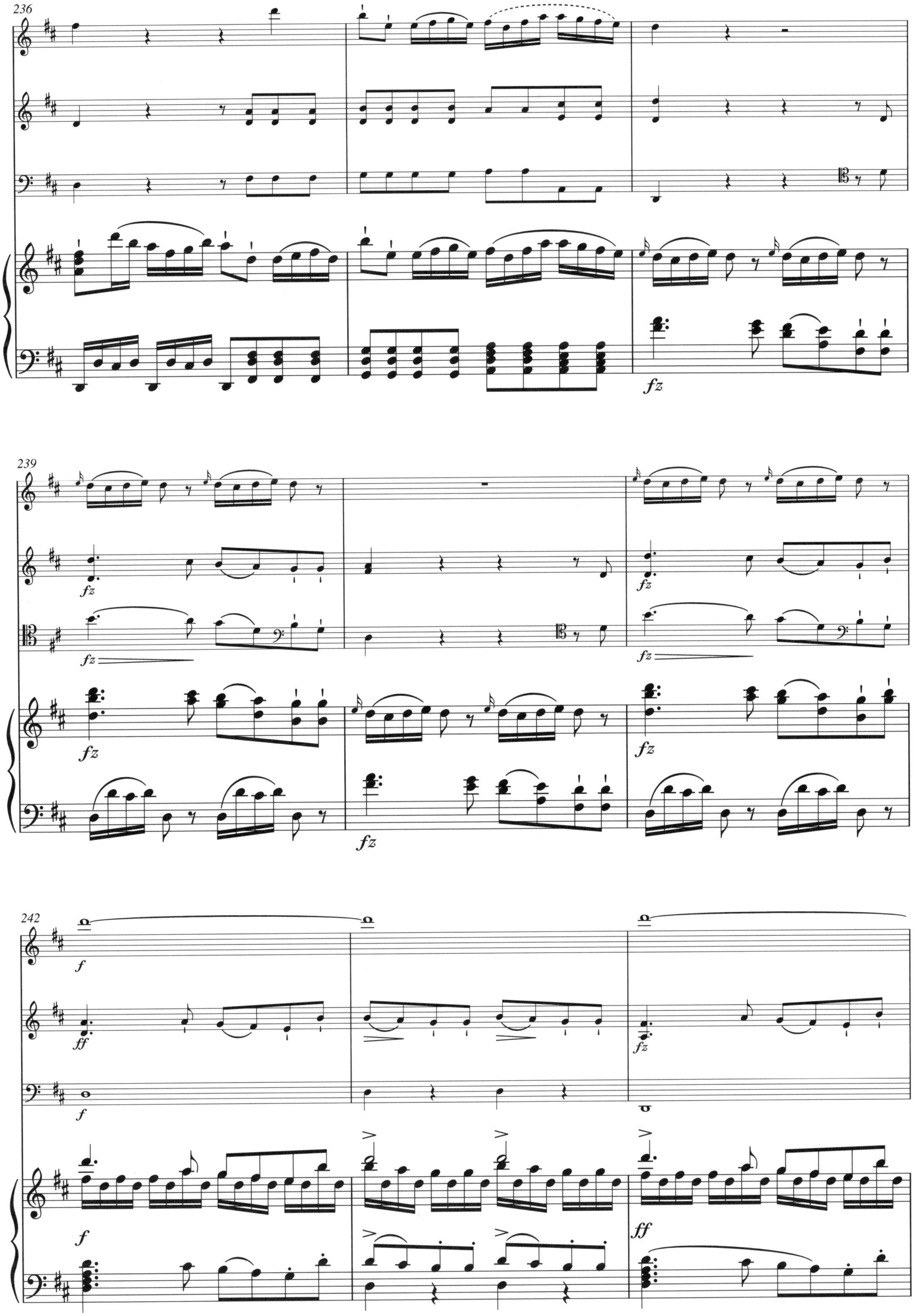
236
fz
239
fz
fz
fz
fz
fz
242
f
ff
fz
f
f
ff

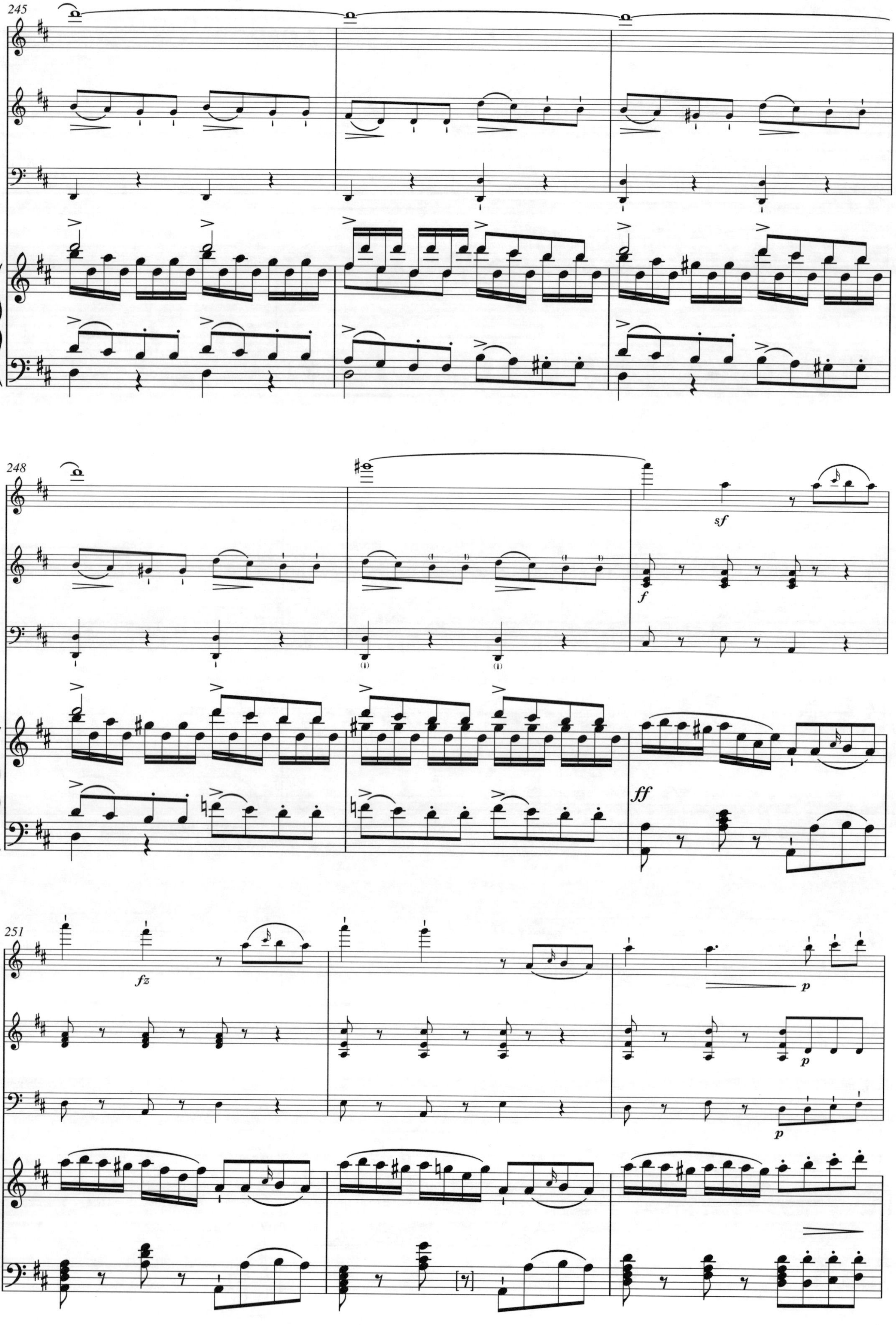
245
248
sf
f
ff
251
fz
p

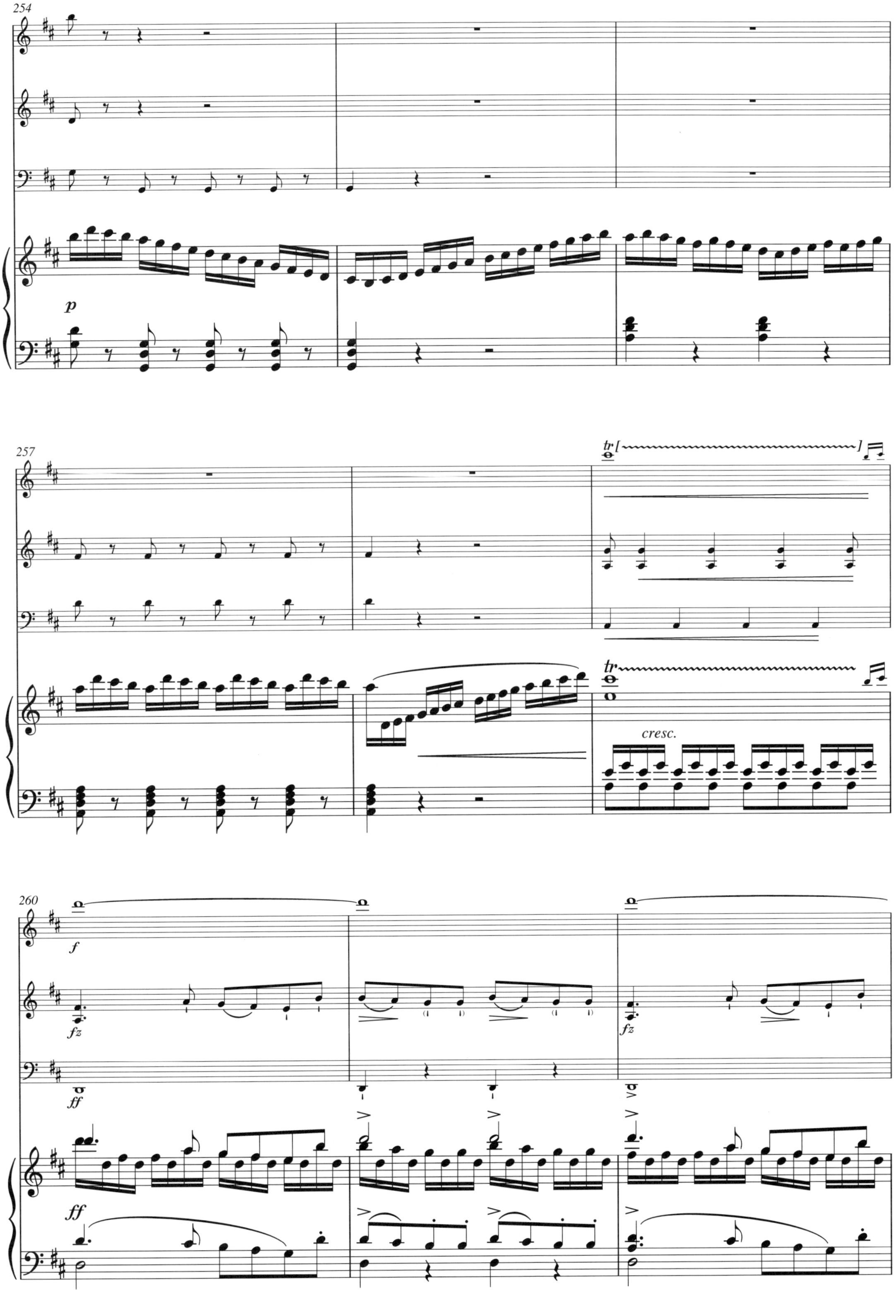
254
p
257
tr
tr
cresc.
260
f
fz
ff
fz
ff

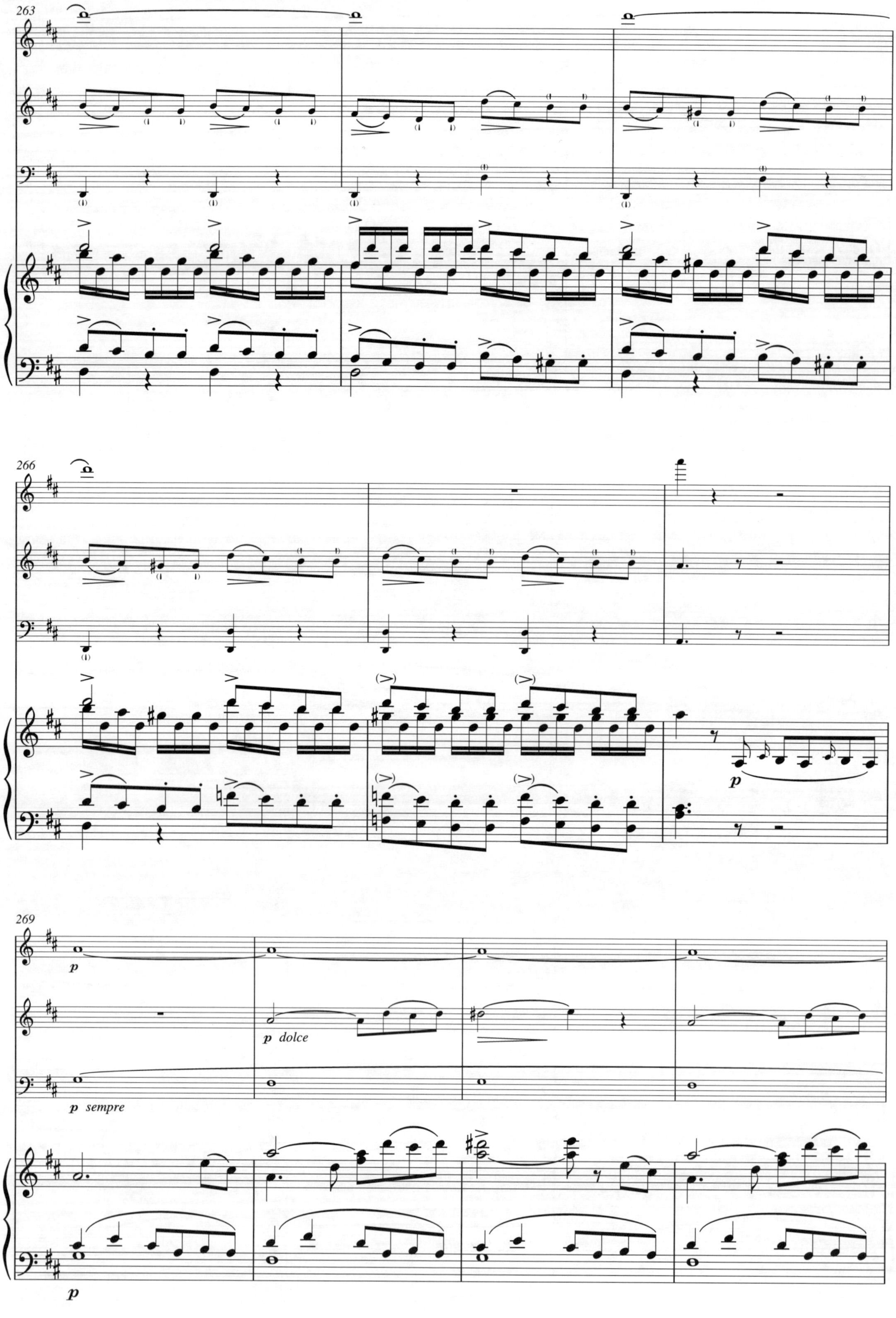
263
266
269
p
p dolce
p sempre
p

281

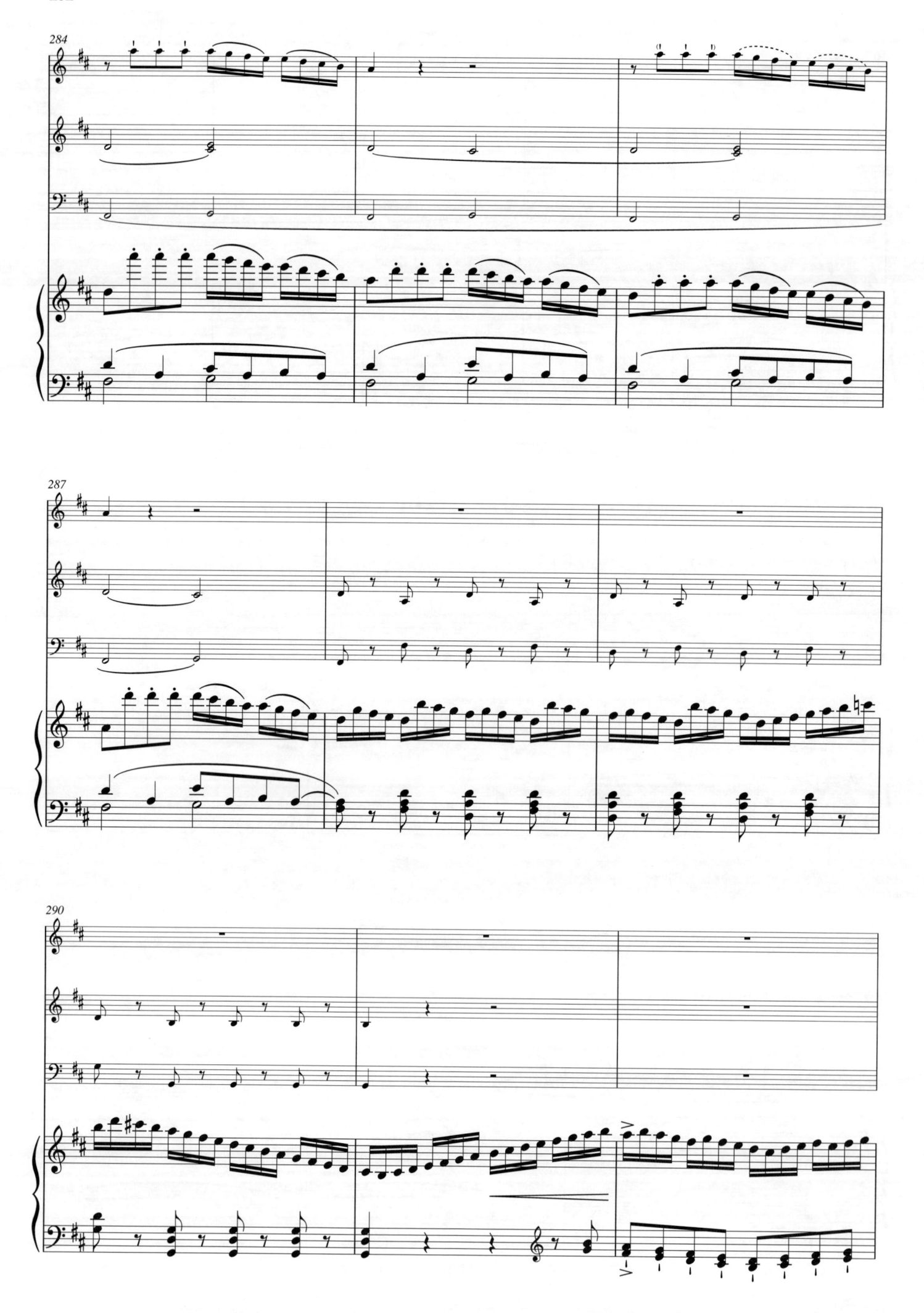
284
287
290

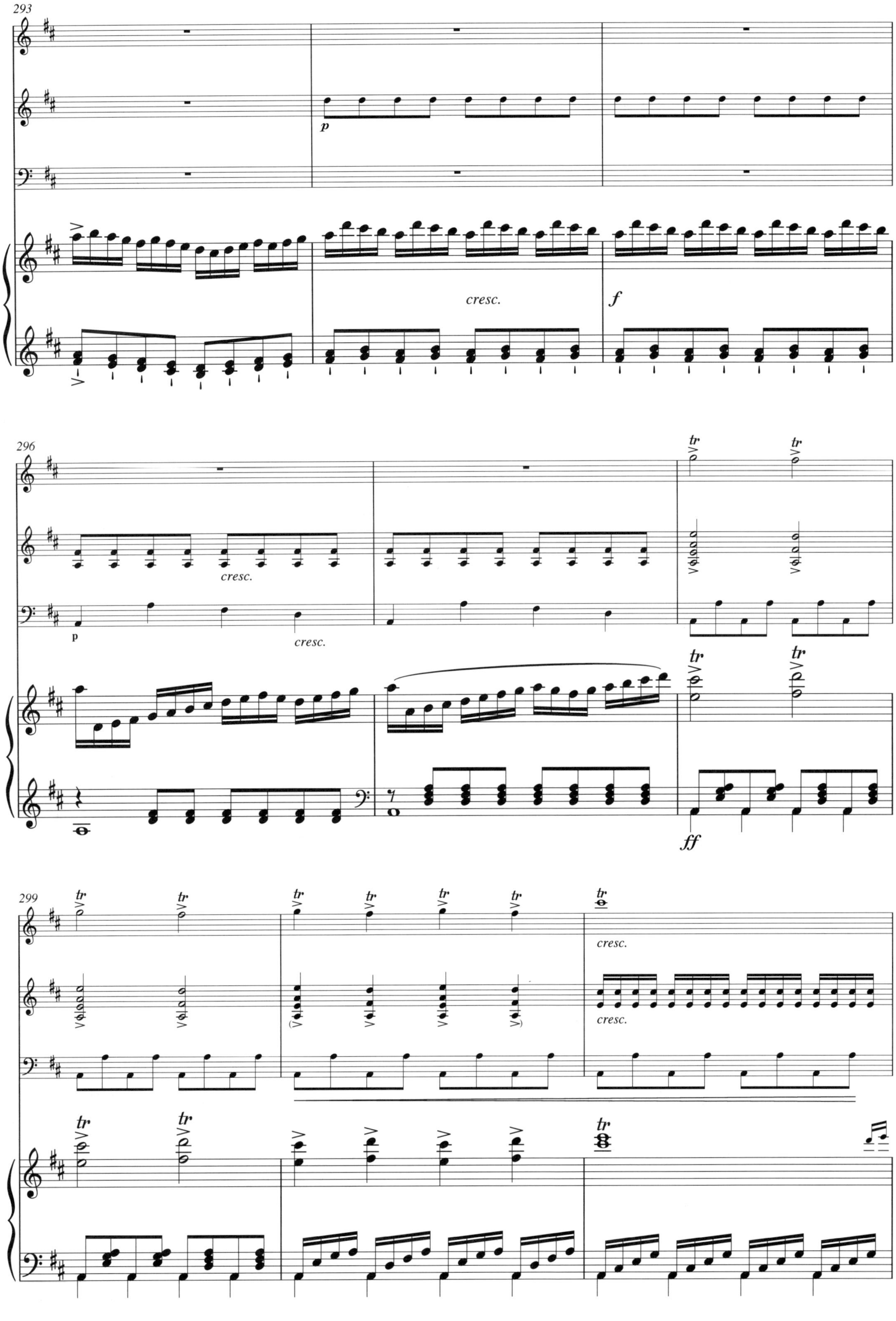
293
p
cresc.
f
296
cresc.
p
cresc.
tr
ff
299
tr
cresc.
cresc.

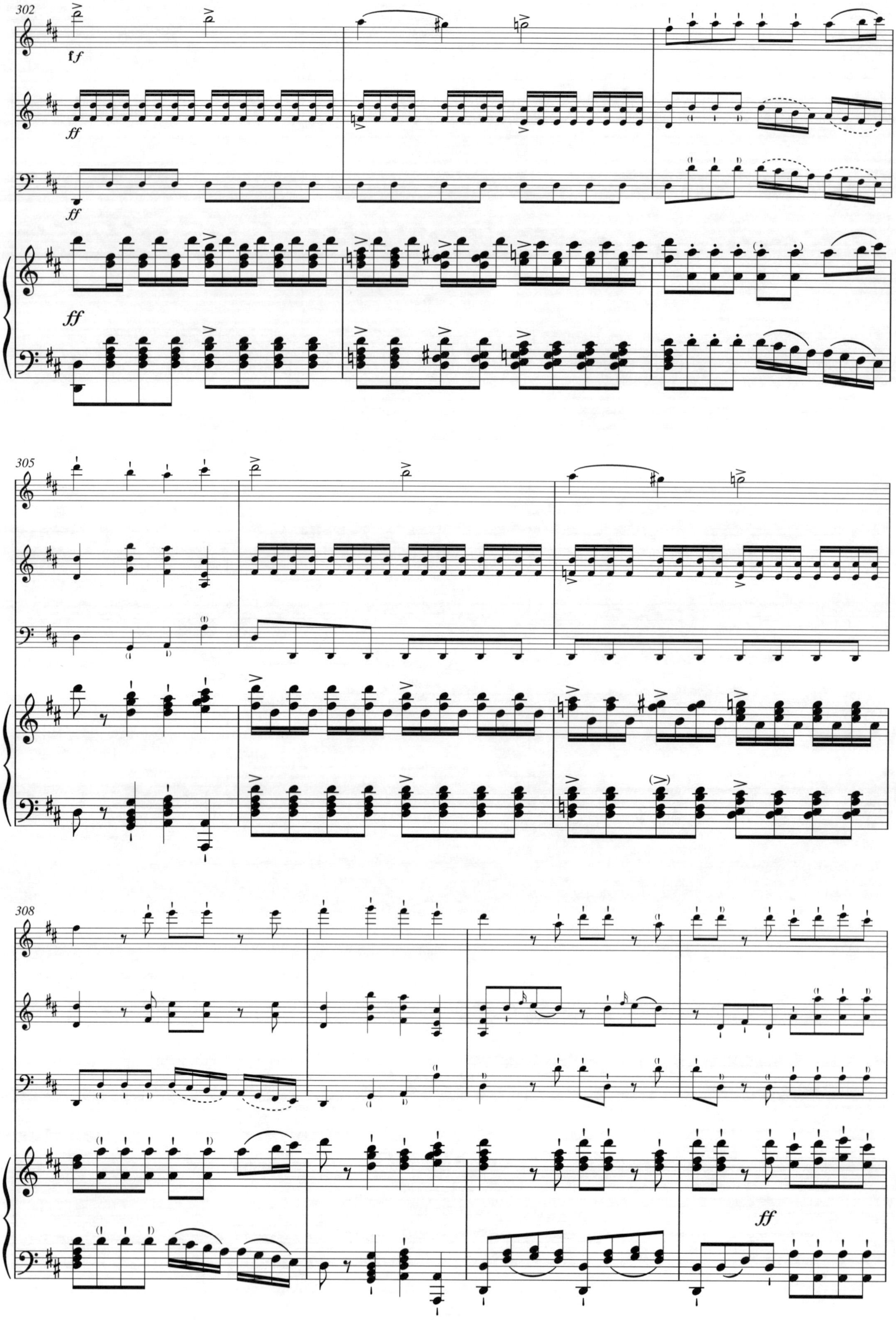
302
ff
305
308

285

Critical Report

The Source

There is only one source, published by T. Boosey and Company. The *Overture to Prometheus* was entered into Stationer's Hall on 1 March 1821. There are no entry dates for the remaining eleven overtures, but it is safe to assume that all were published on this date or shortly thereafter. The original title is:

Twelve | SELECT OVERTURES | of | Beethoven, Cherubini, Gluck, Mozart, Ec. | Arranged for the | PIANO FORTE, | with Accompaniments of | Violin & Flute & Violoncello, | by | J.N. HUMMEL, | Maitre de Chapelle to the Duke of Saxe Weimar. | No. 10 [rule] Price | London, Published by T. BOOSEY & C°. Importers of Foreign Music. | N°. 28 Holles Street, Oxford Street | *The above Overtures may be had without the Accompaniments.*

Editorial Methods

Since there is only one source for the arrangements, it is not possible to compare a second publication for variant readings. The situation is made somewhat more problematic by the fact that the Boosey edition of the overtures was obviously not prepared with the same care and proofreading as were the *Haffner* and *Linz* arrangements. Thus, the modern editor is confronted with an unusually large number of errors, discrepancies, and ambiguous passages. However, by applying accepted norms of performance practice from the period and examining the internal evidence of the arrangements themselves, a reasonable and consistent performing edition can be prepared with confidence. The original versions of the overtures were also compared, and they reveal a variety of fascinating details, but differ from the arrangements on so many levels that their value for this purpose is limited.

The order of the works in the original source is preserved, and the numbering of the overtures is editorial. There is no original score, only parts. The score of the edition is presented in standard format. Titles are based on those in the source, and the original titles and composer attributions are given in the critical notes. Tempo and other written directives meant to apply to the entire score are placed above the top staff and above the upper staff for the piano, with orthography adjusted to modern conventions. The notation of double and final barlines conforms to modern practices, including that in which all key changes are preceded by thin-thin barlines; other adjustments to double barlines are reported in the critical notes.

Stem directions, beaming patterns, and rhythmic groupings of notes and rests in the source are made to conform to modern conventions in the edition. The duration and slurring of appoggiaturas follows the source, unless otherwise noted. A few editorial slurs are added to appoggiaturas when slurs are present in parallel passages. Appoggiaturas are notated with stems up, except in the lower voice of passages with opposing stems in the piano. The notation of suffixes to trills also follows the source. Triplet and other groupette numerals are placed at the beam or stem side of notes, with those added placed in brackets; only two or three are required to establish a pattern and extra ones are tacitly omitted.

Common stemming is employed in the piano except in clear instances of contrapuntal voice leading or when separate stems are necessary to clarify ornaments, articulations, or phrasing. Cross-staff notation is altered to use ledger lines on a single staff where possible. Instances where both hands are combined into a single staff (usually with the unused staff left empty) in the original, presumably to avoid excessive ledger lines or changing clefs, are redistributed to use both staves, incorporating clef changes as necessary, in the edition. Rests have been added in some instances to clarify voice leading, but unnecessary rests have been removed. In a few instances *all'octava* indications and changes of clef are used where they were not in the source.

Measured tremolo and other shorthand methods of notation are realized without comment. In the violoncello part, the source uses either bass clef or notation in treble clef that was understood to be read an octave lower; in the edition, such treble clef passages are realized at the lower pitch level, and tenor clef (C4) is used where appropriate. Indications of octave transpositions in the flute part are also realized.

All editorially added accidentals are placed in brackets. Added cautionary accidentals are placed in parentheses; source cautionaries are retained only where they clarify passages. Accidentals in the source that are redundant by modern standards are tacitly removed. Placement of accidentals in passages involving repeated pitches tied across barlines is adjusted to follow modern convention (that is, the accidentals are moved from the second of the tied noteheads to the next reiteration of the pitch within the same measure).

The spelling, orthography, and placement of expressive and dynamic markings (such as *dolce, marcato, crescendo*) are regularized. Redundant dynamics or accents are tacitly omitted, unless they seem to serve a particular purpose or are necessary for clarity. The disctinction between accent markings and hairpin dynamics is retained as in the original, except for ambiguous cases, which have been tacitly altered and are discussed in the critical notes. Fermatas are placed above the staves. Any added markings, dynamics, or fermatas are placed in brackets or parentheses; added hairpins are dashed; added letter dynamics are set in bold (rather than bold-italic) type. The use of both dots and strokes for shortened notes are retained as in the original. Ornaments are regularized with respect to placement. The placement of slurs and ties is also regularized, and slurs are extended to enclose tied notes (except in no. 8, mm. 1–4); those that are added are dashed. Converging slurs (where one note note marks the end of one slur as well as the beginning of another) are combined into a single slur unless doing so clearly disrupts the indicated phrasing. Instances where the phrasing, articulation, and dynamics differ in parallel passages, or between two or more instruments playing at the same time, are reproduced as in the original, except when an editorial emendation is obvious and necessary. The few pedal indications in the source have been retained, and several others have been added in brackets to passages of similar character or content.

Critical Notes

The following notes document readings of the source where they differ from the edition in ways not accounted for by the editorial methods. Instruments are abbreviated as follows: Fl. = Flute, Vn. = Violin, Vc. = Violoncello, Pn. = piano, r.h. = right hand staff, l.h. = left hand staff. Notes are numbered consecutively within a measure, including appoggiaturas and counting each notehead under a tie separately; notes sounding simultaneously are numbered from bottom to top. Where appropriate, chords or beats are numbered rather than specific notes. Rests are numbered separately from notes. Pitches are named according to the system in which c' is middle C. Consecutive notes are separated with en-dashes; simultaneously sounding notes are indicated with plus signs.

1. Overture to Prometheus

Composer attribution is lacking.

M. 13, Fl., note 1 has *rf*. M. 29, Pn., r.h., notes 1–2 are quarter + quarter. M. 83, Pn., l.h., note 4 is g♯. M. 104, Pn., r.h., beat 1 has *sf*. M. 205, Vc., beat 1 is c 8th–8th rest. M. 231, Pn., beats 2–3 have crescendo hairpin. M. 250, Pn., l.h., notes 1, 3, 5, and 7 are G♯$_1$, notes 2, 4, 6, and 8 are G♯. M. 281, Fl., beats 3–4 are half rest.

2. Overture to Die Zauberflöte

Title is "Overture to the Zauberflöte"; composer attribution is lacking.

M. 3, Pn., l.h., beat 4 is quarter rest. M. 5, Pn., r.h., notes 3–7 are slurred. M. 13, Pn., beats 2–3 have crescendo hairpin (changed to accents). M. 14, Vc., note 1 is E♭ (emendation follows original version). M. 96 has single barline. M. 97, Fl., note 1 has *ff*.

3. Overture to Lodoïska

Title is "Overture to Lodoiska"; composer attribution is "Cherubini."

M. 40, Fl., note 1 is g". Mm. 53 and 54, Fl., note 1 has *sf*. M. 128, Fl., beat 1 has *cresc*. (moved to beat 4). M. 132, Pn., l.h., beat 1 is A + c♯ + e. M. 183, Pn., r.h., notes 3–4 are slurred. M. 193, Pn., r.h., notes 2 and 5 are c♮''', c♮". M. 219, Vn., note 1 is e'; Pn., r.h., note 1 is e". M. 263, Pn., r.h., notes 1–5 are slurred. M. 290, Vn., beats 1–2 are d' half. M. 307, Pn., r.h., notes 4–7, fingering is 4 3 2 +.

4. Overture to Figaro

Composer attribution is lacking.

Mm. 16 and 33, Pn., l.h., beat 3 has *p* (moved to r.h.). Mm. 139 and 141, Vc., note 5 has staccato dot.

5. Overture to Iphigénia

Title is "Overture to *Iphigenia*"; composer attribution is "Gluck."

M. 1, Vn., note 1 has stroke. M. 9, Vc., note 1 has stroke. M. 19, Fl., Vn., and Vc., rest 2 has fermata (moved to rest 1). M. 29, Vn., beats 3–4 are e' + c" half. M. 31, Vn., beats 3–4 are g' + d" half. M. 33, Fl., note 5 has staccato dot. M. 39, Pn., r.h., note 9 has stroke. M. 43, Pn., r.h., note 2 has stroke. M. 57, Fl., beats 1–3 are c''' half–quarter rest; Pn., r.h., notes 10 and 13 are c♯".

6. Original Overture

Composer attribution is "Himmel."

M. 10, Pn., r.h., beat 4, note 1 is double-dotted 8th. M. 36, Vn., note 1 has *sf* (moved to m. 37, note 1). M. 42, Vn., note 1 has *ff*. M. 55, Vn. and Vc., beats 2 and 4 are 8th rest–64th rest–32nd–32nd–32nd. M. 60, Vn., note 1 has *p*. M. 75, Pn., r.h., chord 1 has accent. M. 110, Vn., note 1 has *p* (moved to m. 109, note 1). M. 153, Pn., r.h., note 3 is dotted half. M. 190, Pn., r.h., notes 1–3 are 16th–16th–16th. M. 191, Pn., r.h., notes 2–4 are 16th–16th–16th. M. 193, Pn., r.h., notes 4–6 are 16th–16th–16th. M. 194, Pn., l.h., 8th rest is e 8th. M. 196, Pn., r.h., notes 2–3 are 8th–8th. M. 249, Fl., note 2 has *p* (moved to note 1).

7. Overture to Sargino

Composer attribution is "Paer."

M. 6, Pn., r.h., beat 3 is a' + d" + f♯" quarter; l.h., beat 3 is d' quarter. M. 15, Fl., note 2 has accent (changed to decrescendo hairpin). M. 18, Pn., r.h., beats 3–4, fingering is 4 3 2 +. M. 30, Vc., notes 9–10 have staccato dots. Mm. 47 and 49, Fl., note 1 has p (moved to note 2). M. 58, Fl., notes 7–9 are 32nd–32nd–32nd (with triplet indication). M. 59, Fl., notes 2–4 are 32nd–32nd–32nd (with triplet indication). M. 83, Vc., notes 2–5 are slurred. M. 84, Pn., l.h., notes 3–6 are slurred. M. 87, Vc., notes 2–4 have strokes. M. 92, Pn., r.h., note 7 is e♭". M. 96, Pn., l.h., notes 3–6 are slurred. M. 127, Vc., beat 4 is a quarter. M. 147, Vn., beat 3 is quarter. M. 187, Pn., l.h., chords 2 and 4 have strokes. M. 190, Fl., note 1 is f♯'''. M. 196, Pn., l.h., beat 2 is 8th rest–D + d 8th.

8. Overture

Composer attribution is "A. Romberg."

Mm. 32–33, Vn. and Vc. have 64ths. M. 57, Vc., note 2 has f (moved to note 1). M. 65, Fl., note 1 has stroke. M. 76, Pn., beat 1 has p (moved to beat 2). M. 84, Vn., note 1 has stroke. M. 90, Fl., beats 3–4 are e''' double-dotted quarter–e" 16th. M. 152, Pn., note 1 is e'''. M. 154, Vc., notes 1–7 have strokes. M. 163, Pn., r.h., note 7 is d♮'. M. 176, Vn., note 6 is f♯'. M. 265, Pn., beat 1 has ff (moved to beat 2). M. 301, Pn., r.h., notes 1–2 are g♭ + b. M. 325, Pn., r.h., note 2 is half. M. 356, Pn., r.h., upper voice, note 4 lacks ledger line. M. 391, Pn., l.h., beat 4 has stroke. M. 396, Fl., Vn., and Vc., rest 3 is dotted 8th rest.

9. Overture to Der Freischütz

Title is "Overture Der Freischütz"; composer attribution is "C. M. de Weber."

M. 64, Vn., note 1 is half. M. 211, Fl., beats 3–4 have decrescendo hairpin (moved to m. 212). M. 287, Pn. has single barline.

10. Overture to Euryanthe

Composer attribution is "C. M. de Weber."

M. 33, Pn., r.h., beat 4, note 1 is a♭'. M. 114, Vn., superfluous measure identical to m. 113 precedes m. 114. Mm. 156, 157, 162, 163, 168, and 169, Pn., r.h., lower voice, notes 2 and 4 are dotted quarter. M. 182, Vc., note 1 is A♮. M. 188, Vn., note 9 is b♮. M. 212, Pn., r.h., beat 4, note 1 is a♭'. M. 214, Pn., r.h., note 1 is e♭'. M. 241, Vc., note 8 is f. M. 258, Fl., note 1 has f (moved to m. 259, note 1).

11. Overture to Tancredi

Composer attribution is "Rossini."

M. 4, Vn. and Pn., both staves, notes 11–13 are slurred. M. 30, Fl., beats 3–4 contain cues for Pn., r.h. M. 56, Vc., note 1 has ff and *arco* (both moved to m. 50, note 1). M. 59, Vn., beats 3–4 are f♯' + a'. M. 93, Vn., notes 2–3 are slurred. M. 101, Vc., note 2 has *cre-* (moved to m. 100, note 2). M. 120, Pn., l.h., chord 1 is E + G + c + e quarter. M. 155, Fl., notes 2–6 are slurred. M. 185, beat 3 is d''' quarter preceded by a" 16th–b" 16th–c♯'" 16th appoggiatura.

12. Overture to Anacreon

Composer attribution is "Cherubini."

M. 4, Vc., note 2 has stroke. M. 10, Pn., l.h., notes 1–3 lack ledger lines. M. 44, Vn., notes 4–7 are e'–g'–f♯'–e'. M. 71, Fl., notes 4–6 are 16th–32nd–32nd. M. 90, Fl. has superfluous 8th rest after note 2. M. 120, Pn., r.h., note 1 is half. M. 144, Vc., notes 1–2 have strokes. M. 169, Vc., note 1 has ff. M. 199, Vn., beat 3 through m. 200, beat 2 are 8th rest–f♯" 8th with stroke–d" 8th with stroke–f♯" 8th with stroke–d" 8th–8th rest–quarter rest. M. 201, Vn., beat 3 through m. 202 are half rest–whole rest. M. 268, Vc., beats 1–2 are a half. M. 308, Vc., notes 9–12 are G–F♯–E–D. M. 184, Vn., note 3 is e'.